The Troubles of Journalism

A Critical Look at What's Right and Wrong With the Press

Second Edition

William A. Hachten

LEA LAWRENCE ERLBAUM ASSOCIATES, PUBLISHERS
2001 Mahwah, New Jersey   London

Lawrence Erlbaum Associates, Inc., Publishers
10 Industrial Avenue
Mahwah, NJ 07430

Cover design by Kathryn Houghtaling Lacey

Library of Congress Cataloging-in-Publication Data
Hachten, William A.
The troubles of journalism: a critical look at what's right and wrong with the press / by
William A. Hachten—2nd ed.
    p.   cm.—(LEA's communication series)
Includes bibliographical references and indexes.
ISBN 0-8058-3816-3 (cloth : alk. paper)—ISBN 0-8058-3817-1 (pbk. : alk. paper)
1. Journalism—United States—History. I. Title. II. Series.

PN4855.H24 2001
071'.3—dc21   00-056212
                                                                                      CIP

Books published by Lawrence Erlbaum Associates are printed on acid-free paper, and their bindings
are chosen for strength and durability.

Printed in the Untied States of America
10   9   8   7   6   5   4   3   2   1

The Troubles of Journalism

A Critical Look at What's Right and Wrong With the Press

Second Edition

LEA'S COMMUNICATION SERIES

Jennings Bryant/Dolf Zillmann, General Editors

Selected titles in Journalism (Maxwell McCombs, Advisory Editor) include:

For a complete list of other titles in LEA's Communication Series, please contact Lawrence Erlbaum Associates, Publishers

In Memory of Harold "Bud" Nelson (1917–1996)

Contents

Preface

During the early 1930s when I was a youngster in Huntington Park, California, I could hear the cry of newspaper boys walking through the neighborhood, sometimes at night, hawking the *Los Angeles Herald Express* or the *Los Angeles Times* calling out EXTRA! EXTRA! to announce some breaking news story, such as FDR's first election, which required a special edition—an *extra!*—to get the news out faster.

Soon, news "bulletins" on radio supplemented and in time replaced the newspaper extra. During World War II, we listened to radio for breaking news, but with wartime constraints, the time element of major battles and other wartime events was often vague and often several days old. Newspapers were still important, but so were newsreels, which in the dark of movie theaters provided moving pictures of distant events—Hitler haranguing Nazi crowds in Germany, the abdication of King Edward VIII, but again the immediacy of the newspaper *extra* was not there.

During the 1936 presidential campaign I can remember my family huddling around our radio set listening to ex-President Herbert Hoover addressing the Republican Convention. We were all Republicans and hoped that the GOP would nominate Hoover to take on FDR again as in 1932. Forlorn hope. My uncle was an International News Service reporter in Washington, DC, and an admirer of Hoover. I later rejected his politics but not his work. He was my role model for a career in newspapering.

When I studied journalism at Stanford in 1947, the curriculum still required students to learn to set type by hand using the California Job Case. Some weekly papers, despite the widespread use of Linotype machines, were still doing it the old way.

During my newspaper days from 1948 to 1956, daily papers were still being put together much as they had been for the previous 75 years—local news stories were written on typewriters (preferably Underwood or Royal Standards), "wire" or telegraph news stories came clattering in on Associated Press or United Press teletypes. News stories, after being funneled through the city and news desks and then to the copy desk for close editing and headlines, were set in type by Linotype operators. Then galleys of lead body type and headlines were made up on page forms; stereotype mats and lead castings were made and transferred to a rotary press which printed out the newspapers.

In those days, there was a sense of romance and excitement about working on newspapers that appealed to idealistic young people who wanted to change or improve the world, or at least have fun and interesting jobs, despite the obvious reality that salaries were meager and the hours long. (When he retired, John Chancellor of NBC News recalled that when he began as a young reporter on the *Chicago Sun-Times* in 1948, the management didn't know it but he was having so much fun that he would have worked for nothing.) Then, few worried about the future because there was a certain amount of social prestige and cachet in just being a newspaperman. Then (and now) journalists were interesting and stimulating people to be around.

World War II had produced its journalistic heros, Ernie Pyle, Edward R. Murrow, Hal Boyle, Eric Sevareid, and others. Still in its salad days, radio news was much admired and relied upon. One of its early giants, Eric Sevareid, later said he was in the broadcast end of the news business, not the news end of the broadcasting business as he would later be. As seen later, that was an important difference.

Much has changed since I had my first newspaper job in 1948 at the Santa Paula (California) *Daily Chronicle* (circulation 3,000 but now defunct.) (I later worked as a reporter for the *Long Beach Press Telegram* and as a copy editor for the *Santa Monica Outlook, Los Angeles Examiner*, and the *Minneapolis Star*.) As a newspaperman and later journalism educator, I have been dazzled by the changes, for better or worse, that have occurred over the last half century.

Some of those changes were technological—new cold-type production methods and computer terminals revolutionized the news room and the backshop. Computerized high-speed data transfers assisted by communication satellites greatly accelerated thespeed and volume of news and photos. The old-time newspaper city room with its clattering typewriters and its floors strewn with copy paper and galley proofs began to look more like an insurance company office—rugs on the floor, reporters and editors quietly peering into computer terminals and perhaps Muzak playing in the background.

Changes in daily newspaper journalism, however, have been overshadowed in the past half century by the impact of television. In many diverse ways, television news has remade, glamorized, and expanded the reach and impact of daily journalism. But at the same time, the small, flickering screen has distorted, trivialized, and, in many ways, corrupted the news business.

Many of the changes in American journalism—economic, social, cultural, technological—seem mostly related to what television has done *for* and *to* journalism and to society. We have seen how television continues to modify and transform the Olympic Games (away from sport to entertainment) as well as our national political conventions, which no longer choose candidates but merely crown them. The earlier ethic of the near-anonymous reporter has given way to celebrity journalists appearing on television news and talk shows and commanding huge salaries and large lecture fees.

This volume looks at these and other criticisms and evaluates some of the changes in journalism, both positive and negative, and suggests what they may have meant for this nation and indeed for the world at large because American journalism—its methods and its standards—has markedly influenced the way many millions overseas receive news and view their world.

As the century ended, deeper and more disturbing concerns about a perceived crisis in the practice of journalism have surfaced. Media critic Howard Kurtz of *The Washington Post* said the crisis has three essential elements:

> First, a crisis of confidence. Journalists no longer see journalism as the business they got into and are worried about the erosion of fundamental values. Second, a crisis of credibility. More and more people do not believe journalists, don't trust journalists, and think we put our spin on the news. Third, a crisis of tabloidism. The whole business has channel-surfed lately, from Marv Albert to Diana to the nanny trial to O.J. and back again. We are complicit, in varying degrees, in the paparazzi phenomenon. (Kurtz, 1998, p. 44)

Another prominent press critic, Tom Rosenstiel, said of contemporary journalism that

> What is going on in the so-called serious press is a crisis of conviction, a philosophical collapse in the belief in the importance of journalism and the importance of news. When supposedly responsible news organizations stop pursuit of the best obtainable version of the truth and reproduce rumor and gossip, they are shedding long-standing principles. The same is true when they fill space with sensational celebrity news to the exclusion of significant matters.(Kurtz, 1998, p. 45)

I share these views and acknowledge a personal bias: I believe that serious public affairs journalism is an important resource of American public life that should be nurtured and shielded from the various influences that have been marginalizing and trivializing serious news. This is an inquiry into the causes of the malaise that seems to grip the news business today.

THE PRESS AS A DISTORTED MIRROR?

The mirror is often a metaphor (as well as a name) for the daily newspaper; two of the largest, the defunct *New York Daily Mirror* and the flourishing *Daily Mirror* of London, were sensationalist tabloids. Today there is a sense that the bright, shiny mirror of American journalism has received some serious cracks, becoming at times a distorted mirror. One astute journalist, Kenneth Walsh (1996), wrote: "The media are no longer seen as society's truth-sayers. In holding up a mirror to America, journalists too often have filtered out the good and embellished the bad, resulting in a distorted image" (p. 281). I suggest that sometimes our admirable press, as a "false mirror," like Francis Bacon' s human understanding, "distorts and discolors the nature of things" by bringing at times its own preconceptions and biases to bear in reporting the news.

ACKNOWLEDGMENTS

This book is based on a 50-year involvement with newspapers and journalism education. My colleagues, teachers, and students, particularly during my 30 years at the University of Wisconsin–Madison, have helped to educate me about the press. Aware that I will omit some, let me name several of the most influential. Among my teachers, I am indebted to Chilton Bush, Ralph Casey, Edward Gerald, Ray Nixon, Mitch Charnley, Bob Jones, and Harold Chase. Among friends and colleagues, I learned a good deal from Ralph Nafziger, Harold "Bud" Nelson, Wilmott Ragsdale, John McNelly, Graham Hovey, Alex Edelstein, Jim Baughman, Charles Higbie, Jim Fosdick, Steve Chaffee, Jack McLeod, Scott Cutlip, Anthony Giffard, Raymond Louw, and Hartley Howe. Students who later became colleagues and friends include Dave Nimmer, Don Pember, Al Hester, Jim Scotton, Dwight Teeter, John Stevens, Bob Stevenson, Don Dodson, Don Shaw, Earl Hutchison, Frank Kaplan, and David Gordon. I owe much to all of them. Finally, as with everything I have written for many years, this book has benefitted from the careful editing and insightful suggestions by my wife, Harva Sprager Hachten. I alone am responsible for any errors in this book.

—*William A. Hachten*

Introduction

*Most journalism is not about facts but about the interpretation of
what seem to be facts.*

—Walter Lippmann (1922)

As the 21st century begins, it hardly needs repeating that journalism and
mass communication play a central role in modern society. Over time, our
newspapers, magazines, radio, television, cable, video cassettes, computers, and movies have been demanding more and more of our attention and
leisure time. The media markedly affect our politics, our sports, our recre-
ation, our education, and in general and profoundly, our culture, our perception, and our understanding of the world around us.

Although the news media may lack coercive power (a newspaper cannot draft you and send you off to a foreign war or put you in jail), their
influence and pervasiveness are beyond doubt. Yet there are wide disagreements and conflicting views about just how, for better or worse, we
are influenced by media in general and by journalism in particular.

The media, in their diverse, ubiquitous manifestations, are everywhere. As Pember (1992) wrote:

> Perhaps no nation in the history of mankind has enjoyed a communication system
> equal to the one that currently exists in the United States. It must be regarded as one
> of the technological marvels of the modern world. It is a multi-faceted system of
> interpersonal and mass communication elements, and some parts of the network
> touch virtually everyone in the nation. (p. v)

Further, much of the greater world is influenced as well by U.S. mass communications and their cultural by-products and relies heavily on English-language journalism to report global events.

THE IMPORTANCE OF NEWS

Much of the essential and useful information we require for our personal lives and livelihoods comes from the news media. Our economy, our government, and our society would have great difficulty functioning without the continuing flow of news and information—the lifeblood of our body politic. An open, democratic society without independent news media is impossible to imagine.

Many Americans have a strong need for, and attachment to, news and use a variety of news sources at least several times a week; about half of the people in the U.S. say they get most of their news from television. A January 1997 Roper poll found that 70% of the public believe that news is either very or somewhat useful to them in making practical decisions. Half of the respondents said they consume news at least one hour a day; for many it is two hours or more. Two-thirds said it would matter some or a lot if they could not get news for a week.

Journalism or what is often called the news business—the gathering, the processing, and delivery of important and interesting information and developments by newspapers, magazines or broadcast media—is inextricably entangled in the giant, whirling entity often referred to as "the media."

Journalism, of course, is concerned with news, which is somewhat different from information because of its public nature. Michael Schudson believes that news is a form of culture, which he terms "public knowledge," which he defines as "this modern, omnipresent brand of shared knowing" (Schudson, 1995, p. 3). Many millions of Americans pay close attention on a daily basis to the news.

James Fallows argued that the real purpose of journalism (and news) is to satisfy both the general desire for current information and its meaning. "People want to know the details but they also want to see what the details add up to. Journalism exists to answer questions like, 'What is really going on?' and 'Why is this happening?'" (Fallows, 1996, p. 134).

By definition, news reports should be accurate and objective in order to be believed or to be credible. Objectivity means that a news story should be free of a reporter's feelings or opinions and should be based on verifiable facts. Verification of a news story means that the story should be convincing so that there can be no argument about its truth or accuracy.

In explaining the meaning or importance of any event, a journalist always runs the risk of being considered biased or partial, hence the need to be fair and evenhanded. Objectivity and fairness may be difficult, if not impossible, goals to achieve, but it is essential that the journalist try.

News provides perspective by telling people what is considered important and significant and what is not. Page location and size of headlines can indicate this; any story placed on the right-hand column of page one of a metropolitan newspaper is considered important, usually what an editor considers that day's major story. Most of the time, the first item on a television or radio newscast is considered of prime interest. The news, on whatever medium, is not all the news available but only a small selection of it.

Fallows (1996) pointed out that

> During times of scandal our media abandon the pretense of maintaining perspective, and in times without scandal, it hopes for a scandal to come. The financial press does the same thing waiting for the next big takeover deal. The foreign affairs press does so waiting for the next big international disaster. All of them are too busy looking for what is "urgent" to do the daily chore of telling us what is important and why. (p. 134)

This illustrates a long-standing contradiction and dilemma for daily journalism. News should also provide placement in time by not only reporting what is happening but explaining to us the background or the history of a particular story. When genocidal warfare breaks out suddenly in Kosovo or Rwanda, the press should tell us the background and detail of similar tragic instances in that land and elsewhere. News should also point out the similarities and differences in events because many events are important because they fit a certain pattern and as such have added significance. When an airliner, such as the ill-fated TWA Flight 800, explodes in midair, people want to know about similar catastrophes of recent years.

News is not usually a discrete, singular event, although television news often gives that impression. News is a process with a recent past, present, and future, hence, the importance of giving background and context to a story as well as providing follow-up stories. It has also been said that news is a liquid, not a solid.

Much news is interesting and diverting but may be important mainly because many people find it useful. A crisis in the Middle East can mean that gasoline will be more expensive at the pump. Other examples: Next Tuesday is election day and polls are open from 8 a.m. to 8 p.m. Here are the candidates. . . . Here is the weather forecast for today. Business sections of newspapers are replete with useful information about changes in the markets and the shifting prices of investments and commodities. Sports pages provide scores. Scores and scores of scores.

In more abstract terms, Harold Lasswell (1971) wrote that the communication process (including serious journalism) in society performs three broad functions: (a) surveillance of the environment, disclosing threats and opportunities affecting the value positions of the community and of the component parts within it, (b) correlation of the components of society in making a response to the environment, and (c) transmission of the social inheritance to the next generation. According to Lasswell, in democratic societies, rational choices depend on enlightenment, which in turn depends on communication; and especially on the equivalence of attention among the leaders, the experts, and the rank and file. A workable goal of democratic society is equivalent enlightenment among expert, leader, and laymen. If, for example, the president, leading scientists, and the public disagree over the potential threat of global warming, then the society has a problem.

News, as useful public knowledge, is a lot of things as distinct from rumor, titillation, diversion, gossip and, particularly, scandal, although any of these elements may contain kernels of news and unfortunately often become involved in news stories. News has a long and fascinating history; one man's news is another man's titillation, entertainment, propaganda, or diversion.

Nonetheless, news in whatever form seems essential for any society. Gossip, or just idle talk or rumors about the private affairs of others, is not without purpose and seems to be a human requirement; inquiring minds really do want to know. Gossip is all mixed up with and an integral part of journalism and always has been. Much of what is "news" is also gossip, that is, idle talk and rumors, often about the private affairs of others. A large portion of "news" in a newspaper concerns human interest stories, interviews, items about "personalities" or celebrities, and so on. This is true of serious publications as well as tabloids.

Anthropologists and evolutionary psychologists tell us that gossiping is not only a very human activity but is perhaps central to social relationships. At whatever level, at the family, in the workplace, or the broader community, we require and seek out information about other people in order to adjust our relationships with each other. This includes people close to us as well as distant public figures and celebrities of all kinds.

Robin Dunbar (1996) writes that

> Most of us would rather hear about the doings of the great and the not-so-good than about the intricacies of economic processes or the march of science. It is a curious fact that our much-vaunted capacity for language seems to be mainly used for exchanging information on social matters; we seem to be obsessed with gossiping about one another. Even the design of our minds seems to reinforce this. Language makes us members of a community, providing us with the opportunity to share knowledge and experience in a way no other species can do. (p. 6)

A central problem for serious journalism is how to manage gossip as news, how to keep it from overwhelming the significant news that must be reported. Often important stories are rife with gossip and titillation, as in the prolonged Clinton-Lewinsky scandal, and what separates the serious from the trivial media is the way these stories are reported. Continued and repetitious coverage with emphasis on salacious details of a "scandalous" story is often an indicator of bad journalism. The excessive and prolonged attention to the death of Princess Diana was a case in point. Media attention often creates celebrities who then become lifelong "newsworthy" persons. Charles Lindbergh was a notable example of the 1920s and 30s. Similarly, for several decades there has been a continuing interest in any morsel of news or gossip about the Kennedy family. One sociologist's definition of news as "organized gossip" is not far off the mark.

What kinds of news do people want to read about? A Pew Research Center for the People and the Press (1996, May) survey found that crime, the local community, and health were the news subjects that most interest the American public. Culture and the arts, news about famous people, and business and financial news were the least interesting of 14 subjects tested. Other topics of interest included: sports (4th place); local government (5th place); science and technology (6th place); religion (7th place); political news (8th place); international news (9th place); and entertainment (10th place).

Of course, there are marked differences between, say, listeners to National Public Radio (NPR) and C-SPAN and those who watch MTV and tabloid, tell-all television shows. The former were less interested in crime news whereas the latter followed news about crime very closely.

STORIES OF HIGH INTEREST

Other surveys conducted over five years by the Pew Research Center for the People and the Press (1997, April) found that relatively few serious news stories attract the attention of adult Americans, except those that deal with national calamities or the use of American military force. Only one in four Americans (25%) followed the average story closely. Of 480 stories reported over five years, the survey found that most attention went to natural or man-made disasters, such as the Challenger spacecraft explosion, and stories about wars and terrorism involving American citizens. Most notably, only 5% of Americans paid close attention in late 1991 to news about the outbreak of civil war in Yugoslavia.

The public also has a taste for trivia. In early 1990, for example, when only 21% of Americans were following the fall of Communist regimes in Eastern Europe, 74% of Americans had "heard a lot recently" about the Teenage Mutant Ninja Turtles, 78% knew about the recall of Perrier water, and 76% could name George Bush's least favorite vegetable—broccoli.

Sometimes an event of no apparent importance takes on a media life of its own and becomes a consuming passion for many millions of people for weeks or even months on end. In early 2000, no one could have predicted that the plight of a six-year-old Cuban boy, Elian Gonzalez, who was washed ashore in Florida in November 1999 after his mother drowned, would become the center of a media-driven custody controversy involving Cuban exiles in Miami, Fidel Castro, the immigration service and other legal bodies, as well as various politicians. This prolonged media event, a cross between a Cold War skirmish and a soap opera, enthralled many people and dismayed many others, but it was undeniably news.

In a broad sense, the term *media* encompasses most of commercial entertainment—movies, popular music, television, radio, books, and video programming as well as print journalism and broadcast news. But more often media are separated into the entertainment media and the news media and that is a distinction I follow in later chapters. *News media*, or simply the *press*, is used to designate newspapers, journals, news magazines, and those aspects of electronic organizations primarily involved with news and information of public interest and concern. But I quickly add that the intermixing and overlapping of news and entertainment and/or sensationalism is a central concern about today's journalism. Along with this is a trend for opinions and predictions to replace facts, particularly in political reporting.

Increasingly, the media, and sadly some serious journalism and some of its best-known practitioners, have become ensnared in the various orbiting worlds of advertising, publicity, public relations, promotion, and that pervasive commercial activity, marketing. In modern America, apparently no organization is too proud or pure to refrain from trying to market or sell its ideas, its by-products, its people. The aim is to "brand" your name or product so that everyone recognizes it.

The serious news media, which are mainly, but not exclusively, concerned with public affairs news, can at times pursue the same stories and share the news values of trivial or entertainment-oriented media. Even worse, the serious news media sometimes emulate the trash journalism as typified by the supermarket tabloids and various television magazine shows such as *Hard Copy* and *Entertainment Tonight*.

Today, even the best and most responsible of news media are often a mix of hard news, self-help and lifestyle stories, news about celebrities and pop culture, and some scandal and crime news. The editor's goal is to maintain a balance between the important and the fascinating but yet trivial. That essential balance is easier to achieve on daily newspapers than in broadcasting because print media have much larger news holes than the network television news' usual 21 minutes to tell everything. (A news hole is the space left over after advertising, comics, features, etc., have been allocated.)

After all, from its beginnings the press has sought to entertain its readers. Even today, a great many people will be interested in or diverted by a good story. (The press is still not too far removed from Hearst's definition of real news: a story whose headline causes a reader to first stagger back in disbelief and then to rush to buy the paper and read all the shocking details.)

Further, due to pressures for profit-making or just economic survival, some news media and their journalists are facing an identity crisis—they are becoming increasingly involved in the entertainment business. "Infotainment" is a pejorative term used to describe the mixing of news and titillation that is so widespread today. (Historians may say the press has always sought to profit by seeking the greatest possible audience with content as low or enticing as necessary.)

NEWSPEOPLE'S NAMES MAKE NEWS

A fairly recent trend is that some journalists, from network anchors to television talk show regulars, have become highly paid celebrities whose names appear in gossip columns and who command large speaking fees. They are famous because they appear regularly on television talk shows and may appear in *People* magazine. Some people, with no apparent accomplishments, are famous because they are famous.

Many in journalism are distressed by this trend. The journalist as celebrity, it is argued, has undermined press standards and fueled public animosity toward the press.

The identity, if not the soul, of American journalism appears to be threatened. At times, it seems that the news media have made Faustian bargains with the devil in order to increase their circulations, audience sizes, corporate profits, and, in the case of individual journalists, to maximize their personal wealth. For a few, journalism is a very lucrative career. The best newspapers and magazines, as well as broadcast outlets, have always been in business to make money and indeed must prosper in order to survive in the marketplace. But critics detect a recent willingness to unduly compromise journalistic standards to increase monetary gain. In the past, there were always some news organizations for whom public service was a higher calling than merely making money. Today, that seems to be the case less often.

DISAPPEARING FIRE WALL

Public communication today appears to be marked by a kind of Manichaean struggle—a battle between good and evil propensities of journalists and their masters. There is a sense that public affairs journalism has become seriously tainted.

Veteran newsmen say there used to be a "fire wall" at responsible news organizations—such as *The New York Times*, *The Washington Post*,

Time, *Newsweek*, and CBS News, and a few other media—between serious news reporting and mere sensationalism and entertainment. Some feel that wall has almost disappeared or at least has too frequently been breached in the competitive scramble for audiences, circulations, and profits. This scramble has been exacerbated by the intense competition provided by 24-hour cable news outlets and increased use of the Internet to spread rumors and dubious assertions as well as news.

Certain kinds of lurid stories come along that seem to cause some of the most reputable news organizations to forget the fire wall and compete with the "bottom feeders" (i.e., supermarket tabloids) for juicy tidbits about the travails of some celebrity or public figure well known to television viewers. Examples come along too regularly—the Bobbitt case, the Amy Fisher trial, the Menendez brothers trial, the Tonya Harding–Nancy Kerrigan episode, and the JonBenet Ramsey case, among others. Perhaps, the prime example of recent journalistic waywardness was the way the press reported the prolonged murder trial of O. J. Simpson, the story that had everything—a brutal double murder, a well-known athletic celebrity, spousal abuse, celebrity lawyers, racial overtones, and a prolonged, televised trial. During election campaigns, scurrilous and often unfounded rumors make their way into the news cycle of even the most responsible media.

These trends toward trivialization of content and decline of serious news reporting are seen as somehow related to the consolidation of newspapers, magazines, television, and radio stations into bigger and more pervasive media conglomerates with great economic power and influence both here and overseas. Well-regarded news organizations, such as *Time* magazine, the three networks, Cable News Network (CNN), and a long string of once-prestigious daily newspapers such as *The Louisville Courier-Journal* and *The Des Moines Register*, have been swallowed up by media mergers into giant conglomerates. In these multibillion-dollar operations, news organizations devoted to serious journalism represent only a small fraction of a media giant dedicated to maximizing profits from highly profitable entertainment divisions. How have such organizational changes affected the quality and integrity of serious journalism?

For these and other reasons to be discussed later, the American public has become increasingly annoyed and dissatisfied with the news media. Public opinion polls of various kinds show widespread scorn and dislike of much popular culture, the media, and of journalists in general. High-profile journalists such as Diane Sawyer, Sam Donaldson, Cokie Roberts, Barbara Walters, and Dan Rather, among others, have been singled out at times for failing to meet the standards of public affairs journalism.

Public dismay or unhappiness with the media is often confused—and confusing. When the "media" are under attack, one should ask which medium or media personalities are being criticized—one's local daily newspaper, Tom Brokaw on NBC News, Russ Limbaugh on talk radio, shouting anchors on *Crossfire*, or smart-aleck comments in *Newsweek*? Equally unclear is what aspects of the media are undergoing scrutiny—violence or sex in the entertainment media or the lies and distortions of the news media? That is part of the problem. Critical readers and viewers usually treat the media as a monolith, forgetting that media is a plural noun (although the usage is changing) that refers to a complex and multifaceted activity composed of many diverse elements.

Widespread distrust and suspicion of the press exists across the political spectrum from the far left to the far right and among many political moderates. A few critics such as Fallows (1996) believe the press' cynical distortions of political reporting are undermining American democracy.

The public itself, however, is not blameless. The usual comeback of criticized media has long been, "we're just giving the public what it wants." In a sense that is true, and a major failing of Americans today is that too few people are adequately concerned and informed about the serious issues and problems facing the nation. People under 30 years of age read less in general and are not reading many daily newspapers; further, recently a dramatic drop in watching news on network television occurred among this group.

Many young people get their political news, especially during presidential campaigns, not from serious media, but from entertainment sources such as Music Television (MTV), late-night television comedians such as Jay Leno and David Letterman, and from talk radio's call-in shows. There is an obvious need to create and expand a more attentive and critical audience for serious news.

The crisis in journalism may be related to the reality that we are becoming an increasingly polarized society—a small, affluent, and well-educated upper class that attends to news and public information and the swelling bottom 85% of our population (especially those under 30) that reads less and pay less and less attention to public information, opting instead for pop culture and entertainment. The news media themselves reflect these schisms.

I agree with Stephen Hess that the United States is a one-nation-with two-media society, especially in the case of foreign news. Hess (1996) wrote:

Our society is awash in specialized information, available to those who have the time, interest, money, and education to take advantage of it. The other society encompasses the vast majority of Americans, who devote limited attention to subjects far removed from their necessary concerns. They are content to turn to the top stories of television networks' evening news programs and their community's daily newspaper for their information. (p. 5)

This distinction is central in understanding the strengths and weaknesses of American journalism.

THREE MODES
OF DAILY JOURNALISM

This analysis may be helped if we consider that the press often seems to operate under three different modes in covering the day-to-day news. Mode One is a routine, normal news day when no one major story or "blockbuster" dominates the news. The better newspapers will cover a variety of stories, perhaps even reporting foreign news and highlighting a few features or "soft news" stories. Television will do likewise, probably stressing stories of self-help, medical news, personal advice, or human interest.

Mode Two is when a story of major significance breaks: the mysterious explosion of an airliner, results of a presidential election, outbreak of war overseas or the assassination of a major world leader. Both print and broadcasting will throw all their resources into covering these stories. Evening television may devote an entire program to the story—excluding most or all of the other news. *The New York Times* may give the story four or five full pages. This mode shows U.S. journalism at its best.

Mode Three is when a major scandal or sensational story of high interest such as the Simpson case, JonBenet Ramsey murder, or even the air crash death of John Kennedy, Jr., takes over the news spotlight. The most sensational story of the late 1990s, the scandal involving President Clinton with Monica Lewinsky, also had major implications for public affairs and created serious dilemmas for the news media. Television news will respond to stories appearing first in tabloids and pick up the story even while decrying such journalism. Often, the coverage of the coverage becomes a compelling story as well. This mode shows the national media at their worst due to the unseemly scramble over tidbits of news in the scandal. It is worth noting that the current unhappiness with news media and journalists comes during a period of rapid technological change in news communication and entertainment media and their economic underpinnings as well as in a period of societal change. Media—movies, television, pop music, videos, cassettes, CD-ROMs, and computer-generated exchanges such as the Internet—are the main conveyor belts of our vast popular culture, mostly generated in America, that have been sweeping the world, for better or worse.

As noted, American journalism in all of its forms is a small but important part of that cultural flow. The old distinction between foreign and domestic news has all but disappeared as well.

Change brought on by electronic media, especially the Internet, as well as computer-assisted information transfers, threatens the viability of traditional ways of reporting the news, yet offers promising new ways of disseminating information.

The focus in this book is on serious news coverage, primarily American journalism, and how news is gathered, edited, and disseminated here and abroad. Although faced with such recent disturbing trends as tabloidization, mixing of facts and opinion, lowering of standards, and trivialization, as well as media consolidation and commercialization to increase profitability, American journalism is still arguably the most informative and most free anywhere and is an influential and significant source of news for news organizations of other nations.

A great advantage of the free and independent journalism Americans have enjoyed is its ability to correct its own excesses through the process of self-criticism. American journalism has had a long tradition of self-examination throughout the 20th century—from Will Irwin to A. J. Liebling to various journalism reviews and a current bumper crop of astute critics, several of whom are quoted here. Some newspapers have ombudsmen, who act as representatives of the public in responding to complaints about media performance.

Many within the field of journalism are deeply concerned about its shortcomings and want to see changes made. So if it will recognize its faults (some say U.S. journalism is in denial), U.S. journalism can potentially correct and improve itself. Recently, a good deal of self-criticism has been going on *within* U.S. journalism, a reassuring sign. The power of embarrassment and shame to convince journalistic peers to mend their ways should not be underestimated. There are some indications that media criticism has been bringing results.

This volume examines recent trends and current problems that beset American journalism in its schizophrenic, love-hate relationship with the burgeoning entertainment industry—typified by such names as Rupert Murdoch, AOL-Time Warner, Disney-ABC, the Gannett and Knight-Ridder newspaper chains, NBC, CBS—and with a wary and sometimes hostile public. People often do not like the media, but they still pay attention to the media.

Chapter 1, "Best News Media in the World?," examines the American news system as it operates today. It is usually considered the best, most comprehensive, and reliable in the world. Chapter 1 also looks at its key players and major organizations—the so-called national media.

In our rapidly changing world of interdependent economic systems and political uncertainties, American news media have become major players in global news exchanges and mass culture diffusion. In chapter 2, "Global Impact of American Media," I analyze the expanded international role of American journalism and note how changes in media structures are impacting on major news events, which in turn influence diplomacy and the relations between nations.

American journalism has enjoyed unusual freedom from government interference and has broad constitutional protections when criticizing public officials. Chapter 3, "Freedom of the Press: Theory and Values," shows how the First Amendment and political theory undergird the news media, protecting rights of expression enjoyed by all of us.

A brief historical overview in chapter 4, "Recent History of the Press," provides some perspective on current press difficulties. Monopoly, sensationalism, tabloidization, irresponsibility, and public unhappiness with the press have all been around for quite a while. No one designed our news system. It has expanded rapidly and is still evolving.

Bigness, fewness, and like-mindedness are the concerns of chapter 5, "Bigger, Fewer, and More Like-minded," which examines how profit opportunities at home and abroad, as well as innovative media technologies, are driving our mass media into bigger and more concentrated conglomerates. Recent megamergers have markedly changed the structure and possibly compromised the integrity of mass communication. Further, the number of truly independent news organizations is fast diminishing.

The pervading perceptions of decline in electronic journalism—diminishing audiences, lower status for downsized news staffs, compromised news standards and infotainment trends, all driven by profit squeezes—are analyzed in chapter 6, "News on the Air: A Sense of

Decline." An examination of the similar malaise of the newspaper business is the focus of chapter 7, "The Fading American Newspaper?" Comparable concerns about downsizing to increase profits, declines in readership and, for big city papers, in retail advertising, are analyzed.

Chapter 8, "Why the Public Hates (Some) Journalists," examines widespread dismay with political journalism and with celebrity journalists seen on television talk shows and lecture tours. Some believe that the political culture has been debased by the cynicism and negativism of the political press.

Chapter 9, "The Clinton Scandal and 'Mixed Media,'" examines the crisis within the news media over the ways that the long-running controversy involving the president and Monica Lewinsky was reported to the American public. Chapter 10, "Changes in Foreign News Coverage," looks at problems of reporting foreign news and the changing role of the foreign correspondent. Chapter 11, "The Press and the Military," reports on the often-abrasive relations between the press and the U.S. military in the news coverage of military incursions abroad from Panama, Grenada, Persian Gulf War, Somalia, and the air war over Kosovo and Serbia.

Chapter 12, "News on the Internet," speculates about some of the short-term changes to be expected in the collection, collation, and distribution of news via cyberspace. Change is coming rapidly but no one knows for sure how journalism will be affected. Chapter 13, "Educating Journalists," focuses on how to prepare young journalists within the context of journalism education in universities. The final chapter, chapter 14, "Conclusions: Journalism at a Time of Change," offers several ways to improve press performance.

1

Best News Media in the World?

There is much to criticize about the press, but not before recognizing
a ringing truth: the best of the American press is an extraordinary
daily example of industry, honesty, conscience, and courage, driven
by a desire to inform and interest readers.

—Ben Bradlee (1996)

A major news event can occur unexpectedly somewhere in the world at any moment—the explosion of a jet airliner in midair, a terrorist bombing of an American military facility, the assassination of a world leader, an outbreak of war in the Middle East, a major oil spill in a ecologically sensitive region.

On hearing about an important news story, millions of Americans turn to their television sets or radio to learn more—to CNN perhaps, or to an all-news radio station for the first details from the Associated Press (AP) or Reuters or from broadcast reporters. The evening network news shows will give a more full picture and one of the networks—ABC on Ted Koppel's *Nightline* or maybe NBC or CBS—may put together a special report later in the evening. In addition, the news will be available on cable networks and the Internet.

The next morning more complete stories with additional details will appear in more than 1,500 daily newspapers and hundreds of radio and television stations will recap the story with more developments. If the story is big enough, if it "has legs," *The New York Times* may devote three or four inside pages to more details, related stories, and news photos. Other major dailies may do the same.

Within a week, the news magazines, *Time*, *Newsweek*, and *U.S News and World Report*, will publish their own versions, complete with cover stories, more background, and commentary.

If the event is important enough, aware Americans will know the basic essentials—"Terrorists bomb U.S. military housing in Saudi Arabia"—within 24 hours, and the "news junkies" and interested specialists among us will know a great deal more.

Such extensive communication of so much news and information, driven by high-speed computer systems, communication satellite networks, and various databases, is commonplace today. Many Americans will pay little attention and will not be impressed, but to some of us, such an impressive journalistic performance will be dazzling. For when it is good, American journalism is very good indeed—as any careful examination of the annual Pulitzer Prizes, DuPont-Columbia Awards, National Magazine Awards, and Peabody Awards reminds us. Probably no newspaper covers the day's news as well and as thoroughly as does *The New York Times*. Rivals that may outperform the *Times* at times (and they often do) would be other major U.S. papers such as *The Washington Post*, *The Los Angeles Times*, *The Wall Street Journal*, or *the Philadelphia Inquirer*, winner of numerous Pulitzer Prizes for excellence in reporting.

There are good newspapers, of course, in other open, democratic societies, many of which serve their readers well. Newspapers are edited for the interests and concerns of their own readers in their own cultures, so comparisons of papers across national boundaries are often interesting but probably pointless.

NATIONAL MEDIA SET AGENDA

These daily papers plus *Time*, *Newsweek*, *U.S. News*, and the television networks—ABC, NBC, CBS, and CNN—plus NPR are often referred to as the national media, and to a large extent they set the news agenda for other media across America.

What the national media decide is major or important news in New York City and Washington, DC, will be important news, or at least noted, in Pocatello and Peoria, because electronic news, as well as AP news, reaches almost every community. This nationalizing of the American press took place over several decades. News magazines and nationwide radio news were well established before World War II. A national television news system took on real importance after the 30-minute format took over in 1963. The highly successful *60 Minutes* appeared in 1968 and *Nightline* in 1979 becoming important supplements to the evening news and imitated later by lesser broadcast newsmagazines. C-SPAN also started in 1979 and CNN in 1980. In the 1990s, other cable channels from NBC and Fox became players, while more and more of the public turned to the Internet for late-breaking news as well as sports results.

In 1970, educational and noncommercial radio licensees formed NPR and out of it came two superior daily national news programs "All Things Considered" and "Morning Report."

Due to facsimile and satellite publication, several major newspapers, *The Wall Street Journal*, *The New York Times*, and *U.S.A. Today* are now available to many millions through home delivery, by same day mail, or on newsstands almost everywhere in the nation. Today, an American interested in significant news has almost the same access to these national media as anyone in New York City or Washington, DC.

In this sense, "national" has two meanings. These media are available across the country and they provide news and information of national, not of local or parochial, interest. This agenda-setting function of the national media flies in the face of the reality that most news is local, as the perusal of page one of any small daily newspaper or local television news show will attest. People are most interested in what happens close to home, whatever seems to most directly affect their own lives. A small airplane crash at a nearby airport is a bigger story than a jet going down with 250 aboard in Europe. But for important news from distant places, the national media decide what is significant or at least highly interesting, and regional and local media generally take heed. The national media also collect and edit foreign news.

The dissemination of that news is assisted greatly by the AP, the cooperative news service owned by U.S. press and broadcast outlets, which is instantly available to almost every daily paper and most broadcasters.

Reuters and the news syndicates of The New York Times, The Washington Post, and The Los Angeles Times companies supplement the AP's round-the-clock coverage. News video on television and cable networks is often syndicated or cooperatively shared with local broadcasters in much the same way. United Press International (UPI) is no longer able to compete with AP and Reuters.

Televised news has evolved as an elaborate process of gathering and disseminating news and video from domestic and foreign organizations. For many millions, the television and perhaps the car radio may be their only source of news. A major reason for the steady decline of afternoon papers in big cities was that the papers' midday deadlines enabled the evening television news shows to offer major stories breaking too late to be reported by those papers.

Although declining in audiences and profits, the three networks news shows, identified with ABC's Peter Jennings, NBC's Tom Brokaw, and CBS's Dan Rather, usually maintain professional standards. Until 1996, Jennings' report was considered the best; ABC's news resources, especially in foreign news, were superior, and Jennings was seemingly less tempted than CBS or NBC to present more entertainment-oriented and trivial features at the expense of hard news. More recently, NBC has topped the ratings and CBS has made something of a comeback. But essentially the highly competitive networks stay fairly close together in the size of their audiences as well as their popular appeal and choice of content.

Broadcast media and print media each have different strengths in reporting major news stories. For epochal events from the opening night of the Gulf War to the election returns of a presidential contest, network television can command the nation's attention for hours on end. Network news, including CNN, easily switches locales to bring information and comment from a variety of sources; at times, widely scattered reporters or experts can be brought together electronically to engage in group discussions—all of which we now take for granted. Through video and spoken reports, television viewers get the headlines and the first available facts.

Newspapers and news magazines, however, have the space and the time to provide more details, background, and analysis than broadcasting. Moreover, print media are much better on follow-up stories to inform the public about what really happened during, say, the air war over Kosovo and Serbia and its complex aftermath.

NEW CATEGORIES OF NEWS

This volume is critical of some current journalistic practices, so it is important to realize that in many ways the news media today are better than they have ever been.

Forty years ago, most newspapers considered the news to be covered adequately if they reported some government affairs and politics; a smattering of foreign news, local crime and disaster stories; some business news; and sports. In addition, light and human interest features to divert and entertain were often included.

In recent years, this same subject mix is still being covered but in much more detail and depth, for journalism is very much a part of the information explosion and news media now have far larger amounts of news available. More importantly, the definitions of what is news have been greatly expanded to include news and developments about science, medical research, reviews of movies, the arts and popular culture, the entertainment business, a wide range of social problems, education, legal affairs, information technology and the computer revolution, personal health, nutrition, and many facets of the business and financial world here and abroad. Much of this expanded reporting is done by specialists with professional training in their fields. (These expanded news categories should not be confused with the gossip, trivia, and celebrity-oriented sensationalism that have also expanded but that so many deplore in some of today's media.)

A recent study of media in the last 20 years found that the current news media are producing fewer stories about "what happened today" than two decades ago, and are devoting less coverage to government and foreign affairs. More prevalent now are features on life style, human interest, personal health, crime, entertainment, scandal and celebrities. Why the shift? The Cold War is over, and technology, medical science, and the environment have taken on new importance. Another harbinger of change was *Time*'s announcement in October 1999 that it would publish in five special issues a serialized novel by Caleb Carr, a writer of historical thrillers. It may have been the first time a news magazine had published serialized fiction and departed from its tradition of news only.

This broader newspaper and broadcast coverage is supplemented by a plethora of specialized magazines, journals, and books that deal with such topics in a more leisurely and detailed manner.

Any person living anywhere in America who is determined to be well informed and be on top of the news can do so by owning a television set with cable, subscribing to a national newspaper such as *The New York Times* or *The Wall Street Journal*, listening to NPR, selectively watching CNN and C-SPAN, and subscribing to several magazines such as *Newsweek, Harper's The New Republic, The New Yorker, Atlantic, Foreign Affairs,* or *The Economist*, plus getting a good state or regional daily newspaper.

Further, our hypothetical news junkies can gain access to a lot more news and information, if they also own a computer with a modem to scan the news and information available from online services such as America Online, Yahoo, CNN, MSNBC, Slate, or the interactive editions of hundreds of newspapers on the World Wide Web (see chap. 12).

At this time of media bashing, it is well to remember that a lot of good reporting still gets done by newspapers. Phillips (1996) commented:

> Anyone with an hour for a Nexis computer search can come up with 50 courageous exposes of special interests buying congressional favors, lobbies run amok, the plight of the Middle Class and such like in *The New York Times, The Washington Post, The Wall Street Journal, The Chicago Tribune, The Philadelphia Inquirer, The Los Angeles Times,* and *The Boston Globe*. The ghost of Lincoln Steffens is not gone from the nation's newsrooms. (p. 8)

Press critic Ben Bagdikian (1992) commented that newspapers are much better today than they were 40 years ago and report a great deal more news than before. But, he added, newspapers now need to be better than before because much more and varied information is required to cope with today's complex and changing world; further, many Americans today are better educated and desire, indeed require, more sophisticated and specialized news for their lives and their jobs.

As always, what some people consider to be very important news does not get reported. Most news is mainly of local or parochial interest and does not make it beyond city or state borders. Sometimes, major stories, such as the savings and loan scandals of the 1980s, will be reported in some national media but fail to make an impression on other media and, hence, do not attract the attention of the public in general.

Further, despite the availability of so much news each day, similar space and time constraints persist. ABC, CBS, and NBC have only 21 minutes each evening for their major newscasts. Sometimes a major breaking story, such as the TWA Flight 800 disaster, will take the entire 21 minutes; as a result, no other news gets reported on that broadcast. Radio's news-on-the-hour broadcasts usually last 5 minutes or less. Many daily newspapers have small news holes for the day's news after all the retail advertisements, features, comics, advice columns, classifieds, stock market reports, and sports have been included. Most people probably devote less than one hour a day to news from various media.

Journalism, as that proverbial "watchman on the hill" keeps its eyes open and sees more because news gatherers can penetrate almost all corners of the world, but not always. Between 1928 and 1938 an estimated 10 to 20 million people were killed or starved to death in the Soviet Union as a result of Stalin's brutal and disastrous policies, but little news about this horror reached American readers. Similarly, in the early 1960s little was reported about the 20-30 million Chinese who perished during Mao's Great Leap Forward. Today, it is less likely that an autocratic regime could hide calamities of such proportions from the world's view.

To better understand what is ahead, we need to provide a concise overview of the American press as it exists today.

THE "MIGHTY WURLITZER" OF U.S. JOURNALISM

The two main arms of U.S. journalism today, print media and electronic media, are divided as well into three main approaches:

1. The "new news" of daily journalism as exemplified by the daily newspaper, evening television news, or radio "news-on-the-hour" with the latest from AP; plus cable and Internet sources;
2. weekly or periodical journalism as typified by *Time* as well as the better television discussion shows like *Meet the Press* and *Washington Week in Review*;
3. commentary or opinion journalism in various periodicals; *The New Republic*, *Nation*, *Foreign Affairs*, *Atlantic*, and Sunday editions of some dailies, as well as books, are examples.

The expectations for objectivity, balance, and fairness are much higher, naturally, for daily journalism, which reports the first version of events, than for the more leisurely weekly and opinion publications or the talk shows of weekend television. Daily journalism also has room for editorial comment and interpretation, but the expectation is that comment and predictions should be clearly identified and separated from hard or just-appearing news.

The Print Media

Daily Newspapers.   Although viewed by some as a twilight industry, the daily newspaper is still the most effective means of supplying large amounts of serious late-breaking news to the American public. A total of about 1,500 dailies are published—roughly 40% in the morning and 60% in the afternoon—with a total circulation of about 63 million. Almost all metropolitan papers come out in the morning to better compete with television.

Circulations vary widely. Fifteen dailies have a circulation of more than 500,000, whereas more than 1,129 dailies have circulations under 25,000 and are primarily concerned with serving small cities and communities.

The backbone and intellectual leadership of daily journalism comes from the 40-45 dailies each with circulations of more than 250,000 and includes all those considered the best plus a number of mediocre or fading dailies.

A December 1999 survey by the *Columbia Journalism Review* of 150 daily newspaper editors produced the following rankings for what they considered to be America's 21 best daily newspapers:

1. New York Times; 2. Washington Post; 3. Wall Street Journal; 4. Los Angeles Times; 5. Dallas Morning News; 6. Chicago Tribune; 6. Boston Globe; 8. San Jose Mercury News; 9. St. Petersburg Times; 10. The Sun (of Baltimore); 11. Philadelphia Inquirer; 12. The Oregonian; 13. USA Today; 14. Seattle Times; 15. Newsday; 16. Raleigh News & Observer; 17. Miami Herald; 18. Star Tribune (of Minneapolis); 19. Atlanta Journal-Constitution; 20. Orange County Register (of Santa Anna); Sacramento Bee. (America's best, 1999, p. 16)

From this elite group, the largest and presumably the most influential dailies include:

The *Wall Street Journal* (daily circulation about 1.7 million) is primarily a business publication but is noted for its excellent news coverage and fine writing on nonbusiness topics. Owner is the Dow Jones Co., which has 14 other papers.

USA Today (circulation about 2 million) is also distributed nationally and is owned by the Gannett Co., which has 74 dailies and a total daily circulation of more than 6.6 million. The paper has received mixed reviews but is considered to be improving and is carrying more hard news.

The New York Times has a Sunday circulation about 1.7 million, of which about 200,000 comes from its national edition. Although undergoing marked changes in recent years, the *Times* is still considered by many as the nation's most influential newspaper and targets an elite readership.

As mentioned, the large circulations of *The Wall Street Journal, USA Today*, and *The New York Times* are due in part to their national distribution; facsimile newspaper pages are sent via satellite to regional printing plants around the nation.

The Los Angeles Times (about 1.3 million Sunday) is one of the notable success stories in U.S. journalism, changing in the past 40 years from a parochial, partisan paper into the finest newspaper west of the eastern seaboard. (In March 2000, the paper and the Times Mirror Company were purchased by the Tribune Company of Chicago.)

The Washington Post (Sunday circulation about one million) is highly regarded and wields great influence in the political vortex of the nation's capital. The Washington Post Co. also owns *Newsweek* as well as broadcast and cable properties. The paper competes head-to-head with *The New York Times* on major stories in Washington but targets the greater Washington area for readers.

The New York Times, Washington Post, Los Angeles Times and *Wall Street Journal* all maintain significant numbers of their own reporters in key capitals overseas. In truth, concern about the global economy and political instability of the world beyond our shores and the willingness to report foreign news is one of the hallmarks of a great news medium. Much of this outstanding reporting finds its way to other dailies through syndication.

Another major newspaper group is Knight-Ridder Inc. with 29 papers enjoying a circulation of 4,136,770. Highly regarded among its properties are *The Miami Herald, The Charlotte Observer, San Jose Mercury News*, and *The Philadelphia Inquirer*, each an outstanding daily with great influence in its city and suburbs. For $1.65 billion, Knight-Ridder acquired two big additions, *The Kansas City Star*, circulation 291,000, and *The Fort*

Worth Star-Telegram, circulation 240,000, from the Disney Co. in April 1997.

Finally, Newhouse Newspapers has 26 dailies with a circulation of 2,960,360, including *The Oregonian*. Newhouse also owns *The New Yorker* and the Conde Nast magazines.

Weekly Newspapers.   At the other end of the circulation scales are the 7,400 to 7,500 weekly newspapers that average about 7,500 subscribers each. Total circulation of these publications, so important in so many small communities, is about 55 million, more than double the mid-1960s total. Although often small and unimposing, these papers are close to their readers and usually serve their communities well. Local news dominates these papers (Strentz & Keel, 1995).

Magazines.   Certainly the most diverse and perhaps the most change-able, yet resilient of the media have been magazines, of which about 4,000 are published, up from 2,500 in the mid-1980s. Carmody (1995) reported that 832 new magazines started in 1994; 67 of these were about sports and 44 were related to sex. Each year about 80% of newly launched magazines fail.

Comparatively few magazines are mainly concerned with journalism and news but, overall, magazines contribute tremendous amounts of diverse information and entertainment available to the public. As seen later, U.S. magazines are increasingly popular overseas.

Leading news magazines and their approximate circulations are: *Time* (4.1 million); *Newsweek* (3.2 million); and *U.S. News and World Report* (2.3 million). Business magazines such as *Money* (2.2 million), *Business Week* (900,000), and *Fortune* and *Forbes* (each about 770,000) contribute to the public affairs news as do *Atlantic*, *Harper's*, and *The New Yorker*.

Though modest in circulations, opinion journals such as the *New Republic, Nation,* and *National Review* have a disproportionate influence on politicians, opinion makers and intellectuals, particularly in Washing-ton, DC and New York City.

Books.   Over 50,000 new book titles are published annually in the United States and a significant number contribute directly to the swirling cauldron of journalism. Ever since Theodore H. White wrote *The Making of the President, 1960*, after John Kennedy defeated

Richard Nixon, journalists have been writing numerous books on national politics and public affairs. However, the two political best sellers of 1996—*Primary Colors* by Anonymous (Joe Klein) and *Rush Limbaugh is a Big Fat Idiot* by Al Franken—were essentially satire and entertainment, not political journalism.

Nowadays, almost all candidates for the presidency kick off their campaign by publishing a book to publicize themselves and their political ideas; such efforts qualify as political journalism. Of interest here is that journalists have been writing books critical of media performance. Important recent efforts include *Breaking the News* by James Fallows, *Hot Air: All Talk, All the Time* and *Spin Cycle* both by Howard Kurtz, *Feeding the Beast* by Kenneth T. Walsh, *Don't Shoot the Messenger* by Bruce Sanford, *Warp Speed* by Bill Kovach and Tom Rosenstiel, *Life: The Movie* by Neal Gabler, and *What the People Know* by Richard Reeves.

Electronic Media

Radio.   Radio is ubiquitous and has been for most of the 20th century. Receiving sets are everywhere—in almost every car, scattered around the house, and carried by young people and joggers. There are 500 million sets in America. The nation is served by more than 8,454 radio stations of which 3,764 are AM stations and 4,690 are FM stations. About 70% of the audience listens to FM. Many big city radio stations today are quite profitable.

Hard hit by the advent of television, radio was slow in finding a new niche. It no longer seeks its previous mass audience and offers instead narrow formats in various kinds of music and news, plus a smattering of network programming, especially in news. Radio's survival has offered additional proof that older media are supplemented by new media, not replaced by them.

Radio's journalistic contributions appear to consist mainly of brief newscasts stressing local and regional news, as well as headlines and brief reports on national and foreign events. As mentioned, two shining exceptions are National Public Radio's *Morning Report* and *All Things Considered* heard all over the nation on public stations. These programs make important contributions to the reporting and analysis of public affairs. Public radio has disproved the conventional wisdom that government support of broadcasting compromises journalistic quality and independence.

Television.   A good deal is written about television news and its ups and downs. To set the scene briefly, here are a few basic facts: More than 1,290 commercial licenses have been granted by the Federal Communications Commission (FCC). Of these, about half are VHF, with a far-reaching signal, and half are UHF stations, more numerous and limited in reach.

Viewers have access to about 350 noncommercial or public television stations. More than 400 commercial stations are independents, not affiliated with the four major networks—CBS, ABC, NBC, and Fox. (Two fledgling networks, UPN and WB, are trying to break into prime time.) Television markets vary widely from New York City with about 7 million television households, all the way to Alpena, Michigan, with just 15,600 households with television sets (Strentz & Keel, 1995).

Ninety-eight percent of homes have television sets and research suggests that sets are on seven hours a day in a typical home. About 80% of homes have a video cassette recorder (VCR) and 60% receive cable. Both VCR and cable percentages are steadily increasing as are satellite receivers. In 1997, there were 1,594 total cable systems across the nation. Cable channels such as CNN and MSNBC have become major outlets for both news and public affairs programming.

Most Americans are aware of television's importance as a news medium. If at any time there are rumors of a disaster or other ominous event, people will first turn on their television sets or, if away from home, their radios. But they are more likely today to find the breaking news on a cable station than a broadcast outlet.

Public television stations have made their own significant contributions to broadcast journalism primarily in recent years through the *News Hour with Jim Lehrer* and various documentary news programs such as *Frontline, Nova, The American Experience*, and so on. With the exception of CBS' *60 Minutes*, news documentaries or news magazines on commercial networks rarely reach the journalistic quality of those on PBS.

Another important contributor to broadcast news is C-SPAN, the nonprofit cable channel created to report on the legislative process in the U.S. Congress. In addition, it provides television coverage, without comment or interpretation, of a wide variety of meetings, conferences, or seminars, all of which have some connection to public affairs. C-SPAN has a small but devoted group of listeners who care about public affairs.

Finally, the Internet has been rapidly growing in importance as a medium for news as computer users have been increasing at exponential rates. Broadcast and print news organizations all seem now to have their outlets in cyberspace. In 1994, there were 20 newspapers on online; in 1999, there were 4,925 worldwide with 2,799 of them in the United States. As the year 2000 began, the Web sites with most visitors were, in order, *MSNBC.COM*; *CNN Networks*; *ABC News*; *USATODAY.COM*; *NY TIMES.COM*; *CBS.COM.*; and *WASHINGTONPOST.COM*. (See chap. 12, "News on the Internet," for more details.)

As mentioned, we are largely concerned with the so-called national media, all of which have the capability of reaching most of the nation— either directly on indirectly. There are, of course, other important regional news media—in Chicago, Boston, Philadelphia, Detroit, Los Angeles, San Francisco, Seattle, Phoenix, Houston, Dallas, Miami, Denver, Atlanta, and numerous other urban areas but the national media have an agenda-setting capability and influence extending beyond their locales.

These national media have overlapping audiences and, to a great extent, reach the movers and shakers of the American establishment— leaders in government, politics, social affairs, business, and academia, especially along the eastern seaboard from Boston to Atlanta and throughout the midwest and the West Coast.

As shown later, these trends raise concerns about just where the news media are headed. For one thing, it means that the great majority of Americans are not being reached by serious journalism. Whether the U.S. news media are the best in the world or not may be a pointless argument. The more important question is whether they are as good as they should be or could be. Nonetheless, as seen in chapter 2, the impact of American journalism on the world has been significant.

CHAPTER

2

Global Impact
of American Media

*Mankind has become one, but not steadfastly one as communities or
nations used to be, nor united through years of mutual experience. . .
nor yet through a common language, but surpassing all barriers,
through international broadcasting and printing.*

—Alexander Solzhenitsyn

Most Americans who keep up with the news are unaware of the influence
and reach of American journalism beyond the borders of their nation. During the past 50 years, the U.S. news media, in doing their basic job of
reporting the news for local audiences, have participated in and helped
shape a world that is economically more interdependent while being, since
the end of the Cold War, more politically fractured and still threatening.

In addition to American-generated news in print and broadcasting, our
movies, pop music, television programs, and lifestyles have penetrated the
minds and cultures of European and non-Western people with tremendous
impact. With results both positive and negative, transnational communication is undeniably evolving toward a single, integrated global communication system that espouses free, independent journalism as well as favoring
market economies and Western popular culture. As seen later, the current

wave of major media mergers can be viewed in part as corporate strategies to better compete for overseas markets and profits in both entertainment and news.

The enhanced ability of Western journalism (Britain and other industrial democracies contribute as well) to report quickly and fully on global crises and trends enables leaders of nation states, the United Nations, and business and nongovernmental organizations to respond to such challenges. News media can and do alert nations to a kaleidoscope of such dangers as environmental disasters, changing facets of terrorism, human rights clashes, economic trends and crises, and incipient political crises whether in Bosnia, Central Africa, Chechnya, or Kosovo.

It has been said with some but not much exaggeration that an American's right to know is the world's right to know. For any news story that gets into the American news media can and often does flow rapidly around the world and can appear in local media anywhere if it gets by the various gatekeepers that select and reject the news of the day. Since the end of the Cold War and the demise of Communist news systems in the Soviet Union and other Eastern-bloc nations, the American approach to international news, based on independent and wide-roving journalists free to report (at least in theory) whatever they want and wherever they wish, has gained influence and acceptance.

English is the dominant language of global news just as it is of computers and the Internet. Global news gathering is now more cooperative and less confrontational (or competitive) than it was in the Cold War days, and more countries are now open to foreign journalists.

Autocratic regimes still exist, of course, and many often restrict their own journalists, as well as foreign reporters while trying to control the news, but they have not been as successful as they once were. Despite press controls in such currently authoritarian states as China, Cuba, and Algeria, the news does get out sooner or later.

GLOBAL NEWS SYSTEM

This global news system, although largely American, is greatly enhanced by such British media as the great BBC World Service (mainly shortwave radio) and BBC World television (a recent competitor to CNN International), Reuters news agency, *The Financial Times*, *The Economist*, and the long tradition of foreign coverage in several elite newspapers such as *The Guardian*, *Times of London*, *Sunday Times*, *The Independent*, and *Daily*

Telegraph. Reuters Television (successor to Visnews) and World Television News (WTN), two Anglo-American enterprises, daily gather and distribute video news packages to television stations all over the world.

Among U.S. daily newspapers, most of the foreign reporting, some of high quality, comes from just seven publications—*The New York Times*, *The Washington Post*, *The Los Angeles Times*, *The Wall Street Journal*, *The Chicago Tribune*, *The Christian Science Monitor*, and *The Baltimore Sun*—which all maintain overseas news bureaus. (The Tribune Co. now owns the *L.A. Times* and *Baltimore Sun*.) These papers, whose total daily circulation is about 11 million, represent only about 20% of newspaper circulation of all U.S. dailies. Companies controlling 80% of daily newspaper circulation have been making little effort to produce sustained international coverage; the list includes such prominent newspaper owners' names as Newhouse, Thomson, Hearst, McClatchy, and Pulliam.

A survey by the *American Journalism Review* reported that as of September 1998, there were 186 full-time staff writers working in newspaper foreign bureaus. *The New York Times* had 38 reporters in 26 bureaus; *The Washington Post* had 25 reporters in 19 bureaus; and *The Los Angeles Times* had 28 reporters in 22 bureaus.

The big explosion in overseas coverage has been due to the expanded interest in business and financial news—a key aspect of the expanding global economy. This explains the 100 staffers for *The Wall Street Journal* with its business focus and overseas editions. Reuters and Bridge News (formerly Knight-Ridder financial news) have hundreds of overseas staffers to report its specialized economics news. Bloomberg News, another financial news service, had 226 reporters in 62 countries (Arnett, 1998).

Most dailies rely on the Associated Press' widespread correspondents for news from abroad. AP is probably the single most important agency that collects and distributes news globally. By the agency's count, more than 1 billion people have daily access to AP news. To collect foreign news abroad, AP maintains bureaus in 93 countries staffed by 400 full-time foreign correspondents. Like Reuters, its closest competitor, AP uses an extensive network of leased satellites circuits, submarine cables, and radio transmissions, and even the Internet, to supply newspapers and broadcasters with up-to-the-minute news around the world 24 hours a day. AP broadcast services are used by 6,000 radio and television stations. Three key centers—New York, London, and Tokyo—channel the millions of words and pictures daily to both U.S. and foreign subscribers.

The New York Times, *The Washington Post*, and *The Los Angles Times* syndicate their foreign news stories, thereby extending the impact of U.S. journalism overseas. The New York Times News Service, including Cox newspapers and *The Boston Globe*, sends more than 50,000 words daily to 550 clients, of which more than 130 are newspapers abroad. Its close competitor is the Los Angeles Times/Washington Post News Service, which transmits about 60,000 words daily to 50 nations or about 600 newspapers, half of which are outside the United States.

Hess (1994) reported that major broadcasters of news (and the number of bureaus) are ABC (5), ABC Radio (9), CBS (4), CBS Radio (4), CNN (19), Mutual Radio/NBC (1), NBC (11), and NPR (3).

Time, *Newsweek*, and *U.S. News and World Report* have long maintained substantial bureaus overseas in major news capitals but numbers of staffers has been shrinking in recent years.

Since 1980, CNN has added a new dimension to global television journalism—the ability to broadcast news around the clock via satellite, aided by cable, to millions of television sets in foreign nations. Broadcast news from ABC, NBC, and CBS is also found on foreign cable and satellite systems.

U.S. global journalism is augmented by two important U.S.-owned daily newspapers. *The International Herald Tribune* (IHT), published in Paris, is a joint venture of the New York Times and Washington Post companies and carries stories and features from both papers in addition to reports generated by a staff of 40. IHT, a marvel of newspaper distribution, sells about 200,000 copies six days a week in 164 countries (in Europe alone sales number about 135,000) and is printed by plants in London, the Hague, Marseilles, Rome, Zurich, Singapore, Hong Kong, and Miami. Although still an American paper in outlook and content, it has acquired an important non-American readership. Nearly half its readers are an elite group of European internationalists—businessmen, diplomats, and journalists fluent in English. IHT is the first newspaper in history to publish the same edition simultaneously for distribution to all continents.

The Asian Wall Street Journal covers a 16-country, 6,000 square-mile business beat from Manila to Karachi. Averaging about 12 pages an issue and roughly one third the size of the domestic edition, the paper tries for the same mix of authoritative business and political news, a risky effort for a region with so little press freedom. *The Wall Street Journal* also has a European edition, written and edited in Brussels and printed in the

Netherlands. The Asian *Journal* has nearly 33,000 circulation and the European *Journal* about 47,000.

American magazines are influential abroad as well. Two international-ized versions of *Time* and *Newsweek*—in English—are widely read glob-ally. Among non-news U.S. magazines, Hearst publishes *Cosmopolitan*, *Esquire*, *Good Housekeeping*, and *Popular Mechanics* in 14 languages in 80 nations. For example, the Russian language edition of *Cosmopolitan* carried 110 pages of ads and sold 225,000 copies in 1995. A long-time overseas success is *Reader's Digest*, which in 1995 had 47 international editions in 18 languages, circulating 13 million copies a month overseas. Many millions reading the *Digest* overseas are unaware that it is an Amer-ican magazine.

Also important in disseminating U.S. and world news abroad is the U.S. government's Voice of America (VOA), which broadcasts via short-wave radio in 48 languages and has an audience in the tens of millions. A BBC study found that 200 million people daily tune in to shortwave radio on about 600 million shortwave receivers around the globe—half in Asia and Africa. In the last 20 years, the total number of nations that broadcast internationally has risen to more than 100 and the number of hours broad-cast has risen to about 30,000 hours annually, almost double that of the 1960s. Most international broadcasters carry some news programming.

MAJOR EFFECTS OF GLOBAL NEWS

The increasing capability to broadcast and publish news globally has changed our world as well as our perceptions of our world. Some effects have been global or geopolitical in nature, others are more media-related, and some are felt mainly by individuals. (Several of the following topics are expanded later in this book.)

Triumph of Western Journalism

Since the fall of the Communist "second world," the Western concept of journalism has become the dominant model around the world and is widely emulated. Non-Western nations have adopted not only the gadgets and equipment of the U.S. press and broadcasting but also its practices, norms, ethical standards, and ideology. Journalists abroad increasingly seek edito-rial autonomy and freedom from government interference. These journal-ists aspire to the professional values of fairness, objectivity, and responsibility as well as the so-called "checking effect," that is, the role of the press as a watchdog and critic of government and authority. They want to report the news as they see it, not as their government wants it seen.

Electronic Execution of Communism

Today many experts agree that news and popular culture from the West contributed to the demise of the USSR and Communist regimes in Eastern Europe. Western media, including Voice of America, BBC World Service, and Radio Free Europe, provided news not otherwise available and delivered the forbidden fruit of Western movies, video cassettes, rock music, lifestyles, as well as promises for a better life—democracy, market economies, and a higher standard of living. Western mass communication, by going over, under, and around the Iron Curtain, played a significant role in raising expectations and breaking the Communists' monopoly on news and pop culture.

Some observers believe the breakup of the Communist system began with the successes of the Solidarity trade union in Poland. There the Communists' monopoly on information was broken in two ways: the rise of alternative newspapers challenging the government and supporting Solidarity goals, and a triangular flow of news among the alternative newspapers inside Poland, foreign reporters, and international broadcasters. It worked this way: Foreign journalists reported news of Solidarity to their Western media; this news was beamed back to Poland via international shortwave radio, particularly BBC, Deutsche Welle, and Radio Free Europe; these stories were then picked up by listeners and by the alternative papers inside Poland.

Western media suggested that political change was possible, that times were changing, and that the world was watching. Potential demonstrators in other nations saw that the unthinkable was indeed possible. Thus events in East Berlin, Budapest, Prague, and Bucharest reinforced each other.

Mass Culture Accepted

In recent decades, Western mass media have also conditioned much of the world to use the media for entertainment and leisure. (Political indoctrination by the media has been rejected, at least currently, by peoples everywhere, including even China, the last great Communist nation.) Ever-growing audiences appear to accept and enjoy the movies, television, and even the ever-present commercials. Parents everywhere find it difficult to prevent the influence on their children of the most powerful engine of mass education the West has yet produced: commercial advertising. (The pervasiveness of entertainment in Western media has become a controversial issue.)

Global Audiences Growing

Each year many millions of people are drawn into the global audience, mainly through competing satellite and cable services of television as well as shortwave radio, which carry news as well as entertainment. With satellite dishes and antennas proliferating everywhere, even in the face of governmental opposition, the populous lands of Asia, particularly China and India, are flocking to join the global village. Since the Tiananmen Square crisis, China has felt the impact of heightened international communications. Western television networks—CNN, ABC, NBC, CBS, BBC—carried words and pictures of the 1989 Beijing uprising to the world, while VOA and BBC reached hundreds of millions of rural Chinese with its Chinese language newscasts. After the crackdown on demonstrators when all Chinese media were brought under party control, shortwave radio continued to report news into China.

Since then, China has been facing a quieter but more serious challenge in the form of hundreds of thousands of satellite dishes. Millions of Chinese people can hook in via satellite to global television programs bypassing the Communist Party commissars. Some believe the information revolution threatens to supplant China's Communist Revolution, which was long sustained by the now crumbling government monopoly on news and propaganda. Besides shortwave radio, fax machines are widely available in private homes and direct-dial international phones and computers with modems are multiplying as well, enabling many Chinese to use e-mail and interactive news sources on the Internet.

In China and throughout Asia, Comsat-delivered television programming has been flooding in—Star TV in Hong Kong, HBO Asia, CNN, ESPN, MTV Asia, BBC World—bringing news, information, and entertainment to many millions for the first time. Some Asian nations welcome satellite television but others see it as a threat to their cultural identity and political stability.

Governments across the former Third World have tried to suppress global television with mixed success. Satellite services may be discouraged but educated Chinese can still get world news from BBC and VOA on shortwave radio. Governments are finding it nearly impossible to stop people from taking their news and entertainment from the skies. Dishes are easily put together from imported kits, which are growing smaller, cheaper, and more powerful.

Vast Audiences for Global Events

Great events—a regional war in Yugoslavia or the quadrennial Olympic Games—can attract huge shares of the global audience. An estimated 2 billion people watched a Live Aid rock concert to help starving people in Africa. About 3½ billion people watched some of the 1996 Olympics in Atlanta. The games were probably watched by more people in China than anywhere else, because more than 900 million Chinese had access to television sets, and three channels broadcast events all day long.

Some of the effects of expanded global news communication have subtle political and diplomatic effects.

History Is Accelerated. Nations and peoples react faster to important news because global television information moves so quickly and widely. War breaks out in the Middle East and the price of gas at the pump goes up immediately around the world. A bomb explodes in an airliner and security measures tighten in airports everywhere. Actions that would have been taken later are taken sooner, thus speeding up the pace of change—and of history.

"The Whole World Is Watching." The reality that many millions around the world can watch on television as tanks rumble across national borders, or as troops storm ashore on an African coast, or as police fire on peaceful protestors, can give heightened consequences to a television report. For example, an amateur's camcorder tape of Los Angeles policemen beating Rodney King set off repercussions lasting for years. Vivid and dramatic video of several years of the tragic civil war in Bosnia, Croatia, and then Kosovo, seared the world's conscience and had political consequences. Ditto for Tiananmen Square: The Chinese regime won the battle of ruthlessly squashing the demonstrators but lost greatly in the world court of public opinion for its abuses of human rights.

Diplomacy Has Changed. Foreign relations and the ways that nations react to each other are affected by public (and world) opinion, now often quickly formed by global communication. The editor of *Foreign*

Affairs expressed concern about the dramatic increase in live television reporting of international crises. James F. Hoge (1994) wrote:

> These capabilities of modern media to be immediate, sensational and pervasive are unsettling the conduct of foreign affairs. . . . The technology that makes possible real-time, global coverage is truly revolutionary. Today's correspondents employ lap-top computers, wireless telephones that transmit directly to satellites and mobile satellite dishes to broadcast vivid pictures and commentary from the scenes of tragedy and disorder without the transmission delays, political obstructions or military censorship of old. (pp. 136–137)

Nonstop coverage by CNN and its new rivals, BBC World and others, does provide the opportunity to constantly monitor news events and disseminate timely diplomatic information. However, Hoge believes politicians are more concerned than elated by global, real-time broadcasting: "They worry about a 'loss of control' and decry the absence of quiet time to deliberate choices, reach private agreements and mold the public's understanding" (p. 137).

Autocrats Lose.   An authoritarian regime can no longer control and censor the news as completely as in the past. Shortwave radio, fax, direct-distance telephone, the Internet, and Comsats carrying CNN International or BBC World have changed all that and have blunted the power of censorship. The Chernobyl disaster in the USSR showed the impossibility of keeping a nation's bad news from its own people and from the outside world. During times of crisis, dictators can no longer seal their borders and control information. The news will get out.

Surrogate Media for Fettered Peoples.   U.S. and other Western news media now provide news and information for people who are captives of their own governments. By publicizing human rights violations, torture, and political imprisonments, outside media often help victims to survive by reminding the outside world of their plight. It can be argued that a famine never occurs in a nation with a free press because the press by reporting incipient food shortages, will bring pressures on its government to act before people begin dying. During a famine in autocratic Ethiopia, the people endured suffering for many months as the world largely ignored their plight. But after dramatic BBC video reports appeared on the NBC evening news program night after night, Americans were galvanized to support relief efforts generously.

Reporting Pariah Nations. The Western press' persistent reporting about pariah states, such as South Africa under apartheid or Iraq under Saddam Hussein, can help facilitate political change. Such reporting forms world opinion, which, in turn, can lead to actions by concerned nations. Persistent American and European press reporting of the civil war in Bosnia and the growing evidence of genocide by Bosnian Serbs undoubtedly pushed the Clinton Administration and NATO to intervene and impose a military truce. After the bombing war over Kosovo and Serbia, Milosevic was still an outcast leader.

Effects of No News. Sometimes the failure to report major news events can have unexpected political consequences. Because Western journalists were largely barred from reporting the prolonged war in Afghanistan between Soviet forces and Afghan rebels, the impact of that major event on the world's awareness was minimized. In past years, numerous small wars and insurrections in Africa—Western Sahara, Angola, Sudan, and Algeria—have passed largely unnoticed because the world's news media could not, or would not, report them. The prolonged war between Iran and Iraq was largely ignored because both sides barred Western reporters; yet the conflict lasted for years and had major significance.

Terrorism: News or Theater? Global television, which is capable of bringing the world together to share a common grief, such as the death of a president, or exultation, as during Neil Armstrong's walk on the moon, can also be manipulated to shock the world. Terrorism is still very much with us although the forms keep changing: plane bombings, hijackings, political kidnapping, assassinations, civilian bombings, and more recently, bombings of American embassies in Nairobi, Kenya, and Dar es Salaam in Tanzania.

Such acts are perpetrated, some feel, to capture time and space on the world's media. Terrorism has been called "propaganda of the deed."—violent criminal acts, usually against innocent people, performed by desperate people seeking a worldwide forum for their grievances.

Terrorists have learned a lesson of this media age: Television news can be manipulated into becoming the final link between terrorist groups and their audiences, and as with sensational crimes, the more outrageous and heinous the act, the greater attention the media will give it.

Yet, terrorism is news and poses worrisome questions for broadcast journalists: Does television coverage encourage and aid the terrorists'

cause? Is censorship of such dramatic events ever desirable? Most journalists agree that terrorist acts are news and must be reported. Most
believe that self-censorship is undesirable and usually not feasible. Some
television organizations have established guidelines for reporting terrorism incidents in a more restrained and rational way. Journalists agree they
should avoid giving sympathetic support or endorsement to the aims of
terrorist organizations.

"Revolution" by Personalized Media.   The spreading information
revolution, characterized by personal computers, desktop publishing,
CDs, VCRs, the Internet and World Wide Web (WWW), has turned individuals into communicators—even revolutionaries—who can reach out to
others abroad. The overthrow of the Shah of Iran in the 1970s was substantially aided by photocopiers and audio cassettes bringing in revolutionary messages from abroad. Now, the implications of the Internet for
international journalism are just beginning to be realized. In East and Central Europe, personalized media—video and audio cassettes and shortwave radios—were key weapons in the overthrow of Communist regimes
because they broke government communication monopolies and piped in
the siren songs of the West.

   Hachten (1999) quoted Peter Lewis who wrote: "Today, political dissidents of all nationalities are discovering a homeland in the worldwide
web of communication known as cyberspace. . . . Today, many human
rights advocates are exploring an even more powerful medium (than fax)
the computer web called Internet, as a way of defying censorship" (p. 65).

Copy Cat Effects.   With global news so pervasive and widely available, a particular act or occurrence can be imitated elsewhere. A terrorist's
car bombing in one country, widely shown on television, is repeated 3,000
miles away. Somali clansmen defied U.S. soldiers in Mogadishu and a few
days later, Haitian thugs were encouraged to stage a near riot as U.S.
troops tried to land at Port-au-Prince, causing U.S. forces to withdraw.

   Economic and financial considerations undergird the transnational
news system that has expanded so in recent years.

Profit-Driven Media.   The fact that money was to be made has fueled
the rapid expansion of international news and mass culture. INTELSAT,
the communication satellite consortium that was such a crucial early component in extending the reach of global news, grew so quickly because of
the profitability of a more efficient and cost-effective way to make inter-

national telephone calls. For whatever their shortcomings, the new media barons, Rupert Murdoch, Ted Turner, Steven Case, Silvio Berlusconi, and others, have been entrepreneurs who are risk-takers and innovators. Of course, news media have followed (and profited from) the expanding economy as it has become increasingly globalized.

Globalization of Advertising and Public Relations.   The two persuasive arms of Western mass communication, advertising and public relations (PR), have become globalized along with journalism. Here again, the Anglo-American model, speaking English, is the pacesetter. Although often criticized, advertising and PR are necessary and inevitable components of market economies and open democratic societies. Moreover, advertising and PR often make news themselves and are an integral part of marketing.

DILEMMAS OF GLOBAL TV NEWS

If all politics is local, then it also may be true that all news is local, although most of the best journalists believe that foreign news is important and that the news media should carry more of it. Yet, U.S. journalism and that of other nations is clearly marked by provincialism. Unless there is a compelling story of global impact, most newspapers and broadcasters stress local news. Dennis (1992) reported that InterMedia published a global survey, "A Day in the Life of TV News," that measured country-by-country uses of domestic and foreign news on one day in 1991. The study found that 85% of television news on Middle East television was about the Middle East, 92% of Latin American television news was about Latin America, 80% of news on Eastern European television was about Eastern Europe, 78% of news on Japanese television was about Japan, and so on. The study illustrated the parochialism of news in most countries of the world.

A comparative study of television network news in Japan and the United States over seven months between 1992–1993 found 1,121 reports from the United States on Japanese television and only 92 from Japan on American television. U.S. Ambassador Walter Mondale commented, "I thought our trade imbalance with Japan was bad, but now I see that the news imbalance is even worse" (Hess, 1996, p. 10).

This confirms the impression that most people abroad know more about Americans than American do about foreigners. But, on the other hand, these differences may not be that significant if one accepts the view that the old distinctions between foreign and local news have largely disappeared. The fact that the best news media place high value on news from afar, whereas more entertainment-minded media do not, may indicate that it may be in our self-interest to know more about the outside world.

As we have seen in this chapter, the flow of news and mass culture throughout the world has had a variety of important effects on our global community. Some of those effects have been due to the success of CNN. CNN became the first 24-hour cable news network and as such attracted news viewers away from the evening news shows of ABC, CBS, and NBC during the Gulf War and other periods of international crisis. When a big story breaks, CNN comes on the air and stays with the story. As a result, ABC, NBC, and CBS have become even more reluctant to interrupt scheduled programs with news bulletins or extended reporting.

From its beginning, CNN supplied television news to many foreign broadcast services, homes, and hotels via cable and direct broadcast satellites in many nations. CNN has provided independent Western news to many millions overseas, who previously had received only government-controlled information. CNN has had its great and not-so-great moments: live and global coverage of the Gulf War versus CNN's gavel-to-gavel coverage of the O. J. Simpson criminal trial, thus abdicating for many months its self-proclaimed major role in reporting foreign news. CNN gets low marks on its programming and low ratings when crisis news is lacking. However, during the 1999 bombing war over Serbia and Kosovo, CNN greatly expanded its audience both at home and abroad.

Technologically speaking, however, CNN is a major innovation because of its ability to interconnect so many video sources, newsrooms, and foreign ministries to television sets in so many remote places in the world. In this way, CNN has influenced diplomacy; coverage of a crisis in North Korea or Chechnya makes not only other journalists but diplomats everywhere tune in to get the latest.

A television news channel of true global reach was an innovation whose time had come, and CNN now has its imitators and competitors. In 1991, the BBC started its own World Service Television (WST), now called BBC World. Plans call for BBC news and entertainment channels in Europe, Asia, and the United States. By 1997, BBC World had started to challenge the dominance of CNN International, which, according to CNN company figures, reaches 113 million homes in 210 countries and territories outside the United States. CNN's domestic services reaches another 71 million homes.

After two years in Europe, BBC World has gained an audience of 30 million homes outside of its worldwide viewership of 50 million homes in 174 countries and territories. BBC World is not yet received in Britain due to regulatory restrictions but is expected to soon start a 24-hour broadcast news operation there.

BBC World Service (radio) and BBC World (television) are now widely heard on U.S. public and nonprofit stations. In 2000, various PBS television stations were carrying two British television news programs nightly—Independent Television News (ITN) and BBC World—thus providing American viewers an opportunity to watch two services that still take world news seriously.

Another characteristic of the domestic CNN—as an around-the-clock, cable news channel—has elicited competition from other U.S. networks. In late 1995, ABC News announced plans for a 24-hour cable system to compete with CNN, but in May 1996, the idea was shelved by ABC's new owners, the Disney Company. NBC, however, moved ahead aggressively, launching MSNBC—a 24-hour cable news channel, owned jointly with Bill Gates' Microsoft—with great fanfare in July 1996. Another NBC cable channel, CNBC, stressed financial and business news and is considered a success as well.

Rupert Murdoch's Fox Network has joined the 24-hour cable news steeplechase with its own Fox News Channel or FNC. CBS has been trying to get into the 24-hour cable news competition but, so far, has lagged behind the others

Despite this headlong rush, there were serious reservations about whether even two, much less three or four, cable news channels could survive financially. CNN itself has not been very profitable lately. The average number of homes that tuned in to CNN, for instance, dropped from 572,000 in 1995 to 372,000 in 1996 and to 274,000 in 1997. CNN's prime time ratings sank 33% in 1996, in part because the O. J. Simpson trial ended. In 1997, MSNBC's nightly cable news with Brian Williams averaged 27,000 households. Its rival, the Fox News Channel, drew just 10,000 homes. But such ratings are quite volatile and can change quickly as when a blockbuster story like the Clinton-Lewinsky scandal breaks.

In any case, this stampede to provide cable news channels probably reflects a sea change in broadcast news. People seem to be getting their electronic news more and more on the run in small snippets from car radios or at home (radio ratings have stayed high), or from cable news flicked on at odd hours, and increasingly from the Internet. Less and less are people getting the news from the evening network news shows, which have been steadily losing viewers.

Multiple 24-hour cable TV news channels also have important implications for global television. Both Rupert Murdoch and NBC's Jack Welch have had their sights on global television networks similar to CNN International and BBC World. Murdoch is well on his way to achieving that goal with his existing Star TV satellite service based in Hong Kong for Asia and Sky Channel, a satellite TV service in England with a 24-hour news channel drawing on the staffs of his *Times* and *Sunday Times* of London.

NBC has similar global ambitions, and its well-regarded CNBC channel in Europe and the Middle East is widely available overseas. Emphasizing daily business news from New York, it is seen as a precursor for such a global network (Auletta, 1995a). But again, reservations have been expressed about the economic feasibility for global television news at least along the lines envisaged by media tycoons Murdoch, Turner, and Welch. A careful and persuasive study by Richard Parker argues against the growth of more global television news. Citing the InterMedia study mentioned above, Parker (1995) wrote:

> The overwhelming interest of audiences globally is not about global news per se but, rather in a much more focused sense, of region as the relevant domain of concern. For organizations such as CNN International and other global broadcasters, this further erodes the mass-audience potential for a standardized global news wheel, and stresses the importance of national—and regional—broadcasters in delivering news to audiences that meet a broad audience interest. (p. 78)

Yet when the next major world crisis erupts, as it surely will, global television news services like CNN and BBC World will take center stage again in reporting, explaining, and, yes, greatly influencing, if not manipulating, the world's response to those events.

CHAPTER
3

Freedom of the Press: Theory and Values

The First Amendment reads more like a dream than a law, and no other country, as far as I know, has been crazy enough to include such a dream among its fundamental legal documents. I defend it because it has been so successful for two centuries in preserving our freedom and increasing our vitality, knowing that all arguments in support of it are certain to sound absurd.

—Kurt Vonnegut (1982)

Americans have long had lively, irreverent, rambunctious, and scurrilous newspapers, often disrespectful of authority and at times outrageous. People often despise the news media, but they still value their right to freedom of the press.

Thomas Jefferson had strong and ambivalent feelings about the press, as his quoted words indicate: "Newspapers serve to carry off noxious vapors and smoke" (p. 85), and later, "Nothing can be believed which is seen in a newspaper" (p. 85). In addition, "The man who never looks into a newspaper is better informed than he who reads them, inasmuch as he who knows nothing is nearer the truth than he whose mind is filled with falsehoods and errors" (Rafferty, 1975, p. 26).

And yet, our most intellectual of presidents also wrote these words: "When the press is free and every man able to read, all is safe" (p. 61), and

"No government ought to be without censors; and where the press is free none ever will" (p. 61), "The press is the best instrument for enlightening the mind of man, and improving him as a rational, moral, and social being" (Rafferty, 1975, p. 61).

Jefferson's ambivalence has been shared by other leaders because newspapers can sometimes be excellent, even indispensable to our political life, and at other times, they can be offensive, dishonest, and hateful. Yet the importance of the concept of a free press as essential to a democratic republic has long been recognized, and the American press has been given more protection in our constitutional law than in any other democracy.

The First Amendment to the U.S. Constitution states clearly and unequivocally that "Congress Shall Make No Law . . . Abridging Freedom of Speech or of the Press." Freedom of the press in the United States is more than a legal concept—it is almost a religious tenet. The Constitution, as interpreted by the Supreme Court of the United States, is itself virtually a sacred text, and the First Amendment, which also protects religion, rights of assembly and association, and expression in many forms, is a central part of the value system proclaimed by most Americans (Soifer, 1985).

ORIGINS OF THE FIRST AMENDMENT

America's high regard for the principle of press freedom derives from the Enlightenment and the liberal political tradition reflected in the writings of John Milton, John Locke, Thomas Jefferson, James Madison, John Stuart Mill, and others. A democratic society, it is argued, requires a diversity of views and news sources available—a marketplace of ideas—from which the public can choose what it wishes to read and believe about public affairs. For no one or no authority, spiritual or temporal, has a monopoly on truth. Underlying this diversity of views is the faith that citizens will somehow make the right choices about what to believe if enough voices are heard and government keeps its hands off the press.

In American Constitutional theory, Blasi (1977) saw this libertarian view as based on certain values (and hopes) deemed inherent in a free press: (a) by gathering and publishing public information and scrutinizing government and politicians, the press makes self-government possible; (b) an unfettered press ensures that a diversity of views and news will be read and heard; (c) a system of free expression provides autonomy for individuals to lead free and productive lives; and (d) it enables an independent press to serve as a check on abuses of power by government.

Our press freedom, rooted in English Common Law, evolved slowly during England's long 17th- and 18th-century struggle between the crown, the courts, and Parliament; when none of the three could dominate the others, a free press slowly began to emerge. In the American colonies and later republic, a press relatively free from arbitrary government controls evolved as printers and editors asserted their freedoms and gradually established a tradition of a free press. The American press today is freer of legal constraints than is the press of other countries.

In American history, however, press freedom has suffered great lapses and defeats, especially at the state and local level. In fact, the key constitutional decisions supporting claims for press freedom have been decided almost entirely since the 1930s, beginning with the great Supreme Court decision on *Near v. Minnesota* (1931), which protected the press from prior restraint or censorship especially when involved with reporting news of government.

How to define it? Our definition of *freedom of the press* means the right of the press to report, to comment on, and to criticize its own government without retaliation or threat of retaliation from that authority. This has been called the right to talk politics. By this demanding test—the right to talk politics—press freedom is comparatively rare in today's world. A free or independent press is usually found in only a dozen or more Western nations that share these characteristics: a system of law that provides meaningful protection to civil liberties and property rights; high average levels of per capita income, education and literacy; legitimate political oppositions; sufficient capital or private enterprise to support news media; and an established tradition of independent journalism. In any case, freedom of the press really has meaning and can survive only within a framework of law.

Through the decisions of the courts in adjudicating legal disputes involving newspapers, pamphleteers, broadcasters, radical speakers, and others over basic conflicts between written, printed, oral expression and other competing claims, the framework of our system of press freedom has been delineated. In our law, free speech and free press are identical rights; only the form is different. Print and broadcasting are equally protected but radio and television seem less free because they are licensed by the Federal Communications Commission (FCC) and because broadcasters are not as assertive in demanding their rights as are the print media.

Great Supreme Court justices such as Oliver Wendell Holmes, Louis Brandeis, Charles Evans Hughes, Hugo Black, William Douglas, and William Brennan, in particular, have contributed to our expanding freedom of expression. Legal scholars Zechariah Chafee, Alexander Meiklejohn, Thomas I. Emerson, Vincent Blasi, and others in their commentaries have filled out the picture.

Some of the press-related issues decided by the courts have involved highly charged loyalty and national security issues; freedom from prior restraint and censorship; freedom to report legal proceedings and to criticize judges; libel immunity when criticizing public officials; freedom of distribution, pretrial publicity, and defendants' rights; press rights versus right of privacy; freedom of expression versus obscenity; protection of confidential news sources; and access to information about public records and meetings. In most of these areas, press freedom has expanded significantly in the previous century.

ESSENTIAL TO DEMOCRACY

That the American press plays a key role in our democratic system and, in fact, is a central requirement for it, is due in part, Emerson (1985) believed, to several factors. First, instead of representing only private or partisan interests (as in the earlier days of the political party press and yellow journalism), the press has moved to representing the public interest. The growing stress on professionalism, the role of investigative reporting as a regular feature of serious newspapers, and even claims made for special treatment such as shield laws (protecting confidential news sources) are all indicators that the press perceives itself as serving the public interest. Certainly not all (or even many) of the news media share these goals (much less achieve them), but the mere existence of the concept is important.

Second, this concept of the press as serving the public interest has become the popular as well as legal justification for protecting freedom of the press. Despite widespread criticism of the media, residual support remains for this press tenet among the general public, opinion journals, and legislatures because the serious press does contribute independent and counterbalancing voices to public discourse.

Third, it can be argued that the press, as an institution, constitutes a viable base from which to stand up to government and concentrated corporate power. With the great expansion of state power and the proliferation of giant corporations, the serious press, despite its own links to many large corporations, still provides a significant potential for independence. So, if not constrained by government, the press in a general way, remains an important factor in generating political and social ideas and programs.

Finally, the constitutional and legal doctrines that protect the press are stated in general terms and are applicable to all sectors of the press. Freedom of the press is an individual right, we all are protected by it; it is misleading to hear, as is often stated, that newspapers are the only business specifically protected by the Constitution. Corporations are only claiming a right we all enjoy, including minorities, even especially unpopular ones. The First Amendment not only protects NBC and Gannett but also Noam Chomsky or any unpopular dissident or malcontent handing out inflammatory pamphlets in a mall.

In fact, the First Amendment and the rest of the Bill of Rights can be seen as primarily concerned with protecting minority or dissident rights. Thus a free society must tolerate irresponsible, reckless, and tasteless expression in order to protect the rights of all. The majority rarely feels the need for First Amendment protection, yet the survival of the First Amendment, as both Alexander Hamilton and Alexander Bickel averred, relies on the support of the people. That is the paradox of the First Amendment and a reason for its fragility.

VALUES OF THE
FIRST AMENDMENT

Several scholars have elaborated on various values they deem central to the theory of the First Amendment.

Emerson (1966) saw four major values all of which stressed individual rights. The first was the right of an individual purely in his own capacity to seek his own self-fulfillment. "In the development of his own personality, every man has the right to form his own beliefs and opinions. Hence, suppression of belief, opinion and expression is an affront to the dignity of man, an affront to man's essential nature" (p. 5).

Second, free speech is the best method of searching for and attaining truth. This value is similar to values found in both academic freedom and the scientific method of inquiry. A journalist seeking important public information must be free to go wherever the leads take him or her to get the story, just as a scholar should be free to follow the indications of truth wherever they may lead.

Third, free speech makes self-government possible by encouraging the participation of citizens in social and political decision making. And fourth, by so doing, the system of free expression becomes a safety valve that helps maintain a balance between stability and change in an open, dynamic society. If people have access to information and are free to express their views and address their grievances to authority, they are less likely to take up arms against their rulers and resort to civil strife.

Diversity is a value directly relevant both to the ownership and performance of a free press. A related concept, the marketplace of ideas, which goes back to Milton, has come into some disrepute because critics say that truth does not always seem to come to the top and win out in the clash of ideas and programs. Propaganda, PR, and other persuasive and manipulative communications have made many of us skeptics. Still, even if communication channels are polluted, diversity ensures that press freedom is served if people are given a wide choice of information sources, as well as alternative proposals from which to choose rather than having an authoritarian selection imposed on them.

In an anti-trust case, *Associated Press v. United States* (1945), Judge Learned Hand expressed well the value of diversity:

> That (newspaper) industry serves one of the most vital of all general interests: the dissemination of news from as many different sources, and with as many different facets as possible. . . . It presupposes that right conclusions are more likely to be gathered out of a multitude of tongues than through any kind of authoritarian selection. To many this is, and always will be, folly; but we have staked upon it our all. (p. 20)

This view reflects Hand's skeptical view of free speech. The spirit of liberty, he said, is the spirit that is not too sure it is right. Therefore, many views must be available for consideration.

Diversity implies the necessity of competition and a variety of differing and even conflicting views. The steady decline of local newspaper competition coupled with the trends of concentration and monopoly of news media have placed this value in some jeopardy.

Another value, also directly linked to press performance, is the checking value, which sees the press as a watchdog on excesses and malfeasance of government. Blasi (1977) revived this neglected value, on which the drafters of the First Amendment had placed great stress, the ability of free expression to guard against breaches of trust by public officials.

Influenced by 20th-century wars, Blasi argued that government misconduct is a more serious evil than misconduct by private parties because there is no concentrated force available to check it. The potential impact of government on the lives of individuals is unique because of its capacity to use legitimized violence. "No private party—not Lockheed, not United Fruit, not the Mafia—could ever have done what our government did to the Vietnamese people and the Vietnamese land. Private forces could never have exterminated such significant portions of the domestic population as did the Nazi and Soviet governments of the 1930s and 1940s" (Blasi, 1977, p. 527).

The checking value has been rarely invoked by the Supreme Court, but Justice Hugo Black did so in his last written opinion, in the Pentagon Papers case, *New York Times v. United States* (1971), giving it eloquent expression.

In the First Amendment the Founding Fathers gave the free press the protection it must have to fulfill its essential role in our democracy. The press was to serve the governed, not the governors. The Government's power to censor the press was abolished so that the press would remain free to censure the Government. The press was protected so that it could bare the secrets of government and inform the people. Only a free and unrestrained press can effectively oppose deception in government. And paramount among the responsibilities of a free press is the duty to prevent any part of the government from deceiving the people and sending them off to distant lands to die of foreign fevers and foreign shot and shell. (*New York Times v. United States*, 1971, p. 717)

KEY CONCEPTS
OF THE FIRST AMENDMENT

The values of press freedom are further buttressed by several key concepts that are well established in constitutional law. One of the oldest—no prior restraint—means that government is barred from censoring any printed matter before its publication, a principle that goes back to Blackstone in 18th-century England. The landmark decision, *Near v. Minnesota* (1931), dealt with prior restraint or prior censorship and struck down a state statute that barred publication of a local smear sheet, *The Saturday Press*, which had been highly critical of Minnesota state officials. The key point about Near is that a publication was prohibited from future publication because it had criticized official conduct; the court found this to be an unacceptable restraint on a free press.

Chief Justice Charles Evans Hughes relied on Blackstone's rather narrow view of press freedom:

> The liberty of the press is indeed essential to the nature of a free state; but this consists in laying no previous restraints upon publications, and not in freedom from censure for criminal matter when published. Every freeman has an undoubted right to lay what sentiments he pleases before the public; to forbid this, is to destroy the freedom of the press; but if he publishes what is improper, mischievous or illegal, he must take the consequences. (*Near v. Minnesota*, 1931, p. 702)

And in referring to the sleazy publication barred, Hughes wrote: "The fact that liberty of the press may be abused by miscreant purveyors of scandal does not make any the less necessary the immunity of the press from previous restraint in dealing with official misconduct. Subsequent punishment for such abuses as may exist is the appropriate remedy, consistent with constitutional privilege" (*Near v. Minnesota*, 1931, p. 705).

As Near and other cases demonstrated, press immunity from prior restraint in other situations such as obscenity or war-time security needs was not absolute, but the principle of no prior restraint of press criticism of government conduct (the right to talk politics) took on great and lasting importance from then on.

Another key concept, the press' right to criticize government, even wrongly, was spelled out in the celebrated *New York Times v. Sullivan* (1964) decision in the turbulent 1960s. The case involved a civil libel judgment against the *Times* for an advertisement, signed by civil rights supporters, critical of the conduct of public officials during civil rights demonstrations in Montgomery, Alabama. L. B. Sullivan, Montgomery police commissioner, sued for defamation, winning a $500,000 judgment. Upheld by the Alabama Supreme Court, the case went to the U.S. Supreme Court where it was unanimously reversed. The court famously announced a constitutional standard that a public official may not recover libel damages regarding official conduct unless he or she can prove actual malice—that is, knowledge on the part of the critic that the statement was false or "showed reckless disregard of whether it was false or not."

Justice William Brennan's decision stressed that Alabama's libel law was unconstitutional because it failed to protect freedom of the press.

(Previously, no one ever thought civil libel had anything to do with the First Amendment.) Brennan said that at issue was: "a profound national commitment to the principle that debate on public issues should be uninhibited, robust, and wide-open, and that it may well include vehement, caustic, and sometimes unpleasantly sharp attacks on government and public officials." Brennan rejected the argument that falsity of some statements in the ad destroyed any protection the paper may have had. He said protection did not depend on the "truth, popularity, or social utility" of the ideas and beliefs expressed. He wrote: "A rule compelling the critic of official conduct to guarantee the truth of all his factual assertions—and to do so on paid libel judgements virtually unlimited in amount—leads to a comparable 'self censorship'" (*New York Times v. Sullivan*, 1964, p. 278).

Brennan pointed out a civil libel suit brought by a public official was as dangerous to press freedom as seditious libel. He added that "the court of history" had found that the Sedition Act of 1798 that had authorized punishment for criticism of public officials and government was inconsistent with the First Amendment. Professor Harry Kalven hailed the *Times* decision as a great constitutional event because the "touchstone of the First Amendment has become the abolition of seditious libel and what that implies about the function of free speech on public issues in American democracy." Kalven felt that the absence of seditious libel as a crime was the true pragmatic test of a nation's freedom of expression, because politically relevant speech is what press freedom is mostly about (Blasi, 1977, p. 568).

Another key concept of press freedom is the more general proposition that expression itself is protected and only actions can be proscribed. This is related to the view that there are no false ideas, that is, all views and ideas, however heretical or illogical they may seem, enjoy the same protection under the law. Only when the fighting words are closely linked to illegal action can the state step in.

In the long history of national security and sedition cases, the clear and present danger test and similar measures were devised to give as much protection as possible to political speech in the face of sedition laws. Since 1969, the Supreme Court has moved to an even more objective standard. In *Brandenburg v. Ohio* (1969), the court said a speaker could not be convicted for "mere advocacy" of illegal action; to be constitutional, a statute can only prohibit advocacy where it is "directed to inciting or producing imminent lawless action and is likely to incite or produce such actions" (p. 448). In so doing, the court reached back and adopted a standard used by Judge Learned Hand in the *Masses Publishing Co. v. Patten* (1917) case and greatly expanded freedom of political speech.

Of more direct interest to the news press is the key concept of the right to know, which implies that the press not only can publish and comment on the news but also has the right of access to news itself at all levels of government. (One murky question is whether the right belongs to the press or to the public.)

Long ago, the press won the right to be present at open meetings of Parliament and legislatures, including Congress. The Fourth Amendment's guarantee of a fair and public trial has ensured the right of a reporter, standing in for the public, to attend and report on public trials. Further, evolution of U.S. contempt-of-court law has given the American press broad powers to criticize judges, report on pretrial news and criticize the conduct of trials—as the O. J. Simpson trial so well demonstrated.

The right to know about the executive branch with its numerous bureaucracies and vast classified files and records has been a long and contentious problem for serious journalism. Some progress has been made, however, through the Freedom of Information Act and various sunset laws that require the release of classified government records after a specified time lapse.

The famous Pentagon Papers case (*New York Times v. United States*, 1971) involved overclassification of government records—a secret history of the Vietnam War—and the alleged potential danger to national security posed by *The New York Times'* publication of them. U.S. Judge Murray Gurfein ruling for the *Times*, wrote:

> If there be some embarrassment to the government in security aspects as remote as the general embarrassment that flows from any security breach, we must learn to live with it. The security of the nation is not at the barricades alone. Security also lies in the value of our free institutions. A cantankerous press, an obstinate press, a ubiquitous press must be suffered by those in authority in order to preserve the even greater values of freedom of expression and the right of the public to know. (p. 715)

The Supreme Court upheld the favorable ruling for the *Times*.

Another key concept, journalistic autonomy, supports the independence of newspapers from government intrusion into their operations. In *Miami Herald v. Tornillo* (1974), the Supreme Court said a right of reply requirement was unconstitutional when applied to the print media. The Court had ruled just the opposite in a broadcasting case, *Red Lion v. FCC* (1969). In Tornillo, *The Miami Herald* challenged a Florida statute that required newspapers to print free replies to political candidates that the papers had attacked. The Supreme Court ruled unanimously for the *Herald*, supporting editors and publishers. Chief Justice Warren Burger said it was unconstitutional to require a newspaper to print what it otherwise would not. Press responsibility, he said, was a desirable goal, but it was not mandated by the Constitution and "like many other virtues" could not be legislated. Burger said the law was unconstitutional simply because it intruded into the function of editors. He wrote:

> The choice of material to go into a newspaper, and the decisions made as to limitations on the size and content of the paper, and the treatment of public issues and public officials—whether fair or unfair—constitute the exercise of editorial control and judgment. It has yet to be demonstrated how governmental regulation of this crucial process can be exercised consistent with First Amendment guarantees of a free press. (*Miami Herald v. Tornillo*, 1974, p. 248)

The values of U.S. press freedom may have influenced the professional values of journalists in other nations. One particularly influential concept is that of a free flow of news, which captures the spirit of the First Amendment. This concept refers to the need to report foreign news fully, accurately, and quickly across national borders and without interference from foreign governments. Timely and accurate news and other reliable information is deemed essential to the needs of an increasingly interdependent global political economy. This concept collides with the counter view that every nation has a sovereign right to control news and information passing back and forth across its borders. The free flow of news may be often one-sided, erratic, or delayed and, in some parts of the world, may seem a hopeless ideal. Yet the trend is favorable for more open and free journalism in more and more nations.

CURRENT CHALLENGES TO PRESS FREEDOM

Most of the basic law protecting freedom of the press is considered settled, yet the news media have met several important challenges recently. Here are several:

- American news publications operating in Southeast Asia have been facing increased restrictions on distribution posed by authoritarian regimes, especially by the government of Lee Kuan Yew and his successor in Singapore. *The International Herald Tribune, The Asian Wall Street Journal, Time, Newsweek,* and *The Far Eastern Economic Review* have all been repressed at times by Singapore's authoritarianism and, sadly, the publications have not really fought back (for more details, see chap. 10).

- A rare case involving prior restraint of a publication, with echoes of *Near v. Minnesota*, was settled in 1996 when a federal appeals court in Cincinnati threw out a lower court's ruling blocking *Business Week* magazine from publishing sealed court documents from a lawsuit brought by Procter & Gamble. The appellate court was somewhat incredulous that the trial judge seemed unaware he was engaged in the unconstitutional practice of preventing a news organization from publishing information in its possession on a matter of public concern.
- Two major confrontations between the news organizations of ABC and CBS with two tobacco giants, Philip Morris and Brown and Williamson, over broadcasts about the deadly effects of cigarette smoking had major press freedom implications. Neither network acquitted itself well (both controversies are discussed in chap. 5).

But here it should be noted that some critics are concerned that the ever-expanding media conglomerates are backing away from aggressive news coverage and subsequent legal challenges in order to placate their investors. Some media companies have taken legal actions that critics consider to be capitulation. These include ABC, NBC, *Business Week,* and *The International Herald Tribune.* The national press, it is felt, may be backing away from a long-time principle: that the best way to ward off challenges to news coverage is to rigorously fight each and every one, particularly high-profile cases. James Goodale, a First Amendment lawyer, said, "The press lawyers have lost sight of the fact that for press freedom to exist, it's a continuous, constant fight" (Glaberson, 1995b, p. A3). Some feared the effect it might have on journalism elsewhere. Jane Kirtley of the Reporters Committee for Freedom of the Press said: "Never mind what happens to CBS, NBC, or CNN. What about the small news organizations all over the country? When the big guys won't fight those battles against the likes of the tobacco company, how can the small news organizations stand up to its local equivalent, or even more unthinkable, take on the tobacco industry?" (Glaberson, 1995b, p. A3).

- Recently, television journalism has been facing a new form of legal attack, as individuals and corporations have been successful by charging in courts that hidden cameras and other undercover reporting techniques trample on their rights. In January 1997, a jury found ABC News liable for $5.5 million in punitive damages for using deceptive research techniques, amounting to fraud, in a 1992 *Primetime Live* broadcast that accused Food Lion supermarket chain of selling spoiled food. The show's producers faked resumes to get jobs at Food Lion stores and used hidden cameras to show workers dealing with tainted meat.

ABC said the *Primetime* staffers were being punished for being journalists. Critics in journalism (and apparently the jury) said ABC was punished for trickery and deception. Increased use of hidden cameras by news magazine shows such as *Primetime Live* and NBC's *Dateline* was called part of a ratings-driven descent by major networks into the swamp of tabloid television. It was suggested that this and similar verdicts stem from a growing public skepticism about television. Jurors seemed to be showing more sympathy for the subjects of television news reports than for aggressive reporters.

However, in August 1997, a federal judge reduced the punitive damages from $5.5 million to $325,000. Then, in October 1999, a federal court of appeals threw out all but $2 of the damages ABC had been ordered to pay Food Lion. The court said that the attempt to win a fraud verdict because two ABC employees had lied their way into jobs at Food Lion was an "end run" around First Amendment protection of journalists.

Nevertheless, one critic of ABC News said that such stunt journalism saps the credibility of the press and makes life more difficult for serious investigative journalism. Such rulings, however, certainly make it more difficult for smaller media, often the most visible consumer watchdogs in their communities, but that can ill afford punitive damages, while reporting truthful information.

- A particularly disquieting decision for the press came in March 1997 when a Federal jury in Houston awarded $222.7 million to a local bond brokerage firm in a libel suit over a 1993 article in *The Wall Street Journal*, which the plaintiffs claimed was false and drove away customers, forcing the company to close. The *Journal* claimed it was just chronicling the difficulties of the company, not causing them.

The award was four times the next biggest libel award ever and shocked media lawyers who denounced the outsize award as dangerous to First Amendment rights. As with ABC News in the Food Lion case, the outsize award reflected public dissatisfaction with media performance. In May 1997, a U.S. judge threw out the $200 million in punitive damages but let stand the $22.7 million in actual damages. (Libel suits pose a continuing problem for the news media.)

- Finally, in 1996, after four years of legislative struggle, Congress rewrote the nation's communications laws, passing major legislation that would transform television, telephones, and the emerging frontiers of computer networks, but without much discussion in the nation's news media. It remains to be seen just how freedom of expression will be affected (see chap. 12 for details), but certainly the public as consumers are expected to gain in various ways.

Viewers will be offered attractive new choices for news and entertainment. They will be able to turn to their telephone company for cable service, to their cable company for telephone service, and to their electric facility for both kinds of service. The bill offers increased competition, which in turn may mean lower prices and innovation.

However, since then the dilatory pace of competition concerned consumer advocates. Not only were cable television bills going up but cable companies were retreating from the phone business.

Nonetheless, overhaul of the nation's communication laws was long overdue to bring them in line for the competitive and technological needs of the 21st century. Because so much news and other public information is carried on television, cable, phone lines, and the Internet, it will be essential to keep track of how well journalism and press freedom fare in this rapidly changing information age.

CONCLUSION

As this overview of U.S. press law shows, our news media enjoy a wide range of legal rights and privileges enabling them to carry out their essential roles of providing meaningful news and commentary on public affairs. A free, vigorous, and outspoken press is indeed essential to a healthy society. It is important, too, that the principles and theory of our press are deeply embedded in our Constitutional law and are not just the yearnings of a handful of radicals and dissidents. All supporters of the U.S. Constitution, including the most conservative or reactionary judges, should uphold freedom of the press when they enforce the law.

Yet there remains the very real question of how well the American public understands and supports the First Amendment. The 1997 Roper poll, mentioned earlier, found that few Americans are familiar with the five rights guaranteed by the Constitution's First Amendment. Further, few believe that the right to freedom of the press should be guaranteed at all times. The poll found people see the role of news media as "crucial to the functioning of a free society," but the legal processes of press freedom are not well understood. Eighty-five percent could not name press freedom as one of the five First Amendment freedoms. Nearly two thirds said "there are times when the press should not be allowed to publish or broadcast certain things." That, of course, would be prior restraint, clearly illegal under the First Amendment.

One of our greatest judges, Learned Hand, in speaking of the spirit of liberty, sounded a cautionary note:

> I often wonder whether we do not rest our hopes too much upon constitutions, upon laws and upon courts. These are false hopes. Believe me, these are false hopes. Liberty lies in the hearts of men and women. When it dies there, no constitution, no law, no court can even do much to help it. While it lies there it needs no constitution, no law, no court to save it. (Gunther, 1994, p. 548)

CHAPTER
4

Recent History
of the Press

*The press as it exists today, is not, as our moralists sometimes seem
to assume, the willful product of any little group of living men. On the
contrary, it is the outcome of an historical process in which many
individuals participated without foreseeing what the ultimate product
of their labors was to be.*

—Robert Park (1923)

To understand the flaws of the press today, we must first examine several
trends in journalism during the previous century. The dismaying shortcomings as well as the encouraging strengths we see in U.S. news media
today have their roots in the past.

The 20th-century history of American journalism has been dealt with
in all its complexity and fascination by numerous scholars and writers,
some of them journalists. Among other things, our press history is a
morality tale with plenty of sinners and bad guys, some high-minded
heroes, and even a few saints.

This brief historical overview focuses on several topics related to the
main concerns of this book: the rise of the great metropolitan newspapers;
trends toward group or chain ownership of daily newspapers; roots of the
gossip or scandal-mongering tabloids and their obsession with celebrities;

the advent and growing influence of radio and television journalism; new technologies for reporting the world; and criticism of the press.

BIG CITY NEWSPAPERS

By 1900, the press was poised to become big business—the leading papers had attained large circulations, high capitalizations, and profits. High-speed rotary presses that made possible automated printing on both sides of the paper at once, the Linotype machine, which speeded typesetting, the typewriter, and the telephone all helped create the big city dailies. Important, too, was the telegraph, invented in 1844, which enabled newspeople to collect and send news from great distances.

These tools for putting out a newspaper were still used well into the 1960s. Then the new technologies of offset printing, computers (for writing, editing, and storing news), communication satellites, and high-speed data transfers (for instant global news distribution) again revolutionized journalism as well as telecommunications in general.

The great rivals of the 1890s, Joseph Pulitzer and William Randolph Hearst, set the tone for 20th-century journalism, especially for the more lurid and sensational variety. Pulitzer's *New York World* combined a crusading editorial page and thorough news coverage with some sensationalism for mass appeal. The *World* had the first sports section and comics, featured brightly illustrated pages and campaigned against corrupt public officials. By 1892, the *World* had reached a circulation of 374,000. (By 1900, the *Daily Mail* of London was selling 1 million copies a day.) The first mass medium for a mass audience had truly arrived.

Pulitzer's success influenced the young Hearst, who did the same things with his father's *San Francisco Examiner*. In 1895, Hearst bought *The New York Journal* and began his famous circulation war with Pulitzer. Hearst hired away some of the *World*'s staff, expanded the use of photography and introduced color printing to newspapers. The circulation competition led to lurid stories about sin and corruption, sensational pictures, and expanded use of the newly popular comics. The intense rivalry produced the shrill debate and jingoistic coverage of the Spanish American War. *Yellow journalism* was the term critics used for the formula of sensationalism that has persisted in varying forms to the present.

Interestingly, intense competition for circulation was a factor in the enduring tradition of objectivity as a standard for reporting. The papers, as well as the budding press associations—AP and later United Press—

wanted all the readers they could possibly attract so it made sense not to turn off some customers with partisan or one-sided stories. Striving to be first—to get a "scoop"—was another enduring newspaper goal and a reason for extra editions to boost street sales. The UP motto of "get it first, but first get it right" animated journalists even after radio and television provided instantaneous delivery of spot news.

Democratization of news was also a hallmark of Pulitzer and Hearst, both of whom championed the little person and the working class. To maximize circulation meant targeting news to the masses, often recent immigrants, whose tastes and interests affected the newspapers' content. Despite its faults, yellow journalism did much to help the new arrivals off Ellis Island learn about and adjust to a strange, new land. Pulitzer's famous motto, "To comfort the afflicted and to afflict the comfortable," had an underlying commercial motive. Publishers like Hearst, Pulitzer, and E. W. Scripps also acquired readers through the inclusion of some serious social and political content. Bagdikian (1992) wrote, "They secured deep loyalties among readers because their papers crusaded in direct and unmistakable terms for reforms most needed by the powerless majority of the times" (p. 126). The young Hearst wrote, "I have only one principle and that is represented by the effort to make it harder for the rich to grow richer and easier for the poor to keep from growing poorer." Pulitzer's editorial position was "Tax luxuries, inheritances, monopolies . . . the privileged corporation" (p. 127). Such sentiments are rare in today's mainstream press.

The acquisition of *The New York Times* by Adolph S. Ochs more than 100 years ago in 1896 marked the real beginning of modern serious journalism and acceptance of a responsibility to stress news, not trivia and sensation. Ochs stated, "It will be my aim to give the news impartially, without fear or favor" (Johnston, 1979, p. 55). He eschewed yellow journalism and left out comics and other purely entertainment features. Ochs and his editor, Carr Van Anda, stressed persistent and full coverage of significant national and international events. The reporting was objective, the tone somber (some thought it dull) and the contents thorough enough for the *Times* to be considered a "newspaper of record" providing as its front page has long proclaimed, "All the News That's Fit to Print" (Johnston, 1979, p. 55). Following that approach, the *Times* outlived both the *World* and the *Journal* and prospered to become, 100 years later, perhaps today's leading newspaper.

After 1900, running a big city paper had become expensive and required revenue, not just from street sales but from advertising, which came from the newly arising department stores, like Macy's and Gimbel's. In circulation, number of pages per issue, and volume of advertising, the papers grew to sizes never dreamed of before, and the figures representing investments, costs, and revenues reached astonishing totals. Mott (1947) noted that the biggest U.S. paper, *The New York Times*, had an annual expenditure of some $2 million and a full-time force of 1,300 men and women in the mid-1890s. Combined circulation of its morning and evening editions hit 1 million in March 1897. The *World* was said to be worth $10 million and earning 10% of that sum annually.

Mott (1947) quoted Lincoln Steffens in 1897: "The magnitude of financial operations of the newspaper is turning journalism upside down. Big business was doing two things in general to journalism: it was completing the erection of the industrial institution upon what was once a personal organ; and it was buttressing and steadying the structure with financial conservatism" (p. 547). Prophetic words indeed.

Corporate newspapers marked the end of the personal journalism of earlier America. As Mott (1947) wrote:

> The roar of double octuple presses drowned out the voice, often shrill and always insistent, of the old-time editor. . . . Yet, as was often said in this period, the soundly financed and well-established journal was in a far better position to resist undue interference with proper journalistic functions than the insecure sheet of an earlier day. Ochs of the *Times* could defy even an angry advertiser. And many of the papers of the period were inveterate crusaders against moneyed interests. (p. 548)

GROUP OWNERSHIP OF DAILY NEWSPAPERS

Early in the century, New York City had 14 highly competitive dailies. Many papers lacked the money to compete and were forced to close down, consolidate with a rival, or be bought out. This was the beginning of chain publishing or later, group publishing, whereby several newspapers were owned and operated by one publisher or publishing corporation. (From a peak of 2,460 daily newspapers in 1916, the number of papers declined after World War I and leveled off at mid-century to around 1,750.)

Group ownership, although it made good business sense, was not necessarily good for democracy and the values of diversity and competing viewpoints. In 1900, 10 chains controlled 32 papers, just 1% of all dailies, and about 12-15% of total circulation. Chains boomed during the 1920s;

the number of chain newspapers doubled between 1923 and 1933. By 1935, 63 groups controlled 328 papers and 41% of total circulation. In 1960, the figures were 1,09 groups with 560 papers (30%) and 46% of circulation (Emery, Emery, & Roberts, 1996).

Around 1900, the eccentric E. W. Scripps was the first to establish a major U.S. newspaper chain, 34 papers in 15 states. Scripps broke all of the later rules for acquiring papers: He created new papers (sometimes in competition with existing ones) instead of acquiring established publications. He charged readers as little as he could and took in few ads. He crusaded for socialist reforms and against abuses of working people. Nevertheless, in 20 years, he was a major publisher worth about $50 million.

His success was followed by that of William Randolph Hearst, also a proclaimed socialist and populist early on. By the end of 1922, Hearst owned 20 dailies and 11 Sunday papers in 13 of the largest cities including New York, Chicago, Los Angeles, Baltimore, and San Francisco. By 1931, Hearst had taken control of 42 papers. With the largest chain in 1935, Hearst controlled 13% of daily circulation and 24.2% of Sunday sales.

Hearst was active in politics and used all his papers to push his own ambitions and favorite causes—he was opposed to entering World War I and later waged a long-time national campaign against radicals, which was sometimes called "Hearst's red hunt." Mott (1947) noted that Hearst's vast empire, which included numerous major magazines, began to crumble during the 1930s. By 1986, Hearst had 14 dailies, which represented only 1.6% of daily circulation.

The press associations or wire services expanded during the rise of newspaper groups. The AP, which was started in 1848 by New York City papers to pool shipping news, expanded greatly in the new century, and although a cooperative, it mainly served morning papers in the larger cities. Scripps founded the United Press (UP) in 1907 because he feared an AP monopoly of news. Two years later, Hearst started the International News Service (INS) to serve his papers. (In 1958, UP and INS merged to form UPI, which today is nearly moribund.) Few papers could afford to station reporters in Washington or abroad or even to cover news outside their local regions. The wire services filled the gap by cooperative news gathering and distribution by telegraph or leased wires.

Group ownership of daily papers has flourished and expanded throughout this century. The expertise acquired in handling and merchandising news, boosting circulations, selling advertising space, and the promotion and marketing of their newspapers was, logically enough, carried over to other media—magazines, radio stations, book publishing, television stations, and in some cases, motion pictures. So after World War II, various newspaper chains, including Scripps' and Hearst's and others, were transformed into the great media conglomerates of today.

TABLOIDS: SCHOOLS FOR SCANDAL

The Roaring Twenties, following World War I, brought a revival of sensationalism in the form of tabloids patterned after the successful *Daily Mirror* of London. With pages half the size of broadsheet newspapers, which made them easier to read in subways or on buses, tabloids were intended for workers and the foreign-born and stressed crime and sex, ample photographs, and large eye-catching and irreverent headlines. ("Tabloid" refers to both the half-page format and the racy style of journalism.)

The most successful and enduring U.S. tabloid was *The New York Daily News* launched by Joseph Medill Patterson in 1919. Within six years, the *News* went to a million circulation, and before World War II had reached 2 million sales. Two competitors, Hearst's *Daily Mirror* and Bernarr Macfadden's *Evening Graphic*, which was the most lurid and irresponsible of the three, had joined in by 1924. In addition to stressing photos, the tabloids introduced composographs (i.e., faked photos), crime, and lurid stories of show business personalities. The intense circulation war led to what was called the battle of gutter journalism. The *Graphic* folded after six years and the *Daily News* gradually moved toward more straight news and less trivia and sensation.

Few tabloids in other big cities were as racy as the New York tabloids, but the quest for sensational news did not end with the 1920s. Today's bawdy and irresponsible tabloids sold in supermarkets, such as *National Inquirer* and *The Star*, continue the questionable practices of the 1920s tabs but are more directly related to the cynical Fleet Street practices of British journalism.

One tabloid journalist who left an indelible mark (or perhaps blemish) on American journalism was Walter Winchell, who wrote for *The New York Graphic* and then for *The Mirror* in the 1920s and early 1930s. Gabler (1994) wrote that Winchell invented the gossip column, breaking journalistic taboos in the process by chronicling the marital problems, peccadilloes, frailties, finances, and personal information of the prominent and famous, often basing his items on vague rumors or gossip. Winchell successfully kept at it for 40 years, and by one estimate, 50 million Americans either listened to his weekly Sunday radio broadcast or read his daily syndicated column in more than 2,000 newspapers. It was, according to one observer, "the largest continuous audience ever possessed by one man who was neither politician or divine" (Gabler, 1994, p. xi). Winchell's impact on journalism and mass culture was tremendous and deleterious.

Frank Rich (1994) commented, "The whole oppressive idea of celebrity as we know it today—a fame more often conferred by the press than earned by achievement—also owes its birth to Winchell. The Winchell column may have done more than any other single feature to spread tabloid journalism in its infancy and to speed the rise of the nascent public relations industry" (p. 1).

The way that Winchell and others reported the Hauptmann trial for the kidnapping of the Lindbergh baby in 1935 was a precursor, Rich believes, for the media circus of the O. J. Simpson criminal and civil trials.

In his fine biography, Gabler (1994) wrote (quoting columnist Leonard Lyons): "It was Walter Winchell who rewrote the rules for what was permissible in a major daily newspaper; it was Walter Winchell who first created a demand for juicy tidbits about celebrities and then spent 40 years trying to satisfy it" (p. 552). Gabler went on in his own words:

> If Winchell was responsible for having enlivened journalism, he was also responsible in the eyes of many for having debased it. Once loosed, gossip refused to confine itself to columns. Once loosed, it danced all over the paper, sometimes seizing headlines, sometimes spawning whole publications and television programs, sometimes, and more insidiously, infecting reportage of so-called straight news by emphasizing gossip and personalities at the expense of objectivity and duller facts. Once gossip had been loosed, WE would become jaded. We would always want more and the media would bend to accommodate us. . . . The legacy remained. We would believe in our entitlement to know everything about our public figures. . . . Above all, we would believe in a culture of gossip and celebrity where entertainment takes primacy over every other value. (p. 553)

Winchell did not do it all alone. There were others—Broadway and Hollywood gossip columnists (Louella Parsons, Hedda Hopper) *Confidential* magazine, and a panoply of Hollywood fan magazines, as well as press agents and studio publicists, all working overtime to feed the public's appetite for gossip, rumor, and scandal. Winchell, of course, became a celebrity himself, and in part because of him, the circle of celebrities has been widened today to include many prominent journalists and broadcasters.

RISE OF BROADCAST JOURNALISM

In the 1920s, radio provided newspapers with a new form of competition in the news arena. At first, radio's offerings were limited. However, radio had the advantage of involving listeners with events taking place thousands of miles away with a flip of a switch. Also, radio could report news immediately and directly, many hours before newspapers could print and distribute their papers. Radio was the death knell for the extra edition; big city papers soon cut back on the number of editions published daily. (Although radio could get the news out faster, the newspapers still did—and do—gather most of the day's news.)

On November 2, 1920, the Westinghouse Electric Corporation inaugurated the first commercial radio station, KDKA in Pittsburgh. That day, a crackling KDKA kept a small number of listeners in a restricted area up to date on the tabulations of the presidential election of 1920. At that time, interested voters in remote rural regions of America far from telegraph lines, without telephones, and beyond population centers with daily papers, had to wait two weeks before news reached them that Warren K. Harding had defeated James M. Cox for the presidency. (Now, there is not a place in the United States where one cannot follow election night tabulations instantaneously and, indeed, be told the winner's name even before all the polls are closed. Broadcasters have been widely criticized for announcing winners before polls have closed in western states.)

By the end of 1922, some 576 commercial radio stations were operating in America. Local stations started offering news summaries, often in cooperation with local newspapers. Johnston (1979) reported that in 1926, NBC, a subsidiary of David Sarnoff's pioneering Radio Corporation of America, initiated the first network with 24 stations interconnected; in the next year, the first coast-to-coast hookup was achieved with the broadcast of a football game. In 1927, CBS was organized, the Mutual Broadcasting System followed six years later.

For years, NBC operated two networks, the Red and the Blue, so dominating radio broadcasting that the FCC later forced the company to give up one. In 1943, NBC sold the Blue network, which became the ABC. Significantly, the three major radio networks, NBC, CBS, and ABC, all moved on in postwar years to dominate the next medium, television, and today each is a major part of giant entertainment conglomerates. (Mutual opted not to go into television.)

Radio's entertainment shows—Jack Benny, Amos 'n' Andy, Burns and Allen, and others—drew large national audiences and interest in instantaneous, on-the-spot news reports became popular due to the Lindbergh kidnapping trial in 1935, presidential nominating conventions, and FDR's fireside chats. Radio commentators—H. V. Kaltenborn, Gabriel Heatter, and Lowell Thomas—became household names. Radio expanded greatly between 1935 and 1945, when commercial stations reached 900. Daily newscasts were routine and the networks and most major stations had news staffs and reporters in key cities.

Radio played a major role, of course, in reporting World War II with direct reports from the fronts and key cities abroad. Edward R. Murrow and his colleagues, William L. Shirer, Eric Sevareid, and Charles Collingwood, reported with distinction for CBS. Murrow became famous for his "This is London" broadcasts.

Radio as a news medium, however, was to be eclipsed a few years later by a new and more immediate broadcasting force. Television came in soon after World War II but it is often forgotten that television was essentially an outgrowth of radio, which provided the norms and the format for early television news as well as entertainment programming. Television took its viewers to the event itself—to show the president speaking, the touchdown being scored, or the sights and sounds of deadly combat. And from the 1950s, the news reports were in color.

The first regularly scheduled network newscasts began in 1948 with Douglas Edwards on CBS-TV and John Cameron Swayze on NBC. As on radio, these were only 15-minute newscasts with the "talking head" reading most of the news. Until the technology improved, live or taped video reports were slow in coming. When the television report finally did present the actual witnessing of an event on a screen, rather than reading a journalist's report, it had considerable impact.

Great social and political impact was felt throughout the nation by televised coverage of the Senate's McCarthy-Army hearings in the 1950s, space exploration, the Watergate hearings, the Vietnam War, and the tumultuous Democratic convention in Chicago of 1968. Americans felt these traumatic events deeply and viscerally because of what they saw and heard on that little screen.

The nightly newscasts expanded to 30 minutes and drew huge audiences. In the 1970s, an estimated 41 million Americans watched the 7 p.m. news on the three networks. The faces of the newscasters—Walter Cronkite, Chet Huntley, David Brinkley, Howard K. Smith, John Chancellor, and Harry Reasoner—became well known and trusted. Broadcast journalists were on the way to becoming celebrities. For a time, television news was supplemented by some serious in-depth documentaries. Leading the way was the *See It Now* series and the later *CBS Reports* of Ed Murrow and Fred Friendly. Although technically better today, television news, and its familiar reporters, no longer enjoy the prestige they had in the 1960s and 1970s. Before they died, Murrow, Sevareid, and Chancellor all expressed disillusionment with current trends in television news.

Television news did not replace news on radio or in newspapers and news magazines; it supplemented them. Radio was hardest hit but slowly adapted to television news and has developed its own niche by adopting many new formats. Cronkite once called the evening television news a "headline service," and that is still the case. Some big afternoon dailies were hard hit by television, but the press generally, especially the serious press, adapted and survived. The number of daily newspapers has been generally stable in recent times. However, several journalistic magazines, such as *Colliers*, *Saturday Evening Post*, *Look*, and *Life*, were electronically executed, not because their circulations declined, but because national advertising moved to television. Magazines, by finding niche readerships, generally prospered after television; the same can be said for books.

NEW TECHNOLOGY FOR REPORTING THE WORLD

From Gutenburg on, technology has always shaped the way that news is gathered and disseminated. The persistence of certain anachronistic terms attests to the importance of earlier mechanisms. The *foreign correspondent* was the journalist abroad who literally wrote letters transported by ship to his newspaper at home. The *wire editor* handled out-of-town stories that came clattering in over telegraph wires from around the country. The *cable editor* (not cable television) was the foreign news editor sifting through news reports coming from the underseas cable, mainly from London and the British Empire, which long controlled the cables. *Cablese* was a shorthand method used by news services to combine words to save on cable charges, which traditionally cost a British penny a word.

As mentioned, in the first half of the century, newspapers depended on the telegraph, the telephone, the typewriter, hot type (i.e., Linotypes), and the rotary press to get out the newspaper. But from about 1960, a wide range of innovations, loosely called the new technology, came along and markedly affected journalism and especially news from abroad.

A much-deepened reservoir of information and its rapid dissemination among many more people are the hallmarks of this quiet revolution, which in its broader context, came to be called the *information revolution*. In the print media, high-speed transmission and electronic processing have accelerated and expanded the gathering, storing, and transferring of words for newspapers, magazines, and books. Computized composition and offset printing techniques have simplified production, leading to desktop publishing. (Today small newspapers exist that are published using a computer, printer, copying machine, and a staff of two or three people.) In broadcasting, minicams, videotape, and remote location transmissions have simplified the delivery of video to the television screen.

International journalism has been greatly facilitated by the vast improvement of telephone service, including fax, provided by the INTEL-SAT system. Foreign correspondents in remote places can be in close telephone or Internet communication with their supervising editors.

A major innovation for global television reporting was the development of portable satellite uplinks, which can be disassembled, checked as luggage, and flown to the site of a breaking story in order to send back live reports. Costing about $250,000 each, a flyaway dish can become a temporary CNN or ABC bureau in just the time it takes to get one on the scene.

Perhaps the major impact of communication satellites on the news industry has been the capability to relay color television reports instantly and globally, often significantly influencing world public opinion and understanding, as during the Gulf War or in Kosovo and Bosnia. The U.S. networks daily incorporate satellite news feeds from their correspondents in various parts of the world.

What are some of the implications for journalism of the four decades of innovations in communication technology? Here are several suggestions:

- The unit cost of communicating news will continue to drop as usage of world news systems increases and the efficiency, speed, and reach of the hardware become greater. However, the same is not true for the print media due to the rising costs of newsprint.
- Technology has made it possible to send and receive news from almost anywhere in the world at increasing speed. Researchers have succeeded in transmitting information at a rate of 1 trillion bits per second through an optical fiber. That is the equivalent of sending the contents of 300 years of daily newspapers in a single

second through a wire of glass. The continuing integration of computers with television means much more interactive, or two-way, communication will occur.

- The two-way capability of cablevision, tied in with Comsats and personal computers, means that information users can seek out or request specific kinds of news and not remain a passive audience.
- The two way capability of telecommunications means that a two-way flow of information and news is more likely, with consumers having more choice about what they receive. And each of the increasing millions of Internet users worldwide becomes a potential communicator of news and participant in the exchange of ideas and information.

CRITICISM OF THE PRESS

Criticizing the press has long been a favorite sport in America, if only because the press has long been so outspoken about our public officials and the establishment. H. L. Mencken once said, "The only way for a newsman to look on a politician is down." He also said: "All successful newspapers are ceaselessly querulous and bellicose. They never defend anyone or anything it they can help it" (Bartlett & Kaplan, 1992, p. 642). If so, they asked for it.

Like the government it supposedly keeps an eye on, the press itself needs watching and throughout the previous century, the press has not lacked critics, including many from its own ranks. One of the earliest critiques was a series of articles titled "The American Newspaper" for *Colliers* written by Will Irwin in January-July 1911. *The Brass Check* by Upton Sinclair in 1919 pictured a false, cowardly press dominated by advertisers and business interests. Walter Lippmann's *Public Opinion* in 1922 raised serious questions about the validity of journalism standards and values.

Hearst and other press lords triggered a series of critical books: Oswald Garrison Villard's *Some Newspapers and Newspapermen* in 1923 and in the turbulent 1930s, George Seldes' *Liberty of the Press* and *Lords of the Press*, Harold Ickes' *America's House of Lords* in 1939, and Ferdinand Lundberg's *Imperial Hearst* in 1936. In those depression years, the largely Republican press was much on the defensive. Newspapers still endorsed political candidates and President Franklin Roosevelt claimed that 85% of the press opposed him; he blamed the owners, not the reporters.

A major effort to study the responsibilities and character of the U.S. press came from an academic study financed by Time publisher Henry Luce and headed by Chancellor Robert M. Hutchins of the University of Chicago, called the Commission on Freedom of the Press. Several books, but little research, by noted social scientists, came out of the effort. Its summary report, *A Free and Responsible Press*, in 1947, provided a statement of principles, which were largely rejected by newspapers but studied closely in journalism education programs.

Out of the tempestuous 1960s came a spate of journalism reviews, written by journalists themselves and highly critical of press performance. Before 1968, only two reviews existed, *The Montana Journalism Review* and *The Columbia Journalism Review*. *The Chicago Journalism Review*, published from 1968–1975, inspired about 40 or so similar publications, but fewer than a dozen survived after 1977, including *More*, a national review; *Accuracy in Media* (AIM), a conservative newsletter; *Media Report to Women*, *Twin Cities Journalism Review*, and feed/back.

Among newsmen who wrote for those reviews, the model of press critics was provided by A. J. Liebling, whose insightful "Wayward Press" pieces in *The New Yorker* entertained readers as he skewered newspaper errors and ethical lapses throughout the 1950s and 1960s. Throughout the considerable literature of press criticism, Johnston (1979) noted that certain themes have persisted: The media are too big and powerful, too tightly controlled by too few people, too standardized in their presentation of news and information; too much "managed" news; and too much attention is paid to gossip, trivia, sex, and violence and not enough attention to significant social, economic, and political trends. Current press criticism echoes and rephrases some of these themes.

As seen later, criticism of the press is alive and prospering, and there is some evidence that the news media heed their critics.

CHAPTER
5

Bigger, Fewer,
and More Like-Minded

Freedom of the Press is guaranteed only to those who own one.
—A. J. Liebling (1960)

News has become a big business controlled not by powerful families but by media moguls who place a higher priority on the size of the profits than on the value of their contributions to society.
—Marvin Kalb (1999)

A continuing and inexorable trend throughout 20th-century America has been for more and more newspapers, radio and television stations, magazines, book publishers, and other media organizations to become owned and controlled by corporate giants—usually called *conglomerates*—that have become bigger, fewer, and, in significant ways, more like-minded. The trends continues into the 21st century.

This thrust toward monopoly or concentration of ownership has developed in stages, each of which represents potential threats to diversity of ideas and views as well as to independent and vigorously competing news media. First came the newspaper groups noted in the previous chapter whereby a number of similar papers are held by one owner. The Gannett Co. is currently the largest, with 74 dailies and 6.6 million circulation in 2000. Next comes Knight-Ridder with 31 dailies and 4 million circulation. Similar patterns of group ownership of radio and television stations have characterized broadcasting as well.

Next there were the increasingly common one-newspaper cities with local media oligopolies whereby the only newspaper in particular city also owned local radio and television outlets. (The spread of national newspapers plus more suburban papers has allayed this concern somewhat.)

Another stage was cross-media ownerships whereby one company— such as the Tribune Co. of Chicago, Times Mirror of Los Angeles, Washington Post Co., and others—acquired newspapers, radio and television stations, book publishers, and magazines, scattered around the country. In such companies, media properties come and go as corporate strategies change.

In television broadcasting, groups of stations and networks have been swallowed by bigger fish. In 1986, the ABC network was acquired by the much smaller Capital Cities for $3.5 billion; General Electric, original owner of RCA, bought it back, including the NBC network, for $ 6.4 billion. In 1990, Rupert Murdoch assembled the Fox network out of the Metromedia television station chain and the film studio, 20th Century Fox. And in 1994, Hollywood film studios started two more networks— WB (Warner) and UPN (Universal and Paramount).

These various media companies have evolved to the most ominous creature on the media landscape: the giant conglomerate that owns not only news and entertainment media, but production and distribution companies as well. They deal in all of the products of entertainment and popular culture, including sometimes, over in a small corner, news media.

The world's largest media company was, at a recent count, Time Warner (and now AOL-Time Warner) but others are in the chase, particularly Disney/ABC and the far-flung empire controlled by Rupert Murdoch operating under the misnomer of News Corporation.

No one has followed the continuing trends of media consolidation more closely than Ben Bagdikian (1992), who has shown that ownership of most of the major media has been consolidated into fewer and fewer corporate hands—from 50 national and multinational corporations in 1983 to just 20 in 1992. In that nine-year period, the companies controlling most of the national daily circulation shrunk from 20 to just 11. Among magazines, a majority of the total annual industry revenues, he said, earned by 20 firms in 1983, was amassed by only 2 in 1992; in book publishing, revenues divided among 11 firms accrued to just 5 in that same nine-year period. This media merger frenzy has continued unabated with no end in sight.

The sheer size of media conglomerates makes them, as publicly held companies, active players in the financial markets, hence they are under pressure to compete for earnings with highly speculative investments. Bagdikian (1992) commented, "For the first time in the history of American journalism, news and public information have been integrated formally into the highest levels of financial and non-journalistic corporate control. Conflicts of interest between the public's need for information and corporate desires for 'positive' information have been vastly increased" (p. xxx).

Driven by visions of expanding profits and ever-larger markets as well as the opportunities created by new technologies of telecommunications, the media giants have been acquiring each other at a quickened rate. Grow or perish seems to be the credo; bigger is apparently better.

A flurry of mergers of major U.S. media organizations has been occurring since 1995. The continuing trend has broad implications both for the quality of journalism and the nature of the entertainment business here and abroad. The mergers also illustrate the complexity and global reach of these behemoths.

DISNEY SWALLOWS ABC

In August 1995, the Walt Disney Company announced acquisition of Capital Cities/ABC in a deal valued at $19 billion—the second largest media takeover ever. The merged company brought together ABC, then the most profitable television network, including its highly regarded television news organization and its ESPN sports cable service, with an entertainment giant—Disney's Hollywood film and television studios, its theme parks and its repository of well-known cartoon characters and the merchandise sales they generate. For example, in 1995, the Disney Company sold more than $15 billion worth of Disney merchandise worldwide—a figure more than seven times the global box office for Disney movies (Auletta, 1996).

Both companies announced they would grow faster together. Disney/ABC became the first media company to have a major presence in four distribution systems: filmed entertainment, cable television, broadcasting, and telephone wires through its connections with three regional phone companies. So, ABC's news media operations, including its national news shows, *World News Tonight with Peter Jennings*, *Nightline* with Ted Koppel, and the admirable ABC television news organization, plus 20 radio stations and eight television stations, publishing operations, *The Kansas City Star*, *The Fort Worth Star Telegram*, Fairchild and Chilton trade publications, and international broadcasting interests were all merged, or better, submerged, into an entertainment giant that generates about $17 billion in revenues yearly. Heretofore, Disney had no involvement with any activity remotely concerned with news or journalism. Now Peter Jennings and Ted Koppel and colleagues were all working for Mickey Mouse. At the time of the merger, no top executive from either Disney or ABC made any statement about how the merger would affect news media and journalists in the new company. (In early 1997, Disney announced it was putting up for sale the publishing businesses, including the newspapers, it acquired from ABC. The *Kansas City Star* and *Fort Worth Star Telegram* were both purchased by Knight-Ridder.)

TIME WARNER, TURNER AND AOL

The next merger bombshell came one month later when Time Warner Inc. and Turner Broadcasting System announced they would merge their sprawling operations, reinforcing Time Warner's position as the world's largest communications giant. Time Warner said it would buy the 82% of Turner that it did not already own—at a price tag of $7.5 billion.

In this case, both companies had major news-related media. (Time Inc. and Warner Communications had merged in a $14 billion deal in 1989.) Time Warner's major publishing interests included *Time*, *Life*, *Money*, *Fortune*, *People*, and *Sports Illustrated* as well as Time-Life Books and Warner Books. However, just in money terms, these publications were overshadowed by the Warner Bros. film and television studios, television and cable channels such as HBO, Cinemax, and others, 50 record labels, the world's largest music publisher, film libraries and other businesses such as Six Flags theme parks, and so forth. The Turner company, of course, had CNN, CNN International, and Headline News cable channels, in addition to its film and television production, other television and cable channels, film libraries, and assorted sports franchises such as the Atlanta Braves baseball team, the Atlanta Hawks basketball team, and World Championship Wrestling. As with Disney/ABC, the news and journalism operations were in monetary terms a fraction of the corporate pie, and presumably of less importance in the corporate scheme of things.

But all of this was just a prelude to the richest media merger to date when on January 11, 2000, America Online (AOL), which provides the

Internet to many millions, announced that it had agreed to buy Time Warner for $165 billion, providing the best evidence yet that the old and the new media were converging. Time Warner thus admitted that the Internet was central to its music, publishing, and television businesses. AOL with its 22 million paying subscribers gained access to Time Warner's cable systems. For consumers, the merger portended further mergers and alliances among media giants that could lead to the development of and access to high-capacity information and entertainment networks.

Concerns were expressed that the Internet, with its many thousands of sources of information, had itself become prey to corporate consolidations. Some journalists were concerned not that there would be fewer outlets—the opposite was true—but that a few people would have control over them. This biggest of all media mergers was forcing journalists and those who care about journalism to be cognizant of the need to build walls among the multiple compartments of these new information, entertainment, and marketing giants. Some saw the independence and diversity of journalism in peril all across a media world that was being reshaped more rapidly than anyone could have predicted.

WESTINGHOUSE, CBS, AND VIACOM

Another blockbuster merger came in mid-1995 with Westinghouse Inc.'s takeover of CBS Inc., creating the nation's largest broadcast station group with 39 radio stations and 16 television stations reaching 32% of the nation. This merger brought together two pioneers of broadcasting—CBS started its radio network in 1927 and Westinghouse had launched KDKA Pittsburgh in 1920. However, currently 90% of Westinghouse's sales are in manufacturing with only 10% in broadcasting. There were concerns about how well it could run a major network. CBS, once a leader in both ratings and quality of broadcast news, had slipped. The former Tiffany network had lost some important affiliates and had no holdings in cable. By the scale of today's mergers, once-mighty CBS was sold for an embarrassingly low price—only $5.4 billion.

Another significant merger was the marriage of a hot cable television company, Viacom, with a legendary Hollywood studio, Paramount Communications, Inc., for $8.2 billion in 1993. The new company, called Paramount Viacom International, fused Viacom's ubiquitous MTV and Nickelodeon cable channels and Showtime pay television channel with

Paramount's film company, Paramount television, and publishing firms—Simon & Schuster, Prentice-Hall, and Pocket Books—and several sports properties, Madison Square Garden, The New York Knicks, and The New York Rangers (Fabricant, 1996a).

The mega-merger pot kept boiling and in September 1999, Viacom said it would acquire the CBS Corporation for $37.3 billion, creating the world's second largest media company. For the news division of CBS, it meant probably more cost-cutting and the realization that, even more than in the recent past, news would be a small slice of a big media pie.

CBS brought to the merger $1.9 billion in radio properties including 190 radio stations; $4.4 billion in television holdings, including the CBS Network, CBS Entertainment, CBS Sports, 17 television stations, and $546 million in cable properties including two country music networks, CMT and TNN, and two regional sports networks.

Another piece was added in March 2000 when Viacom made a deal to acquire full control of the UPN television network for $5 million. If this deal is approved by the FCC, Viacom would be the first company to own two networks—CBS and UPN.

In May 2000, the FCC approved the merger of Viacom and CBS, which will give Viacom control of 35% of the broadcasting market.

As media properties are traded back and forth, the size and annual revenues of the media entertainment giants rise and fall. As of late 1999, the estimated total annual revenues of the major players were: Time Warner (before AOL), $26.9 billion; Viacom (including CBS), $18.9 billion; News Corporation (Murdoch), $13.6 billion; Bertlesmann, $12.7 billion; Seagram, $12.3 billion; General Electric, $15.3 billion in media revenues out of $100.4 billion of total GE revenues (Mifflin, 1999).

MURDOCH ROLLS ONWARD

Although smaller than several of its U.S. rivals, News Corporation had expanded into satellite television and programming abroad and had global clout far beyond its size.

During these recent mega-mergers, Rupert Murdoch, the most conspicuous big roller among media owners, had not been idle. In 1996, his News Corporation acquired the New World Communications Group, Inc. for $3.4 billion, making him the biggest owner of television stations in this country. The purchase gave Fox network ownership of television stations in 11 of 12 of the nation's largest television markets, extending the company's reach to 40% of American homes. Murdoch's reach was extended even further in 1997 when he agreed to pay $1.9 billion to acquire the cable channel controlled by Pat Robertson, the religious-right purveyor of programs reaching 67 million homes.

In August 2000, Murdoch proposed to add to his vast media empire by buying WWOR Channel 9 in New York City and nine other television stations around the country from Christ-Craft Industries. If approved, the $3.5 billion purchase would give News Corporation two television stations each in New York, Los Angeles, Phoenix, and Salt Lake City.

Since starting out with a small group of Australian newspapers, Murdoch has been continually reshaping his media empire and juggling his considerable debts. Although long involved in journalism and newspapers, Murdoch has consistently shown a cynical and hypocritical disdain for responsible journalism, apparently considering news just another commodity to be sold. His Fox network has notably lacked respectable news programming and he has been criticized for using his news operations to satisfy his own political goals. One critic, Alex Jones, said of him: "News is a commodity that is of no more importance to Rupert Murdoch than a television sitcom. He crafts news for the audience, but in fact his sense of what the audience wants is skewed to sensation and a lowering, not an elevation, of standards" (Fabricant, 1996a, p. C7).

Murdoch makes no excuses. "Look," he said, "the first thing you have to do in a public company is to survive, and I don't make any apology for a paper or a magazine" (Fabricant, 1996a, p. C7).

His strategy apparently is to own every major form of programming—news, sports, films and children's shows—and beam them via satellites or television stations he owns or controls to homes in America, Europe, Asia, and South America. He commented: "We want to put our programming everywhere and to distribute everybody's product around the world" (Fabricant, 1996b, p. C1). Some believe the recent media deals came about because Disney and Time Warner felt they had to catch up with Murdoch.

Murdoch has more than 150 media properties in his constantly shifting empire, based mainly in the United States, United Kingdom, and Australia, and with it, he has carefully put together a vertically integrated global media empire. In the United States, he owns the Fox television network, 20th Century Fox movies and television, *The New York Post*, *Weekly Standard*, and Harper Collins Publishers. (In October 1999, Murdoch sold his *TV Guide*, America's best-selling magazine with a weekly circulation of 12 million for $9.2 billion to Gemstar International Group.) In Britain, he owns *The Sunday Times, Times* of London, *The Sun, News of the World*, and other media companies. In Australia, he owns Fox Studios Australia for movies; seven television networks; one national newspaper, *The Australian*, and 117 other newspapers giving him two-thirds of newspaper circulation; and two magazines and other media-related companies. Further, through various holdings including ASkyB, SkyMCI, Fox News Cable, Sky Entertainment Latin America, British Sky Broadcasting, Sky TV in Asia, and Vox in Germany, he has satellite coverage of five continents.

THE RACE FOR GLOBAL MARKETS

These mega-mergers positioned the evolving giants—Disney Co., AOL-Time Warner, NBC, and Murdoch—to better penetrate and dominate the growing international markets for television, movies, news, sports, recordings, and other media products. At the time of the merger with ABC, Disney president Michael Eisner spoke glowingly of India's middle class of 250 million as a great potential audience for Disney/ABC movies, cartoons, news, and sports programs. Further, NBA and NFL professional games have been gaining large audiences overseas, hence the importance of the ESPN networks.

The competition between CNN, MSNBC, and Murdoch's Fox network for a 24-hour cable news channel has strong international potential as well. Broadcast networks have been looking to international markets as a way of gaining hundreds of millions of new viewers. NBC's international holdings currently are about 20% of the network's worth of $10 to $12 billion; in 10 years, half of the network's value will come from international holdings. Asia is expected to be the main area of growth because about 25% of the continent's homes are expected to receive cable by the year 2000. By contrast, the U.S. market, with cable in 65 million of its 97 million households, is nearing saturation. Numbers of cable viewers are expected to rise abroad in time for the start of NBC Europe and related NBC services in Latin America as well.

Other competitors in the global race after CNN and NBC are Disney, British Broadcasting Corporation, and NHK of Japan.

In 1999, the European televison industry was suddenly in the grip of an American-style consolidation. Responding to the thrust of the global economy and the power of the Internet, media companies in Europe were forging cross-border links as media giants like Microsoft, Disney, and Murdoch were getting into the action. The resulting alliances offered an opening for advertisers to reach wide audiences and an opportunity for Europe to challenge American supremacy in television programming. Europe, in fact, seemed headed for a future, much like America's present, in which the television industry would be dominated by a few huge conglomerates.

OTHER BIG MEDIA PLAYERS

Other overseas media barons are also competing for the growing international media markets. Among the bigger players are Bertelsmann A.G. of Germany, which built up a media giant with book and record clubs in Germany, Spain, United States, Brazil, and 18 other countries. Bertelsmann owns Bantam, Doubleday, and Dell book publishers in America, 37 magazines in five countries, and radio and television properties.

In 1998, Bertelsmann surprised and shocked the American book industry when it purchased Random House, the dominant general book publisher in the U.S., making the German firm by far the most important book publisher in the world. With Random House combined with its other U.S. book properties, Bertelsmann controls a substantial share of the American adult trade-book market.

Possibly the most swashbuckling of the media tycoons has been Silvio Berlusconi of Italy, who built a multibillion dollar television and newspaper empire, Fininvest, of unusual power and influence. With 42% of Italy's advertising market and 16% of its daily newspaper circulation, ownership of Italy's three main private television channels, plus other properties, Berlusconi dominated Italy's media and influenced its politics. Using that power, he won election as prime minister in 1994. However, he was forced to resign after his media empire was linked to bribes of tax auditors. In 1998, he was sentenced to two years in jail for illegal political contributions and for bribing tax inspectors. The future of his media empire is uncertain.

Japanese corporations have invested heavily in Hollywood movie studios. MCA, owner of Universal Studios, Universal Pictures, MCA Records, theme parks, and Putnam's publishing firm, was acquired by Matsushita Electric Industrial Co. for $6.13 billion in 1990. Another Japanese giant, Sony, owner of CBS Records, Columbia Pictures and Tristar Pictures, and Matsushita controlled more than a quarter of the U.S. motion picture market. However, the Japanese owners have not done well financially with these media properties.

Such transnational acquisitive media activities are a natural and the expected result of the globalization of the economy and the free flow of investment capital across borders. But the U.S. and other democracies may need to update and revise their own communications policies that were formulated before news, mass culture, entertainment, and other information moved so freely around the world.

IMPLICATIONS AND CONCERNS FOR JOURNALISM

A principal concern for public affairs journalism is that the news operations—broadcast news divisions, newspapers, and news magazines—have become just a small part of these giant entertainment companies. The future of independent news gathering appears threatened when news media are submerged into entertainment companies.

Bill Kovach (1996), head of the Nieman Foundation at Harvard, wrote,

> Though the trend is not new, with the Disney/ABC merger the threat to a form of journalism that serves the interests of a self-governing people crosses a new threshold. Even with the best of intentions, owners and managers are influenced by the fact that they now preside over a corporation that, by the simple act of merger, has drastically reduced the proportionate importance of the news department. . . . ABC's news division will now have to compete with the enormous energy of Disney's entertainment productions in a company in which ABC's value as an outlet for entertainment is paramount. (p. A17)

The future of journalism as watchdog on the government (and corporations) is threatened when big organizations that do business with the U.S. government, like General Electric (NBC), have swallowed major news media. Communications companies in recent years have almost ingested most news organizations, yet these same companies are involved in lobbying government and buying government favors. In the 1994 elections, the communications industry was the sixth largest contributor to candidates, giving almost $10 million to political action committees.

A major concern is whether reporters within these entertainment giants will be permitted to objectively and critically report news about their own organizations. Lawrence Grossman, former head of NBC news, reported that when the stock market crashed in 1987, he received a call from Jack Welch, chairman of General Electric, owner of NBC, telling him not to use words in NBC news reports that might adversely affect GE stock. Grossman said he did not tell his NBC news staff about the call (Bagdikian,1992).

"You cannot trust news organizations to cover themselves," said one critic, citing as example television's meager coverage of the telecommunications debate in Congress that led to major communications legislation in 1996 (Gunther, 1995, p. 36).

Gunther (1995) raised this question regarding mega-deals: "Will film critic Joel Siegel of ABC's *Good Morning America* feel free to deliver a withering critique of Disney's next big animated movie?" (p. 37).

Will ABC news be able to report critically about the Chinese government at a time when Disney may be trying to get its movies via satellite into China? We already know what Rupert Murdoch will do: In 1994, in an effort to curry favor with the Deng regime in China, which had criticized BBC news, Murdoch summarily dropped BBC's World television news from his Star TV satellite service in Hong Kong.

The word *synergy* has become a mantra for the CEOs of the recent mergers. When he bought ABC, Disney chief Michael Eisner used the term five times in four sentences to illustrate the advantages of merger. When Westinghouse purchased CBS, its CEO said that combining the two companies' broadcasting assets would save hundreds of millions of dollars a year and bring about "tremendous marketing synergies" (Auletta, 1995b, p. 31). "Whether these wonders will come to pass remains to be seen. What is already apparent is that synergy is no friend of journalism. The business assumptions behind the word—cost savings, a team culture, the leverage of size—can be actively hostile to the business of reporting" (p. 31).

Rich (1996) defined synergy as the "dedication of an entire, far-flung multimedia empire to selling its products with every means at its disposal." Another critic said, "When you hear the word synergy, you might as well read 'conflict of interest'" (p. 15).

Investigative reporters like Brian Ross of ABC News have been learning how far they can go in reporting about their own companies. In October 1998, Ross had what he thought was a solid story involving accounts of pedophilia and lax security at theme park resorts, including Disney World. But his story for *20/20*, ABC's newsmagazine program, was killed by ABC News executives, who refused to discuss the decision. The Disney Company issued a statement that its executives had nothing to do with the decision. An important question was whether other ABC journalists would feel inhibited from pursuing stories about Disney.

When the Warner movie *Twister* was released, *Time* magazine just happened to run a cover story on tornadoes, and Time Warner was criticized for committing synergy. Another example: After joining with Disney, ABC broadcast a special on the making of *The Hunchback of Notre Dame* to coincide with the release of the animated Disney film. Several television stations owned by ABC also covered, as news, a gala celebration that Disney threw for the movie in New Orleans.

Some critics think the big problem is not compromised news coverage, but compromised news distribution, whether over radio, television, or satellite. A squabble between media barons over scarce television channel space came sooner than expected. In October 1996, Rupert Murdoch went to court in New York City charging that Time Warner was out to destroy his Fox network by refusing to offer Fox's new 24-hour news channel to Time Warner's New York cable subscribers. Instead, the cable channel went to MSNBC, the new Microsoft/NBC joint venture. New York's mayor, Rudolph Giuliani, got into the act, hoping to force Murdoch's news network onto the Time Warner channel, by trying to air it on a municipal channel. (Murdoch was a political ally of the mayor.) However, a federal judge issued a broad ruling barring Giuliani from the action, rebuking the mayor for what she said was a thinly disguised effort to help a political supporter. She said the mayor violated Time Warner's First Amendment right to choose the channel it transmits. At its simplest, it was a battle over a precious commodity in the information age, channel space, but it also raised questions about competition in the news business and relations between politicians and news organizations.

Another and more ominous dispute between media giants occurred on May 2, 2000 when Time Warner Cable removed ABC stations from cable systems it operates in seven cities serving 3.5 million customers including New York, Los Angeles, and Philadelphia. Viewers found themselves without access to "Who Wants To Marry A Millionaire" as well as the ABC *Evening News* and *Nightline*. The dispute involved how much Time Warner should pay Disney (owner of ABC) for carrying its cable channels. But it also touched on larger issues relating to the distribution of entertainment and news programs, including the friction between cable and broadcast industries, the growing competition between cable and satellite firms, and Disney's opposition to the merger between Time Warner and America Online.

Time Warner backed off 24 hours later but for critics, the shutting down of a major news outlet, even for a day, was seen as a blow to the public interest and should not be tolerated in a democracy. By the blunt use of its monopoly power, Time Warner suffered an instant public-relations disaster and critics called for a closer scrutiny of its merger with AOL. One critic said the incident made the theoretical danger of media consolidation and control and into a very real problem. The incident provided a wake-up call for those concerned about media monopolies.

By comparison, synergy seemed like a modest concern but yet it has a lot to do with diversity—and marketing. Critic Edward Rothstein commented,

> Disney can produce related movies, toys, books, videos, shows and infomercials so that each format feeds the others. A video game turns into a television show, a computer game into a novel. A newspaper reviews its own corporation's products; news shows promote made-for-TV movies with tie-ins. It can seem that much of culture has become a series of products being transported from one technological medium to another, with fewer and fewer hands manipulating the software. (Rothstein, 1996, p. B1)

The media giants' timidity and aversion to controversy was illustrated by recent legal clashes of both ABC and CBS news organizations with major tobacco corporations. In 1994, ABC on its *Day One* magazine show carried a hard-hitting investigative piece called "*Smoke Screen*" about the manipulation of nicotine in cigarettes and the behavior of tobacco companies. As a result, ABC spent 17 months and millions in legal fees fighting a potential $10 billion dollar lawsuit from Philip Morris. Both the producer and on-air correspondent said the story was accurate and ABC lawyers were confident they could win. But soon after the merger with Disney was announced, Capital Cities/ABC management forced the news division to issue a humiliating public apology, which Philip Morris reprinted in newspapers all over the nation. Many journalists were stunned. Why had ABC settled? Most agreed it was not a matter of journalistic ethics ("We were wrong") but more of corporate convenience ("We can't impede the merger"). Auletta called it "the logic of negative synergy" (1995b, p. 9).

A similar ethical embarrassment hit CBS' *60 Minutes* news program soon after and was even more of a cause celebre. In November 1995, in an atmosphere of increased tension between the tobacco companies and the press, CBS' lawyers ordered *60 Minutes* not to broadcast a planned on-the-record interview with a former tobacco company executive who was harshly critical of the industry. Many in journalism and the law felt that

CBS, facing a multibillion-dollar lawsuit, had backed off from a fight it probably could have won. *60 Minutes* was faulted for not saying that the decision came at a time CBS stockholders were considering a merger with Westinghouse. *The New York Times* editorialized:

> This act of self censorship by the country's most powerful and aggressive television news program sends a chilling message to journalists investigating industry practices everywhere. . . . But the most troubling part of CBS' decision is that it was made not by news executives but by corporate officers who may have their minds on money rather than public service these days. With a $5.4 billion merger deal with Westinghouse Electric Corp. about to be approved, a multi-billion dollar lawsuit would hardly have been a welcome development. Some of the executives who helped kill the *60 Minutes* interview, including the general counsel, stand to gain millions of dollars themselves in stock options and other payments once the deal is approved. . . . The network's action shows that media companies in play lose their journalistic aggressiveness when they let lawyers and corporate executives make decisions that ought to be the province of news executives. The same issue was raised when ABC settled its lawsuit with Philip Morris. ("Self-censorship at CBS," 1995, p. 14E)

Both ABC and CBS took a critical lambasting from the press in general and from academic critics, *Columbia Journalism Review* and *American Journalism Review*. Many in journalism were asking whether the corporate executives of the big conglomerates will back their in-house news media in future legal clashes with government or economic power as, for example, *The New York Times* and *The Washington Post* had done in the Pentagon Papers case. So far the outlook was not promising.

DOMINANCE OF GROUP OWNERSHIP IN DAILY NEWSPAPERS

The great majority of U.S. daily newspapers have not been swallowed by the huge entertainment conglomerates described earlier. This is important because the daily newspaper is a medium that is mainly involved with marketing news. However, more than 500 of the 1,516 dailies in 1997, including almost all of the largest and most influential, are owned by the 20 largest U.S. newspaper companies, that is, firms mainly concerned with putting out newspapers.

In early 2000, the 8 largest newspaper groups, all with total daily circulations of more than 1 million, are in order of daily circulation: Gannett Co., 74 papers; Knight-Ridder Inc., 31 papers; Times Mirror Co., 7 papers; New York Times Co., 20 papers; Dow Jones & Co., 31 papers; E.W. Scripps, 19 papers; (Chicago) Tribune Co., 4 papers; and Washington Post Co., 51.

TRIBUNE CO. BUYS THE LOS ANGELES TIMES

This lineup was changed abruptly on March 14, 2000 when the Tribune Company of Chicago announced that it was buying the Times Mirror Company for $6.3 billion, creating the nation's third largest newspaper company. *The Los Angeles Times*, operated for 118 years by the Chandler family, along with *The Baltimore Sun*, *The Hartford Courant*, and Long Island's *Newsday*, plus 18 magazines, passed over to the Tribune Company, which along with the *Chicago Tribune*, had interests in three other newspapers, regional cable programming, plus 22 television stations, 3 radio stations, as well as the Chicago Cubs and heavy investments in America Online. The seven dailies had a combined 3.9 million circulation and combined 1999 revenues of $6.25 billions. The Tribune Company moved up to second place behind the Gannett company among the top groups in market value of its assets.

The sale of the L.A. *Times* was about more than mergers and financial payouts. The *Times* had played a leading role in the history and growth of Southern California and was a dominant influence on the region's political, intellectual and cultural life. It was a blow to civic pride and to Angelenos' sense of identity to see the great newspaper pass into the hands of midwesterners. Even the *Times'* many critics hated to see the change.

More importantly, the *Times* is one of the four or five best newspapers in the nation and it faced an uncertain future. Would the Tribune Company do what is necessary to maintain its excellence? Would the *Times'* expensive Washington and foreign news bureaus be maintained?

In the aggregate, 455 individual companies own the nation's dailies. Of these, 129 groups now own 80% of the total.

In earlier times, the concept of several daily newspapers competing in one city for news and public support reflected the value of diversity and was considered important for democratic government. New York City once had 14 dailies, whereas Omaha had 7. Today, only eight large American cities have more than one daily newspaper under separate ownership and not involved in joint operating agreements: Boston, Chicago, Denver, Los Angeles, New York City, Trenton, New Jersey, Tucson, and Washington, DC.

However, in most larger communities, the presence of local radio, television, and cable outlets, suburban and weekly papers and local magazines, plus access to national papers, certainly contributes to diversity and a marketplace of ideas.

The steady, inexorable trend toward group ownership seems to go on unabated. The long-standing tradition of the family-owned newspaper may be ending. According to media analyst John Morton (1995), it cannot last because few family dynasties are left. In 1995, he counted only 77 independently owned, family-controlled newspapers of 30,000 circulation or more remaining; this represented about 5% of the 1,516 or so dailies still in business in the United States. According to industry figures, the total number of independently owned daily papers shrank from 1,650 in 1920 to 850 in 1960, and to just 300 in 1998 and most of these papers had small circulations.

Morton says the unusual thing about the growing concentration of newspaper ownership in the past 25 years, compared with other industries, is that it has come rather late to newspapers. Compared with automakers, grocers, steel companies, and retailers, the newspaper industry remains diverse in ownership. Moreover, newspaper ownership is much more concentrated in other Western democracies such as Britain, France, Italy, Australia, and Germany.

When Gannett purchased 11 daily papers in July 1995, Eisendrath commented, "The war is over and the old guys lost" (Glaberson, 1995a, p.1, sec. 4). The "old guys" were independent newspaper publishers, many of whom had close ties to their communities. Gannett's earlier purchases of respected family-owned papers had raised the issue of whether good journalism and corporate ownership can coexist. Now the question does not seem to come up.

Some major newspapers have been able to withstand the pressures of potential buyers by either adopting a two-tier stock ownership plan, retaining voting power with the founding family, or by distributing the company to its employees through employee stock ownership plans. Several of the biggest companies in terms of circulation, New York Times Co., Tribune Co., Dow Jones, and Times Mirror have such arrangements to ward off potential buyers. (At Times Mirror, it was the contentious Chandler family that initiated the sale to the Tribune Co.)

At *The Milwaukee Journal*, an employee-owned trust was established in 1937 by publisher Harry Grant, who also acquired an ownership stake that his descendants control today. Grant felt that protecting the company from a buyout would promote superior journalism. In 1996, an offer of $1 billion was made for the Journal Co., which owns the recently merged *Milwaukee Journal Sentinel* and six subsidiaries. Although the offer was estimated to be twice the value of the company, the offer was rejected.

As noted earlier, most of best papers are in groups. The old days of William Randolph Hearst sending out explicit orders from San Simeon regarding his pet campaigns and editorial positions to be carried in all his papers are over. Most group-owned dailies enjoy considerable local autonomy with editors and publishers establishing their own news and editorial policies. Group ownership provides economic stability by efficient business policies that enable papers to survive where they might otherwise fold. The sharing of news through the group and through news services and other cooperative efforts helps papers to survive. In its first years, *USA Today* was greatly assisted by the seconding of staff members from other Gannett papers who remained on the payrolls of their home papers. Nonetheless, papers within a group tend to look alike in format, typography, features, and editorial tone.

RESEARCH ON CHAIN OWNERSHIP

What does research say happens when a chain buys a highly regarded independent newspaper? The usual expectation is that the quality of the newspaper will deteriorate, the news hole and staff numbers will shrink, and the new corporate owners will squeeze as much profit as possible out of their new acquisition. But this is not always the case. Some research studies show a somewhat mixed picture. The independently owned *Louisville Courier-Journal* was purchased by Gannett in 1986. A careful longitudinal study of the news content of the *Courier-Journal* found a mixed commitment by Gannett to the editorial quality of the paper. Under the group owners, the paper substantially increased the size of the news hole, but the average length of the stories dropped, coverage of hard news declined, and the number of wire-written stories exceeded staff-written pieces (Coulson & Hansen, 1995).

Another scholar used the recession of the late 1980s to compare how the different forms of newspaper ownership—chain and independent—

responded to difficult economic conditions. Twenty-nine daily newspapers were studied from 1985–1992. Chain ownership showed modest and mixed effects. The chain papers had higher average profit margins, supporting a common accusation of their critics. Chains spent more on news editorial as a percentage of all expenditures and showed a consistently higher benefit ratio. The independents were higher on news hole and editorial pages (Blankenburg, 1995).

LOSING READERS AND PROFITS

In the past several years, although profits were still running at about 12%, or twice the Fortune 500 average, daily newspapers have not been as profitable as earlier. The industry has cut about 6,000 newsroom and production jobs and many others have gone unfilled.

Some critics think that newspapers should be spending more, not less, on news gathering and publishing. Newspaper executives are understandably concerned about threats to the industry: advertising dollars moving away from newspapers, circulation slipping, an aging readership, and a younger generation with few of the newspaper habits of its parents. There seems little doubt that most newspapers publishers are more concerned with the bottom line than they are with exerting political influence and control.

Aside from the largest and best-quality dailies, losses of circulation overshadowed gains for most papers in 1999. Morton (1999) reported that in papers under 500,000 circulation, 60% lost or showed no gain in readers. For papers under 25,000 circulation, about 65% showed losses. Such trends contribute to a feeling that the daily newspaper is a fading industry. (And yet many newspaper groups are still very profitable).

For some time now, critics have predicted that the days of the daily newspaper are limited; that it is a sunset industry. Still, daily newspapers persist and provide more news and information today than ever before. For millions of educated and concerned Americans, their daily supplement of news and current specialized information supplied by the dozen or more great metropolitan papers is still essential to their public activities and private lives. On most days, news on commercial radio and television cannot compete with that.

Yet with proliferating new electronic and cable media, computers online, and Internet services providing outlets for clashing opinions and ideologies, the place of daily newspapers in the electronically expanded marketplace of ideas would seem to be diminished. Freedom of expression is much less dependent on the printing press than it has been in the past and that is a reason for concern.

Today's media mix presents a paradox. The sources of news and useful information, however wrapped and disguised in gaudy packages of entertainment and persuasive communication—marketing, advertising, propaganda and PR-driven messages—are greater than ever. This vast, expanding landscape also includes cable channels, magazines, and books (just visit a Border's or Barnes & Noble bookstore), the Internet, CD-ROM and other electronic outlets, and even mail order.

On the other hand, another reality is that the economic units—the media companies and organizations that produce, market, and distribute the news that enlightens us and the entertainment that diverts and beguiles us—are rapidly becoming gigantic in size, fewer in number, more remote, and more like-minded. That is certainly cause for concern.

6

News on the Air: A Sense of Decline

Radio, if it is to serve and survive, must hold a mirror behind the nation and the world. If the reflection shows radical intolerance, economic inequality, bigotry, unemployment or anything else—let the people see it, and rather hear it. The mirror must have no curves and must be held with a steady hand.

—Edward R. Murrow (1945)

For more than 50 years, television has been a powerful information force, focusing a nation's attention on great events—a presidential election, a disastrous war in Vietnam, an historic struggle in the 1960s for civil rights and, more recently, the fall of Communism and prime time wars in the Persian Gulf and Yugoslavia.

In 1963, the three networks began their 30-minute evening newscasts (originally 15 minutes as in radio), which became the "front page" from which most Americans increasingly received their news. But in recent years, things have changed. There has been a pervading atmosphere of unease about television news, a sense that broadcast journalism has lost its way and is in decline.

In addressing the shortcomings of today's journalism, it should be understood that some criticisms are peculiar to television news, others to news on radio, and still others to newspapers and magazines. Yet, many broad-brush indictments of poor journalistic performance blame all news media equally. That is patently unfair. Some criticisms such as mixing entertainment with news may seem to cut across several media but not in the same ways. The problem of journalists as celebrities is peculiar to television. Many media differences persist, exacerbated by the rise of cable and the Internet.

The media are not a monolith, but a complex and heterogeneous collection of diverse organizations and individuals often with quite different motivations and goals. Journalists, whether at *The Daily Chronicle*, ABC news, or *The National Enquirer* are members of a news organization and their performance is shaped by and is a reflection of where they work. Some journalists do their jobs well, others not so well at times. So bear in mind that the criticisms that follow usually apply to only part of the news media. For clarity, television, radio, and the print media are analyzed separately as much as possible.

In its transition from radio to television, broadcast news was for many years a loss leader, a public service intended to attract serious viewers as well as prestige. Profits, if any, from newscasts were incidental. The best-known broadcasters—Edward R. Murrow, Eric Sevareid, Walter Cronkite, Chet Huntley and David Brinkley, Howard K. Smith, and John Chancellor—enjoyed a stature and credibility with the public rarely found among today's anchors.

As the pioneering broadcast giants, William Paley at CBS and David Sarnoff at NBC, faded away, conventional corporate interests took control—General Electric at NBC, real estate magnate Lawrence Tisch (and later Westinghouse and then Viacom) at CBS, and Capital Cities (and later Disney Company) at ABC. News programs were increasingly expected to attract audiences and bring in revenue, and that required higher ratings and mass audiences.

The short television life of the early high-quality but low-rated documentaries soon ended, and the evening news broadcasts began to stress more crime, scandal, and celebrities, all of which tended to crowd out foreign and public affairs news. After the ratings success of CBS' *60 Minutes* in the 1980s, the networks found money was to be made from the so-called newsmagazine shows. Imitators, such as *20/20, Prime Time Live,*

Turning Point, 48 Hours, Dateline NBC, Eye to Eye with Connie Chung, and *Day One,* soon clogged the airways. The quality varied widely from the newsworthy to such trivia as Connie Chung seriously interviewing Tonya Harding, an Olympic skating hopeful who caused injury to a rival, and Heidi Fleiss, a Hollywood madam. These news magazines had a semblance of journalism, but were increasingly emulating the popular pseudo-journalistic television shows such as *Hard Copy, A Current Affair,* and the talk shows hosted by Oprah Winfrey and Phil Donahue.

Don Hewitt, a 50-year veteran of CBS News, doesn't like the recent trends in television news. "For the old news giants, the motto was 'news is news and entertainment is entertainment and never the twain shall meet.' Well, the twain have met. And it's not good," he said. He didn't mean that television news has gone soft or is excessively trying to entertain a fickle audience. He has a broader worry: that television news programs are being used as filler for prime-time slots in which entertainment shows have faltered (Mifflin, 1998a, p. C5)

During the summer of 1999, *Dateline NBC* was on five hours a week; at ABC, *20/20* was on four hours a week; and at CBS, *60 Minutes* was on two hours a week and *48 Hours* was on four hours. Such programs were cheaper to produce than entertainment shows and attracted good audiences. Yet critics considered the journalistic quality of these shows to be diluted and trivialized.

Veteran television anchors have expressed their concerns about all of this. Walter Cronkite, who anchored the CBS evening news for 17 years, wrote that in the face of rising competition from cable, VCRs, and more aggressive local newscasts and tabloid shows, the big three newscasts, "frequently go soft. Their features aren't interpretive to the day's events, and the time could be better spent" (p. 34). Cronkite blamed two developments. First, the networks have cut news budgets "so practically an amputation has taken place. The reduction of the foreign bureaus is a crime. It is simply not possible for anybody to intelligently and adequately cover a distant foreign beat without living there" (p. 35). Second, Cronkite saw television news evolving away from the networks into something in the pattern of daily newspapers. That is, he said, "the local television station really does all the news—some international, some national, and some local. And many local journalists—smaller markets, smaller money—are not as good as those on the network" (Rottenberg, 1994, pp. 34–35).

John Chancellor, long-time NBC anchor and commentator, berated television for neglecting its coverage of politics. The networks, he said, "are spending far less than they ever did on covering politics. I sense in the networks an unwillingness to go into much detail as far as politics is concerned. The people who run the news divisions feel that unless it's an unusual election, the public isn't all that interested" (p. 1C).

Chancellor was the last news commentator on an evening network show. Daniel Schorr, NPR commentator, said, "Television deals badly with talking heads, especially when they are also thinking heads" (Glass, 1992, p. 1C).

The decline of public affairs news on network news was further signaled by the decimation of network news staffs in Washington, DC, the major source for news of government and politics. In a two-year study of 75 Washington correspondents and producers at ABC, CBS, and NBC, Kimball (1994) found not just a slump in coverage but "the end of an era in broadcast history" (p. 5). Overall, the CBS and NBC Washington bureaus, which once had 30 correspondents each, were down to about 13 each; ABC had just eliminated seven reporters. The White House, Congress, and Supreme Court, and federal agencies all received diminished attention. Beats such as the environment and individual agencies were eliminated. Kimball found the networks relying more and more on shared pool coverage and voice-overs, or tape shot by a freelancer or syndicate and narrated by a home-based correspondent who had not been to the scene of the story. (Similar practices became prevalent in foreign news coverage.)

In this regard, the print media did not do much better. A survey of 19 key government agencies in Washington, DC, found that newspapers are also jettisoning their traditional beat coverage. For example, the important Department of the Interior, which controls the use of 500 million acres of public land, including the National Park Service, and agencies like Indian Affairs, Fish and Wildlife, logging, mining, and so on, had no newspaper reporters assigned full time (Herbers & McCartney, 1999).

Further efforts to save money (and incidentally compromise news independence) came in December 1999 when the news operations of CBS, ABC, and FOX agreed to form a cooperative service to supply video pictures of news events to the affiliate stations of each network. NBC News was expressly excluded. It was the first time that the three news organizations, which normally compete in news coverage, agreed to a joint enterprise, which was to be called Network News Service (Carter, 1999b).

Another example of such "strategic alliances" was an agreement made in November 1999 connecting NBC News, *The Washington Post*, *Newsweek*, as well as MSNBC cable and *MSNBC.com* and *Newsweek.com*.

These diverse media agreed to share "news material and technological and promotional resources." Each medium saw advantages in sharing content across print, television, cable and the Internet. Despite protests to the contrary, such (entangling?) alliances raised the potential difficulties of reporting unflattering news about the corporate ownerships involved. *Post* editor Leonard Downie said his newspaper will continue to cover NBC, GE, and Microsoft the same as always. Such agreements are indicative of the rapid changes in the ways that news is reaching the public.

With the decline of television network news, there has been a dramatic rise in alternative news outlets such as prime-time newsmagazines, radio talk shows, cable news and talks show, and Internet outlets.

The soft "infotainment" news that has largely replaced public affairs news on network newscasts has been called "your news," "news lite," or "news you can use." A newspaper ad touted NBC's hottest story, "Marriage 'Boot Camp': Could It Save Your Relationship?" On any given evening, one third or more of the 21-minute news hole is given to features such as "Sleepless in America" (the growing problem of insomnia), "Starting Over" (on keeping New Year's resolutions), "The Plane Truth" (airline safety), or "Going Home" (NBC journalists return to their roots). A consistent leader in ratings, NBC also puts soft news into regular segments like "In Their Own Words," "In Depth," "The Family," "The American Dream," and "Norman Schwarzkopf's America." ABC and CBS have similar non-news segments regularly on their evening network shows.

The Big 3 networks seem to be losing their competency and interest in reporting public affairs news on a regular day-to-day basis. CBS, NBC, and ABC, who have long dominated network television news, can no longer compete effectively with CNN, MSNBC, and Fox News Channel with their 24-hour cable news capability. The networks still cover news but are changing the ways they do it. Evening newscasts have been reshaped, foreign and domestic bureaus closed down, correspondents are asked to move faster and do more, and there is more reliance on non-network people to gather news.

Mifflin (1998b) points out that three powerful forces have caused this change: (a) 24-hour services, like CNN, report big stories sooner and stay with them longer; (b) precarious economics of broadcasting, which spend billions on sports coverage, have forced the Big Three to cut news budgets; and (c) satellite and computer technology have enabled networks to report news faster and easier and to rely on footage from two giant video news agencies: Reuters Television and APTN (Associated Press Television News). So the networks have retreated from original or direct news coverage and become retailers of other journalists' reporting. In 1998, for example, CBS News had 4 U.S. bureaus and 4 foreign bureaus; CNN has 12 U.S. bureaus and 23 overseas bureaus.

The evening news shows identified with Jennings, Brokaw, and Rather can often be technically and visually impressive, especially for special events such as those marking the new millennium. But during the lively political primaries leading up to the presidential election of 2000, to get the latest breaking news and in-depth analysis, viewers had to turn such cable news channels as CNN and MSNBC.

DECLINING VIEWERSHIP
OF TELEVISION NEWS

The changes and decline in quality of television news seems related to its continuing loss of viewers; as audiences splinter or evaporate, network producers seem to use more of these soft features, as well as sensational and entertainment-oriented news to attract a greater audience.

A study by the Pew Research Center for the People and the Press (1996) reported that television news is in trouble with the American public and especially with younger viewers. Fewer adults regularly watch it.

Viewership of evening network news was particularly hard hit. Less than half the public (42%) regularly watch one of the three nightly network broadcasts, down from 48% in 1995 and 60% in 1993. Among viewers under the age of 30, only 22% watch nightly network news, down from 36% the previous year. That is a drop of one third in just 12 months.

Local TV news broadcasts attracted more viewers overall, but their audience declines were also steep. Among all adults, 65% said they regularly watch local TV news; it was 72% the previous year. But among those under age 30, 51% said they watched local news, down from 64% one year before.

Survey director Andrew Kohut said, "The networks are facing a serious problem, with increased competition within their industry (from cable, VCRs, pay TV, Internet, etc.) and with a decreased appetite for news, especially among young people" (Mifflin, 1996b, p. C5.) Network officials said the falloff is due to the fact that news is following the trend of cable—drawing viewers away from networks. As viewers grow older, these executives say, they will watch more news just as today's older viewers watch more news than younger ones do. Kohut partly agrees but is convinced they will be far fewer in number. "They will grow up and watch less news than the previous younger generation that is now middle-aged. I really think it's not a life-cyclical pattern, it's generational" (Mif-flin, 1996b, p. C5).

How does television news viewing compare with newspaper reading? Newspaper reading is a bit more stable. Half of those polled (50%) said they read a newspaper "yesterday" (compared to 52% a year earlier). In contrast, the percentage saying they watched TV news "yesterday" slipped to 59%, the percentage had been as high as 74% in 1994. Regular CNN-watching in 1996 was also less (26%) than in 1995 (30%) and 1994 (33%). Interestingly, the Pew study found that listening to radio was largely unchanged in 1996, as it has been for more than five years.

As mentioned before, it is apparent that many people are getting their news on the run—from car radios, television and cable news snippets at all hours, or newspaper headlines, but the disquieting trend is that young people do not include reading or listening to news in their lifestyle. Apparently a growing number of young people—tomorrow's leaders—are not interested in news.

IMPACT OF TELEVISION ON NEWS
AND ON JOURNALISTS

Newspapers and television both report the day's news, but, more and more, television news is becoming packaged entertainment with less hard news. According to James Fallows, there are two significant differences in methods. In television, news becomes a kind of spectacle, designed to fully engage the viewers for a moment or longer but then move on to other discrete and separate spectacles. This contrasts with the press' view that news is a process and that events have a history that should be explained. Television's natural emphasis is on the now. Fallows (1996) said, "Part of the press's job is to keep things in proportion. TV's natural tendency is to see things in shards. It shows us one event with an air of utmost drama, then forgets about it and shows us the next" (p. 53).

Television's second impact concerns its effect on the concept of being a reporter. Television has shown that the most successful way to be a journalist is to give up most of what is involved in being a reporter. Fallows (1996) argued that "behind the term 'reporter' is the sense that the event matters most of all. Your role as a reporter is to go out, look, learn—and then report on what you have learned" (pp. 53–54). Although TV journalists still call themselves "reporters," it is their personality (i.e., celebrity status) that is the real story they report. When Dan Rather travels to Afghanistan, the subject of the broadcast is not Afghanistan, it is Rather-in-Afghanistan. When Diane Sawyer conducts a high-profile interview, the real story is the interaction between two celebrities. One of them is a politician or movie star or athlete, but the other is a particular sort of TV "journalist." Diane Sawyer, Barbara Walters, Mike Wallace, Tom Brokaw, and Sam Donaldson (among others) are not paid multimillion dollar salaries because they are reporters in the traditional sense.

CREEPING TABLOIDIZATION

The changing perceptions of journalists and other factors have made television news most vulnerable to charges of *tabloidization*. The term refers to the featuring of stories of crime, violence, or scandal in a sensational or lurid fashion, preferably about celebrities, as was the practice of some New York tabloid papers like *The Daily Mirror* and *Daily News* of the 1920s, or the supermarket tabloids of today such as *The Star* and *The National Inquirer*.

Of course, sensationalism and triviality have long been found in American journalism. But during the 1990s, television seemed to erupt with stories of sensation, bad taste, and lurid scandal, usually involving celebrities or notorious persons appearing on the scheduled news programs as well as the newly popular newsmagazines like *Dateline* and *20/20*.

David Shaw (1994), the astute press critic of *The Los Angeles Times*, sounded the alarm.

Twenty years ago, there were essentially seven gatekeepers in the American news business—executive editors of the *New York Times* and *Washington Post*, executive producers or anchors of the CBS, NBC, and ABC evening news shows, and editors of *Time* and—*Newsweek*. Occasionally, someone else—*60 Minutes, Wall Street Journal. Los Angeles Times*, or *The New Yorker*—would break a big story that would force everyone to take notice. If a story didn't make it past one of these, it didn't fly and often the *New York Times* editor was the key one. Now, all of that has changed. Well, almost all. Now the *New York Times* and the other six no longer decide. There are dozens of gatekeepers or none at all. Today, there is a weekly network magazine show on every night—"60 Minutes," " Day One," "Turning Point,"

"Dateline," etc., plus syndicated magazine shows like "Inside Edition," "Hard Copy," "A Current Affair," "American Journal" are each on every night. That's a vast maw craving information, "infotainment," around the clock. Add to this CNN with its big appetite and once a CNN story comes on at any time, everyone scrambles for it. Once a story like the Clinton/Gennifer Flowers story gets on, it takes on a life of its own and the media succumb to it. The big seven cannot resist the pressure not to use it. (p. 4)

The "fire walls" that formerly separated the serious media from the trivial and sordid have disappeared. Another perceptive media critic, Howard Kurtz (1996) of *The Washington Post*, said we have become a talk-show nation,

> pulsating with opinions that are channeled though hosts and reverberate through the vast echo chamber of the airwaves. The Old Media—the big newspapers, magazines and network newscasts—still cling to some vestige of objectivity, the traditional notion that information must be checked and verified and balanced with opposing views before it can be disseminated to the public. (p. 3)

But talk shows, Kurtz said, revel in their one-sided pugnacity, spreading wild theories, delicious gossip, and angry denunciations with gleeful abandon. "Anyone can say anything at any time with little fear of contradiction. . . . The gatekeepers of the elite media have been cast aside and the floodgates thrown open" (p. 3).

Important news events are now discussed, analyzed, and snap judgments made as they are happening. Did George W. Bush win or lose in tonight's televised debate?

Kurtz (1996) believed the talk culture has been further vulgarized by the popularity of tabloid television, which has increasingly set the agenda for mainstream media.

Diane Sawyer was roundly criticized for her sympathetic and uncritical interview of just-married Michael Jackson and his wife on *Prime Time Live*. The show promoted Jackson's latest Sony album and attracted an audience of more than 60 million for the network. TV Critic Walter Goodman (1995) wrote: "It was an expertly modulated hour of synthetic collision and wholehearted collusion. Sony could be sure ABC's star would not put Sony's star in harm's way. Mr. Jackson did a little dance as the credits rolled. Why not? This hour meant millions for him. And then a voice announced, 'This has been a presentation of ABC News'" (p. B1). ABC

News considers Sawyer a journalist, and she often substitutes for Peter Jennings on the ABC evening newscast and on *Good Morning America*.

Earlier commentators at the time of Walter Lippmann or James Reston tried to influence informed readers on public issues, whereas the electronic talkers of today play to the audience. News of public issues is either pushed aside or trivialized in the new media mix of scandal, sensation, gossip, and commercial promotion carried on television and radio talk shows.

Clearly, the more or less respectable news programs or newsmagazines of television have often succumbed to the subjects and techniques of the gossip or tabloid shows—all done in the pursuit of ratings and revenue.

JOURNALISM TESTED
BY O. J. SIMPSON TRIAL

The O. J. Simpson criminal trial—the "trial of the century"—was a major cultural phenomenon that for a year and a half transfixed millions of viewers and raised continuing controversies. When the first verdict was announced at midday on October 5, 1995, about 107.7 million people, or 57% of the nation's adult population, watched on live television. Another 62.4 million watched the recap later in the day.

The drawn-out trial reflected and strained many aspects of American life—race relations, violence against women, the criminal justice system, and the integrity of the news media.

The continuing story had to be reported, of course, but did it have to dominate the news for so long? Coverage of the trial by the mainstream news media left much to be desired. CNN covered the entire trial live from gavel to gavel for months and drew large audiences. Night after night, the network news shows on ABC, NBC, and CBS, as well as local TV news, led off with the day's developments and often devoted large chunks of their daily 21 minutes of news time to Johnnie Cochrane, Judge Lance Ito, Marcia Clark, Mark Fuhrman, and the other characters of the long-running soap opera.

ABC News' highly regarded *Nightline* had aired 55 programs by the summer of 1995 on the Simpson trial—nearly half of its air time during one seven-week period, and boosting its ratings 15%. "There's a point in journalism when you have to accede to the voracious appetite of the consumer," Ted Koppel explained. Koppel had acceded previously with two programs on Tonya Harding, two on Paula Jones, and one on child molestation charges against Michael Jackson (Hume, 1996, p. 54).

When he retired from public television's *MacNeil/Lehrer Newshour* after 20 years, Robert MacNeil had harsh words for the trend in television news toward ever more sensational stories. Singling out CBS and NBC coverage of the O. J. Simpson trial, MacNeil said,

> Here were these prestigious news organs saying in effect night after night last year, "Mr. and Mrs. America, this is the most important thing that happened today." The journalists knew perfectly well that O. J. Simpson was not the most important thing that happened that day. But they were scared to death—at least at CBS and NBC— that all the bottom feeders, as I call them, were going to steal more and more of their audience. (Kolbert, 1995, p. H39)

Newspapers and news magazines, including the most prestigious, were guilty of similar excessive coverage, but a print medium still has space for other news stories; on television news shows, a great amount of significant news was barely mentioned or simply not reported during the trial. CNN, which prides itself on reporting news from abroad, turned its back on the world outside the Los Angeles courtroom. As a result of the Simpson trial, the public gained a new perspective on television news: Some major events will be reported daily unless some sensational or titillating event comes along that will attract a larger audience. When that happens, important news will be ignored as some broadcasters cross the line and become mass entertainers.

The second Simpson trial, the wrongful death civil lawsuit brought and won by the families of Nicole Brown and Ronald Goldman, was a more moderate and low-key media event, mainly because the judge banned television cameras from the courtroom. The trial was thoroughly reported, but this time, the media kept things more in proportion, generally avoided sensationalism, and managed to report other news as well.

During the extended story, however, television news had little reason to be proud. Between June 17, 1994 and January 31, 1997, when the second trial ended, NBC Nightly News had devoted their lead story to O. J. Simpson 73 evenings, for CBS Evening News, it was 66 evenings, and for ABC World News Tonight, the O. J. trial led for 53 evenings. The three networks alone devoted 2,768 minutes or more than 46 hours of their weeknight newscasts during the same period to the story: 46 hours that could have been devoted to important news (Carter, 1997).

GROWING INFLUENCE
OF LOCAL
TELEVISION NEWS

As network television news has declined in both audiences and journalistic quality, local television news programs have gained in influence, especially in the metropolitan areas where local news shows are on the air one hour or more before the evening network shows begin. Because of CNN, the networks are no longer first with breaking national and foreign stories.

According to Tom Rosenstiel (1994), CNN has significantly, if unintentionally, affected broadcast journalism's control over its own professional standards. In the mid-1980s, CNN, in order to generate more revenue, began selling its vast footage to hundreds of local news stations. Before that, the three networks had jealously protected their own footage, well aware that exclusive coverage of the day's biggest story was one of their competitive advantages. CNN did not have that concern. In turn, CNN could make deals to acquire local footage from these subscribing stations, thus expanding its own coverage reach, even if CNN news crews had not produced the pictures.

Next, the networks' local affiliates began pressuring the networks for more network footage so that they could compete in the local markets. Soon the networks' control over national and foreign footage had ended. In 1986, the three networks fed affiliates about 30 minutes of footage a day. By 1990, they had averaged about eight hours a day. This greatly changed the business, and the networks became subservient to local stations. The network shows began doing more "you news" features and less hard-news reporting, as well as sending Tom Brokaw, Dan Rather, and Peter Jennings off to cover floods, fires, and presidential trips live, thus hyping some stories beyond their importance.

Local television news, although often highly competitive, is usually less professional, less responsible, and more sensational than network news. The Rocky Mountain Media Watch in Denver analyzed the tapes of 100 programs in 58 cities on a single night and found a disheartening sameness. The typical 30-minute program offered about 12 minutes of news, more than 40% of it depicting violent crimes or disasters. Commercials averaged more than nine minutes and sports and weather nearly seven, leaving two minutes for promotions. Of the 100 programs, 37 led off with crime, 15 with disasters. On 70 stations, the favorite disaster that night was a mild California earthquake, one of 200 that month, which caused no injuries and little damage.

In commenting on the study, Max Frankel (1995) wrote: "Virtually, no station offers thoughtful coverage of important local issues, including crime. Few ever try to analyze the local economy or the school, transportation and welfare systems" (p. 46). About the late-evening local news, Frankel (1995) wrote:

> Their newscasts are distinguishable only by the speed and skill with which they drive the audience from rage and fear to fluff and banter, leading the way to long commercials that exploit aroused emotions. Sports results, too, are delivered at a manic pace, spiced with scenes of violence or pathetic pratfalls, and even the weather reports are used to drive our moods up and down, from alarm to calm and back again. (p. 47)

Production costs are the usual explanations for this kind of journalism. A television crew takes one to two hours to visit the scene of a murder or a fire; it may take days or weeks to report on the causes of crime or the poor state of housing.

> Murders, fires or accidents—the grist of today's local television news mill—are relatively simple stories to cover. It's not that local newsrooms have a built-in predilection for violence. It's just that it's there—easy to get—and it can be enhanced by production techniques. How many times have you seen on the 11 p.m. news on a New York City channel a reporter standing in front of a precinct house, reporting "live" on a murder that might have happened 15 hours earlier? It happens on Chicago television practically every night. (Frankel, 1995, p. 47)

In some cities, news on public television deviates from this pattern but still is criticized for not covering local news adequately.

PERSISTENCE AND STABILITY OF RADIO NEWS

Although viewers for both network and local television news seem to be disappearing, many people are listening to the news on the radio. In the Pew Research Center for the People and the Press (1996) study cited earlier, the percentage of people who listen to radio news was largely unchanged in 1996, as it has been for the previous five years. Four in 10 people (44%) said they listened to news on radio "yesterday" in the current survey, compared to 42% in 1995. The survey found 13% of respondents reporting they were regular (NPR) listeners, which was not significantly different from the 15% recorded in the 1995 study.

Yet radio news has been undergoing changes just as radio itself has. Developments in radio news have been both good and bad.

First, the positive. Lou Prato (1996) reported that an official at ABC News Radio said in 1996 that radio news overall was stronger than it has been in 15 to 20 years. "Radio is still the medium in which most American first hear a breaking news story. It's fast, ubiquitous, and a growing industry," Bernard Gershon said (Prato, 1996, p. 52).

At the same time, consolidation of ownerships has been proceeding at a rapid rate.

In October 1999, Clear Channel Communications, the nation's largest owner of radio stations, said it would buy the second-largest owner, AMFM Inc., for $17.4 billion in stock and $6.1 billion in assumed debt. This created the world's largest radio company in both revenues and numbers of stations, which reach a weekly audience of about 100 million. The merger brings 830 radio stations into one organization. This acquisition dwarfs the earlier purchase by Westinghouse of CBS radio stations (Carter, 1999a). When Westinghouse acquired CBS, it added several major all-news stations and the CBS radio network to its holdings of all-news and talk stations. The company owned two different all-news stations in the New York, Chicago, and Los Angeles markets.

Another stimulus for radio news came in 1994 when the AP launched a 24-hour all-news radio service to supplement its audio feed and newscast service. CNN Radio, with some 550 affiliates, was considering a new six-hour morning drive-time news program to supplement its scheduled newscasts and impromptu updates.

Not so encouraging is the trend of more and more radio stations to get out of the local news business altogether. In 1994, the percentage of commercial stations with no employees devoted to gathering local news increased to 16.9%. The survey also found that television news staffing had continued to grow modestly since 1987, even as radio news staffs declined at the steepest rate in more than 10 years. Since 1981, station owners no longer have been required to broadcast news and public interest programming in order to maintain operating licenses. Professor Vernon Stone, who did the research for the Radio-Television News Directors Association, reported that another 230 of the nation's 5,500 radio newsrooms went dark that year. Stone estimated that 1,100 radio news operations have ceased since 1981.

Grossman (1998) had some disturbing words to add to this:

> Improbable as it seems, television's unglamorous 75-year-old sibling, radio, now reigns as the most profitable of all media. Radio's recent tidal wave of corporate consolidations, its cheap production costs, and its high cash flow have transformed it into the darling of Wall Street. One troubling result of radio's remarkable financial turn-around: the elimination of serious news reporting. It is fast disappearing from stations across the nation, replaced by talkers, "shock jocks," syndicated headline services, or no news at all. Except at public radio and a few all-news stations, radio reporters have become a vanishing breed. (p. 61)

The radio industry increasingly has relied on syndicated material—news, music, and talk shows—transmitted by satellite and offered by networks on a barter basis in exchange for commercial time. The decline in local news programming was also related to radio's move to specialized music formats ranging from bluegrass to polka; station owners have turned to narrow formats as a way to attract a specific audience desired by advertisers.

Neal J. Conan of NPR, a noncommercial service that does report the news well, commented that the decline in local radio news does not mean that listeners are less well informed, "I'm not sure a three-minute newscast was vastly informative. It's not a tremendous loss" (Adelson, 1994, p. C8).

A different litany of complaints and concerns from the public are of concern to newspapers and magazines. These are discussed in chapter 7.

CHAPTER

7

The Fading American Newspaper?

The newspapers! Sir, they are the most villainous—licentious—abom-inable—infernal—not that I ever read them—I make it a rule never to look into a newspaper.

—Richard Brinsley Sheridan (1779)

At this time of rapid change in public communication, newspapers, as well as news magazines, have been undergoing modifications similar to those of broadcast journalism. Publishers and editors of papers are increasingly under pressure to expand their profits and their attractiveness to Wall Street investors. And they are worried about the Internet. As in other industries, many newspapers have been downsizing to increase their profitability. In addition, many editors, in pursuit of greater circulations, are stressing more entertainment-oriented, celebrity-soaked infotainment, as well as soft features that relate to the personal concerns of readers. Newspapers are not adverse to pick up on the sensational stories carried on television.

SLIPPING MORALE

Morale of reporters and editors on many newspapers is clearly low—a sense that working for a newspaper is no longer an exciting and respected calling. One former newsman, C. S. Stepp (1995) wrote:

> For all the trials of poor pay, lousy hours, and grinding pace, the payoff (in earlier times) was high: deference, entitlement, the buzz of recognition, the glory of it all. Readers grumbled but they paid attention. . . . These are different days. The newspaper person (today) is just one more harried molecule in the maligned Media Horde. Newspapers are old news, byte-sized cogs in giant information conglomerates. . . . The criticisms were bearable, honorable scars from the ramparts. But irrelevance truly singes, the gnawing feeling that the spotlight has moved on forever. . . . The result: angst and anxiety are pandemic across American newsrooms, as newspaper people collectively sense the end of an era. (p. 15)

Similar feelings were found in a 1995 survey ("Nieman poll finds decline in media quality," 1995) of 304 former Nieman Fellows—working journalists who had studied one year at Harvard. General findings were that:

- Overall quality of the media is declining and the basic principles of the journalism profession are being eroded.
- The distinction between news and entertainment is increasingly obscure.
- Television and radio are gaining in influence but declining in journalistic quality whereas newspapers struggle to maintain quality and are losing ground.
- Media proprietors are more concerned with profits than product quality.
- The public is losing confidence in the media.

The Nieman survey was largely validated by a much broader national survey in 1999 of the news media, including newsroom staff, managers, and executives on journalistic values and principles. Sponsored by the Committee of Concerned Journalists and the Pew Research Center on the People and the Press, the survey was headed by Bill Kovach and Tom Rosenstiel, who summarized the findings on the Internet. In brief, the survey found that not only is the public increasingly disaffected by the press but journalists now agree that something is wrong with their profession. News professionals see two overriding trends that worry them: They believe the news media have blurred the lines between news and entertainment and that the cult of argument is overwhelming the cult of reporting. A broad majority feel that way, about 70%, including top executives. These journalists also see problems of reporting the news fairly and factually and avoiding sensationalism. And things are getting worse. Concerns about punditry overwhelming reporting, for instance, have swelled in only four years. In short, the report said, a large majority of news professionals sense a degradation of the culture of news—from one that was steeped in verification and a steadfast respect for the facts, toward one that favors argument, opinion-mongering, haste, and infotainment. (The full report can be read online at www.journalism.org/surveycomment.html)

Although a good many newspapers, when viewed objectively, do a better job then ever of reporting the day's news and serving their communities, many publications no longer enjoy the prestige in their communities that they formerly had. Once great regional newspapers such as *The Minneapolis Star and Tribune, The St.Louis Post-Dispatch, The Milwaukee Journal (and Sentinel), The Louisville Courier-Journal, The Atlanta Constitution*, and *The Denver Post* are *perceived* as having diminished in influence and stature even though they are still excellent newspapers.

Yet, daily newspapers remain going concerns and are more prosperous than most corporations. This fact, however, concerns many in the newsrooms who feel that public service and thorough news coverage are badly neglected in the scramble for profits. "Job satisfaction in newspapering appears to be in significant decline," wrote David Weaver and Cleve Wilhoit in their survey of working journalists. "Only 25 percent say they are very satisfied with their job, about half the satisfaction rate of 20 years ago. . . . More than 20 percent . . . said they plan to leave the field within five years, double the figure of 1982–83" (Stepp, 1995, p. 17).

This crisis of confidence may be caused by a number of factors: the declining number of independently owned papers; the slow but steady drop for some papers in readership and advertising revenue; less interest by the public in serious news; and competition from the "new media"— cable, VCRs, interactive computers, and the exciting prospects of cyberspace and the Internet. In university schools and departments of journalism, newspaper careers have been losing their appeal; the best students more often opt for careers in advertising, public relations, and online journalism.

Newspaper journalists have come to think of themselves as trapped in a sunset industry, and many are more concerned about protecting their financial interests and meager salaries than about serving the public interest. The long-term shift from family-owned to group-owned chains is probably the most demoralizing factor in the newspaper business today.

Family-owned papers had their faults and would often play favorites and beat up on their enemies, yet much of the success of numerous great newspapers was due to their strong-willed and high-minded family owners. One thinks of the Sulzbergers of *The New York Times*, the Grahams and Meyers of *The Washington Post*, the Niemans and Harry Grant of *The Milwaukee Journal*, the Bingham family of *The Louisville Courier-Journal*, John Cowles of *The Minneapolis Star and Tribune*, and the Pulitzers at *The St. Louis Post-Dispatch*.

Group ownership brings the problem of a counting-house mentality determined to downsize the newsroom and cut expenses to satisfy demands for quarterly earnings. The Gannett chain with its 74 newspapers and nearly 24 television and radio stations has been very profitable and is considered a pacesetter in this trend.

Today, four widely admired dailies—*The New York Times, The Washington Post, The Los Angeles Times, and the Wall Street Journal*—have all been protected in some way from the imperatives of quarterly reports. In the first three cases, original family members control enough stock to affect the newspaper's policies.

The *Los Angeles Times*, however, after a loosening of family control, suffered a rude shock and much unfavorable national criticism in October 1999, after an inexperienced new publisher made a major ethical mistake. Publisher Kathryn Downing apologized to an assembled newsroom and asked for the staff's forgiveness for having negotiated a profit-sharing deal with the new Staples Center, a major new sports arena in downtown Los Angeles. The two companies had shared $2 million in advertising revenues from the October 10, 1999 *Times* Sunday magazine that was devoted to publicizing the Center. The deal, reached without the knowledge of the editorial staff and without informing *Times* readers, was a serious journalistic blunder because news media are not supposed to have financial relationships with organizations about which they report. The *Times'* news staff was incensed and then came a scathing open letter from Otis Chandler, former publisher and scion of the Chandler family that had controlled the paper since 1882. Chandler, retired but a major stockholder, criticized what he called management's "unbelievably stupid and unprofessional handling of the special edition." He said, "I am sad to see what I think may be a serious decline of the *Times* as one of the great newspapers in the country" (Waxman, 1999, p. C1). The paper's staff was demoralized by the unfavorable publicity about this breaching of the "wall" between the editorial and advertising departments. Critics blamed the faux pas on the paper's CEO Mark Willes and Publisher Browning, either of whom had prior newspaper experience before joining the *Times*. These events were followed in January 2000 by the abrupt sale of the Times Mirror Company to the Tribune Company of Chicago. The sale was precipitated, some said, by disagreements among Chandler family heirs over how the paper should be managed.

The Wall Street Journal is considered protected by its niche market for financial and industry readers and advertisers, but has been under some pressures from family stockholders to increase profits, as was the case at the *Los Angeles Times*.

The most biting criticism of newspapers today often comes from journalists themselves. *New Yorker* editor David Remnick wrote:

> With one eye on Wall Street and the other shut tight, newspaper owners everywhere except for a few . . . are following the path to deadening mediocrity. Everything that cannot be made blandly profitable is killed outright. Spoiled by the profits of the 1980s, the owners rarely have patience for a more modest future. . . . In a growing number of cities and regions newspaper owners have abused their franchise, slashing staff, cutting the "news hole," dropping aggressive reporting and leaving little behind but wire-service copy, sports, and soft local stories designed to make readers feel all warm and fuzzy and inclined to place a classified ad. (Remnick, 1995, p. 82)

FINDING A PRINT NICHE IN A CHANGING ENVIRONMENT

At a time when news and entertainment seem inextricably mixed, newspapers have been constantly seeking a niche in the changing news picture. The decline of downtown department stores and other changes in marketing from mail-order catalogues to Wal-Mart have led to cutbacks of retail advertising on metropolitan dailies.

After radio and television usurped the first reporting of breaking news, newspapers began offering more interpretive and analytical pieces, thus introducing more opinion into news columns. Professional standards have suffered because the first news reports, as on CNN, are often fragmentary, lacking details and occasionally distorted or incorrect. Then, instead of waiting for fuller and more rounded reporting, both television and print reporters immediately start interpreting the meaning of it all and offering opinions on the event's future impact.

Time, *Newsweek*, and other news magazines also have been struggling to find a role for themselves in an age of television saturation and more in-depth and opinionated newspaper stories. Talk radio, personified by Rush Limbaugh, Gordon Liddy, Don Imus, and Howard Stern, plus the television newsmagazines have also skimmed off more and more news readers.

When television first appeared, newspapers tried to ignore it, in some cases not even carrying program logs, and by fully reporting stories tele-vision news did not cover. Now the printed press tends to report fully on television's big stories plus much news about television itself including its celebrities. A Super Bowl game seen by many millions on television will be fully reported and analyzed by newspapers, following the sound assumption that people like to read about events they already know about, whether it is a movie seen or a televised event or sports competi-tion. Further, comings and goings of television's personalities, programs, gossip, and trends are reported as well. The British popular press carries this trend even further and has become, in effect, a mere adjunct of British television.

The print media have responded to television and radio talk shows' approach to the news by offering readers more and more of the news through the proliferation of signed columns or bylined interpretive pieces. In earlier times, few bylines appeared in newspapers on hard news stories; the story itself was the important thing and the name of the reporter was incidental. In general, bylines were given out sparingly for unusually well-written features or soft news stories. Stories in *Time* and *Newsweek* rarely carried bylines.

Today, *Newsweek*, for example, presents its major news stories through the often lively, irreverent, breezy words of its stable of star writ-ers—Howard Fineman, Jonathan Alter, Evan Thomas, Alan Sloan, Ellis Cose, and others—who not only tell you their version of what happened last week and what it means for you, but what you should think about it. Often, the slant or spin on the story is more important than the content. *Newsweek* assumes most readers already know the basic facts but would still like to read something insightful or at least clever or funny about the story.

The New York Times has joined the trend from mostly straight news to news liberally mixed with opinion. Diamond (1993) noted that until about 1960, there were never more than four or five columnists in the *Times*, one or two on the editorial page, a "Sports of the Times" columnist, and on the local page, Meyer Berger's "About New York" column. By the 1990s, the

Times had about four dozen columnists scattered through the paper, who reported/commented on a much wider and softer variety of subjects than the traditional no-nonsense hard news fit to print. In addition to signed editorials in "Editorial Notebook" and the op-ed page's regular columnists and guest writers, the proliferating columnists reflected a wide variety of reader interests: "The Practical Traveler"; four or more sports columns plus one of commentary on sports on television; "Peripherals" for computer users; "Personal Health"; "Pop View"; "Keeping Fit"; "Parent and Child"; "Runways" for fashion; "Patterns" for the garment industry; "Books of the Times"; "Media," and so on. Other newspapers, of course, have been following the trend; some, like *The New York Daily News* and *The New York Post*, have long been collections of signed columns. Small dailies rely heavily on syndicated columnists.

Proliferation of columns reflects a much more broadened approach to what is meant by "news." This translates as less public affairs news (government, politics, and foreign affairs) and more news and useful information that, as on television news, people relate to personally such as personal health, medical advances, and sundry advice for coping with life's daily trends and challenges. More interpretation and explanation is not a bad thing if it is done carefully and does not sink to just opinion and speculation.

Daily newspapers have been greatly influenced in recent years by Gannett's *USA Today*. This innovative paper was launched in 1982 as a national daily available almost everywhere through satellite production and aimed at travelers. Taking its cue from television, the paper uses lots of color, imaginative graphics—graphs, maps, photos, and large, detailed national weather maps. At first, it reported the news in the print equivalent of sound bites—short takes on complicated matters as well as on lighter themes and without jumps to inside pages. Sports are covered in great detail, but at first the paper maintained no foreign correspondents. Although criticized for reducing news to spoon-sized pellets, and called "McPaper" or "USA OK," many smaller dailies imitated its compacted news presentation and especially its color graphics.

Without a doubt, *USA Today* sells papers: Peterson (1996c) reported the Friday edition, sold throughout the weekend, passed 2 million average circulation in 1996, while the Monday-Thursday editions have reached 1.6 million, making it second only to *The Wall Street Journal*. But 55% of sales came from newsstands and 25% was purchased in bulk for free distribution by hotels and airlines. Millions read the paper but not the same millions every week; hence, there is little reader loyalty, and as a result, advertising has been sparse. The paper finally began to turn a profit in 1993 after more than $250 million in losses since 1982. In 1996, the paper was under pressure to improve its scant profitability and began changing its news approach. Instead of its light, feel-good news, the paper began stressing more hard news in longer explanatory stories, including some important investigative stories. Said one newspaper editor, "Having ruined half of the rest of the newspaper industry with three-inch briefs, they're finally going the other way" (Peterson, 1996c, p. C8). Clearly, *USA Today* was moving back toward the mainstream.

Other newspapers are seeking more personal connections with their readers in order to reverse trends faced by newspapers, an aging reader-ship, declining circulations, and weaker ties between readers and their papers (Peterson, 1997). *The San Jose Mercury News* turns most of a weekly features section, called "Celebrations," over to articles written by readers; it is one of the paper's most popular features. Typical of the more popular articles were "Quotable Kids," "How I Met My True Love," and "The Seven Second Philosopher."

GETTING INTO BED
WITH SUPERMARKET TABLOIDS

The relationship of mainstream newspapers with the so-called supermar-ket tabloids has been uncomfortable and a reason for concern. Headlines for these lurid weeklies can be read at the checkout counters of 29,800 supermarkets in America—"Six Signs that PROVE the World is Coming to an End," "Liz's Hubby's Drug Bust," and "How to Tell If Your Dog Worships Satan." Most stories are not news by any definition.

Until a few years ago, most newspapers did not pay much attention. But nowadays, some of the stories that publications like *The Star* or *The National Enquirer* dig up on political and entertainment celebrities find their way to front pages of the better newspapers and on the networks evening news. These are stories that respectable journalists would not fer-ret out themselves, but once they are published, many editors and broad-casters believe they must go with the story or be left behind.

The National Enquirer's stories and pictures of Senator Gary Hart's escapade with Donna Rice ended Hart's political career. The *Star*'s stories on Gennifer Flowers threatened Clinton's political fortunes in the 1992 campaign. And in the O. J. Simpson criminal trial, the tabloids put out a string of scoops the more respectable media felt they had to follow. *The New York Times'* publishing information first reported by the *Enquirer* about the Simpson case provoked journalistic criticism of the *Times*. But the *Times'* reporter David Margolick (1994) said of the *Enquirer*, "Mainstream reporters may grumble about its checkbook journalism, laugh at its hyperbole, talk vaguely about its inaccuracies. But always, they look at it" (p. 6).

The 1996 political campaign was roiled briefly by *The Star's* revelations that President Clinton's closest political adviser, Dick Morris, had a year-long relationship with a prostitute. The *Star* paid the $200-a-night call girl well for the exposé. The story had short but intense coverage: CNN, ABC, and NBC gave it excited play the first day, and both *Time* and *Newsweek* put Morris on their covers. However, much press reporting was more restrained in part because Morris was so quickly fired and the political impact was minimal.

But as Howard Kurtz noted, "The established media is increasingly covering the same sorts of things as the tabloids and finding that the supermarket papers are often better at the game" (Zane, 1996, p. 2, sec. 4). The paradox is that even as the mainstream media are inexorably moving toward the tabloid style of journalism, the tabloids are gaining relevance and credibility by operating a bit more like their respectable brethren. The tabloids are becoming more conventional in how they gather news and are entering into the political arena more often. Kurtz said the cross-pollination may be sowing the seeds of a new hybrid form of news.

Earlier, the tabloids were staffed mainly by British journalists trained on the more egregious Fleet Street tabloids. More recently, current top editors have come from *The Washington Post* and *The New York Post*. Interestingly, *The Star*, *The Globe*, and *The Enquirer* have each lost about 30% of their circulation in the past five years. Peterson (1996d) said that the tabloids are facing more competition from mainstream media. One response to increased competition has been for the major supermarket tabloids to merge. In November 1999, American Media, which owns *The National Enquirer*, *The Star*, and *The Weekly World News*, announced that it was buying *The Globe* and its sister tabloids, the *Sun* and *National Examiner*. Despite the consolidation, the papers have not improved much in quality.

BAD ATTITUDE: CYNICISM, ELITISM, AND OTHER COMPLAINTS

Fibich (1995) said tabloid journalism contributes to one of the press' major problems today—a feeling by the public, and many thoughtful journalists as well, that the press has become too cynical and negative. "Journalism is too negative, too negative, too negative," said Andrew Kohut, director of the Pew Research Center. "There's criticism of the way the press conducts its business, particularly its watchdog role. And the attitude is more fundamentally negative than in years" (Fibich, 1995, p. 17). Gallup surveys show that from 1981–1993, the share of Americans who felt that journalists had high ethical standards slid from 30% to 22%.

One survey by Kohut found the public had a favorable attitude toward the press but objected to some of its practices. The press was judged as too intrusive, too negative, driving controversies rather than just reporting them.

A 1997 Roper poll, commissioned by the Freedom Forum, found the public critical of journalists. People trust most or all of what ministers, priests, rabbis, and doctors say, but only 53% place similar trust in their local television anchors. Even fewer trust what network anchors say and just under a third trust newspaper reporters.

Ethically, people see journalists not as equals of teachers and doctors, but as being among those with agendas to advance—politicians, lawyers, and corporate officials. The public also believes, according to the poll, that special interests are pulling strings in newsrooms. The public believe that profit motives, politicians, big business, and advertisers, as well as media owners, influence the way the news is reported and presented. Also, a majority of those polled (64%) said a major problem with news is that it is too sensational.

Sometimes the negative comments are entertaining and selectively true, yet they show cynicism for the political scene. Maureen Dowd's now famous page-one lead in *The New York Times* on Clinton's visit to Oxford in June 1994 illustrates the point: "President Clinton returned today for a sentimental journey to the university where he didn't inhale, didn't get drafted, and didn't get a degree" (Walsh, 1996, p. 286). Clever indeed, but did it belong on page one?

It should be noted, said Fibich (1996), that the press owns up to a lot of its criticisms. Kohut's study found that a majority of the news people surveyed thought that public anger with the press was justified, either totally or in part. A majority of journalists agreed about the validity of the charge that "the personal values of people in the news media often make it difficult for them to understand and cover such topics as religion and family values" (p. 19).

During her three years as ombudsman for *The Washington Post*, Joann Byrd received 45,000 telephone calls and she concluded that "people don't see journalism as public service anymore." Instead, they believe "that journalists are engaged in self service—getting ratings, selling newspapers, or making their careers . . . that our ideas about detachment are so much hog wash. . . . They feel cheated, I think, that the rules changed and nobody told them" (Fibich, 1996, p. 18).

Public annoyance at reporters and the bad news they bring is not new; it has a long history. However, there is the feeling that a healthy skepticism has crossed the line to a virulent cynicism that assumes all in public life are guilty until proven otherwise. Cynicism and negativism, some feel, has become a virus that has contributed to a decline in faith in democratic institutions.

A media reporter for *The New York Times*, Iver Peterson (1996a) wrote: "Nobody would dispute the importance of a skeptical mind and tough questioning, and few want reporters to be cheerleaders. What the critics are arguing is that newsroom cynicism has crossed the boundary between being tough and being mean" (p. C7).

The solution, according to Sig Gissler, a former editorial page editor of *The Milwaukee Journal* and now a journalism professor, is to strive for balance. He wrote: "We're great at raising people's anxieties but we don't leave them with much sense of hope or remedy. So I always thought it was a good idea to at least shade in some potential solutions to all those problems we see" (Peterson, 1996a, p. C4).

Elitism and a sense of being out of touch with the rest of the nation is another problem for journalists who work for the national news media. (Elitism is not considered a problem apparently on smaller newspapers and broadcast outlets.) Journalist Richard Harwood (1995) noted the elitist label is being pinned on journalists and journalism in unflattering ways:

Journalism's ills are a symptom of a poison infecting all professional elites. Increasingly removed from the realities of manual labor, community ties, or ordinary life in general, professionals have disdain for those they see as inferiors and for any genuine achievement or heroism. Nothing is properly understood until it is exposed as corrupt, duplicitous, or hypocritical. (p. 27)

Journalists in New York City and Washington, DC, tend to identify with the affluent professional classes and follow their lifestyles. A 1995 survey found significant differences in attitudes between the mainstream media and the public. For example, more than 50% of the public said that homosexuality should be discouraged, whereas 8 out of 10 national journalists said it should be accepted. Two out of five Americans said they attended a church or synagogue regularly, compared with only one out of five national journalists. Further, 39% of Americans said they were politically conservative, compared with only 5% of national journalists. (Nearly 66% of national journalists identified themselves as moderates, and 22% said they were liberals.) More than 50% agreed that the press was too cynical and negative in covering Congress, whereas 8 out of 10 national journalists disagreed (Walsh, 1996).

LOSS OF CREDIBILITY

Many of the ethical problems faced by journalists today, including cynicism and elitism, relate to matters of credibility—the quality or power of inspiring belief, essential for public acceptance of serious journalism. Some say that credibility is the journalists' and the news media's most precious asset. Often, loss of press credibility is self-inflicted as two recent examples illustrate.

The first involved a best-selling novel, *Primary Colors*, a tale of political intrigue and deceit, whose author was identified only as anonymous. The book was a commercial success and after months of emphatic denials, Joe Klein, a political columnist for *Newsweek* and commentator on CBS, admitted publicly that he was indeed the author. Klein offered no apologies for lying to friends and colleagues and said he guarded his secret the way journalists protect their news sources. *Newsweek*'s editor, Maynard Parker, was privy to the secret and not only kept it out of his magazine but misdirected one of his own reporters who wrote a piece about the mystery in the magazine.

The response from the press was mixed. Stephen Hess (1994), a media expert at the Brookings Institution, was amused. "Look, people lie to reporters every day. What annoys journalists was that this was a member of their own community, a friend of theirs" (Peterson, 1996d, p. C5). Most were much tougher on Klein. Rem Rieder (1996), editor of *American Journalism Review*, wrote: "Lying is lying. For a journalist, it is poison. Credibility is crucial. Why should *Newsweek's* readers believe what

Klein writes when they know they can't believe what he says? And we're not talking little white lies here. No coy deceptions for Joe Klein. For God's sakes, I didn't write it, he told the *New York Times*" (p. 6).

Editorially, the *Times* was critical of Klein, reflecting the views of many in the working press. The *Times* said:

> Their behavior (Klein and Parker) violates the fundamental contract between journalists, serious publications and their readers. If journalists lie or publications knowingly publish deceptively incomplete stories, then readers who become aware of the deception will ever after ask the most damaging of all questions: How do I know you are telling me the whole truth as best you can determine it at this time? . . . Mr. Klein wants his colleagues to view his actions as a diverting and highly profitable whimsy. But he has held a prominent role in his generation of political journalists. For that reason, people interested in preserving the core values of serious journalism have to view his actions and words as corrupt and—if they become an example to others—corrupting. ("Colors of Mendacity," 1996, p. A14)

Klein now writes for *The New Yorker*.

Press credibility took another hit a few weeks later amidst the media glare of the 1996 Olympic Games in Atlanta. After the bombing in Centennial Olympic Park, Richard A. Jewell, a security guard, was named in *The Atlanta Journal* as the focus of the FBI investigation because he fit the profile of the lone bomber. A blitz of media coverage raised all kinds of damaging questions about Jewell's possible guilt. Yet Jewell had not been accused by law authorities or charged with anything. The FBI had not spoken on record about their suspicions, nor had he been arraigned, arrested, or taken into custody. Why had the Atlanta paper gone with the story? Apparently, competitive concerns and police leaks of information were involved. The story was out there; people were talking about it and the paper was afraid that local television would get it first. Once the story was published, the feeding frenzy began in earnest, setting in motion worldwide coverage about a man who was never publicly implicated by officials or charged with the crime. The story led the evening news on all the networks and was regularly repeated by Tom Brokaw to the huge audience watching the Olympics on NBC. Major newspapers like *The Washington Post*, *USA Today*, *The Los Angeles Times*, and *The Chicago Tribune* all gave it front-page play.

Almost three months passed before the FBI held a press conference and announced that law enforcement officials had cleared Jewell and said it now believed he had nothing to do with the crime. Jewell sued the

Atlanta Journal-Constitution for libel. NBC and CNN settled out of court to avoid litigation.

Media critics were livid about Jewell's manhandling by the press. Max Frankel wrote:

> Too easily overlooked among the athletic and political entertainments of the summer was the careless abandon with which this uncharged suspect (Jewell) in a murder case was identified, vilified, stalked, and stigmatized before the entire world without a shred of evidence. A journalistic industry that gradually learned to defend itself against the evils of McCarthyism urgently needs some new barriers against this comparable kind of slander. The barriers are best devised now, in the calmer moments between excitements. (Frankel, 1996, p. 60)

Unless such guidelines are established and enforced, the rule seems to be that the press will protect the rights of someone involved in a criminal case, unless there is such overwhelming media interest and competition that the story must be published anyway.

THE DUBIOUS PRACTICE
OF BUYING
NEWS AND PHOTOS

The British press world of quasi-journalism has a long and dishonorable tradition of paying, and paying well, for scoops, exposés, and photos about the rich and famous, especially prominent politicians and the royal family. Fleet Street tabloids will pay $200,000 to $300,000 for a story that has lasting interest. Provocative pictures of Princess Diana commanded prices up to $6 million.

This practice, as much as anything, undermines the credibility of news because of the suspicion that sources will exaggerate to make a better—and more profitable—story or photo. Unfortunately, although resisted by mainstream news media, paying for news has become more commonplace in U.S. journalism and its disreputable tabloid fringe. After the second Rodney King trial, *The Los Angeles Times* reporters found themselves excluded from post-trial interviews with certain jurors because they were not willing to pay them. Today, tabloid television shows routinely pay for interviews, whereas mainstream magazines like *Sports Illustrated* and *Redbook* have paid for news exclusives. Bill O'Reilly, anchor of *Inside Edition*, defends the television show's payments: "The competition for ratings and stories is now so intense that Inside Edition must pay for some big scoops to survive. If we'd didn't pay, we'd be off the air. Simple as that" (O'Reilly, 1994, p. 15).

The practice is not new; in the 1970s, *60 Minutes* paid Nixon aide H. R. Haldeman $25,000 and Watergate burglar G. Gordon Liddy $15,000 for interviews. But the practice (and the prices) have escalated lately, even more bad news for journalism's slipping credibility with the public.

The high (or better, low) episode of checkbook journalism came when President Clinton faced impeachment for the Lewinsky affair. Larry Flynt, publisher of *Hustler* magazine, placed an advertisement in *The Washington Post* in October 1998 offering up to $1 million to anyone who could prove that a member of Congress or a high-ranking public official had carried on an adulterous affair. Before the year ended, information turned up by the ad ended the career of House Speaker-designate Bob Livingston. And in January 1999, Flynt accused Georgia Rep. Bob Barr of adultery but Barr survived politically. Flynt told a well-attended press conference that all news organizations are going to be paying for stories. That has not happened—yet. But the serious press often faces a dilemma of whether or not to pick and use a paid-for news story.

The violent death of Diana, Princess of Wales, in a high-speed car crash while being pursued by paparazzi photographers in Paris had ominous lessons not just for tabloid journalism but for the mainstream press as well. The immediate public reaction was revulsion aimed at the press, even though much of the public are eager consumers of scandal and gossip about the celebrities they have come to know well from tabloids and television.

Tabloids have little interest in serious news but will pay much more for intrusive and revealing photos of the rich and famous and hence have triggered intensive competition among the paparazzi, who use hidden vans, planes, and motorboats to stalk and harass celebrities, often invading their privacy. The problem for mainstream journalism is that such lurid and distorted photos and the companion gossip and scandal find their way into the more respectable publications and TV news. *Time* and *Newsweek* are regular users of tabloid by-products. *People* magazine ran 43 covers featuring Princess Diana. U.S. news media carry little serious news about the United Kingdom but most Americans are well informed about the scandals and peccadilloes of the royal family. The unprecedented public grief and mourning in Britain at the Princess' funeral was stark evidence of the power of celebrity-driven gossip and scandal to affect the lives of many millions. It's also an indictment of mainline media when they give excessive and sustained coverage to such celebrity-driven stories.

Journalism's credibility problems have been exacerbated as well by the antics of certain celebrity journalists whose names and faces, as well as incomes, are almost as well known to the public as are those of rock stars or movie personalities. These are discussed in the next chapter.

CHAPTER

8

Why the Public Hates (Some) Journalists

I should make my bias clear: I have been a journalist for 60 years, in print, on radio, on television. I have been appalled to watch "the press" metamorphose into "the news media" and, ultimately, into "the media," occupying a small corner of a vaster entertainment stage.

—Daniel Schorr (1999)

No question about it, many of the most prominent personalities in journalism today have become unpopular with segments of the American public. This is shown in public opinion surveys as well as in caustic comments from a wide range of commentators including from within the press itself. In general, many people feel that journalists, along with politicians, are not dealing with the real concerns of the people. (This chapter's title suggests that the perception of scorn is not directed at all journalists, just mostly at one group—those in the highly visible national media based in New York City and Washington, DC.)

Public affairs news, the heart of serious journalism, is the focus of this criticism, striking most deeply at a press perceived as estranged from its readers and viewers. Journalist J. Schell (1996) wrote:

> On one side is the America of those who are political professionals. It comprises politicians, their advisers and employees, and the news media. Politicians waste little love on the newspeople who cover them, and the newspeople display a surly skepticism towards politicians as a badge of honor. Yet if the voters I met on the campaign trail are any indication (and poll data suggest they are), much of the public has lumped newspeople and politicians into a single class, which, increasingly, it despises. Respect for the government and respect for the news media have declined in tandem. More and more the two appear to the public to be an undifferentiated establishment— a new Leviathan—composed of rich, famous, powerful people who are divorced from the lives of ordinary people and indifferent to their concerns. On the other side of the division is the America of political amateurs: ordinary voters. (p. 70)

Schell believes that the activity of politics has become an interaction between the media and people running campaigns. Everyone else is an onlooker.

Walsh (1996) believed good reasons exist for concern about the cultural chasm between the public and the Washington press corps. A 1996 survey for *U.S. News and World Report* found that 50% of Americans thought that the media were strongly or somewhat in conflict with the goals of ordinary citizens, whereas only 40% thought the media were strongly or somewhat friendly to their goals. This was the worst approval rating of any group measured—lower than prime-time television entertainment providers, welfare recipients, even lower than elected public officials, whose goals were judged to be in conflict with those of ordinary citizens by only 36%. Even lawyers did better, with 45% of Americans saying attorneys' goals conflicted with the public's.

Clearly, the media were seen as part of a strongly disliked governing elite. When asked about "the people running the government," 52% of those surveyed said they had little or nothing in common with them.

Further evidence of the public's low regard for journalists came in a 1998 survey during the Clinton-Lewinsky scandal and based on 3,000 telephone interviews. The public said the credibility of all news media had suffered in what was perceived to be a ceaseless chase after the saucy, sexy story. Responding to the statement, "journalists chase sensational stories because they think it will sell newspapers, not because they think it's important news," 53% agreed and 27% strongly agreed. Among the more intriguing findings: 76% of respondents said journalists can be manipulated by people in powerful positions; 75% said journalists do not demonstrate consistent respect for their readers and communities; and the people who say that journalists do not slant their reporting to suit their political beliefs are more likely to be Democrats.

One encouraging finding for print media: Only 23% of respondents see print reporters as the worst perpetrators of bias, while another 42% see another more pervasive purveyor of bias: television (ASNE Poll, 1998).

DEBASING
PUBLIC AFFAIRS JOURNALISM?

Instead of reporting the news as carefully and fully as possible, many political journalists today are seen as too arrogant, opinionated, and biased in their comments on major issues, particularly when appearing on television. Rather than just telling the news straight, reporters often go beyond the news report itself and predict the future impact of the news. Needless to say, such predictions, so widely strewn on television talk shows, often prove wrong.

Newspaper reporters covering a presidential campaign were accused of letting opinion replace straight news. Because editors know that by morning most people learn from radio and television what the candidate had said the day before, the usual hard news story was often replaced by an analytical or opinion piece. One critic said that one third to one half of every campaign story reflected some level of analysis. (But interpretive pieces, if carefully done, can be free of opinion or bias. It is a fine line.)

Critical of the cozy relationship between journalists and Washington insiders, columnist David Broder calls this a "blurring of the line" when journalists become pseudo-experts on television talk shows. He told one audience, "On television, the 'punditocracy' has begun to look like the last scene from Orwell's *Animal Farm*. You can't tell the journalists from the politicians, the watch dog from the running dog. It's not just that they're in bed with each other. It's that they have become one and the same" (Fibison, 1996, p. 1).

Matters are not helped when some journalists move back and forth between journalism and high political positions. David Gergen, for example, worked in the White House for both Presidents Reagan and Bush before joining *U.S. News and World Report* and the *MacNeil/Lehrer News Hour*. Then he joined the Clinton White House for a time and later returned to journalism. Pat Buchanan, once a Nixon White House aide, has used talk shows, especially CNN's *Crossfire* and his newspaper column, as springboards to his presidential campaigns of 1992, 1996, and 2000.

A recent high-profile political operator to leap into high-profile journalism was George Stephanopoulos. After four years of advising President Clinton on how to deal with and manipulate the press, Stephanopoulos suddenly became a political analyst for ABC News and he now reports and comments on his former boss as well as politics in general. ABC apparently believed that any conflict of interest of their new star analyst was more than balanced by his celebrity status and good looks.

CBS News joined the trend in 1997 by hiring Representative Susan Molinari to move directly from Congress to its anchor desk. However, after a short and bumpy stint, she withdrew from CBS.

ABC News came in for some sharp criticism for further blurring the lines between news and entertainment when it hired actor Leonardo DiCaprio, star of *Titanic*, to interview President Clinton on Earth Day in May 2000. According to onlookers, the actor was nervous and halting on camera, so after the interview, DiCaprio was given the chance to "re-ask" his questions on camera and these retakes were then spliced into the interview footage.

Critics have long advocated that political journalism should get away from the insider game and move closer to the audience; that, however, is not where the rewards are these days for national journalists. A root cause of this animosity toward the press is the fact that due to exposure on television, many journalists have become well-known celebrities themselves and highly paid ones at that. Many among the public can instantly identify Barbara Walters, Tim Russert, Jane Pauley, Diane Sawyer, Sam Donaldson, or Mike Wallace, but they have no idea what the editors of the *Washington Post* or *Time* magazine look like, nor do they know their names.

As previously explained, news on television is becoming packaged entertainment. The role of celebrity journalists in such circumstances is not just to report the news, but to embellish and "spin" the news with lively and entertaining commentary, much of it opinionated and speculative.

TALK SHOWS LEAD TO LECTURES
AND BIG BUCKS

Newspaper and magazine journalists in Washington, DC, and New York City have learned that the way to become prominent and affluent in journalism is to appear on the television talk shows such as *The Capital Gang, Washington Week in Review, McLaughlin Group, Reliable Sources, Weekend Crossfire, Inside Politics, Hardball,* and others that have proliferated in the nation's capital since 1980. Some talk shows are carried nationally, but all are seen in Washington. Compared to prime-time network television or even the daytime talk shows, these political confabs attract scant audiences but are inexpensive to produce because participants receive little pay. But plenty of journalists want to be on them for the "visibility" and opportunities that can result from their appearances.

Some talk shows have became known as "food fights" because the format requires guests to be opiniônated, loud, witty, and, of course, to disagree with other panelists. One participant said the less she knew about a topic, the better she was able to argue about it. These shows provide little time for measured and thoughtful comments on the news and public affairs. (Some journalists see these shows as pure entertainment but others consider them an embarrassment and disservice to serious journalism.)

But the talk shows provide visibility, and for many, they have been the path to affluence. Rem Rieder, editor of *American Journalism Review* commented: "It is a package. You say outrageous things to get attention on the shows so that you can become a regular, and once you become a regular you can get the speaking fees" (Fallows, 1996, p. 96).

For example, *Newsweek* reporter Howard Fineman, a regular on various talk shows, was hired to speak to a group of lawyers on a 12-day cruise from Holland to Russia. Margaret Carlson, the *Time* columnist, said her speaking fees doubled to approximately $10,000 after she became a regular member on *The Capital Gang.* Kurtz (1996) said a partial sampling of journalists' speech-making income from 1994 shows that Sam Donaldson got $30,000 a speech, Pat Buchanan received $10,000, and William Safire, frequent *Meet the Press* panelist, pulled in $20,000 a talk. ABC's Cokie Roberts got at least $20,000 per lecture and was said to have earned $300,000 a year. Mike Wallace of CBS earned $25,000 an outing while CNN's Larry King received $50,000 for each appearance and was said to earn $1 million per year.

Because these hefty lecture fees usually come from a variety of for-profit organizations and interest groups, it is legitimate to ask whether ethical problems or conflicts of interest are involved here.

Many in the national press have been unhappy at the spectacle of this "buckraking" by so many of their colleagues. Fallows (1996) wrote: "The bluntest way to criticize journalists on the lecture trail is to say, simply, that they are corrupt. Some day, in some form, they may have to write about the groups they are addressing. If they have taken big money from these groups, they can't give the reader an honest—or as honest-sounding—assessment as if they had kept their distance" (p. 103).

Similarly, Alan Murray of *The Wall Street Journal* said: "You tell me what is the difference between somebody who works full-time for the National Association of Realtors and somebody who takes $40,000 a year in speaking fees from realtor groups. It's not clear to me there's a big distinction" (p. 103).

"I call it white collar crime," Tom Brokaw of NBC has said. "That's just what I think it is." Other prominent television journalists who do not accept money for speeches include Peter Jennings of ABC, Dan Rather of CBS, and Brian Lamb of C-SPAN. They make speeches but not for money (Fallows, 1996). Jim Lehrer of the PBS news show no longer accepts speaking engagements.

The drumbeat of intramedia criticism of journalists speaking for lucrative fees has had an effect. In 1995, the ABC network drew up a restrictive policy drafted by Vice President Richard Wald. Before accepting a lecture engagement of any kind, ABC correspondents were ordered to check with their superiors and were specifically told not to accept a fee from a trade association or a for-profit business. Wald said, "We don't tilt what we say to please any special interest, we don't sell special access in the guise of fees—and we don't want to risk looking as though we do. It isn't just how big a fee is, it is also who gives it and what it might imply" (Kurtz, 1996, p. 218).

Later, NBC followed suit when it banned its journalists from accepting speaking fees from corporations and trade associations that lobby government or take public positions on issues. The NBC policy also prohibited staff members from speaking to any group they might cover and required that all paid appearances first be okayed by management. In April 1995, *Time* magazine adopted a similar policy that correspondents may not accept fees or expenses for outside speaking engagements or other kinds of sponsored events. If an appearance is in the magazine's interest, the magazine will pay for it from either the editorial or publishing budget. The policy of *The New York Times* is that a reporter may appear on television only to discuss a story that he or she has been reporting. Such policies cannot cover all contingencies and in some ways are probably unfair to some, but they show a concern about ethics which had been notably lacking for some years.

Kurtz (1996) summarized the ethical dilemma nicely:

> The essence of journalism, even for the fiercest opinion-mongers, is professional detachment. The public has a right to expect that those who pontificate for a living are not in financial cahoots with the industries and lobbies they analyze on the air. Too many reporters and pundits simply have a blind spot on this issue. They have been seduced by the affluence and adulation that comes with television success. They are engaging in drive-by journalism, rushing from television studio to lecture hall with their palms outstretched. Perhaps when they mouth off on television, a caption should appear under their names: PAID $20,000 BY GROUP HEALTH ASSOCIATION OF AMERICA, TOOK $15,000 CHECK FROM AMERICAN MEDICAL ASSOCIATION. The talk show culture has made them rich, but, in a very real sense, left them bankrupt. (p. 227)

This problem is not as serious as it was a few years ago but it does point out the hubris of some national journalists. Another reason why the public resents some journalists relates to the money they earn. Even more than large lecture fees, the huge salaries earned by prominent media figures are fairly accurate indicators of their celebrity status and the extent to which some of them are more entertainers than they are serious journalists.

According to the 1999 salary report of *Brill's Content*, the big names at ABC news seem to do best: Barbara Walters gets $10 million; Peter Jennings gets $8.5-9 million; Ted Koppel, $8 million; Diane Sawyer, $7 million; and Sam Donaldson, $3 to 3.5 million. Over at CBS, Dan Rather gets $7 million; Mike Wallace gets $3 million; and Lesley Stahl, $1.75 million. At NBC, Tom Brokaw earns $7 million; Katie Couric also gets $7 million; and Matt Lauer, $2.5 million.

In the print media, even the most highly placed journalists received considerably less annual remuneration. Walter Isaacson, editor of *Time* earns $975,000 to $1.05 million; Joe Lelyveld, executive editor of *The New York Times* gets $450,000 to $600,000; a senior writer for the *Wall Street Journal* gets $130,000; a senior reporter for the *New York Times* gets $80,000 to $100,000. And at the lower end of salaries: Ed Agre, the news director, anchor, and reporter at tiny KXGN at Glendive, Montana, gets $22,000 and a starting salary for a reporter with two years' experience at the *New Haven Register* is $26,000 to $28,000 ("Who gets paid what," 1999).

SELF-CRITICISM OF THE PRESS

The continuing squabble over the pros and cons over money earned on television talk shows and the speaking circuit reminds us of the importance of self-criticism by the press. The news business does have recognized professional standards, and most journalists are sensitive and often responsive to the criticisms of press performance that come from such regular or occasional media critics as Howard Kurtz, David Shaw, James Fallows, Ken Auletta, Tom Rosenstiel, Bill Kovach, Richard Reeves, Jonathan Alter, Tom Shales, and Jon Katz, among others, as well as from *American Journalism Review*, *Columbia Journalism Review*, and *Nieman Reports*. A major addition to these academically oriented journals is Steven Brill's new slick magazine, *Brill's Content*, which since 1999 has been providing incisive and knowledgeable criticism of media performance as well as entertaining stories and gossip about media personalities.

The Internet has provided further venues for media criticism including online "magazines" *Slate* and *Salon* which regularly take on the media.

A built-in problem for many of these critics—some who critique the media only part-time and do other kinds of editing or reporting—is that they have jobs with various news organizations. Hence, they never seem to zero in on the foibles or errant behavior of their own paper, newspaper group, magazine, or broadcast station, much less the conglomerates of which they are a small part. Further, sometimes critics themselves can get crosswise on ethical concerns.

Incisive intramedia criticism is an important way the press improves itself at times. The talk show and lecture fee brouhaha struck a nerve with both management and individual journalists. Washington journalists are showing more sensitivity and have drawn back from some of the "food fight" shows and questionable lecture stints.

MORE PROFOUND CONCERNS
ABOUT JOURNALISM

The concerns already mentioned about the press' cynicism, negativism, trivialization of news, and decline of serious public affairs journalism have led to some somber assessments of today's journalism, originating from academics, both left and right, and from respected journalists.

Cynicism is at the heart of the new critique. Journalists, Glaberson (1994) reported, are bringing a self-canceling message: everything—from the O. J. Simpson case to the health care debate and on to journalism itself—is a game about nothing more than winning and losing. Thomas Mann of the Brookings Institution, said, "We're now at a point of believing it's all a scam, everyone is looking out for his own narrow interest and the job of the reporter is to reveal the scam" (Glaberson, 1994, p. 1, sec. 4). The longtime concern about liberal bias in the press has been replaced by a concern that a politically neutral bias now shapes news coverage by declaring that all public figures, indeed all people in the news, are suspect.

This journalism, it is felt, is undermining its own credibility. Professor Kathleen Jamieson said: "Journalists are now creating the coverage that is going to lead to their own destruction. If you cover the world cynically and assume that everyone is Machiavellian and motivated by their own self-interest, you invite your readers and viewers to reject journalism as a mode of communication because it must be cynical, too" (Glaberson, 1994, p. 1, sec. 4).

Studies, backed by statistics, strongly suggest that the press nearly always magnifies the bad and underplays the good. Since the 1960s, reporters have served America a steady diet of trends and events of such a fundamentally negative nature that we have undermined the country's faith in itself. Walsh (1996) wrote: "Of course, the press has to report such stories but they have taken their toll. The media are no longer seen as society's truth-sayers. By embellishing the bad and filtering out the good, a negative picture emerges. It is understandable that Americans have come to associate the press with everything that has gone wrong" (p. 281).

Fallows (1996) thought the ascendancy of star-oriented, highly paid media personalities involves a terrible bargain. "The more prominent today's star journalists become, the more they are forced to give up the essence of real journalism, which is the search for information of use to the public. . . . The best-known and best-paid people in journalism now set an example that erodes the quality of the news we receive and threaten journalism's claim on public respect" (p. 7).

Further, Fallows sees an even more ominous future:

The harm actually goes much further than that, to threaten the long-term health of our political system. Step by step, mainstream journalism has fallen into the habit of portraying American public life as a race to the bottom, in which one group of conniving, insincere, politicians ceaselessly tries to outmaneuver another. The

great problem for American democracy in the 1990s is that people barely trust
elected leaders or the entire legislative system to accomplish anything of value.
(p. 7)

Other forces are involved, but Fallows believes the media's attitudes
have played a surprisingly important and destructive role in public affairs.

Unless the press changes its ways, some feel that legal protections of
the press will be rolled back within a decade. The public does not care
anymore about protecting the press, it is argued, because most Americans
no longer think it informs them well. Libel laws may be weakened and
access laws tightened to make it more difficult for the press to cover news
and investigate abuses in government and the private sector. In the 1990s,
jury awards for libel soared as the public's trust in the press declined.

One solution to all these criticisms is that journalists should place
more stress on reporting the news and leave the task of assessing its
impact to others. Criticism of investigative stories, such as Whitewater,
White House fund-raising, or alleged Chinese espionage, some journalists
say, suggests a naive belief that without the press, the news would somehow be better. Richard Wald of ABC thinks the current criticism is based
on nostalgia for a past that never really existed. He thinks there is a broad
societal skepticism today that erodes the influence of all institutions,
including the press.

What may be significant, however, is that growing numbers of working journalists talk more and more about de-emphasizing coverage that
focuses on conflict and scandal, and others say they are rethinking their
aversions to positive news stories. These ideas are related to a significant
but controversial trend in newspaper journalism today called *public* or
civic journalism.

This approach is an attempt to help the public participate in public
affairs without the press taking stands on issues. Instead of covering elections as contests or horse races that reduce citizens to mere bystanders,
public journalism attempts to ground its coverage in a citizen's agenda or
a list of problems and issues that citizens want discussed by the candidates. The press is divided over public journalism but the controversy is a
welcome sign of ferment in the news business.

Journalist Geneva Overholser, former editor of *The Des Moines Register*, said: "The public is right to question whether newspapers are acting
in the public interest. I think what readers are asking is Are you really giving us a reflection of what is happening or are you just discouraging us?

We're so good at reporting all the negatives and all the infighting that we give people a sense it is all hopeless" (Glaberson, 1994, p. 1, sec. 4).

All of these growing concerns seemed to come together and reach a new level of public disapproval of news media performance during the prolonged scandal involving President Clinton and a White House intern in 1998–1999.

CHAPTER

9

The Clinton Scandal and "Mixed Media"

There is an old piece of advice I think every young reporter in a good news room gets: Do your own work. And I think the lesson of this whole thing for reporters comes down to some pretty simple standards like that one.

—Michael Oreskes (1998)

Major scandals that dominate the news, such as the prolonged presidential crisis over President Clinton's involvement with Monica Lewinsky, seem to bring out a bit of the best—the serious press *did* get the basic facts right—but mostly the worst in the news media.

In part because it was a prolonged *political* scandal (as well as a constitutional crisis), with charges and allegations flying back and forth, everyone connected with it was besmirched and discredited—not only President Clinton but also the presidency, many in Congress, Kenneth Starr and his investigation, the impeachment trial, and especially the so-called "mixed media."

"Mixed media" is a new term, popular with media critics, and intended to describe the recent trends, some technological and others organizational and financial, that have altered the news media in mostly deleterious ways.

Critic Steven Brill (1999) wrote that the Monica Lewinsky affair put all the dynamics of that mixed media culture on display:

- The speed of today's never-pausing news cycle that demands instant reactions from the players.
- The way 24-hour cable news channels love to fill the air with two screaming sides of every argument, as if the two sides are always equal and as if there is always credible disagreement about whatever the issue at hand happens to be.
- The brutal competition across a vast array of profit-hungry news providers that are typically subsidiaries of giant corporations.
- The carnivorous appetite for any shred of news that has even the slimmest claim to being "new."
- Sinking standards for sourcing.
- Shrinking attention spans, and the ability of the story du jour to drown out other news. (p. 84)

"Mixed media" in hot pursuit of a scandal seemed to bring out the worst of American journalism. Many journalists were highly critical of their colleagues' performance during the scandal. David Halberstam spoke for many when he wrote:

The past year [1998] has been, I think, the worst year for American journalism since I entered the profession 44 years ago. . . . What is disturbing about the profession today is that, I think, many of the critics are right, and the people who have been performing as journalists in the past year have in fact seriously trivialized the profession, doing what is fashionable instead of what is right. . . . In some ways, this particular crisis, so much of it driven by technological change, has been coming for more than a decade, as the power of cable television and the effect of it on mainstream media have gradually changed the nature of what constitutes television broadcasting, giving us an ever escalating diet of sensationalized tabloid reporting, and an endless, unquestioning search for access to celebrities on their own terms. (Kovach & Rosenstiel, 1999, p. ix)

The most thoughtful and penetrating analysis of media performance during the Clinton scandal was done by Bill Kovach and Tom Rosenstiel in their book, *Warp Speed: America in the Age of Mixed Media*. Their study was conducted within the framework of the "mixed media culture" (and similar to Brill's views), which they said has five main characteristics:

- *A Never-Ending News Cycle Makes Journalism Less Complete:* In the 24-hour news cycle, the press is increasingly reporting allegations, rather than digging out the truth. Stories begin as bits of evidence or speculation, to be filled in and sorted out in public as the news cycle continues. And then journalists vamp and speculate until a response is issued. So stories come out less complete and reporting takes on a chaotic and unsettled quality. This makes it difficult to separate fact from spin, argument, or innuendo.
- *Sources Are Gaining Power Over Journalists:* The move toward allegation over verification is compounded by a shift in the power relationship toward the sources of information and away from the news organizations who cover them. Sources increasingly dictate the terms of the interaction and the conditions and time frame in which the information is used, whether it is a celebrity promoting a new movie or a leaker negotiating which paper or prime time TV show to give the interview to. With more news outlets, it reflects a rising demand for news "product" and a limited supply of news makers. Media manipulators as well are growing more sophisticated.
- *There Are No More Gatekeepers:* The press is now marked by a much wider range of standards of what is publishable and what is not. With so many more outlets, the authority of any one outlet (such as a *New York Times* editor) to play a gatekeeper role over the information is diminished. Journalism maybe coming more innovative and democratic, but there has been an abandonment of professional standards and ethics. In fact, the lowest standards drive out the higher standards, creating a kind of Gresham's Law of Journalism. The news medium with high standards is often faced with the dilemma overusing a story already "out there" of high interest but poorly sourced and of doubtful news value.
- *Argument Is Overwhelming Reporting:* The "reporting culture" (which rewards gathering and verifying information) is being overrun by the "argument culture" which devalues the practices of verification. Due to the information revolution, many new media outlets now merely comment on information rather than gather it. The rise of 24-hour cable news stations and Internet news and information sites has placed demands on the media to "have something" to fill the time. Further, the economics of new media demand the product be produced as cheaply as possible. Comment, chat, speculation, opinion, and punditry cost far less than assembling a team of reporters, producers, fact-checkers and editors to cover the world. Whole new news organizations such as MSNBC are being built around such chatter, creating a new medium of talk radio TV.

- *The "Blockbuster Mentality"* : As the television audiences fragment, television tries to re-assemble the mass audience with a big running story. These blockbusters tend to be formulaic stories that involve celebrity, scandal, sex, and downfall, be it O. J., Princess Diana, or Monicagate. Part of the appeal to news organizations is that it is cheaper and easier to reassemble the audience with the big story rather than by covering the globe and presenting a diversified menu of news. (Kovach & Rosenstiel, 1999, pp. 6–8)

Kovach and Rosenstiel believe these characteristics of mixed media are creating a new journalism of assertion, which is less interested in substantiating whether something is true and more interested in getting it into the public discussion. The trend contributes to the press being a conduit of politics as cultural civil war. Their concern is whether the journalism of verification will soon be overwhelmed by the journalism of assertion. The authors seem to imply that television's lower standards now trample the once dominant standards valued by the best of the print media.

WHAT HAPPENED
AND HOW MEDIA REACTED

Most of the turmoil of the scandal occurred during 1998—the so-called Year of Monica. As most will recall, Linda Tripp's recordings of her phone conversations with Monica Lewinsky, a former White House intern, contained lurid comments about her sexual relationship with President Bill Clinton, and launched the story. (For many months, Clinton vehemently denied them.) Michael Isikoff, a *Newsweek* reporter, had been following events and was readying a scoop when *Newsweek* hesitated and decided to wait a week after Kenneth Starr promised a complete account for the following week. The delayed scoop somehow was leaked to Matt Drudge, one-man Internet gossip and news agency. He decided the public had a right to know the story even if the facts could not be verified. So the biggest political scandal in years broke first in cyberspace—a new player of mixed media.

Needless to say, the story spread like wildfire and in the first hectic days there was a feeding frenzy as media pursued the relatively few tidbits of information—mostly leaks from lawyers and investigators—but various restraints kept the public from knowing with certainty the sources of key elements of the saga. The most important finding of the Kovach and

Rosenstiel study (1999) of the scandal was the extraordinary degree to which reporting and opinion and speculation were intermingled in mainstream journalism. A snapshot of network news, newspaper reporting, and cable news that typified what an American might see showed that 41% of all the reportage in the first six days of the story was not factual reporting at all—"here is what happened"—but instead was journalists offering their own analysis, opinion, speculation, or judgments—essentially commentary and punditry. Another 12% of content was reporting attributed to other news media but unverified by those reporting it. Taken together, it meant that more than half of the reportage of the first week (53%) was either passing along other people's reporting or commenting on the news (Kovach & Rosenstiel, 1999).

Veteran journalist Jules Witcover commented that "Into the vacuum created by a scarcity of clear and creditable attribution raced all manner of rumor, gossip, and especially hollow sourcing, making the reports of some mainstream outlets scarcely distinguishable from supermarket tabloids. The rush to be first or to be more sensational created a picture of irresponsibility seldom seen in the reporting of presidential affairs" (Witcover, 1998, p. 19).

Not until the story settled somewhat did the serious media begin to report in a manner expected of them. Many news media did act with considerable responsibility considering the early demand for news. And the Clinton White House, in full damage-control mode, seized on the leaks and weakly attributed stories to cast the news media as either a willing or unwilling collaborator of sorts with Starr's probe (Witcover, 1998).

Dire predictions of a premature end of the Clinton presidency were heard almost at once. "Is he finished?" asked a coverline on *U.S. News and World Report* and *The Economist* of London commanded, "If It's True, Go." ABC's Sam Donaldson speculated on January 25 that Clinton could resign before the next week was out, "If he's not telling the truth." (Witcover, 1998, p. 19)

After the initial story, there was much piling-on by broadcast and print media and this did not sit well with the public. A *Washington Post* poll taken 10 days after the story broke found that 56% of those surveyed believed the news media were treating Clinton unfairly, and 74% said they were giving the story "too much attention."

The public's sense of overkill was exacerbated by the 24-hour cable channels, and Internet sites which ensured the story of non-stop reportage and rumor, augmented by late night rehashes and TV talk shows. Despite the public's criticisms, viewing and listening audiences swelled as did circulations of print media.

Journalists' methods came in for sharp criticism—for more rumor mongering instead of fact checking, and the unattributed appropriation of the work and speculations of others. The old yardstick applied by *The Washington Post* in the Watergate story, that every revelation had to be confirmed by two sources before publication, was quickly abandoned by many news outlets. Often reports were published or broadcast without a single source named or mentioned in an attribution so vague as to be useless. The public was told repeatedly that this or that information came from "sources," a word that only conveyed the notion that the story was not pure fiction. Seldom in a story of such major importance has the public been left to guess where the allegations came from and why. Leakers were violating the rules while the public was left to guess about their identity and about the truth passed on through the news media, often without the customary tests of validity (Witcover, 1998).

Yet the fact remains that in all the major aspects of the story, the press was essentially accurate. Kovach and Rosenstiel wrote that contrary to White House claims, "the press usually relied on legitimate sources and often was careful about the facts in the first account." This turned out to be the case with ABC News and its story of the stained blue dress, which indeed proved to be accurate and indisputably relevant; and later became the pivotal evidence against the President. But the key words were "first account" because "others then used the reporting from elsewhere to engage in sometimes reckless speculation and propaganda" (Stewart, 1999, p. 8).

TELEVISION'S ARGUMENT CULTURE

Another dimension of the Clinton Scandal coverage was the proliferation of television talk shows in which pundits, in and out of the news media, would face off in loud, argumentative debates either attacking or defending the president. At various stages of the long-running story—the posting of the Starr report on the Internet, release of taped phone conversations between Linda Tripp and Monica Lewinsky, Clinton's grand jury appearance, and the impeachment proceedings in Congress—viewers were besieged with charge and countercharge but little news or rational discussion and analysis in these programs.

These political "shout shows" were mainly a cable television phenomenon on MSNBC, CNBC, CNN, and the Fox News Channel. CNBC's *Rivera Live* with Geraldo Rivera and CNBC's *Hardball with Chris Matthews* were probably the noisiest and the most polarized in their political sentiments. But these cable food fights were soon spilling over into the networks and onto the newsmagazine formats and onto such respected shows as *Meet the Press*. Unwritten rules seem to require that one person or side must, say, defend the president, the other attack him. Critics felt such shows tend to turn off viewers about the political process, by trivializing the news, and turning a difference of opinion into a shouting match.

Former TV newsman Marvin Kalb of Harvard said, "One of the dangers of programs of this sort is that they convey an impression about politics as being a negative, argumentative forum. And politics is a lot more than that. And a lot more serious than that." Moreover, he added that these pundit shows are for those who enjoy "the veneer of news and the essence of gossip" (Shepard, 1999, p. 22).

The cumulative effect of such shouting matches was a public left hopelessly confused about what is true. "The biggest damage being done is not just losing viewers but to our democracy, because viewers just aren't being informed," wrote Deborah Tannen in her book, *The Argument Culture*. "If you reduce everything to two sides fighting, you are not exploring anything. People are not getting the information they need. It also promotes a real cynicism about the political process" (Shepard, 1999, p. 22).

Such talk shows were one more manifestation of the "culture of assertion" overwhelming the "culture of verification" in public affairs news and, as such, contributed to public disdain of the media.

WHAT CAN THE PRESS DO?

The Clinton-Lewinsky saga with its nonstop coverage highlighted many of the journalistic shortcomings of the mixed media age. Journalists no longer had the luxury of taking either hours or days while pondering a news decision or arguing over a story. Today, battered by technology, competition, the rise of pseudo news and the decline of audiences, serious journalists are faced with the task of how to separate honest, serious journalism from the all-encompassing culture of entertainment that has pervaded modern life.

In their thoughtful study of the paradox, Kovach and Rosenstiel conclude that "newspapers, magazines, Web sites, and television stations will have to distinguish themselves—and establish their brands—by what they choose to report on and the values standards they bring to their journalism. Some will publish only what they know is true. Others will publish rumor and innuendo to have the most startling and comprehensive account. Some will separate information carefully from opinion. Some will separate fact from fiction. Others will blend them into a kind of infotainment" (Kovach & Rosenstiel, 1999).

To accomplish this, the authors propose three steps for media to follow:

Step One: Each news organization should do a great deal more to decide what its news values and policies are. News media must make these decisions in advance and not wait until a blockbuster story is breaking.

Step Two: The news organization must make it clear to those who work there that these are the values in place. Reporters are motivated by the values of the institution and by a sense of mission. They need to know what that mission is to thrive.

Step Three: Once a newsroom has defined its standards and values and genuinely made them clear to its reporters and editors, it must then make these values clear to the audience. In effect, a newsroom must make a covenant with the public about what it stands for. The covenant is crucial since it is the only way for the audience to fairly judge what it thinks of a news organization. (pp. 91–93)

Some may doubt the efficacy of such standards and covenants when the next big blockbuster of a story—replete with scandal, sex, celebrity, and malfeasance—hits the new mixed media. But they are certainly three steps in the right direction.

10

Changes in Foreign News Coverage

In an age of real-time, multimedia, interactive forms of communica-
tion, there is a tendency to declare obsolete (or at least dispensable)
the diplomat and the foreign correspondent in the field. We will do so
at our peril. The myriad forms of instantaneous communication
threaten to substitute immediacy for insight, reaction for reflection,
sentiment for judgment, hyperbole for reality, and deniability for
integrity.

—Peter Krogh (1996)

You know, being a foreign correspondent is like being a maitre d' in a
fine restaurant. You meet so many distinguished people under such
humiliating circumstances.

—Quoted by Stephen Hess (1996)

International news gathered by foreign correspondents—that far-flung and glamorous specialty of American journalism—has been undergoing some basic change in recent times. Because of new technologies and financial concerns, less news from abroad is reported and in very different ways. The correspondents are becoming a different breed of journalist than in the bad (yet, journalistically, good) old days of the Cold War.

Today the American public seems a lot less interested in news from abroad, and editors and broadcasters seem inclined to give the public less. Among the print correspondents themselves, as with broadcast journalists, there is a sense of decline. Things were better in earlier times—when *we* were young.

Serious journalists have long held that foreign news *is* important and should be reported well and thoroughly. Much that happens overseas has a direct impact on American lives, as the rise of Hitler and Stalin, World War II, and the Korean and Vietnam wars amply demonstrated. In a democratic society, an interested public, it is argued, must know what is happening in the greater world in order to judge how well its own government responds to threats and challenges from abroad.

Further, foreign news is necessary to inform our leaders and decision makers about foreign dangers and opportunities. (In his mea culpa on disasters in foreign affairs, Robert McNamara interestingly blamed the press for not better informing State Department officials about Vietnam.)

Despite globalization of our economy, for many Americans, foreign news today does not seem as important. Who is to blame? The national press? The "media"—broadly speaking, with its pervasive cultural and social influences? Perhaps the public itself? Without a crisis story intruding on the public's attention—China threatening Taiwan, famine in Ethiopia, civil strife in Kosovo, or terrorism in Israel or Ulster—the typical daily newspaper does not print much news from overseas—usually about six or more short items about eight inches or less—unless American soldiers or hostages are involved. Anyone regularly watching network television is aware that foreign news has been typically reduced to several brief items ("And now the news from abroad"), unless some video with violent footage is available. (Fifty percent of television's foreign news does portray violence.) At the networks, foreign news has been pushed aside in favor of more personalized, self-help, and advice stories—so-called "you news."

Who cares? Apparently, not the public. The Pew Research Center for the People and the Press (1996) survey of the American public found that among the regular users of the news media, the topics of most interest were crime, local news about people and events, and health news. International news ranked ninth, well behind sports, local government, science, religion, and political news.

One cross-national study found that 78% of Germans read a newspaper yesterday, whereas only 49% of Americans did. When asked to identify the current secretary general of the United Nations, 58% of Germans came up with his name, compared with only 13% of Americans. (Kofi Annan is the current secretary general.)

This declining audience interest means that as a culture, we are missing the connective tissue that binds us to the rest of the world. The British have been long involved with far-off places, a legacy of their receding empire. For many Europeans, the consequences of two world wars are still keenly felt. For Americans, the experience of World War II, when everyone knew someone who was in it, and the aftermath of the rising Third World with its involvement with Soviet hegemony and the Cold War, deeply affected two generations of citizens concerned about the outside world.

Now the consensus in the news business appears to be that you can rely on international news to turn a profit only when it is actually domestic news. The most certain way to become domestic news is through a U.S. military intervention—when it is "our boys" who are "over there."

Others blame the news media. "A great shroud has been drawn across the mind of America to make it forget that there is a world beyond its borders," complained Max Frankel (1994), former editor of *The New York Times*,

> The three main television networks obsessively focus their cameras on domestic tales and dramas as if the end of the cold war rendered the rest of the planet irrelevant. Their news staffs occasionally visit some massacre, famine, or shipwreck and their anchors may parachute into Haiti or Kuwait for a photo op, but these spasms of interest only emphasize the networks' apparent belief that on most evenings the five billion folks out there don't matter one whit. (p. 42)

One indicator of this trend: In its heyday, CBS maintained 24 foreign bureaus; by 1995 it had reporters in only four capitals: London, Moscow, Tel Aviv, and Tokyo. (Miami was its base for covering all of Latin America.) Dan Rather has not hesitated to speak out. "Don't kid yourself;" he told Harvard students,

> The trend line in American journalism is away from, not toward, increased foreign coverage. Foreign coverage is the most expensive. It requires the most space and the most time because you're dealing with complicated situations which you have to explain a lot. And then there's always somebody around you who says people don't really give a damn about this stuff anyway. . . . "if you have to do something foreign, Dan, for heaven's sake, keep it short." (Hess, 1996, p. 61)

FEWER COVER STORIES

The covers of the three major news magazines, each of which has long emphasized foreign news gathered by their numerous overseas correspondents, reflect the declining interest in international news. By late September 1996, *Time* had run five covers that year on international topics, versus 11 in 1995. *Newsweek* featured four international covers by September, compared to 11 in 1995. *U.S. News* published no international covers as of late 1996 but ran six in 1995.

Why the difference? The decline in interest surely was greatly accelerated by the major historic event of the late 20th century—the ending of the Cold War. In the still dangerous and confusing post-Cold War period, foreign correspondents and news organizations have been going through an identity crisis over what is news and what is not news. The Cold War provided reporters with a coherent global road map, in terms of what to cover and how to cover it. Don Oberdorfer of *The Washington Post* added, "Since the fall of the Berlin Wall and the end of the Cold War news filter, the task of making sense of global events has become less manageable for the media." The press is not used to reacting to a world full of conflicts and violent encounters that, as George Kennan put it, offer no "great and absorbing focal points for American policy" (Hachten, 1996, p. 123). The American public has been confused as well and has turned inward.

Editors said that since Vietnam and the Cold War demise, there has been a gradual but significant lessening of interest in what happens abroad. "We no longer have enemies, we have dangers. And that obviously has less attraction for a large audience than what existed before 1990," said Morton Zuckerman of *U.S. News* (Pogrebin, 1996, p. C2). Moreover, this trend has been a continuing one. Throughout 1995, *Time* devoted 385 pages to international news, or 14% of the magazine. *Newsweek* used 388 pages or 12% of its coverage and *U.S. News* had 386 pages on foreign news or 14%. This was a significant decline from 10 years earlier. In 1985, *Time* had 670 pages or 24% on foreign news, *Newsweek* had 590 pages or 22% and *U.S. News* had 588 or 22%.

Another view holds that only a very small portion of the American public is seriously interested and concerned about the outside world. These are mainly teachers and scholars, some business executives and travelers, and some public officials and journalists, especially those who have worked abroad. One editor said that at any given time, only about 2 million people in America are really interested in foreign affairs. The great majority of Americans are concerned about matters closer to home ("all news is local") just as people in other countries are (Hess, 1996).

Hess (1996) said that "audiences with more cosmopolitan interests can find detailed information in the prestige press or outside the mainstream media" (p. 88). Maybe so, but that prestige press or national press is covering less and less foreign news. With the three television networks and the big news magazines continuing to slough off serious foreign news coverage, the major journalistic outlets seem to have narrowed down to a handful of papers—*The New York Times*, *The Washington Post*, *The Wall Street Journal*, *The Los Angeles Times*, and a few others. Their combined circulations of less than 5 million daily out of a total daily circulation of 63 million will continue to inform that small group of serious thinkers who do affect public policy and our response to world news events, but they will not have much direct influence on the 250 million other Americans. Hence, knowledge and concern about global events has become one more of the separators between our two media systems. Foreign news may be a main dish for the elite media but is only an appetizer for the popular press. The one exception to this trend, as noted in chapter 2, is the rapid increase in business and financial news from overseas—a direct result of the globalization of the world's economy.

HOW THE WORLD
IS COVERED BY THE PRESS

For many years, the prevailing pattern of international news has been an east-west-east flow across the northern hemisphere. Three cities—New York, London, and Tokyo—comprise the key centers of the axis. From those metropolises, news is relayed and returned from the southern regions: Latin American news to New York, European, Middle Eastern, and African news to London, and Asian news to Tokyo.

Needless to say, the news that Americans receive about most of 190 nations from Afghanistan to Zimbabwe is sporadic and uneven. In a sense, most news comes from where journalists are stationed, and the U.S. television networks keep their crews in residence in England, Japan, Germany, Russia, and Israel covering happenings in those areas. But because U.S. television crews are there, a certain amount of soft news comes out of these capitals as well; for example, one more story, picked up from Fleet Street tabloids about Britain's royal family.

From London, Tokyo, or Tel Aviv, reporters and cameras can be quickly dispatched elsewhere to a breaking story in the world's crisis areas. With modern air travel, broadcast journalists can quickly get to the scene and, standing before mobs of homeless Africans, can report back "live" from, say, Goma, Congo.

As regular television viewers know, most of the major foreign news seems to be coming from several chronic crisis areas: the former Soviet

Union, Chechnya, the Middle East generally, particularly Israel and its immediate neighbors, plus Syria, Iran and Iraq. The breakup of Yugoslavia and the ugly ethnic hostilities in Bosnia, Serbia, and Kosovo set off a major running international story. China, with its economic expansion, uneasy relations with Taiwan, and persistent human rights abuses, has shared the Asian news spotlight with the region's amazing economic growth. Plus, any time the American military get involved overseas, it becomes major U.S. news.

In most of these crises, a case can be made that national interests of the United States were somehow involved. Other crisis stories—the prolonged struggle over apartheid in South Africa, unrest on the Korean peninsula, civil conflict and terrorism in Northern Ireland, and political upheavals in the Philippines—appear erratically on the radar screens and then disappear for a time.

In his seven-year survey of network news, Hess (1996) found that among 190 countries, 6 were "constant (news) countries" (i.e., Russia, Germany, U.K., Israel, Japan, and France); 22 were "crisis countries" and 77 "others" rarely reported. His study looked at 2,300 stories from outside the United States. Most countries are rarely covered, particularly on television, and then only because they host an important event, have well-known tourists, or are the locale for the odd human interest story.

Confirming what other studies have shown, Hess (1996) found that 21 countries accounted for 79% of foreign dateline stories on network television from 1988-1992. Crisis journalism dominated the evening screens. For 16 nations, the news was wholly or mostly about serious unrest in their regions. A major effect of television news was the reinforcing of stereotypes: Stories from Colombia were often about drugs; in Germany, about neo-Nazis; in Italy, the Mafia. Stories from England ignored business, focusing instead on something offbeat or the royal family.

A more disturbing but not surprising conclusion of Hess' survey was television's concern with violence. When combining the categories of combat (32.8%), human rights violations (13.7%), accident/disaster (2.3%), and crime (2.5%), the total showed that more than 50% of the television network news stories were concerned with some aspect of violence. Further, a correlation was found between violence and the distance of the story from New York City: The farther away from home, the more likely the cameras have been lured there by something violent.

In her recent book, *Compassion Fatigue*, Susan Moeller argues that the volume and character of disaster coverage can lull audiences into a "compassion-fatigue stupor" and damage the prospects for remedy and recovery. Comparing such stories as famine in Sudan, war in Iraq, and Ebola fever in Congo, she argues that news coverage is usually formulaic and sensationalized. Such foreign news stories, she says, all sound alike with causes and solutions often oversimplified. As one crisis bleeds into the next one, she claims, it takes more and more dramatic coverage to elicit the same level of sympathy as the last catastrophe (Moeller, 1999).

TECHNOLOGY PRODUCES
A NEW KIND
OF CORRESPONDENT

For most of this century, the foreign correspondent was a journalist who was "posted" to a distant, foreign capital—Paris, Moscow, Cairo, Buenos Aires—often staying for several years, learning the language, making contacts, and closely following politics and various facets of the society. Some stayed a long time: Henry Shapiro of UPI covered Moscow for 40 years, but most reporters were rotated after 4 or 5 years. Because of poor communications, these reporters were pretty much on their own, and they liked it that way. They decided what to report and usually sent back their stories by cable or sometimes by erratic radio telephone, telex, and even by mail. Dispatches were often crafted in a more leisurely fashion with much thought and reflection. Editors back home tended to go along with what their correspondent reported.

Foreign news enjoyed high credibility. A *New York Times* story from Moscow with Harrison Salisbury's byline really meant something as did a CBS television story from Berlin by Daniel Schorr.

Things have changed due to the revolutionary developments in telecommunications, particularly communication satellites, which make it possible to send a news story or video report instantly from one place to many others. The volume and speed of international news has been greatly accelerated. With the great improvement in telephone communication, thanks to INTELSAT, that lone foreign correspondent out there is no longer cut off from an editor, who now may be on the phone several times a day with advice and instructions, often when the reporter is on deadline.

With the availability of impressive gadgets—satellite telephones, lightweight versatile computers, the Internet, reliable phone connections, faxes, and uplinks to send video reports via satellite—foreign reporting, when combined with air travel is made much easier and has become a lot different.

These technological advances have not always been for the better. Mifflin (1996a) quoted Dan Rather on how the traditional foreign correspondent's mobility has changed.

Jet travel and technology—with smaller and better cameras, satellites, and cellular phones—have made it easier to send correspondents in and out of places swiftly. That means bureaus have been closed and correspondents, as well as anchors, make quick visits instead. . . . In 1996, I can literally go any place on the planet, hit the satellite and get up instantaneously. (p. C5)

[By "up" he meant on the air for a live transmission.] But what about thorough news gathering and reflection by a resident correspondent who knows the country?

Foreign news gathering has always been expensive, and many foreign bureaus are being eliminated. Now broadcast news is being collected in other, less costly ways. Just a few years ago, if you saw a foreign news story on the NBC Evening News, chances are that it was reported by an NBC reporter at the scene and the film was shot by an NBC crew. Now the networks are relying more on less expensive, and often less experienced, freelancers and independent contractors as well as video news agencies; their products are rarely identified on the air, leaving the impression the story was covered by networks staffers.

This practice gives rise to a growing concern about quality control. "By the time, the tape gets on the air, nobody has the foggiest idea who made it or whether the pictures were staged," contended Tom Wolzien, a former NBC News executive (Hess, 1996, p. 99).More loss of quality or authenticity results when U.S. network correspondents, based in London, add voice-overs to stories they did not cover.

Bert Quint, former CBS correspondent, said, "There's no reason to believe the person (doing the voice-over) because odds are he or she was not within 3,000 miles of where the story occurred" (Hess, 1996, p. 99). Martha Teichner of CBS's London bureau, recalled, "I was asked to do Somalia for the weekend news and I've never been to Somalia and I think, oh my God, what am I gonna do? I get every bit of research I can find, but even if I'm correct and accurate, I'm superficial. And I don't want to be superficial" (Hess, 1996, p. 100).

When a big story breaks, such as the plight of 500,000 Rwanda refugees in eastern Congo, literally hundreds of journalists and camera crews, few of them knowledgeable about the area, quickly arrive, do their stories and video the reporters standing among the hungry mobs, and then just as quickly get out. Satellites and jet travel have made such parachute journalism not only feasible, but cost effective, often at the expense of serious news coverage.

Lack of follow-up and failure to provide context are two frequently heard criticisms of today's foreign coverage, according to Hickey (1996). The brilliant spotlight of powerful color television pictures of the 1989 Tiananmen Square uprising by student demonstrators played to millions around the world. During those dramatic days, CBS, NBC, and ABC aired 357 stories on China—more than they had done in the entire decade from 1972 (when China opened to the West) through 1981. Afterwards, China reportage plummeted from 14.6% of foreign news dateline stories in 1989 to 1.4% in 1990.

Foreign correspondents are changing in various ways. Fewer of the U.S. media's correspondents abroad are American citizens. Foreign journalists are not only less expensive but often have a grasp of local languages and knowledge of their countries that American journalists cannot match. The AP uses many locals—nationals of the countries they cover in their many foreign bureaus. Journalist Scott Schuster saw the trend as due to a global acceptance of English as a media language and the global influence of American journalistic methods. Schuster said, "American influence is most profound among broadcasters and foreign broadcast journalists need only turn on their TV sets (to CNN) to receive lessons on how to do the news American style" (Hachten, 1999, p. 129).

Increasingly, print has joined the broadcast media in relying more on stringers or freelancers to deal with rising costs and tighter budgets. Another survey by Hess (1994) found that 26% of 404 foreign correspondents working for U.S. news media were freelancers. Moreover, many of these were underemployed, with 40% saying they do other work as well. All suffer the usual fate of freelancers: low pay, no benefits, and a precarious relationship with their employers. Hess found six types of stringers: "spouses" of other correspondents; "experts," who know languages and the area; "adventurers" like Oriana Fallaci, the Italian writer; "flingers," a person on a fling who may be starting a serious career; "ideologues" or "sympathizers," who are often British; and the "residents," who are often long-time residents and write occasional stories. Although stringers and freelancers remain marginal, many famous foreign correspondents started that way including Stanley Karnow, Elie Abel, Robert Kaiser, Elizabeth Pond, Caryle Murphy, and Daniel Schorr.

One of the significant changes has been the increased number of women among foreign correspondents, especially as war reporters. Before

1970, their numbers were small, although there had been a few outstanding reporters: Dorothy Thompson, Martha Gellhorn, Marguerite Higgins, and Gloria Emerson. Hess (1996) found that by the 1970s, about 16% of new foreign reporters were women; this doubled during the 1980s to about 33%. The total leveled off in the early 1990s. This ratio of two men for every woman was also found in Washington media as well as in U.S. journalism generally.

A number of women correspondents have established outstanding reputations. Among them are Caryle Murphy of *The Washington Post*, Robin Wright of *The Los Angeles Times*, syndicated columnist Georgie Ann Geyer, and Elaine Sciolino and Barbara Crossette of *The New York Times*.

Christiane Amanpour, who reported with distinction for CNN, has become something of a celebrity because of her aggressive and frankly committed reporting style. She listed the Gulf War, famine in Africa, and civil war in former Yugoslavia, as her most memorable stories. Other networks bid for her services. She agreed to do some foreign stories for CBS' *60 Minutes* but decided to stay with CNN.

Foreign correspondents today are better educated and have higher status backgrounds than their predecessors. Current salaries for foreign correspondents range from about $50,000 to $90,000 with more experienced reporters earning even more.

PHYSICAL DANGERS FOR CORRESPONDENTS

Because much of foreign reporting deals with war, civil unrest, and other forms of violence, the work is dangerous, perhaps the most hazardous in journalism. In the world's many troubled and unstable nations, journalists, both foreign and domestic, are frequently singled out as targets for arrest, beatings, or all too often, assassination. Sometimes they are just in the wrong place at the wrong time.

Algeria, beset by a long and deadly struggle between an authoritarian government and militant Islamic opposition, has proved a dangerous place to practice journalism. As of late 1999, at least 59 journalists, mostly Algerian nationals, have been slain since 1993; 7 in the first half of 1996. It has been estimated that 300 to 400 of the nation's 1,500 journalists have left the country at least temporarily (Peterson, 1996b).

The Committee to Protect Journalists (CJP), which keeps track of such violence worldwide, reported in 1998 that 118 journalists in 25 countries were imprisoned. The largest number, 27, were in Turkey, while China and Ethiopia each had 12 journalists in prison. In March 2000, CJP reported that 34 journalists had been killed in 1999 in these nations: Colombia, 5; Indonesia, 2; Lebanon, 1; Nigeria, 3; Russia, 3; Sierra Leone, 10; Turkey, 1; Sri Lanka, 2; Argentina, 1; East Timor, 2; and Yugoslavia, 6. For the decade of 1989–1998, CJP reported that 472 journalists had been killed doing their jobs. The most dangerous countries for that decade were: Algeria, Colombia, Russia, Tajikistan, Croatia, Bosnia, Philippines, Turkey, Rwanda, and Peru. The website of the Committee (www.cpj.org) does an excellent job of providing current information on the repression of and violence against individual newspersons around the world.

TAMING THE WESTERN PRESS IN ASIA

As part of the trend toward a global economy, western news organizations are not only reporting the news, but distributing their news and advertising in the newly industrializing nations of Asia; however, not without considerable difficulties. For example, in India, the global television services, CNN International and BBC World, have become targets for Indian politicians looking for scapegoats to blame for secessionist movements, religious strife, and even natural disasters. India's own television network, Doordarshan, owned and controlled by the government, is well known for delaying and sanitizing news broadcasts. CNN International and BBC World came to India in 1991 and aggressively reported the razing of the Babri mosque in late 1993 by Hindu fundamentalists, an act that led to national riots in which 1,800 people died. In response, Indian leaders of both the left and the right demanded strong action against the networks. However, when things go in favor of the politicians, they praise foreign coverage. (When CNN International reported the Gulf War to India, it was the first time that vast nation been exposed to independent television news from abroad.)

Southeast Asian governments have created the most problems for British and American publications. Because of the region's phenomenal economic expansion, the foreign press has been paying close attention to business and political developments in Singapore, Malaysia, Hong Kong, Thailand, Taiwan, and South Korea. With increasing frequency, these Asian governments frown on independent news reports that they feel tarnish their national image and thus diminish their attractiveness to foreign investors.

Western publications, including *Time*, *International Herald Tribune*, *Newsweek*, *The Financial Times*, and *The Economist*, all of which carry periodic stories from roving correspondents, have had run-ins with Asian governments. But two business publications, *The Asian Wall Street Journal*, a daily, and *The Far Eastern Economic Review*, a weekly, have had the most difficulty, particularly in Singapore. Why? Because each publication maintains a full-time resident correspondent who reports regularly and in depth about local business and politics in that Asian nation. A series of incidents in recent years indicate that Lee Kuan Yew, longtime ruler of Singapore, who has the local Singapore media firmly under his control, has decided to neutralize the foreign press as well. These actions against the press have paralleled government suppression of domestic political opposition and dissent (Hachten, 1993).

One of Lee's primary weapons against the western media is Singapore's 1986 law permitting the government to cut the circulation of any publication "engaging in local politics." "Engaging in local politics" was interpreted by the authorities to mean any story that displeased Lee and/or the refusal to print in full any letter from government ministries refuting the offending report. Shortly after the law was enacted, *Time* became the first victim; its circulation was cut from 18,000 to 2,000.

In the following years, *The Asian Wall Street Journal*'s 5,000 circulation was reduced to 400 and two Hong Kong-based publications suffered a similar fate—*The Far Eastern Economic Review* reduced from 10,000 to 500 and *Asiaweek* from 9,000 to 500.

Singapore's libel laws, similar to those of the British, have also been used to intimidate western media. The *International Herald Tribune*, which prints an edition in Singapore for Asian distribution, was sued for libel by Lee Kuan Yew, Lee Hsien Loong (Lee's son), and the prime minister, Goh Chok Tong, for an article calling the island-state's succession policies "dynastic politics" rather than the officially espoused "meritocracy." The paper was found guilty and ordered to pay $678,000 in damages.

Some think Singapore's victories may be short-lived. Everette Dennis said, "The Singapore government is fighting a losing battle because the Internet, fax machines and other technologies have already rendered obsolete their ability to control all the information in their country. This is a last gasp. You cannot stop information" (Durocher, 1995, p. 11).

But the capitulation of the IHT, which chose not to appeal, to an authoritarian government for reasons of business expediency rather than fight for free press principles was disturbing. It is one more example of giant media corporations such as ABC, NBC, CNN, and *Business Week* (see chap. 3) showing themselves unwilling to fight for the principles of press freedom. Hong Kong, which returned to the control of Communist China on July 1, 1997, may in time be lost as the major base for western journalists covering Southeast Asia.

In conclusion, as international news and foreign correspondents continue to evolve due to the imperatives of instantaneous communication and financial pressures, there is real danger that our foreign news coverage will lose something important. Dean Peter Krogh of the Georgetown School of Foreign Service, commented:

> Over the past 25 years, the numbers of foreign bureaus and foreign correspondents have declined. Deeply informed individual insight from the field is fast disappearing. News and media services compound the problem by making the news more homogeneous. The media are reduced to establishing a fleeting physical presence only after CNN announces there is a crisis abroad. . . . Yet CNN itself is, by its very nature, flawed. It provides unevaluated and sometimes exaggerated reports of developments abroad which drive a domestic rush to judgment and a correlated reaction. (Geyer, 1996, p. 10)

Krogh added: "As the world gets bigger, the foreign policy agenda simultaneously grows longer. Replacing the set agenda of the Cold War is a veritable avalanche of pressing international issues. Our diplomats and journalists need to inhabit these issues where they reside in a far-flung world" (p. 10).

There still are a number of the traditional foreign correspondents sending in thorough and thoughtful news reports from distant capitals but their influence may well be diminishing.

The American public may not show much interest in distant and exotic places, but the media and the public do become very concerned when American soldiers, sailors and airmen are sent off to those places. How the press covers our wars is discussed in chapter 11.

CHAPTER

11

The Press
and the Military

The first casualty when war comes is truth.

—Sen. Hiram Johnson (1917)

Two recent wars—the 1991 Gulf War and the recent aerial war over Serbia and Kosovo—have dramatically altered the ways that armed conflicts are reported to the American people. Although long-standing frictions and suspicions still persist between the press and military officials, the use of new communications technology have altered the journalism for better or for worse.

In the 42-day Gulf War, television, and especially CNN, turned much of the world into a global community witnessing a televised real-time war as the brief struggle evolved from armed confrontation to spectacular aerial bombardment and finally to lightning ground action. The war became the biggest-running global news story in years, and the telling of it utilized the full resources of the U.S. news media and much of the international news system. More than 1,600 print and broadcast journalists and technicians were on hand to report it.

The NATO bombing campaign against Serbia as its ground forces were mauling Kosovo was a new kind of war: an effort, dominated by U.S. air power, to bomb a nation into submission without deploying ground troops or even incurring casualties. As in the Gulf, the U.S. press accused the military of withholding information and of "spinning" its combat reports for political and strategic reasons. The 78 days of NATO bombing in mid-1999 at last succeeded in forcing Serbian dictator Slobodan Milosevic to yield and permit 16,100 NATO soldiers to chase the fleeing Serbian forces out of Kosovo and to bring relief to the battered ethnic Albanians. In this last war of a bloody century, news coverage was greatly facilitated by satellite communications, particularly the satellite telephone, 24-hour cable news reporting and, for the first time, the Internet.

The Gulf War was a great television show. But this unprecedented news story provoked a bitter controversy among the U.S. press, the White House, and the Pentagon over how the war, any war, was to be reported. In the air war over Yugoslavia, press-military relations were less abrasive because NATO controlled much of the war news and the press corps was more multinational.

The role of the war correspondent has changed greatly because of vastly improved communications technology, more skepticism of and abrasive relations with the military, and a marked increase in the number of reporters covering the same war.

War correspondents are a kind of specialized foreign correspondent— they work abroad under difficult and often dangerous conditions, and are often subject to restraint or censorship, often from their own government's military, not usually from a foreign regime. In both wars, the U.S. press strongly believed that it had been barred from fully covering the war in the traditional ways of the past.

BACKGROUND OF PRESS RESTRICTIONS

How did the acerbic relations between American journalists and the military come to this point? During the two world wars and the Korean conflict, the relationships had been generally good and mutually supportive. In World War I, some 500 American correspondents covered the conflict for newspapers, magazines, and press associations in France, and, unlike British and French reporters, they were free to go to the front lines without military escorts. Still, everything that well-known reporters like Richard Harding Davis, Will Irwin, or Floyd Gibbons wrote was passed through the censorship of the press section of the Military Intelligence Service. Details about specific battles, numbers of casualties, and names of units could be released only after being mentioned in official communiqués.

U.S. military censorship followed the same general pattern in World War II with the added feature of controlling radio broadcasts. The Office of Censorship was headed by Byron Price, an AP editor, who handled with distinction the most difficult part of his job—the direction of voluntary press censorship—that applied to newspapers, magazines, and other printed materials outside the combat zones.

In scattered combat areas, reporters were generally free to move about and join military units, but were always subject to possible censorship. The U.S. Navy long withheld details of the Pearl Harbor disaster and of the sinking of ships in the Pacific, but in most theaters, the news was broadcast promptly. About 500 full-time American reporters were abroad at any one time and provided war coverage that many considered the best and fullest ever seen.

With mobile units and tape recordings, radio coverage greatly increased. Many broadcasts were memorable: Cecil Brown of CBS describing the fall of Singapore; Edward R. Murrow flying over Berlin in a hazardous 1943 bombing raid; George Hicks of ABC broadcasting under German fire from a landing craft on D-Day in Normandy. The best-known U.S. reporter of World War II was Ernie Pyle, a columnist for Scripps-Howard, who attached himself to U.S. combat troops and followed GIs through North Africa, Italy, France, and the Pacific, where he died in battle. Pyle was widely read and beloved by soldiers, the military brass, and the American public. No war correspondent has approached his stature. Relations between the military and correspondents were mutually trusting and supportive. Despite occasional conflicts over withheld information, everyone seemed to be on the same team. During the Korean War, press-government relations were pretty much the same.

The change began in the Vietnam War, when relations between the American journalists and the U.S. military soured and reached their lowest ebb. Reporters and camera crew, working within military guidelines, were given free access without field censorship to roam Vietnam; some called it the best reported war in history. Yet many in the U.S. military believed critical press reporting contributed to the defeat by over-stressing negative aspects, including graphic pictures of dead and wounded, highlighting scandals such as the My Lai massacre, and misinterpreting key events such as the Tet offensive, which the military pronounced a defeat for North Vietnam, not a victory as the press reported. Such reports, the military argued, aided the antiwar movement at home and turned the American public against the war.

The press felt that the U.S. military had misled and lied to them in Vietnam and that officials consistently painted a much rosier picture of the war than the facts justified. Given the record of deception, the press, it was argued, was correct in being skeptical of the military.

A view prevailed within the military that the free rein given journalists in Vietnam led to reporting that seriously damaged morale and turned American public opinion against its own troops. If news or information is a weapon, then, the generals argued, it should be controlled as a part of the war effort.

The brief war between Britain and Argentina over the Falkland Islands in the South Atlantic in 1982 provided a model for the Pentagon on how to manage the media during wartime. Only British reporters were permitted to accompany the task force, and these reporters were apparently carefully selected. The 17 journalists finally accredited had to accept censorship at the source and were given a Ministry of Defense handbook telling them that they would be expected to "help in leading and steadying public opinion in times of national stress or crisis." The Ministry of Defense effectively imposed censorship at the source, and most war information followed a policy of suppression and subtle control of emphasis. Bad news was either not reported or delayed. After the war was over, the British press gave a very different picture of the war, detailing loses, mishaps, and failures previously unreported.

Philip Knightley (1982) wrote:

> Vietnam was an aberration. The freedom given to correspondents to go anywhere, see everything, and write what they liked is not going to be given again. The Falklands was a model of how to make certain that government policy is not undermined by the way a war is reported. The rules turn out to be fairly simple: control access to the fighting, exclude neutral correspondents, censor your own, and muster support both on the field and at home, in the name of patriotism. Objectivity can come back in fashion after the shooting is over. (p. 54)

For America, the war news issue surfaced again on October 25, 1983 when U.S. forces invaded the tiny island of Grenada. The Defense Department barred all reporters from covering the initial invasion. After two days of vigorous protests by the press, a pool of 12 reporters was flown in with a military escort. By the end of one week with the fighting winding down, 150 reporters were ferried to the island and allowed to stay overnight. The press, however, was not mollified. Walter Cronkite said the Reagan Administration had seriously erred, arguing "This is our foreign policy and we have a right to know what is happening, and there can be no excuse in denying the people that right" (Hachten, 1996, p. 154).

But, as in the later Gulf War, public opinion polls showed the American people generally supported the ban on press coverage. Max Frankel of *The New York Times* wrote, "The most astounding thing about the Grenada situation was the quick, facile assumption by some of the public that the press wanted to get in, not to witness the invasion on behalf of the people, but to sabotage it" (Hachten, 1996, p. 155).

As a result of the furor, the Defense Department appointed a commission that recommended a select pool of reporters be allowed to cover the early stages of any surprise operation and share its information with other news organizations. This seemed a fair compromise between the military's need for surprise and the public's need for information.

The new guidelines were first tested in December 1989 when U.S. forces invaded Panama. The press arrangements failed miserably. The Pentagon did not get the 16-reporter pool into Panama until four hours after fighting began, and reporters were not allowed to file stories until six hours later. Most critics blamed the White House for the mix-up and for not insisting that the military facilitate press coverage. When the Gulf War loomed, the American generals, Colin Powell and Norman Schwarzkopf, and other Vietnam veterans, were ready to deal with the press.

AMERICA'S WAR WITH SADDAM HUSSEIN

Global television came into its own as CNN and other broadcasters stationed in Iraq reported a war as it was happening, or as it appeared to be happening. After hostilities began early on January 17, 1991, reporters described anti-aircraft tracers in the night sky of Baghdad and flashes of bomb explosions on the horizon. On succeeding nights, viewers were provided with live video reports from Tel Aviv and Riyadh of Scud missiles, some intercepted by Patriot missiles, exploding against the night sky and television reporters donning gas masks on camera.

The press talked of the "CNN effect"—millions anchored themselves to their television sets hour after hour lest they miss the latest dramatic developments. Restaurants, movies, hotels, and gaming establishments all suffered business losses. Ratings for CNN soared 5 to 10 times their pre-war levels.

The Gulf War was a worldwide media event of astonishing proportions. Global television never had a larger or more interested audience for such a sustained period of time. Television became the first principal source of news for most people as well as a major source of military and political intelligence for both sides. CNN telecasts, including military briefings, were viewed in Baghdad as they were being received in Riyadh or Washington, DC—as well as in other non-Western countries.

The combatants, particularly the governments of Iraq and the United States, tried to control and manipulate the media with subtle and not-so-subtle propaganda and misinformation messages. Western journalists chafed at the restraints on news coverage of the war itself and complained that there was news they were not permitted to report. Most coalition news came from military briefings and from carefully controlled and escorted pools of reporters. Some official news released at the briefings was actually disinformation intended to mislead the enemy, not inform the public. For example, viewers were led to believe that Patriot missiles were invariably successful in neutralizing Scud missiles; such was not the case.

Information on the war was tightly controlled on television; one observer called it "the illusion of news." For their own self-defined security reasons, the military often held back or distorted the news they did release. In the opening days of the war, much was made of the smart bombs, which allegedly hit their targets with about 90% accuracy. After the war, the U.S. Air Force admitted that smart bombs made up only 7% of all U.S. explosives dropped on Iraq and Kuwait. Television scenes, many of them realistic computer-generated recreations, of precision-guided bombs going down chimneys or through the doors of targets, notwithstanding, the Air Force later said 70% of the 88,500 tons of bombs dropped on Kuwait and Iraq missed their targets (Wicker, 1991).

Peter Jennings of ABC News reminded viewers that much of what was revealed in the opening days of the war was speculation, mixed with some hard facts and some rumors in the rushing river of information. But whether they were getting hard news or not, millions of viewers stayed by their television sets, if only to find out what would happen next. Public opinion polls showed that the overwhelming majority of Americans supported both the war and the military's efforts to control the news; further, some favored more controls on press reporting. A *Los Angeles Times Mirror* poll found that 50% of the respondents considered themselves obsessed with war news, and nearly 80% felt the military was "telling as much as it can." About the same proportion thought that military censorship may be "a good idea."

But after the war, many in the American press felt that the traditional right of U.S. reporters to accompany their combat forces and report news of war had been severely circumscribed. Michael Getler of *The Washington Post* wrote: "The Pentagon and U.S. Army Central Command conducted what is probably the most thorough and consistent wartime control of American reporters in modern times—a set of restrictions that in its totality and mindset seems to go beyond World War II, Korea and Vietnam" (Getler, 1991, p. 24).

President George Bush and the Pentagon followed a deliberate policy of keeping negative and unflattering news from the U.S. public lest it weaken support for the war. Long after the conflict the public learned that some Iraqi soldiers had been buried alive in trenches by U.S. plows and earthmovers and that the military had waited months to tell the families of 33 dead servicemen that their loved ones had been killed by friendly fire. Not until a year after the war did we learn that key weapons like the stealth bomber and the cruise missile had struck only about half of their targets, compared to the 85% to 90% rate claimed by the Pentagon at the time.

American casualties were reported, but there were few pictures of dead and wounded. Details of tactical failures and mishaps in the bombing campaign were not released, nor was the information that at least 24 female soldiers had been raped or sexually assaulted by American servicemen.

The older generation of military leaders felt strongly, despite evidence to the contrary, that unrestricted and critical press coverage in Vietnam had contributed to the U.S. defeat there. They were determined it would not happen again. Some journalists blamed their own top editors and news executives for agreeing to the field censorship and pool arrangements ahead of time instead of vigorously opposing them.

REPORTING THE SHOOTING WAR

All this was a prelude to the shooting war that started just as the evening news programs were beginning at 6:30 p.m. Eastern Standard Time (January 16 in the United States, January 17 in the Middle East). The networks and CNN interrupted their prepared news shows to report that aerial bombing had begun in Baghdad. Then followed one of most memorable nights in television history: the opening phases of a major conflict reported in real time—as it actually happened—by reporters in Iraq, Saudi Arabia, and Washington.

CNN stole the show that night as three CNN correspondents, John Holliman, Peter Arnett, and Bernard Shaw, gave vivid eyewitness descriptions of the U.S. air attack from the windows of their Baghdad hotel room. As in old-time radio, reporters relied on words, not video, that first night. Other networks reported the fireworks, but CNN with its previously arranged leased lines stayed on the longest after the lines were cut for the other networks. Next day, General Colin Powell jokingly said the Pentagon was relying on CNN for military information.

The second night of the war gave prime-time viewers another long, absorbing evening as CNN and NBC television reporters in Tel Aviv reported live as Scud missiles landed. Reporters, often with gas masks on, put out raw and unevaluated information. At one point, NBC reported (erroneously) that nerve gas had been detected in one Scud attack. Tom Brokaw decried the situation for some minutes, but after the report proved false, NBC apologized. Networks expanded to near 24-hour coverage for the first 36 hours of fighting, and even the daytime soap operas were preempted briefly. There was not much to report at that point, and the same facts, theories, and speculations were repeated again and again. Nevertheless, the mesmerized public stayed tuned.

During this early bombing phase of the war, the Pentagon placed restrictions on interviews with troops and returning pilots. Reporters could go into the field only in designated pools. (One reporter likened a press pool to group of senior citizens on a conducted tour.) All interviews with soldiers were subject to censorship before they could be released.

Most information came from the daily briefings held by military spokesmen in both Riyadh and at the Pentagon but much of this information was rather general, vague, and deliberately incomplete. The military had coherent arguments for its restrictive policies. Destroying Iraq's military command and communications capability was a high priority of the bombing strategy, and it was important to withhold useful information, via the media, that would reveal troop movements and intentions of coalition forces. Keeping Iraq's forces off-balance and without reliable information was a key part of U.S. strategy.

However, some news executives and critics claimed the press restrictions went well beyond security concerns and were aimed at both preventing politically damaging disclosures by soldiers and shielding the American public from seeing the brutal aspects of war. If the war had been unsuccessful, the press would have had difficulty reporting the negative aspects. With more than 1,600 reporters in the theater only about 100 could be accommodated by the pools to report news about the 500,000 American force. As the ground war neared, the large press corps became increasingly restive and frustrated at this lack of access.

The response of some reporters was to "freelance"—to avoid the pools and go off on their own. Malcolm Browne (1991) reported, "Some reporters were hiding out in American Marine or Army field units, given G.I. uniforms and gear to look inconspicuous, enjoying the affection (and protection of the units) they're trying to cover—concealed by the officers and troops from the handful of press-hating commanders who strive to keep the battle field free of wandering journalists" (p. 45).

Browne noted that nearly all reporters who tried to reach frontline U.S. troops were arrested at one time or another (including reporters for *The New York Times*, *The Washington Post*, AP, and Cox newspapers) and sometimes held in field jails for up to 12 hours and threatened with revocation of their press credentials. After the ground war began, these freelancers, particularly John Kifner and Chris Hedges of the *Times*, produced some outstanding reports. Forrest Sawyer of ABC News, who traveled unofficially with Saudi forces, provided some of the earliest and best reports on the freeing of Kuwait City. Had the ground war been longer, more heavily contested, and taken a higher toll in U.S. casualties, relations between the military and the freelancing journalists probably would have turned quite acrimonious. But these journalists felt they were doing what they were supposed to do in time of war—maintaining the flow of information that Americans need to know when 500,000 of their countrymen are at risk in a foreign war.

TRIUMPH OF 24-HOUR
GLOBAL NEWS

During the American Civil War in 1861-1865, the demand for news was so great that U.S. newspapers went to seven-day publication. During the 1963 Kennedy assassination, live television emerged as the preeminent medium for reporting breaking news. Such events positioned ABC, CBS, and NBC as major news gatherers but still essentially American media.

During the 42-day Gulf War, CNN established the importance of a 24-hour news network with true global reach. The concept has changed the international news system—at least during times of international crisis and conflict.

The three major U.S. networks were shaken by CNN's success. After CNN's historic scoop on the first night of the war, a number of independent television stations, radio stations, and even several network affiliates relied on CNN in the crisis. Although the three networks had more talented and experienced reporters, they could not compete with CNN either in time on the air or the vast audiences CNN reached in about 100 countries. The success of CNN has encouraged similar services such as BBC's World television, but it remains to be seen how well any 24-hour global news network will do financially during quieter periods when interest in foreign or war news is low.

The Gulf War conditioned viewers everywhere to keep their television sets tuned to CNN (or its future imitators) during times of high crisis. Perhaps the news today places too much emphasis on immediate and fast-breaking news "as it happens." Video shots of F15s roaring off runways, of smart bombs scoring direct hits, of Tomahawk missiles flying through Baghdad, and tank formations rolling through the desert made memorable viewing. Yet after the fog of war had cleared, the press and the public found that the Gulf War had not been quite what they thought it had been.

LESSONS FOR THE PRESS

Wars between nations are major international news stories and should be reported by the press as completely and thoroughly as conditions permit. The American public may be blasé about much foreign news, but it pays close attention when its armed forces go to war and American lives are at risk. Yet governments at war, even the most democratic, will try to control and manipulate war news to their own strategic advantage. The Gulf War provided ample reminders of this generalization. Censorship and propaganda, the twin arms of political warfare, are integral components of modern warfare. Both sides often deny the press the opportunity to report what has occurred objectively.

In the Gulf War, hundreds of journalists were in the war theater, but were allowed little freedom to cover the actual fighting. On the Iraqi side, the few foreign reporters in Baghdad were severely restricted. From all indications, both the U.S. military and the Bush Administration were pleased with the results of their media policy and would do the same thing again. But among the press, the general conclusion was that the press had been unduly and even illegally denied access to information about the war.

Five years later, much of the official version of the Gulf War was beginning to unravel, and it became clear that the war was a lot messier and less well managed than the Pentagon would have the public believe. Further, there were considerable doubts as to whether the Pentagon actually was unaware of U.S. soldiers' exposure to chemical weapons.

After the war, a report calling military restrictions in the Gulf War "real censorship" that confirmed "the worst fears of reporters in a democracy" was delivered to Defense Secretary Dick Cheney. DeParle (1991) reported it was signed by 17 news executives representing the four networks, AP, UPI, and major newspapers, and news magazines. The report bitterly complained that the restrictions placed on reporters by the Pentagon were intended to promote a sanitized view of the war. The war was called the first in this century to restrict all official coverage to pools. "By controlling what reporters saw and when they saw it, the military exerted great power to shape and manage the news," the report said. Also criticized were the use of military escorts and "unwarranted delays in transmitting copy" (p. 4A).

After eight months of talks with news executives, in May 1992 the Pentagon issued a set of principles intended to guarantee that journalists have greater access to future military operations than they had in the Gulf War. However, news media and the government could not agree on whether there should be any official security review of news reports before publication or broadcast. The statement affirmed that "open and independent reporting will be the principal means of coverage of U.S. military operations. The guidelines limited the role of military escorts and said that 'press pools' are not to serve as the standard means of covering operations" (Hachten, 1996, p. 151).

MARINES' INCURSION INTO SOMALIA

The incursion of U.S. Marines into Somalia in December 1992 was intended to provide military protection to the relief organizations trying to feed starving Somalis caught in the crossfire of warring clans. Under these conditions, the Pentagon decided not to place any restraints on the media. Kurtz (1993) called what happened the most embarrassing moment ever in media-military relations:

The infamous night in December 1992 when Navy SEALS hitting the beach in Somalia were surrounded by a small army of reporters and photographers who blinded them with television lights, clamored for interviews, and generally acted like obnoxious adolescents. That sorry performance, turning a humanitarian mission to aid starving Africans into a Fellini-esque photo op, underscored what the Pentagon had been saying for years: that the press simply could not discipline itself, that reporters would blithely endanger the safety of American troops for the sake of journalistic drama. (p. 215)

It was not one of the media's finer days.

David Hackworth (1992) of *Newsweek* wrote, "to lurch from thought control to no control is plain stupid. When the press corps beats the Marine Corps to the beach, everyone loses" (p. 33). The Pentagon wanted full coverage of Somalia so no controls were placed on the press, and what resulted was a confused circus. There are those, however, who suspect that the Pentagon deliberately orchestrated the fiasco to make the media look bad.

The situation in Somalia raised the question of whether the media, by its heavy barrage of pictures and stories of starving Somalis, pushed President Bush to send troops on their humanitarian mission. The answer is unclear, but Bush did react by committing U.S. armed forces to a limited and supposedly doable assignment of famine relief. (On the other hand, despite horrific pictures of death, destruction, and "ethnic cleansing" from Bosnia, the United States refused for many months to get involved militarily.)

When the Somalia assignment expanded in the early Clinton Administration to include warlord hunting, it provoked a devastating firefight in the streets of Mogadishu. When 18 U.S. soldiers were killed and the pictures shown on U.S. television, the American public was unprepared to accept casualties when vital U.S. interests were not at stake. The White House soon announced the U.S. was getting out of Somalia. So it was said that television pictures got the Marines into Somalia and more pictures got them abruptly out.

James Hoge, editor of *Foreign Affairs*, commented:

From its understanding of Vietnam came the military's subsequent emphasis on quick solutions, limited media access and selective release of smart weapons imagery. The public, however, will not remain dazzled when interventions become difficult. As in Vietnam, public attitudes ultimately hinge on questions about the rightness, purpose and costs of policy—not television images. (Hoge, 1994, p. 139)

The "peaceful" landing in Haiti in September 1994 provided more perspective on military and media relations. When it appeared that a full-scale military invasion to oust the military rulers would take place, U.S. media were planning the most minutely documented war coverage ever. Several hundred reporters and photographers from television networks, newspapers, and magazines were already in Haiti, with the most advanced equipment ever brought to a war zone. The Pentagon had promised more cooperation than ever, and journalists said they would not be relying on the military for primary access.

However, White House and Pentagon officials, in a meeting with television representatives, asked for a broadcast blackout of eight hours. The Clinton Administration also wanted to restrict reporters to their hotels until military commanders gave them permission to go to the fighting. In this case, a press and military showdown was avoided when U.S. forces landed without incident in Haiti.

Nor were there any frictions between press and military in Bosnia when NATO imposed a military truce and thousands of U.S. and NATO peacekeeping troops occupied that troubled land in late 1995. There the Pentagon policy was to encourage friendly relations with reporters and broadcasters. GIs carried a 16-page guide to Bosnia with a section devoted to "Meeting the Media," which instructed a soldier that he or she "can be an excellent unofficial spokesperson."

NATO'S AERIAL WAR AGAINST YUGOSLAVIA

After NATO bombs started falling on Serbia and Kosovo in 1999, military relations with the press deteriorated abruptly. Critics said the lack of detailed after-action reports—routinely provided in past conflicts—had made it impossible to assess NATO's claims that they were steadily dismantling Milosevic's war-making powers. At both the Pentagon and at NATO headquarters in Brussels, spokespersons stubbornly refused to provide specific information about bombing sorties. These policies were considered even less forthcoming than in the Gulf War, which the press had considered overly restrictive. Of course, NATO had its reasons: the need to hold the somewhat reluctant NATO alliance together and the need to retain the support of American public opinion for the military action. But most journalists covering the war were highly critical.

Yet, the war was reported and, in some basic ways, differently than any previous battlefield coverage. After being forced to watch 78 days of bombing through the lenses of official video cameras, some 2,700 journalists had a chance to see for themselves when NATO troops rolled into Kosovo in June. Even though military censors blocked specific information, satellite communications enabled reporters from Brussels to Kukes, Albania, and other points, to triangulate information more easily than in previous conflicts.

The multinational nature of the war also facilitated coverage. Disagreements among the NATO allies produced self-serving leaks from various capitals as did the differences in the United States over the need for ground troops as well as the effectiveness of the bombings. News filtered in from many sources.

According to editors, the key device for putting together information into coherent stories was the satellite telephone and, more broadly, satellite communications. Just as CNN's 24-hour cable TV service first caught on in the Gulf War, the satellite uplink was the information medium for the air war. "Instantaneous communication has changed things," said Andrew Rosenthal, foreign editor of *The New York Times*. "The ability of a reporter on the Macedonian border to call a reporter on the Albanian border or to call a reporter in Brussels or Washington instantly made a huge difference. Newspapers were able to put together groups of reporters to do joint efforts in a way that was previously impossible," he said (Barringer, 1999, p. C16).

For television, the same satellite technology allowed a profusion of images to be transmitted at great speed. When the vivid images were of the fate of Kosovar refugees or fleeing Serbian troops, the emotional impact of television was great indeed. Some thought such reportage helped justify the humanitarian aspects of the hostilities and convinced otherwise dubious viewers to support the NATO effort.

Because of NATO involvement, there were more reporters than ever covering all sides of the war. Even though Serbia expelled most Western reporters, enough journalists managed to get back in and report on both bomb damage and ethnic strife, even while operating under Serb restraints.

The expanded role for the Internet and cable television news meant there were far more outlets for instantaneous reporting and analysis. CNN, MSNBC, and Fox News Channel also offered loud and compelling debates about the conflict, even though much of it was discounted by critics as lacking in serious depth and context. For the first time, the Internet was a player in war reporting, providing a plethora of Web sites presenting war issues and some information from diverse angles: Serb, Albanian, Republican, Democratic, and ranging from the depth of BBC to the fervid nationalism of Belgrade news outlets. Also, several of the online versions of the *New York Times, Washington Post, Wall Street Journal, San Jose Mercury News*, and others used the Internet to provide fuller and more documentary coverage of the war between publication of their print editions.

As a result, some observers thought that the sum total of these trends amounted to sharper, speedier coverage. David Halberstam said, "Despite all the restrictions and just God-awful limitations and dangers, there were enough different people in different places to give you the dimensions you needed" (Barringer, 1999, p. C1).

Even though CNN had more competition this time—BBC World, MSNBC, Fox—than in the Gulf War, the Atlanta cable network emerged from the Yugoslav conflict in a much enhanced *international* role for its news dissemination as a global 24-hour cable news channel. During the Gulf War, some 10 million households outside the United States had access to CNN. In the Yugoslav conflict, that number jumped to 150 million households. Its subsidiary, CNN International, has become a truly international news channel and its staff reflects that diversity. CNNI has split its programming into four international networks: one for Europe, Middle East, and Africa; one for Asia; one for Central and South America; and one for the United States (available at nights and weekends for those who get CNNfn, its business channel. There are also ancillary networks, including a Spanish-language network for Latin America.

The air war in Yugoslavia demonstrated that the democracies of America and NATO are still unwilling to be candid and forthcoming with reliable information to their own peoples when engaged in hostile actions against other states. As in the Gulf War, the Pentagon gave misleading and exaggerated accounts of the effectiveness of the aerial campaign over Kosovo. Joint Chiefs Chairman Gen. Henry Shelton claimed that NATO's air forces had killed "around 120 tanks," "about 220 armored personnel carriers," and "up to 450 artillery and mortar pieces." But months later, *Newsweek*, quoting a suppressed Air Force report, reported on May 15, 2000, that the number of targets verifiably destroyed was a tiny fraction of those claimed: 14 tanks, not 120; 18 personnel carriers, not 220; and 20 artillery pieces, not 450. Out of the 744 "confirmed" strikes by NATO pilots during the war, the Air Force investigators later found evidence of just 58.

Yet, despite such deceptions, the events surrounding the air war also showed that today's news organizations can still get much of the news out if they pursue the story with vigor and imagination and make full use of the varied tools of communications technology. Unlike the Gulf War, which most Americans supported enthusiastically, the air war, with its heavy damage to Serbia and the loss of civilian lives, was viewed by most as a necessary but unsavory business for American forces to be involved in. Most could not see how the bombs were saving the lives of ethnic Albanians as Serbs seem undeterred in killing and driving Kosovars out of the country. At the end of hostilities, the American public was relieved that no American lives had been lost, but there was no sense of victory comparable to the euphoria after the Gulf War ended.

All too often, though, in recent times, the U.S. press has been inhibited or even barred from fully covering wars that it has historically and traditionally reported. So far, there are no real indications that the White House and Congress will modify those policies. This is important because the U.S. Supreme Court has ruled that the press, in order to inform the public, has a First Amendment right to be in those places that "historically" and "traditionally" it has had the right to cover such as trials and town meetings.

The Supreme Court has also ruled that the press has a First Amendment right to be present at all "public" events. Certainly an invasion by American forces lasting more than several hours or a full-scale war is a public event.

The press has no right to report sensitive military information that could aid an enemy and would not want to do so, but it does have a right to be there, to keep a watchful eye on the military just as it does at a criminal trial. No modern war has been fought as quickly and effectively and with as few allied casualties as by the American-led forces in the Gulf War and in Yugoslavia, although we know now that much unflattering and negative news was kept from the public.

And when wars are unsuccessful, as they often are, with incompetent leadership, confused tactics, and unnecessary casualties, it is essential that the press, as independent representatives of the public and of the soldiers, be there to report what has occurred. The citizens of Iraq had no independent press reporting to them about the military disasters and political incompetence that led to the battlefield deaths of thousands of their young men—a basic difference between a democracy and a dictatorship.

The Supreme Court is unlikely to come to the defense of the U.S. press in this matter. Perhaps the best hope of the press is to protest and complain until a significant portion of the public supports their right to know. In the Gulf War, the U.S. news media and their owners did not complain loudly and vehemently enough about the pool and censorship restrictions before the bombs started dropping. Nor has the press expressed much concern about NATO's news restrictions. A sitting president like George Bush or Bill Clinton is not likely to modify such restrictions of free expression in wartime until forced to by political pressure.

Ironically, the greatly expanded capability of global television to report instantly on a modern war provides another rationale for governments to control and censor war news. Yet when American or European journalists are denied access to war news, the rest of the world is denied access as well.

CHAPTER

12

News on the Internet

Like some raging computer virus, the Net seems to be devouring the media culture, shattering the usual definitions of news and eclipsing more traditional subjects. The so-called old media are invading this brave new world with near-revolutionary fervor, fueling a growth industry that might be called e-news.

—Howard Kurtz, 1999

The news media are rapidly becoming involved with the Internet; so rapidly in fact that what is stated here may be largely outdated by the time this book is published. News on the Internet is a moving target and we can only offer a snap shot of this bird on the wing. Everything about the Internet and the World Wide Web, it's been said, is about the future—and the future has been arriving faster than anyone predicted.

The relevance of the Internet for journalism and the news business is perhaps apparent. Publishers, broadcasters, and journalists were "early adopters" of this explosive information revolution. However, neither they, nor anyone else, seem to know just where this brave new world of communication is headed. (A few years ago, few had even foreseen the potential of the Internet itself.)

No consensus exists as to how journalism will be changed by the Internet, but no one doubts that change is coming—and fast. The future of cyberspace itself is murky and yet exciting. Newspaper publishers and other media managers worry about how they can fit into the changing scene and still prosper. Concerned journalists wonder as well how the traditional values and standards of good journalism can survive in the turbulent world of the Internet.

A newspaper is a business enterprise and must survive in the marketplace. At a time when some publishers are downsizing staffs and trimming costs to increase profitability, many other newspapers (and broadcasters) are investing heavily in the new electronic or interactive journalism. Although no one seems to know when they will make real money on the Web, the Internet multimedia information retrieval system is on the verge of becoming a mass news medium itself.

In 1994, there were 20 newspapers online; by mid -1999, there were 4,925 worldwide, 2,799 of them in the United States. The numbers will only go up and the Web sites will carry more and more news and information. The media conglomerates as well as cable and network broadcasters are in hot competition with print media for the proliferating Internet viewers.

In late 1999, the 10 most popular Web sites for news, based on the number of "unique visitors" as (contrasted with "repeat viewers") they attracted in that December were:

Web site	Visitors
MSNBC.com	6,674,000
CNN.com	4,468,000
ABCNEWS.com	3,231,000
USATODAY.com	2,278,000
NYTIMES.com	1,841,000
Washingtonpost.com	1,653,000
BBC.CO.UK.com	1,037,000
LATIMES.com	948,000
Foxnews.com	834,000
APBnews.com	815,000

("Eye ball magnets," 2000, p. 29)

In its April 2000 issue, *Brill's Content* rated the following Web sites as the best for news: 1. *MSNBC.com*, 2. *CNN.com*, 3. *New York Times (nyt.com)*, 4. *Washingtonpost.com*, 5. *APBNEWS.com*, 6. *Slate.com*, and 7. The Obscure Store and Reading Room *(obscurestore.com)*

PROFITS AND LOSSES

For the news media, two basic uncertainties persist about interactive journalism:

First, will the public pay for electronic news on a medium where information, after a basic user's fee, is free? Second, will advertising displayed on web pages "sell" and lead to profitable results on such an anarchic medium?

Hence, the press' rush to online services can be seen as driven by both fear and greed. The fear comes from the threat to the newspapers' advertising base, especially classified advertisements, from the computer's point-and-click technology and the ease of getting answers quickly, complete with pictures and sound from great amounts of electronic information. Greed is stimulated by the possibility of large sums to be made when a profitable "model" is developed that counts and categorizes every visitor to a Web site. Internet publishing could then be a profitable marriage of newspapers' advertising bases with franchise strengths. Publishers also hope to attract the younger Internet users who no longer read newspapers.

Internet journalism has been producing a lot of red ink but recently there have been signs that a small but diverse range of journalistic sites have begun to turn a profit or are near to it. But most sites still lose money and no business model has emerged that so far seems to offer a key to success. Success may depend on a combination of approaches: banner and classified advertising, as well as subscriptions for niche publications and electronic commerce.

But in the meantime, some big newspaper companies have made a comeback on Wall Street in part because so many Internet ventures—all those new "dot coms"—have spent lavishly on advertising in the "old media" to make their brand names better known.

For those who just want to read *about* journalism and the media on the Internet, *Brill's Content* recommended the following sites: 1. Romenesko's Media News *(poynter.org/mediagossip.)*; 2. Arts and Letters Daily *(cybereditions.com/aldaily)*; 3. Salon Media *(salon.com/media)*; 4. Online Journalism Review *(ojr.org)*; 5. Feed Daily *(feedmag.com)*; and 6. *Slate.com*. ("Best of Web," 2000, p. 68)

RAPIDLY EXPANDING USE OF INTERNET

So far, the numbers of potential users of interactive news media are still small compared with total newspaper readership but the numbers are growing fast. Kohut (2000) reported that numerous recent polls have shown the public's appetite for Internet news and information is growing exponentially. At the end of 1999, half of the American public had access to the Internet, up from about 40% a year before and from 23% just three years ago. About two in three of those people say they go on line for news at least once a week. About 12% say they read the news online every day. (Only 6% reported doing so in April 1998.)

For many Americans, these news sites have become primary sources of information. Eleven percent of adults said in an October 1999 survey that they mostly rely on the Internet for national and international news. (That figure was 6% the previous January.) The findings are more impressive among key demographic groups. Among college graduates, under 50, Kohut found that 23% said they principally depend on the Internet for national and international news, rivaling the percentage who said this about network TV news (26%), radio (27%), and local TV (21%). Only cable news (32%) and newspapers (46%) scored better in this important demographic category. (Kohut, 2000). So for that influential segment, the Internet is already a mass medium.

Now the downside. There is some evidence that the Internet may not be a great boon to civic engagement. These surveys show people use the Internet for information that interests them rather than to seek out general enlightenment. Thirty-eight percent go online for updates on stock quotes and sports scores, 41% to follow up on news they had heard about that interests them, and 44% are motivated by the ability to search the news for a particular topic. Considerably fewer (29%) say they go on for general news updates or to keep informed about the day's events. Kohut cautions that trends may be slow to emerge because the news habits of Internet newcomers evolve slowly. It takes time for people to understand how to use the Internet to suit their needs. And at any given time there are a lot of newcomers trying to work it out (Kohut, 2000).

Another study, done at Stanford, found that the Internet is leading to a rapid shift away from the "old" mass media. The study reported that 60% of regular Internet users said they reduced their television viewing, and one third said they spent less time reading newspapers. The study found that 55% of Americans have access to the Internet and of these, 36% said they were online five hours a week. Overall, the study found the Internet is causing many Americans to spend less time with family and friends, less time shopping in stores, and more time working at home after hours, thus creating a broad new wave of social isolation in the United States, raising the specter of an atomized world without human contact or emotion. Similar concerns were expressed when television first became pervasive (Markoff, 2000).

THE INTERNET
AS THE NEXT MASS MEDIUM?

The Associated Press announced in 1995 that it would adopt the WWW to begin distributing its news articles and photographs over the global Internet. In so doing, AP followed other old-line media organizations onto the Web. In January 2000, the AP began distributing the work of Cnet News.com , a four-year-old Internet site as part of the AP's overall offering of financial news. The deal with Cnet Inc., which specializes in coverage of the Internet and related industries, is the AP's first with a non-traditional news organization and provides another validation of Internet journalism.

AP's great rival, Reuters, is also moving onto the Internet. In February 2000, the Reuters Group said it planned to reposition itself as a high-flying Internet concern. Reuters plans to invest $802 million in the next four years to shift its content delivery systems to the Internet, including the creation of a Reuters-branded World Wide Web portal that will compete directly with the sites that now license content from the company. Word of the plans caused shares of Reuters to soar 23%, their biggest one-day gain in more than a year.

The Web incorporates many elements of various print and electronic media that have preceded it; computers can be used to send and receive text, sound, still images, and video clips. Yet for all its versatility, the Web is not expected to replace its media predecessors but to take a place alongside them as a social, cultural, and economic force in its own right. The history of mass communication has taught us that new media do not replace old media, but instead supplement and complement them; radio did not replace newspapers and television did not replace radio.

The Web's complementary role is already evident: Along with the steadily increasing numbers of newspapers and magazines with Web sites, many radio stations and all the major television networks have Web sites, publicizing and providing additional information about their programs and performers. One of the big players is NBC, which with its partner, Microsoft, puts out the top-rated Msnbc.com site—an elaborate online version of MSNBC, its 24-hour cable news channel. So NBC's various news outlets—NBC Evening with Tom Brokaw, the *Today Show* on broadcast TV, MSNBC and CNBC on cable, and Msnbc.com online—all share content as well as anchors and reporters and mutually publicize and promote each other.

Another recent trend is for the media to provide "portals" rather than just Web sites for their online publications. When the *Boston Globe* created *Boston.com* in 1995, it did more than create a Web site for the paper, it started a regional online site and invited all other Boston media to become a part of it. A "portal" becomes a starting point for computer users when they surf and it guides them to a wide variety of services. (Portals are not new; *Yahoo* and *Lycos* are well- known examples.) Recently, the online sites for Dow Jones & Co., New York Times Co., Washington Post Co., and Knight-Ridder have all announced intentions to establish portals.

The idea is that if a portal offers enough services in a single place, its online audience will grow, convincing advertisers to buy more space. The strategy is that the newspaper would be the first stop on everyone's electronic journey into a metropolitan area. The shift to portals suggests a change in news media strategy: To be successful, online newspapers must be more than merely newspapers online.

The British press is moving in the same direction. In London, the *Financial Times* announced in late 1999 that its Web site would be reinvented as a full Internet portal, featuring a search engine for business readers, diary and e-mail capabilities and expanded use of columnists and analysts to provide an early look into the paper's thinking. Changes were planned too in the newsroom: The ideological barrier between online news and the printed page will be erased and in its place will be a redesigned, integrated newsroom where journalists will work to feed both the Web site and the newspaper.

NEW JOURNALISM CAREERS ONLINE

Interactive journalism is already developing a new generation of young journalists who are attracted to online jobs for the money, opportunity, excitement, and a way to avoid unpaid internships and small-town news-paper jobs. The *Chicago Tribune*, for example, has a staff of 20 who work exclusively for the Internet edition—writing stories, taking pictures, using video cameras, and even creating digital pages.

Many of today's journalism graduates are heading for such jobs because that is where the opportunities are. Michael Hoeferlin, placement director at the University of Missouri's journalism school, said, "Online publications are generating more jobs at higher salaries than we have seen for a long time" (Jacobson, 1996, p. C7). Geoffrey Cowan, dean of the Annenberg School of Communication at the University of Southern California, estimated that 10% of journalists who graduated in June 1999 went to Internet concerns. And he added, "The dot.coms are paying in the high 40's and low 50's, whereas the print media are paying their journalists in the low-20's" (Barringer & Kuczynski, 2000).

The young people entering the uncertain world of digital journalism now are the ones who will bring about the great changes later. The older generation of journalists who wonder whether it is really journalism have been much slower to recognize the changes that are coming. However, there has been a clear trend for a good number of print journalists to move over to jobs on the Internet. Exact numbers are hard to come by but the peak has not yet been reached. One of the lures are the possible stock options that net journalists might receive.

Such reporters are in great demand often because of their expertise with computers and the Internet that they have learned on their jobs. Simon (1999) commented:

> Sometimes we fail to appreciate the pace at which technology has been changing our jobs. Think for a moment: palm-sized computers provide features useful to news gathering that were not available on the most powerful laptops just five years ago. With a well-organized laptop and a good Internet connection, a reporter in virtually any part of the world has access to the same information—whether from his own archived files or another database—as someone in the newsroom. With digital cameras, photographers file their shots through e-mail so quickly that an editor can look at the image and, before the event is over, call back on a cell phone to request a different angle. It is in computer-assisted reporting where the real revolution is taking place, not only on the big analytical projects but also in nuts-and-bolts reporting. New tools and techniques have made it possible to for journalists to dig up vital information on deadline, to quickly add depth and context. (Simon, 2000, p. 19)

Without question, print journalists have been benefitting immensely from the Internet. A 1999 survey of managing editors and business editors found that 73% said they went online at least once a day, compared with 48% in 1998. In 1994, only 17% went online daily. The study also found changing trends on how print journalists use the Internet. In 1999, the most popular use was research, displacing e-mail, although both were up from 1998. Ninety percent of respondents used the net to research articles or as a research source, up from 74% in 1998. Some 83% used e-mail, up from 80% in 1998. Half of the respondents used the Internet to search for ideas for articles, up from 30% in 1998 (Fass, 2000).

WHAT ABOUT THE INFORMATION UNDERCLASS?

Interactive journalism is just one aspect of what has been called the information revolution and the information superhighway. One nagging question has been: Who will participate in this revolution and who will be left behind? From a global perspective, the information revolution has been mainly in the United States, Japan, Western Europe, and other industrialized nations. These information societies, mostly in the rich, industrialized north, are further widening the gap between themselves and less developed nations. A highly industrialized nation like Sweden can utilize any new technological innovation much faster or more completely than, say, Pakistan or Nigeria, hence resentments by developing nations over information inequities persist and are exacerbated. Poorer nations want the new media, but lack the economic and social infrastructures to utilize and sustain them.

Only 12 or so of Africa's 54 countries are linked to the Internet and international experts warn that unless Africa gets online quickly, what is already the poorest continent risks ever greater marginalization. "Everyone realizes that Africa is lagging, that it is the only part of the world that does not have network connectivity," said Lawrence Lanweber, president of the Internet Society, which aims to promote the network's development. "Latin America and all but a very few Asian nations are on the Internet. But then you look at the map of Africa and you see huge gaps all over that will prevent this continent from participating in so many aspects of life on this planet as it is developing" (French, 1995, p. A8).

CHALLENGES TO PRESS FREEDOM

On its 21st birthday in 1996, the personal computer's potential as a medium for ideas, information, and news flowing freely around the globe was being recognized. At the same time, the virtual press was already facing serious legal challenges over what could and could not be transmitted over computer networks. Legal restrictions, imposed here or abroad, could very well prevent the personal computer from reaching its full potential.

The sweeping communications bill passed by Congress in February 1996 banned pornography over computer networks and set penalties for those convicted of distributing indecent material to minors. Civil liberties groups quickly vowed a court battle over the provisions that would block the free flow of material, even smut, over computer networks.

Congressional committees debating the communications bill rejected the idea that the Internet is the electronic equivalent of the printing press, thus enjoying the full free speech protections of the First Amendment. Instead, Congress opted to regard the Internet as a broadcast medium, subject to Government regulation and eligible for only some of the Constitutional rights given to newspapers.

The irony is that the same words, printed on ink and paper, are fully protected by the First Amendment, but once those words go on the Internet and become bits traveling in packets over wires and fibers, they lose their protection. But the protection returns when the words are reprinted on paper.

The potential erosion of free speech is due in part to sincere efforts to protect children from pornography being transmitted over the Internet. Despite the existence of current laws punishing those who make and distribute child pornography in any medium, some saw the opportunity in this new medium to banish words and images that heretofore had been considered indecent but not illegal expression.

At about the same time, CompuServe voluntarily denied its 4 million subscribers access to over 200 newsgroups, because a prosecutor in Germany found them offensive and had threatened legal action. Many technologies already exist to let parents restrict areas of the Internet and online services that children can visit. But these are only partial solutions. Some advocates of the Internet fear the possibility that this freest and most open of all media may be restricted to carrying ideas and information only suitable for children. It may be years and many hard-fought legal battles before guidelines defining legal protections for the Internet are firmly established.

However, a major advance for free speech occurred in June 1997 when the U.S. Supreme Court declared unconstitutional the Communications Decency Act, which made it a crime to send or display "indecent" material online in a way available to minors. The unanimous decision was the court's first effort to extend First Amendment principles into cyberspace. The court held that speech on the Internet is entitled to the highest level of First Amendment protection, similar to that given to newspapers and books. This is in contrast to more limited First Amendment rights accorded to expression on broadcast and cable television, where the court has tolerated a wide amount of government regulation. This decision, of course, was not the final word. Other legal challenges are still to come. But the decision bodes well for the future of the Internet as a purveyor of serious news and information on what is being recognized as the most participatory marketplace of mass expression the world has yet seen.

INTERNET
VERSUS FOREIGN DESPOTS

The potential of the Internet as a technology of freedom has been demonstrated in recent years by clashes between computer users and authoritarian regimes in Serbia, Singapore, and China.

In Belgrade, President Slobadan Milosevic, faced with large antigovernment demonstrations, forced the last of the independent media, the station Radio B92, off the air and thus set off a technological revolt in December 1996. Tens of thousands of students, professors, professionals, and journalists connected their computers to Internet Web sites around the world. B92 soon began digital broadcasts in Serbo-Croatian and English over audio Internet links, and its Web site took over the reporting of the protests that had been triggered by annulled elections.

Milosevic quickly backed off, and the radio station was soon back on the air, but the event showed the protesters the potential for bypassing government transmitters, news agencies, and television studios to get their message out across Serbia and abroad. (In the 1999 bombing war over Serbia and Kosovo, the Internet played a significant role as an alternative to official government propaganda.)

On the other side of the world, the small, affluent, and authoritarian nation of Singapore believes it can control the technologies of freedom that threaten its one-party rule. To control television, satellite dishes have been banned and the country has been wired for cable television, which enables the government to screen out objectionable material.

Controlling cyberspace will be harder, but Singapore is trying. Use of the Internet is encouraged by equipping schools with computers and urging Singaporeans to link up with the computer network by dialing a local telephone number. Thus, the government is able to monitor use of the Internet that goes through the local servers. Singapore has already blocked material it considers pornographic. Local officials concede that some users can bypass this system by dialing into the Internet through foreign phone systems. In the future, however, Singapore is not expected to be able to maintain controls over the flow of electronic information.

The People's Republic of China is also trying to regulate and monitor the Internet, which has been used by human rights groups to communicate with dissidents within China.

On January 26, 2000, the Chinese government issued stern new regulations intended to control the release of information on the Internet, underscoring the love-hate relationship between the government and cyberspace. The new regulations specifically govern the posting and dissemination of "state secrets"—a vague term relating to information the government has not sanctioned. The regulations may have little direct impact because other laws already cover such situations. Enforcement would be difficult as China now has over 9 million Internet users, up 2 million from a year ago, plus many Internet cafes and free e-mail services. However, a computer technician recently was given two years in prison for providing 30,000 Chinese e-mail addresses to dissidents overseas.

RUMORS AND CONSPIRACY THEORIES

One of the strongest arguments for increasing the presence of serious journalism on the Internet concerns the wild rumors and unfounded conspiracy theories that often fly through cyberspace in an age of easy global communication. Often mainstream media reports are distorted and gross assumptions are made about the government's capacity for malevolence; and on occasion, some stories and theories are just fabricated.

When TWA Flight 800 exploded off Long Island in July 1996 killing everyone on board, investigators focused on three possible causes: a bomb, mechanical failure, or a terrorist missile. Within 36 hours after the disaster, a message posted on an Internet discussion site suggested a darker possibility: "Did the Navy do it? It is interesting how much evidence there is that it was hit by a missile." Within days, numerous net writers speculated that the jet was downed by accidental friendly fire from a U.S. Navy ship on a training cruise. Such a blunder, according to the evolving theory, was quickly covered up by a conspiracy involving U.S. investigators, the military, and President Clinton. Although it was weak, the rumor hung around despite official efforts to discredit it.

Four months later, the theory gained new life when Pierre Salinger, a veteran journalist and former spokesman for President John Kennedy, told an audience in France that he had a document showing that Flight 800 had been shot down by the Navy. Because of Salinger's reputation, the theory once again bounced around the news media, particularly on television news. The story had a familiar ring to it, so CNN called Salinger and confirmed that Salinger's document was a printout of the Internet message posted anonymously four months earlier.

What formerly was considered just gossip takes on a new credibility when it appears on the Internet. Clifford Stoll, an Internet critic, said "Gossip's been blessed by the computer and sprinkled with techno holy water. The gossip that comes across the Internet comes in precisely the same format as does professional news, Wall Street reports, and other important factual information" (Wald, 1996, p. 5). Net watchers say that such wild, unfounded rumors and conspiracy theories can run into the hundreds at any one time.

Obviously, the news media can play an important role by providing reliable, disinterested, and professionally sound news and information to counter and shoot down some of the wild rumors or just plain gossip on the Internet.

In conclusion, one thing that can be said with some certainty about the future of journalism on the Internet is that more changes and innovations are coming fast. But for many millions, the Internet has already taken its place as a *news* medium.

CHAPTER
13

Educating Journalists

By maintaining close relations between journalism and liberal arts,
the [journalism] faculty hopes that the students will not only come to
see how much the exercise of their technique depends on content but
will habitually employ their humanistic knowledge in their journalis-
tic exercises.

—Professor David P. Host (1966)

Journalism has been taught at a number of colleges and universities for about 100 years. Willard G. Bleyer began teaching a journalism course at the University of Wisconsin in 1905, and his scholarly interests later greatly influenced the field. The country's first separate school of journalism, with newspaperman Walter Williams as dean, began in 1908 at the University of Missouri. The Pulitzer School of Journalism at Columbia University, backed with a $2 million gift from the *New York World* publisher, enrolled its first class in 1912.

There was a widespread belief that the nation's newspapers could be improved and elevated if the journalists themselves were better educated as well as more ethical and public-spirited. Some impetus for journalism education came from public revulsion toward the sensationalism and excesses of yellow journalism, which was so prominent at the time.

The growth of journalism education has been steady and at times explosive, especially since broadening its curriculum to include radio and television, advertising, public relations, plus communication theory and processes. As such, the field has paralleled and mirrored the growth of mass communication in general.

INFLUENCE OF WILLARD BLEYER

Journalism education generally had its beginnings in English departments with an emphasis on technique courses—reporting, news writing, editing, design, photography—often taught by former journalists. Among the pioneer teachers, perhaps the most influential was Bleyer of Wisconsin, who was an English professor from a family of Milwaukee newspapermen. Bleyer advocated integrating journalism education with the social sciences, and, through his own history research, he provided an example and impetus for scholarly research about journalism.

In 1906, he laid out a junior-senior curriculum of course work in economics, political science, history, English, and journalism; he subsequently added sociology, psychology, and the natural sciences. He took journalism out of the humanities into social studies; in time, the new field followed his lead. He specified a four-year bachelor's program of courses that would be one fourth journalism and three-fourths social sciences and humanities. This became the model for many journalism programs and decades later became the basic command of accreditation, of which he was an early advocate.

Bleyer gave high priority to reporting of public affairs, was often critical of the press, and advocated academic study and research about the press and its interaction with politics and society. Besides techniques courses, Bleyer stressed the study of journalism history, legal aspects, ethics, and professional concerns.

Like most of his colleagues, Bleyer thought journalism should be taught by teachers with professional newspaper experience. However, he wanted them to be scholars as well. During 1925-1935, he attracted a number of former journalists to do graduate work at Wisconsin—some took master's degrees, but others earned a doctorate degree in a social science discipline, often political science, combined with a double minor in journalism. A partial list of Bleyer's graduates who later greatly influenced programs at other universities includes Chilton Bush of Stanford, Ralph Casey of Minnesota, Ralph Nafziger of Minnesota and Wisconsin,

Robert Desmond of California-Berkeley, Kenneth Olson and Curtis Mac-Dougall of Northwestern, Fred Siebert of Illinois and Michigan State, Henry Ladd Smith of Washington, Ray Nixon of Emory and Minnesota, Neil Plummer of Kentucky, Blair Converse of Iowa State, Roy French of Southern California, H. H. Herbert of Oklahoma, Fred Merwin of Rutgers, Hillier Kreighbaum of New York University, and numerous others.

Bleyer believed in internships for students and that credits should be given for practical experience, as on a college newspaper. He was active as well in establishing a professional organization of teachers and scholarly publications such as *Journalism Quarterly*.

The focus on newspapers dominated journalism education through the 1940s at leading schools such as Missouri, Columbia, Northwestern, Minnesota, Wisconsin, Illinois, Iowa, and others. But important changes were taking place in J-schools as radio and television emerged as major news and entertainment media. More courses and, in time, sequences of courses were offered on radio news, television news, and on broadcasting production techniques.

Speech departments, also offshoots of English departments, became involved in the preparation of students for careers in broadcasting. In some universities, the speech or communication arts departments were merged with the journalism programs; on some campuses, they were kept separate.

Concurrently, more and more journalism programs were offering courses in advertising and public relations. Here, too, courses proliferated, with some schools offering sequences in both specialties. Even separate departments of advertising appeared. Obviously, advertising and public relations were distinct from journalism, giving rise increasingly to the term "mass communication" to describe this new amalgam of college courses on newspapers, radio, television, magazines, advertising, PR, and an increasing involvement with the study of communication itself.

The Bleyer model of journalism education was particularly influenced by this closely related field—the study of communication, a new academic discipline in American higher education. Wilbur Schramm, who taught at Iowa, Illinois, and Stanford, was the leading scholar in communication studies and is credited with inventing and popularizing the field through his prolific writings as well as passing on the word to his graduate students.

The earlier strands of communication study are found in various social sciences. Communication can be defined as the study of mass media and other institutions dedicated to persuasion, communication processes and effects, audience studies, information interpretation, and interpersonal communication. Yet, it was more, because communication is one of the few fundamental processes through which virtually any social event can be portrayed. The field grew enormously because its perspective proved a useful one for perceiving society.

Rogers and Chaffee (1994) made a persuasive case that communication study found a lasting home in the branch of journalism education identified with Willard Bleyer and his protégés, Ralph Casey, Chilton Bush, Ralph Nafziger, and Fred Seibert, all administrators as well as scholars, whose journalism programs developed major components of communication studies, especially at the graduate level.

The universities also produced the new PhDs who staffed the next generation of journalism and (mass) communication faculties from the 1950s onward. Increasingly, graduate work was concerned with communication theory whereas undergraduate courses stressed preprofessional training for careers in news media, advertising, and public relations.

By the 1960s, many of the former journalism departments and schools had been transformed and acquired new names such as School of Journalism and Mass Communication, Department of Communication, School of Communications, College of Communication Arts, and other variations. Some did not change their names: At Missouri, it was (and is still) the School of Journalism and at Columbia University, the Graduate Department of Journalism.

EDUCATION FOR JOURNALISM AND MASS COMMUNICATION TODAY

Professor Lee Becker's annual reports tell us that in 1998, some 149,188 students were studying for a bachelor's degree in journalism and mass communication in over 400 four-year institutions. Teaching these students were 5,038 full-time faculty and 3,771 part-time faculty in 1998. Journalism education has indeed become a giant academic enterprise, yet a somewhat amorphous one with great variations in quality, size, and focus (Becker et al., 1999).

Today, there are some excellent programs and others that can only be described as marginal and weak. (Becker's surveys do not include another flock of related programs, some with such names as Speech Communications, Communication Arts, or Media Studies, which have come out of the speech departments and study aspects of communication as well.)

A variety of journalism and mass communications-related subjects is taught in today's universities. In the Department of Journalism at the University of Texas' College of Communication, sequences (related courses) are offered in broadcast news, magazine journalism, news and public affairs reporting, public relations, photojournalism, media skills, and media studies. The University of Florida, which granted 584 undergraduate degrees in 1998 and has a regular faculty of around 60 full-time instructors, grants separate BS degrees in advertising, journalism, PR, and telecommunication, as well as masters and doctoral degrees in mass communication.

By whatever name, journalism and mass communication study is not a discipline in the sense that political science and history are but a rather loose interdisciplinary field covering a wide range of concerns somehow related to public communication.

The various research and teaching interests of today's faculties are reflected in the names of the divisions or interest groups within their professional organization, the AEJMC—advertising, communication technology and policy, communication theory and method, history, international communication, law, magazine, mass communication and society, media management and economics, minorities and communication, newspaper, public relations, qualitative study, radio-television journalism, scholastic journalism (high school), and visual communication. In addition, there are other interest groups on gays, lesbians, family diversity, media and disability, religion and media, and civic journalism.

BACK TO EDUCATION FOR JOURNALISM

Journalism education, in the narrow sense of preprofessional training and education for careers on newspapers, broadcast news, news services, magazines, or other publications, has become a diminishing fraction of what goes on in today's academic programs just as news operations are a small fraction what goes on at the giant media conglomerates.

A high school graduate intent on a career in news journalism usually has three options. First, look carefully at the journalism programs offered at well-regarded universities and select one that fits your needs; pick your

courses carefully, work on the college newspaper, and try to get an intern-
ship or two while still in school. A second option is to obtain a BA degree
in a social science and then go on for a professional master's degree in
journalism at, say, Columbia, University of California-Berkeley, or Northwestern. Finally, the would-be journalist can obtain a good college education and perhaps work on a college paper. After graduation, look for a
news job. Graduates of Ivy League and Big Ten universities who lack
journalism degrees often have been hired on the national media in the
East.

There are several advantages in studying journalism in college.
Clearly it is a path to a news career that many thousands of professional
journalists have followed. A student learns about the field—its relevant
history, legal controls on the press, ethical and social concerns—and
acquires some basic skills of reporting, writing, and editing news. In most
programs, the student also studies social science courses relevant to journalism—history, political science, economics, and sociology. One pitfall
for some students is spending too much time on techniques courses—how
to run a video camera or radio broadcast gadgets—to the neglect of substantive courses that develop critical and informed thinking. Many journalism teachers believe that a university degree should prepare a student
for lifelong learning and not just for the first few weeks on a job. In other
words, for a career and not a vocation.

Should a student interested in journalism take communication theory
courses in college? Yes and no. Communication and media studies, it has
been argued, have very little to do with the practice of journalism. On the
other hand, many top communication professors had newspaper or magazine backgrounds, scholars such as Wilbur Schramm, Paul Deutschmann,
Ralph Nafziger, John McNelly, and Philip Meyer.

CONTROVERSIES AND PROBLEMS
WITHIN THE FIELD

The evolution from small, newspaper-oriented departments of journalism
to larger schools, and even colleges of journalism and mass communication, has engendered a number of controversies, some long-standing and
unresolved.

Some journalism professors as well as newspaper executives have
been suspicious of academic research, especially the more theoretical

communication variety, feeling with some justification that it has little to do with the news media or the training tomorrow's journalists and, in fact, impedes the process.

This controversy has been around a long time; 40 or more years ago it was characterized as the "green eyeshades," who thought journalism could only be learned on the job or from ex-journalists versus the "chi squares," the college teachers who measured and counted phenomena but could not teach a student how to cover a police beat.

More and more, the professors on journalism faculties doing the most research usually have PhDs in communication and have lacked significant professional media experience. Yet these professors or their teaching assistants have been teaching undergrads how to report and write the news.

This controversy surfaced again in a 1996 report of a year-long survey by Betty Medsger, a former journalism teacher and ex-*Washington Post* reporter. Medsger argued that journalism schools need a major overhaul, including changes in the curricula and the credentials that they require of new faculty hires. Medsger found that journalism students are being trained by people with doctorates but little or no experience as reporters or editors. She also reported that journalism courses are giving way to generic communication courses, a trend opposed by news professionals and many journalism educators. The increased emphasis on communication theory at the expense of basic reporting and writing skills has been accompanied by the elimination of journalism as a stand-alone major at some schools.

Some journalism educators agreed with the Medsger report, but noted that a number of schools have resisted the trend and have continued to emphasize news reporting and writing "from the sidewalk up." More than half of the journalism educators that Medsger polled reported the number of students intending to become journalists was declining. Most students were heading instead for a related field.

Low beginning salaries for journalists was certainly part of the problem. She cited an annual survey on job recruiting on the Michigan State University campus as evidence. There the starting journalist's average salary of $20,154 in 1996 was the lowest of any college-educated workers entering the workforce. However, it should be added that journalism salaries tend to increase quickly with experience.

By November 1999, the job picture had clearly improved. Becker and his colleagues reported that median salary for bachelor's degree recipients was $24,000—up $1,000 from a year earlier and up $2,500 from two years earlier. Similarly, the percent of graduates who had a full-time job six to eight months after graduation was at a record level.

Journalism schools cannot be blamed for low starting salaries. Instead, the responsibility lies with the news media themselves who place so little value on their new hires and make so little effort to attract the best and brightest of college graduates. It is a reflection on our society's values that a Washington media star like Cokie Roberts or Sam Donaldson can make twice as much money for one public appearance as a new reporter can earn in a year.

In general, financial support for journalism education by major media organizations has, with a few exceptions, been tentative and reluctant. Still, over the years there have been some major benefactors: particularly, the philanthropic foundations associated with Gannett, Knight-Ridder, Dow Jones Newspaper Fund, Cox Newspapers and others. The largest financial contributions to journalism education have come from Gannett's Freedom Forum, which has supported the Media Studies Center at Columbia (since moved) and other activities for journalism education and free press concerns. Some critics regard the Gannett influence on journalism education as too heavy-handed and intrusive into academic prerogatives at times and, as such, created resentment among some journalism professors.

DECLINE AND FALL OF THE BLEYER MODEL

The model of journalism education forged by Willard Bleyer and followed by so many universities is clearly in decline, particularly at the major universities where it once flourished. A number of reasons account for this shift.

First were changes in higher education. Before World War II, universities were primarily concerned with teaching, which journalism departments stressed. Since then, we have seen the rise of the research university and the primacy of research over undergraduate teaching. The better the college or university, the greater the rewards—higher salaries, research grants, research leaves, named professorships, lighter teaching loads—go to professors who can get grants and their results published.

To keep abreast of this trend, universities and even small colleges have placed high priority on hiring new faculty with doctorates. In journalism education this has meant hiring PhDs in communication or other social sciences. Significant professional media experience—five or more years—is no longer a prerequisite and, in fact, may be considered a drawback because those years might have been better spent doing advanced graduate work.

It is ironic that at the universities where Bleyer's protégés had the greatest influence—Stanford, Wisconsin, Minnesota, Michigan State, and Illinois—have produced many of the scholars and PhDs who have rejected or downplayed Bleyer's ideas about the importance of preparing young people for news careers.

Further, the research university has often been dubious of any kind of professional training at the undergraduate level whether it be in journalism, social work, or library science. For this reason, California-Berkeley, Columbia, and Michigan have provided journalism training only at the master's level. The Ivy League universities have never taught undergraduate journalism. The University of Pennsylvania's Annenberg School has focused on communication studies. Big Ten universities with their land grant tradition of public service were early leaders in journalism education because of a perceived need to provide trained graduates for a state's dailies and weeklies.

In today's research-oriented universities, journalism faculties are expected to do more than teach beginning reporting classes. In fact, in some schools, these basic courses are often taught by teaching assistants with slight or no media experience. Most professors prefer to teach substantive or theoretical courses or, better yet, seminars for graduate students that relate to their own research specializations.

Today, the faculties of a number of well-known schools and departments of journalism and communication are collections of diverse social science scholars, each with his or her own research interests and priorities. For example, the excellent journalism faculty at the University of Wisconsin-Madison pursues such diverse scholarly interests as history of media and popular culture, communication theory, communication of science news, feminist studies relating to Africa, radical political economy and the media, media in developing countries, history of motion pictures and movie censorship, economics of newspaper publishing, communications law, and problems of misleading advertising among other interests. Understandably, this talented faculty, as do others, lacks both the professional background and apparently much interest in preparing undergraduate students for jobs with the news media.

ACCOMPLISHMENTS
OF JOURNALISM/COMMUNICATION EDUCATION

What then has the field of journalism and communications education accomplished in the past 100 years? In short, a great deal.

Literally thousands of would-be journalists and communicators have been prepared for careers in news and other related fields of advertising, PR, specialized publications, and so on. Some editors believe that those who study journalism in college tend to be more committed to the field as a career than those who enter it casually. A list of distinguished journalists and public communicators can be compiled, for example, from the journalism alumni of Missouri, Columbia, and Minnesota. (Much the same can be said of students who studied advertising and PR.)

Of course, anyone is free to enter and practice journalism. No license or certification is needed; the First Amendment prohibits that. However, a century of journalism education deserves credit for establishing the precept that anyone in journalism or media occupations should have a college education or better, a master's degree. In the specific field of journalism, many useful textbooks, monographs, and journal articles, including a great deal of press analysis and criticism, have been written by journalism faculties. Much of this work on the history, legal aspects, social, political, and economic aspects of journalism has found its way into journalism courses as well as everyday journalistic practices. Many of the numerous books and articles by practicing journalists and broadcasters also are used in journalism courses and reading rooms. A careful look at the impressive *Mass Media Bibliography: Reference, Research, and Reading* by Eleanor Blum and Frances Wilhoit (1988), with its 1,200 annotations, gives an idea of what has been accomplished. Published by the University of Illinois Press, it covers all fields except communication law.

Research by journalism and communication professors has contributed substantially as well to a long list of pressing public issues, such as the effects of television on children, improved public opinion polling, media relationships with politics, and a variety of legal issues such as pornography, access to government news, free press and fair trial, privacy, and so on.

A bibliography of the books, monographs, textbooks, and major journal and magazine articles produced in the past 40 years by the faculties of the leading 24 journalism faculties would be impressive.

In the much broader realm of mass communication and communication studies and research, similar contributions by faculty members have added to our knowledge of persuasive communication, including advertising, PR, public opinion, and propaganda, as well as other facets of communication processes and effects. The academic study of communication, as described earlier, also has had interactions with and mutual benefits from like-minded scholars in political science, sociology, history, economics, and education.

The field of international communications studies has had global impact in Europe, Asia, and Africa due to work done by American scholars in journalism schools. In fact, the American concepts of journalism education and communication research have been widely emulated in many nations.

Journalism and communications programs have helped, too, to educate the public—the consumers of mass media—to be better informed and more critical of the media. Many non-journalism students in colleges, as well as journalism dropouts, have taken journalism courses, such as introduction to mass communication or mass communications and society. Of course, it will take far more than this to build a critical and concerned public at a time when young people are reading less and paying less attention to the news media.

MID-CAREER EDUCATION
FOR JOURNALISTS

Mid-career working journalists who wish to broaden their expertise into new areas have ample opportunities to return to college campuses for specialized study. At least 20 such programs are available, including the John S. Knight Fellowships at Stanford, Michigan Journalism Fellows at Ann Arbor, Fellowships in Law for Journalists at Yale, the National Arts Journalism Program Fellowships at Northwestern, and the progenitor, the Nieman Journalism Fellowships at Harvard since the 1930s. Participating journalists are well remunerated: At Stanford they get a $40,000 stipend and benefits; at Michigan, they get a $30,000 stipend, plus tuition and a travel allowance.

Surprisingly, applications for these programs have been dropping off in recent years; yet such programs have had an impact on journalism. For example, the Knight Center for Specialized Journalism at the University of Maryland offers intensive week-long seminars on science, technology, business, economics, law, and social issues. More than 950 journalists from some 250 news organizations, both print and broadcast, have attended the 43 courses since 1988.

Another major center for external training for working journalists is the highly regarded Poynter Institute for Media Studies at St. Petersburg, Florida. Since 1988, for example, *The Washington Post* has sent 84 staff members to intensive writing and editing seminars at Poynter. Training conferences are also offered by the National Institute for Computer-Assisted Reporting and Investigative Reporters & Editors. NICARs national conference in Boston in 1999 drew 560 journalists and its week-long "boot camps" held mainly at the University of Missouri, have led 752 journalists through statistics and databases since 1994.

CONCLUSIONS AND COMMENTS

Education for both journalism and the broader area of mass communication has both considerable strengths and dismaying weaknesses. Outside critics, for example, fail to understand its research and other contributions of the academy; on the other hand, many professors arrogantly ignore the real concerns of news media about the way students are being prepared to enter the field.

Perhaps, we need fewer and better schools of journalism; yet the same thing can be said about law schools, business schools, and schools of social work. Some downsizing seems to be going on, with several universities such as the University of Michigan, University of Washington, Ohio State, and University of Arizona, among others, who are reevaluating and modifying their journalism and mass communication programs.

Gene Roberts, former managing editor of *The New York Times*, has a good perspective because he teaches journalism at the University of Maryland. Roberts sees no problem with the disappearance of some programs as long as an adequate number of good ones remain. He added:

> The country probably needs 30 or 40 or 50—some reasonable number of journalism schools that are really good at what they do. . . . They should emphasize writing but also emphasize enough of a history of journalism that people really emerge with some sense of where we've been and how we developed as newspapers—and that is missing even more than writing. (Kees, 1996, p. 6)

Important as that view is, the field is changing rapidly, and the academic community can play a helpful role in dealing with the challenges and opportunities presented by online publications and other innovations. It's significant that the highest salaries for new journalism graduates are going to those who work on the World Wide Web.

A curriculum task force was appointed by AEJMC in 1993 to look at the mission and purpose of journalism and mass communication education. The final report, "Challenge: Responding to the Challenge of Change" (1996), showed that much more consensus than contention exists in the field.

Here are some of the highlights:

The purpose of media education is to produce well-rounded graduates who have critical-thinking skills and who have an understanding of the philosophy of the media and a dedication to the public service role that the media have in our society.

Media education has at least five objectives: 1) to provide students the competencies they need for successful careers in media-related professions, 2) to educate non-majors about the role of the media in society, 3) to prepare students to become teachers or to undertake graduate work, 4) to prepare liberally educated graduate students to become media analysts and critics, and 5) to provide mid-career education for media professionals. ("Challenge: Responding to the Challenge of Change," 1996, p. 102)

Change, after all, is what journalism and education for journalism are all about. At the same time, I personally regret the decline in the teaching of journalism as such.

More than any other sequence such as advertising, PR, communication, or media studies, journalism has the greatest claim on being a profession. By objectively and dispassionately gathering all the important news of the day and making it available to the public, journalism performs an essential public service for our democracy and our society.

14

Conclusion: Journalism at a Time of Change

In this question, therefore, there is no medium between servitude and license; in order to enjoy the inestimable benefits that the liberty of the press ensures, it is necessary to submit to the inevitable evils that it creates.

—Alexis De Tocqueville (1835)

For journalism in America today, the news has been both encouraging and dispiriting. At its very best, during a time of crisis or a momentous event, the news media can do a marvelous job of telling the news thoroughly, yet quickly, then following up with needed interpretation and explanation to inform and reassure the public. For example, on the day of the death of China's top leader, Deng Xiaoping, *The New York Times* provided five full pages of news and informed analysis. Several days later, *Newsweek* published a 25-page special report, "China After Deng," written by 11 experts. Some thorough coverage of major news events is not unusual.

But at their worst, even the best news media, when caught up with a riveting but essentially trivial story that may combine varying elements of celebrity, sex, crime, or scandal (preferably all four), can compete vigorously and persistently with the bottom-feeding tabloids for tidbits of scandal. The long-running saga of O. J. Simpson and the death of Princess Diana were only glaring examples of occasional journalistic excesses. This kind of journalism has at times turned much of the public against the news media.

REASONS FOR CONCERN

This book has been concerned about the fate of serious news and public information at a time when our vast popular culture apparatus has engulfed legitimate journalism into a churning melange of entertainment, celebrity, sensation, self-help, and merchandising—most of which is driven by corporate entities devoted to advertising, promotion, PR, marketing, and above all, a healthy bottom line.

Much of the time, the day's news menu seems dull and routine, so news media have always reported frivolous stories or gossip that may intrigue the public but were without serious consequence. Reporters are always alert for the good story that will appeal to a wide swath of readers or listeners—regardless of its true merit. The history of journalism reminds us that newspapers and journalists primarily concerned with reporting significant news have always been a minority.

Further, since the time of Gutenberg, the press has always had its critics and enemies, beginning with kings and other autocrats who controlled the printing press ruthlessly for several centuries. Yet today, a widespread feeling exists that serious journalism is in trouble not because of a threat of censorship, but because the news itself—accurate and informative—has become a diminishing portion of what Americans glean daily from their television sets, newspapers and magazines, radios, computers, and televisions. Further, news as public knowledge too often seems all wrapped up in a glitzy package of entertainment and diversion. News has too often become trivialized.

Equally distressing is the trend that a smaller portion of Americans, especially young people, are paying attention to news from any medium in their reach. Serious news about the public sector and the world beyond our borders does not seem as important and compelling to the public anymore. Polls show that fewer Americans are paying attention to the news—

whether on broadcasts or in print. Even if the media provided more serious news, it is questionable whether the public would pay more attention.

There is ample evidence as well that much of the public holds the press in diminished regard and, when asked, expresses irritation and animosity toward journalists. Journalists are not trusted by the public and are equated in their ethical standards with lawyers, elected officials, and corporate officials—all with self-serving interests. The public views journalists as part of the political elite, not their independent representatives.

Television news, with its tremendous power to inform, educate, and influence public opinion, has largely failed to report much significant news beyond providing an erratic, headline service. Among the print media, a few of the national publications still do a competent job of reporting a comparatively wide range of news developments, but news coverage in many newspapers is bland, unimaginative, and incomplete.

Probably the principal concern the news media face, then, is the increasing intermixing of news with entertainment in various forms—gossip and scandal, promotion of pop culture products (movies, television programs, etc.), publicity about celebrities, and eye-catching self-help features on personal health, and so on. Daniel Boorstin argued in his classic 1961 book, *The Image*, that Americans have been overwhelmed with pseudo-events, celebrification, and seductive imagery that seemed to drown out reality (including the real news.).

Neal Gabler expands on this in *Life: The Movie: How Entertainment Conquered Reality* (1998) and argues that entertainment values have come to dominate the mass media as well as personal conduct. The headline stories of recent years—O. J. Simpson trial, death of Princess Diana, bombing of the federal building in Oklahoma City, President Clinton's alleged dalliances and thousands of other episodes that life generates—these are the new blockbusters that preoccupy the traditional media and dominate the national conversation for weeks, sometimes months or even years at a time while ordinary entertainments quickly evanesce and the day's serious news is ignored.

Public affairs journalism—the life blood of democracy—has been particularly trivialized and corrupted. Top-of-the-head opinions and predictions, whether on television talk shows or in signed columns or even in news stories, often replace careful reporting and cautious interpretation, particularly during political campaigns. Journalists see a deterioration of their professional standards. Highly paid celebrity journalists are perceived by the public as cynical, arrogant, and out of touch with the needs and interests of the average citizen.

Another cause for concern has been the persistent trend toward larger media conglomerates primarily concerned with providing entertainment and diversion for a mass public. News organizations within such behemoths represent a small part of those diverse companies whose main concern is to make profits for their stockholders.

The corporate mentality of these mega-corporations seems at odds with vigorous efforts to aggressively report the news and defend freedom of the press, as did *The Washington Post* during its confrontations with the Nixon White House in the Watergate and Pentagon Papers affairs. The majority of the biggest and best news organizations are controlled by these large corporations that seem to put profitability ahead of public service. Further, corporate journalism, with some exceptions, seems less able or willing to counter or question the overwhelming influence of great corporations on public policy here and abroad.

WHAT IS TO BE DONE?

Here are several modest suggestions for reversing some of the discouraging trends discussed throughout this book.

First, most critics believe the immediate problem is somehow to restore the well-known fire wall that separated news from entertainment and sensation on most responsible news organizations. Editors and broadcast producers in the national media need to make their own news decisions, stand by their standards and values, and forego chasing after scandalous or titillating stories that surface in the mixed media. Television news—both broadcast and cable—as well as *Time* and *Newsweek*, seem to be seriously corrupted by this scramble for competitive advantage. Change will not be easy because much of the public seems conditioned to equate news with diversion and entertainment. (Another fire wall, the one separating the editorial and business sides of a news medium, has also been breached at times and is a further reason for concern.)

Second, the news business must find ways to improve the stature of journalists, whose public image has become badly tarnished. To do this, the news media must improve their performance and do their own reporting. Political journalists must work to be again viewed as reliable, objective, and dispassionate news gatherers, rather than highly visible and opinionated performers. The task of winning back the public's respect and admiration for journalists will be a difficult one.

The public must understand that there is a real difference between a journalist carefully reporting and explaining an important and complex story and a well-paid television celebrity interviewing a rock star or entertainment personality on a TV news magazine show. One is a public servant and the other is a quasi-entertainer.

Journalism has some, but not much, claim to being a profession such as law, medicine, or the clergy. The principal virtue that good journalism does have is that, like recognized professions, journalism does provide an essential public service: the reporting and presentation of important news or public knowledge in a disinterested and objective manner. When journalism is practiced in that manner—and eschews the temptations to pontificate, mislead, sensationalize, or entertain—the press merits the unusual protection it enjoys under the First Amendment that "Congress shall make no law . . . abridging freedom of speech or of the press."

Another perquisite of an emerging profession that journalism can some day become is the practice of monitoring and criticizing its own errant colleagues. In an open system of free expression, no journalist can be or should be coerced or restrained by government or by any private source, but no journalist or news medium is immune from incisive, scalding criticism or censure from their peers or the public.

As mentioned, a real strength of U.S. journalism is the longtime and still common practice of criticism of press performance from within the ranks of journalists. Such exchanges are healthy and evidence indicates that some egregious conduct has been modified. For example, in recent years, some prominent journalists are avoiding conflicts of interest by steering clear of the lecture circuits and irresponsible television talk shows.

Media criticism may be inhibited, of course, by the complications and practices of multimedia corporate giants. Will *Time* magazine critically report on Time Warner's control of cable channels or AOL's Internet policies? Will NBC News ever look into General Electric's dealings with the U.S. government? Not likely. Despite such problems, more diversity still exists among U.S. news media than in any other democracy.

In the final analysis, diversity—the dissemination of news from as many different sources and different facets as possible—may be the most important value to cherish. The media, as well as the public and the courts, must ensure that the public will continue to have a variety of sources of information and opinions to choose from. When diversity disappears, in its place come orthodoxy and conformity.

Third, the news media must broaden and expand their audiences for serious news, particularly among younger readers and viewers. Newspapers and news itself is often viewed as obsolete or irrelevant among the 50 million who make up the 15-30 age group in America. Each new generation tends to read more news as it gets older but still reads less than the previous generation.

News organizations are well aware of the problem but are not having much success in dealing with it. In general, most agree that news content must be more relevant to the needs and interests of young people. Partly, this is an education problem; many in the current generation do not read much and lack the general knowledge of modern history required to absorb and make sense of significant news. Schools must do a better job.

In an open, democratic society, members of the public have an obligation to keep themselves informed, to be discerning and skeptical users of the media, and to demand and reward substance and relevance from the news media.

The growth of interactive newspapers on the Internet offers the potential of creating more news consumers among computer users who are mostly younger people.

Fourth, the Internet and other communication innovations have already greatly impacted on journalism and will probably play a crucial role in redefining the future directions and format of news. One editor, Rem Rieder (1996), believes the Internet needs the traditional values of journalism—news judgment, accuracy, fairness, and context—to make sense out of the tremendous volumes of information, much of it inaccurate, tendentious, and misleading that is available to computer users.

As the Internet matures, journalistic skills and values should play a key role. The onrush of raw data, including much garbage and misinformation, will require validators, that is, trusted editors and other experts, to separate the wheat from the chaff. The Internet will require interpretation and context, hence a need for individual, online judges to tell the surfers what it all means. Nonetheless, no one knows just how important a role journalism will play in cyberspace or how, in time, journalism itself will be transformed. Adapting to the Internet and the new mixed media culture is perhaps one of the greatest challenges to journalism in the years just ahead.

Fifth, another priority for journalism is to restore and expand the importance of world news on the news agenda. It is ironic that at a time when the big players, Murdoch, AOL-Time Warner, Disney, and NBC, are all expanding their international operations and seeking foreign markets, the news media they own, as well as the public, are paying much less attention to the world outside our borders.

Two of America's best newspapers, *The Washington Post* and *The Los Angeles Times*, rose to prominence in the 1970s, in part, by expanding their corps of foreign correspondents and carrying much more authoritative news from overseas. Attention to world affairs seems a litmus test of quality journalism but too few other publications have emulated those two dailies. America's pivotal role in the world today requires greater attention to world affairs. Yet TV news, news magazines, and many daily newspapers have been moving away from public affairs news, instead featuring more self-help and personalized news on health, self-improvement, or whatever story du jour might appeal to a large audience. Similar to what is found in women's magazines, this soft news has the effect of pushing aside other more pressing news.

Despite the shortcomings of today's journalism and the low esteem in which many journalists are held, there are reasons for hope and encouragement. The U.S. press still is the freest and most unfettered press in the world and enjoys the most Constitutional protection. The values and standards of good journalism and press freedom are firmly established in the hearts and minds of thousands of working journalists, even if lacking in some of their corporate bosses. Most news organizations are sound financially and make money. Americans like to criticize journalists, just as they do politicians and football coaches, but all of us are dependent on the press to know what is happening in our communities and the world. We need the news to know what there is to criticize about the news.

Good journalism has a way of being there when we need it most. During times of national crisis in the previous century—World War I, the Great Depression, World War II, the Korean and Vietnam wars, the civil rights struggle, the Cold War, the information revolution—Americans struggled to understand these momentous events and were largely able to do so because they had access to independent and reliable information from their newspapers, radio, and television stations.

The importance and need of good journalism has not decreased in our society; if anything, we need it more than ever. Take a careful look at any of several leading publications—*The Washington Post*, *The Wall Street Journal*, or *The New York Times*—and glance at the headlines or tune in NPR's "All Things Considered," and you will be reminded of how important a free flow of reliable public knowledge is to our personal well-being and to the welfare of the Republic.

Good journalism does matter.

References

Adelson, A. (1994, May 9). More radio stations drop coverage of local news. *The New York Times,* p. C8.

America's best newspapers. (1999, November/December). *Columbia Journalism Review,* 14–16.

Arnett, P. (1998, November). Goodbye world. *American Journalism Review,* 51–67.

ASNE Poll. (1998, December 28). Another glum portrait of American journalists. *The New York Times,* p. C6.

Associated Press v. United States, 326 U.S. 1 (1945).

Auletta, K. (1995a, March 6). The race for a global network. *The New Yorker,* 53–54, 79–83.

Auletta, K. (1995b, November 27). The wages of synergy. *The New Yorker,* 8–9.

Auletta, K. (1996, July 29). No honeymoon, no marriage. *The New Yorker,* 29.

Bagdikian, B. (1992). *The media monopoly* (4th ed.). Boston: Beacon Press.

Barringer, F. (1999, June 21). A new war drew on new methods for covering it. *The New York Times*, p. C1.

Barringer, F., & Kuczynski, A. (2000, February 28). Net draining talent from print media. *The New York Times*, p. C1.

Bartlett, J., & Kaplan, J. (1992). *Bartlett's familiar quotations* (16th ed.). Boston: Little, Brown.

Becker, L. (1999). Enrollment and degrees awarded continue 5-year growth trends. *Journalism & Mass Communication Educator, 54/3*, 5–22.

Best of the web media 2000. (2000, April). *Brill's Content, 68*.

Blankenburg, W. B. (1995). Hard times and the news hole. *Journalism Quarterly, 72*, 634–641.

Blasi, V. (1977). The checking value in first amendment theory. *American Bar Foundation Research Journal, 3*, 521–649.

Brandenburg v. Ohio, 395 U.S. 444 (1969).

Brill, S. (1999, July/August). War gets the Monica treatment. *Brill's Content*, 84–95.

Browne, M. (1991, March 3). The military vs. the press. *The New York Times*, p. 45.

Carmody, D. (1995, June 12). On the annual scoreboard of new magazines, it's sports, 67, sex, 44. *The New York Times*, p. C5.

Carter, B. (1997, February 6). After verdicts, will case still sell? *The New York Times*, p. A15.

Carter, B. (1999a, October 5). The leader in U.S. radio buys no. 2. *The New York Times*, p. C1.

Carter, B. (1999b, December 21). 3 TV news operations unite to provide video to affiliates. *The New York Times*, p. C8.

Challenge: Responding to the challenge of change. (1996). *Journalism & Mass Communication Educator, 50*, 101–119.

Color of mendacity. (1996, July 19). *The New York Times*, p. A14.

Coulson, D. C., & Hansen, A. (1995, Spring). The *Louisville Courier-Journal*'s news content after purchase by Gannett. *Journalism Quarterly, 72*, 205–215.

Dennis, E. (1992). Comment on the survey. *Intermedia, 20*, 31, 33, 36.

DeParle, J. (1991, July 3). 17 news executives criticize U.S. for "censorship" of gulf coverage. *The New York Times*, p. A4.

Diamond, E. (1993). *Behind the Times: Inside the New York Times*. New York: Villard Books.

Dunbar, R. (1996). *Grooming, gossip, and the evolution of language*. Cambridge: Harvard University Press.

Durocher, D. (1995). Times and Post Cos. bow to mighty Singapore. *American Journalism Review, 17*, 11.

Emerson, T. (1985). Foreword. In P. Lahav (Ed.), *Press law in modern democracies* (pp. xi–xiii). New York: Longman.

Emerson, T. (1966). *Toward a general theory of the first amendment.* New York: Vintage Books.

Emery, M., Emery, E., & Roberts, N. (1996). *The press and America* (8th ed.). Boston: Allyn & Bacon.

Eye ball magnets. (2000, March). *American Journalism Review, 22,* 29.

Fabricant, G. (1996a, July 20). Murdoch's world from a to z. *The New York Times,* p. C7.

Fabricant, G. (1996b, July 29). Murdoch bets heavily on a global vision. *The New York Times,* p. C1.

Fallows, J. (1996). *Breaking the news.* New York: Pantheon.

Fass, A. (2000, March 20). Journalists among the online crow. *The New York Times,* p. C14.

Fibich, L. (1995). Under siege. *American Journalism Review, 17,* 16–23.

Fibison, M. (1996). Washington Post's Broder aims at media dishonesty, "punditocracy." *Murphy Reporter, 43,* 1–2.

Frankel, M. (1994, November 27). The shroud. *The New York Times Magazine,* 42–43.

Frankel, M. (1995, December 17). The murder broadcasting system. *The New York Times Magazine,* 46–47.

Frankel, M. (1996, September 22). An olympian injustice. *The New York Times Magazine,* 60–61.

French, H. (1995, November 17). On the Internet, Africa is far behind. *The New York Times,* p. A8.

Gabler, N. (1994). *Winchell: gossip, power, and the cult of celebrity.* New York: Knopf.

Gabler, N. (1998). *Life the movie: How entertainment conquered reality.* New York: Knopf.

Getler, M. (1991, March 25–31). The gulf war "good news" policy is a dangerous precedent. *The Washington Post National Weekly Edition,* p. 24.

Geyer, G. A. (1996, April). *Who killed the foreign correspondent?* Red Smith Lecture in Journalism, University of Notre Dame, South Bend, Indiana, 3–16.

Glaberson, W. (1994, October 9). The new press criticism: News as the enemy of hope. *The New York Times,* p. 1, sec. 4.

Glaberson, W. (1995a, July 30). The press: Bought and sold and gray all over. *The New York Times,* p. 1, sec. 4.

Glaberson, W. (1995b, November 17). "60 minutes" case illustrates a trend born of corporate pressure. *The New York Times,* p. A3.

Glass, A. (1992, August 18). The last of an era. *Wisconsin State Journal,* p. 1C.

Goodman, W. (1995, June 16). In Jackson romp, echoes of two mergers. *The New York Times,* p. B1.

Grossman, L. (1998, September/October). The death of radio reporting: will TV be next? *Columbia Journalism Review,* p. 61.

Gunther, G. (1994). *Learned Hand: The man and the judge.* New York: Knopf.

Gunther, M. (1995, October). All in the family. *American Journalism Review, 17,* 36–41.

Hachten, W. (1993). *The growth of media in the third world.* Ames: Iowa State University Press.

Hachten, W. (1999). *The world news prism* (5th ed.). Ames: Iowa State University Press.

Hachten, W. (1992). African censorship and American correspondents. In B. Hawk (Ed.), *Africa's media image* (pp. 38–48). New York: Praeger.

Hackworth, D. (1992, December 21). Learning how to cover a war. *Newsweek,* 33.

Harwood, R. (1995, June). Are journalists elitists? *American Journalism Review, 17, 27–29.*

Herbers, J., & McCartney, J. (1999, April). The new Washington merry-go-round. *American Journalism Review, 50–56.*

Hess, S. (1994, April). The cheaper solution. *American Journalism Review, 16,* 28–29.

Hess, S. (1996). *International news and foreign correspondents.* Washington, DC: Brookings Institution.

Hickey, N. (1996, November/December). Over there. *Columbia Journalism Review,* 53–54.

Hoge, J. (1994, July/August). Media pervasiveness. *Foreign Affairs, 73,* 136–144.

Hume, E. (1996, March/April). Something's rotten. *Columbia Journalism Review,* 53–54.

Jacobson, G. (1996, May 20). For journalism graduates opportunities in new media. *The New York Times,* p. C7.

Johnston, D. H. (1979). *Journalism and the media.* New York: Barnes & Noble.

Kees, B. (1996, July). Some universities begin to rewrite the story of journalism education. *Freedom Forum,* 4–8.

Kimball, P. (1994). *Downsizing the news: network cutbacks in the nation's capital.* Washington, DC: Woodrow Wilson Center/Johns Hopkins.

Knightley, P. (1975). *The first casualty.* New York: Harcourt Brace Jovanovich.

Knightley, P. (1982). The Falklands: How Britannia ruled the news. *Columbia Journalism Review,* 53–54.

Kohut, A. (2000, January/February). Internet users are on the rise, but public affairs interest isn't. *Columbia Journalism Review,* 68–69.

Kolbert, E. (1995, October 15). Robert MacNeil gives a thoughtful goodbye. *The New York Times,* p. H39.

Kovach, B. (1996, August 3). Big deals, with journalism thrown in. *The New York Times,* p. A17.

Kovach, B., & Rosenstiel, T. (1999). *Warp speed: America in the age of mixed media.* New York: Century Foundation Press.

Kurtz, H. (1993). *Media circus.* New York: Times Books.

Kurtz, H. (1996). *Hot air: All talk, all the time.* New York: Times Books.

Kurtz, H. (1998, March/April). The erosion of values. *Columbia Journalism Review,* 44–47.

Lasswell, H. (1971).The structure and function of communication in society. In W. Schramm & D. Roberts (Eds.), *The process and effects of mass communication* (pp. 84–99). Urbana: University of Illinois Press.

Margolick, D. (1994, October 24). The Enquirer required reading in the Simpson case. *The New York Times,* p. 6.

Markoff, J. (2000, February 16). A newer, lonelier crowd emerges in internet study. *The New York Times,* p. A1.

Masses Publishing Co. v. Patten, 224 Fed. 535 (S.D.N.Y. 1917).

Miami Herald v. Tornillo, 418 U.S. 241 (1974).

Mifflin, L. (1996a, March 1). For Rather, technology has drawbacks, too. *The New York Times,* p. C5.

Mifflin. L. (1996b, May 13). Media. *The New York Times,* p. C5.

Mifflin, L. (1998a, March 22). An old hand's view of TV news. *The New York Times,* p. C5.

Mifflin, L. (1998b, October 12). Big 3 networks forced to revise news gathering methods. *The New York Times,* p. C1.

Mifflin, L. (1999, September 8). Viacom to buy CBS, forming 2nd largest media company. *The New York Times,* p. C16.

Moeller, S. (1999). *Compassion fatigue: How the media sell disease, famine, war and death.* London: Routledge.

Morton, J. (1995, October). Farewell to more family dynasties. *American Journalism Review, 17,* 67–69.

Morton, J. (1999, July/August). Bad news about newspaper circulation. *American Journalism Review, 21,* 77.

Mott, F.L. (1947). *American journalism.* New York: Macmillan.

Near v. Minnesota, 283 U.S. 697 (1931).

New York Times v. United States, 403 U.S. 713 (1971).

New York Times v. Sullivan, 376 U.S. 270 (1964).

New York Times v. United States, 403 U.S. 713 (1970).

Nieman poll finds decline in media quality. (1995, Fall). *Nieman Reports,* 38–39.

O'Reilly, B. (1994, February 26). We pay for news. We have to. *The New York Times,* p. 15.

Parker, R. (1995). *Mixed signals: The prospects for global television news.* New York: Twentieth Century Fund Press.

Pember, D.R. (1992). *Mass media in America* (6th ed.). New York: Macmillan.

Peterson, I. (1996a, January 12). Media. *New York Times,* p. C7.

Peterson, I. (1996b, March 15). More journalists jailed, but fewer are killed. *The New York Times,* p. A5.

Peterson, I. (1996c, August 19). USA Today. the fast food of dailies, is expanding menu. *The New York Times,* p. C1, C8.

Peterson, I. (1996d, September 9). Media. *The New York Times,* p. C5.

Peterson, I. (1997, May 19). Rethinking the news. *The New York Times,* p. C1.

Pew Research Center for the People and the Press. (1996, May). *TV news viewership declines* (news release). Washington, DC.

Pew Research Center for the People and the Press. (1997, April). *The Times-Mirror news interest index 1989–1995* (news release). Washington, DC.

Phillips, K. (1996, January 28). Bad news. *The New York Times Book Review,* 8.

Pogrebin, R. (1996, September 23). Foreign coverage less prominent in news magazines. *The New York Times,* p. C2.

Prato, L. (1996, September). Still tuning to radio news. *American Journalism Review, 18,* 52.

Rafferty, K. (1975). *That's what they said about the press.* New York: Vantage Press.

Red Lion Broadcasting Co. v. FCC, 395 U.S. 367 (1969).

Remnick, D. (1995, September 18). Last of the red hots. *The New Yorker,* 76–83.

Rich, F. (1994, October 24). He got the poop on America. *The New York Times Book Review,* 1, 31–33.

Rich, F. (1996, May 18). Media amok. *The New York Times,* p.15.

Rieder, R. (1996, September). Primary values. *American Journalism Review, 18,* 6.

Rogers, E., & S. Chaffee (1994, December). Communication and journalism from "Daddy" Bleyer to Wilbur Schramm: a palimpsest. *Journalism Monographs, 148,* 1–49.

Rosenstiel, T. (1994, August 22 & 29). The myth of CNN. *The New Republic, 211,* 27–33.

Rothstein, E. (1996, August 26). Anxiety in the land of gargoyles and giants. *The New York Times,* p. B1.

Rottenberg, D. (1994, May). "And that's the way it is." *American Journalism Review, 16,* 34–37.

Schell, J. (1996, August). The uncertain leviathan. *Atlantic, 278,* 70–78.

Schudson, M. (1995). *The power of news*. Cambridge: Harvard University Press.

Self-censorship at CBS. (1995, November 12). The *New York Times,* p. 14E.

Shaw, D. (1994, Spring). Surrender of the gatekeepers. *Nieman Reports,* 3–5.

Shepard, A. (1999, February). White noise. *American Journalism Review,* 20–25.

Simon, J. (1999, March/April). We're all nerds now. *Columbia Journalism Review,* 19–27.

Soifer, A. (1985). Freedom of the press in the United States. In. P. Lahav (Ed.), *Press law in modern democracies* (pp.79–133). New York: Longman.

Stepp, C.S. (1995, October). The thrill is gone. *American Journalism Review, 18,* 15–19.

Stewart, J. (1999, July 4). Consider the sources. *The New York Times Book Review,* 8.

Strentz, H., & V. Keel (1995). North America. In J. Merrill (Ed.), *Global journalism* (pp. 355–394). White Plains: Longman.

Wald, M. (1996, November 10). Cyber-mice that roar, implausibly. *The New York Times,* p. 5.

Walsh, K. L. (1996). *Feeding the beast.* New York: Random House.

Waxman, S. (1999, November 9). Los Angeles' troubled times. *The Washington Post,* p. C1.

Who gets paid what. (1999, May). *Brill's Content,* 84–95.

Wicker, T. (1991, March 20). An unknown casualty. *The New York Times,* p. A15.

Witcover, J. (1998, March/April).Where we went wrong. *Columbia Journalism Review,* 19–25.

Zane, J. P. (1996, September 29). Liz's love life! Oprah's diet! Dole's foreign policy! *The News York Times,* p. 2, sec. 4.

Zuckerman, L. (1997, January 6). Don't stop the presses. *The New York Times,* pp. C1, C7.

Author Index

Subject Index

BABY

ANNALEESE JOCHEMS

SCRIBE
Melbourne •

Scribe Publications
18–20 Edward St, Brunswick, Victoria 3056, Australia
2 John St, Clerkenwell, London, WC1N 2ES, United Kingdom

First published in New Zealand by Victoria University Press 2017
Published by Scribe 2019

Printed and bound in China by 1010 Printing Co Ltd

Scribe Publications is committed to the sustainable use of natural
resources and the use of paper products made responsibly from
those resources.

9781925849349 (Australian edition)
9781912854271 (UK edition)
9781925693799 (e-book)

CiP records for this title are available from the National Library
of Australia and the British Library.

scribepublications.com.au
scribepublications.co.uk

'This year's best local debut novel.'

—*METRO*

'*Baby* is a funny, taut, relentless fever-dream of a
novel. Buy it and read it now, and you can brag
about it one day the way people who bought and
read Emily Perkins' *Not Her Real Name* in 1996
do today.'

—LOUISE KASZA, *THE SPINOFF*

'An amazing, fresh voice in New Zealand fiction.'

—JENNA TODD, *RNZ*

'In Cynthia, she has crafted a memorable monster.
Creepy and subversive, *Baby* is a classy debut.'

—LINDA HERRICK, *NZ LISTENER*

'Sparse and tantalising in its unfolding, it never quite
allows you to get your sea legs.'

—RUTH SPENCER, *NZ HERALD*

to Nicholas

1

Cynthia can understand how Anahera feels just by looking at her body. Today Anahera's wearing a pair of loose orange shorts. Their quality is obvious from the way they stretch at the crotch when she lunges. Her singlet is very tight, and Cynthia thinks it must be one of those sophisticated ones that button up between the legs. Anahera's quite tall, so if it is that sort it must be extra tight down below when she leans or bends.

That's just it, the leaning and bending – that's how Cynthia knows. Anahera yearns for strain, she courts it with her every movement, and Cynthia can see this, because she feels precisely the same way herself. She's squatting now, and she's been squatting for minutes. The agony in her thighs and ass is desperate and profound, but she continues to squat, as instructed by Anahera.

Classes are held on Anahera's lawn, surrounded by bushes; forceful, gloriously cultivated bushes that spill against each other and onto the lawn, pressing against the seven members of Anahera's class. It hurts, the squatting, but Anahera wants it to, so Cynthia holds the pose. Anahera herself is over by a lavender bush, kneeling and telling motivating things to a very puffed-out middle-aged woman. She can't always be motivating all of them, Cynthia understands. They've got to take turns because Anahera doesn't have a microphone and her throat gets sore. Now she yells that it's time for everyone to plank.

How to describe Cynthia's feelings? How to catch the

sensations so hot in her body, and hold them still enough to mea-sure their edges? It's out of exhaustion, not disrespect, that she stops planking, and sinks down into the grass for a brief rest. Her whole body hurts in the most exquisite way. There are daisies, and she spots three of them by her nose in a near-perfect line, evenly spaced. She picks one and dabs the soft yellow at its centre, smears gold on her wrist. The lawn isn't wet, but it's got that good grassy taste and smell. Something big is happening inside Cynthia, and all around her. She feels herself on the cusp of some enormous event of infinite meaning. She licks some grass thoughtfully, then nibbles a bit and spits it gently back out. She loves the blades, furry and soft on her tongue, and pauses to wonder – how must it feel to be Anahera, to instruct? There's such luxury to Anahera's body, such glory in it. All of her is the same brown, flexing into shades under the sun. Just looking at her helps Cynthia feel the stirring and readiness for action held in her own belly.

Soon, she feels sure, Anahera won't be able to resist her in such repose among the other exercisers. She'll press a shoe into Cynthia's back, and Cynthia will get up, panting, and work out a bit more. For now, she watches the little bugs. They're very fit, clearly, jumping from blade to blade and scuttling along the edges. Bugs don't have feelings, and if there's one thing Cynthia's learned from Anahera's classes, it's that feelings are a hindrance in the game of physical excellence.

The shoe doesn't come. Cynthia looks up, and Anahera's marching past a big bush to stand on the deck beside her barbecue. 'Alright,' she shout-talks hoarsely, 'weights.'

Cynthia puts 1 kg on either side of her bar. Everyone else has at least 2.5 kgs, but that doesn't matter. Anahera's already told her not to compare herself to the other ladies, and to put her bar right down each time she needs to change her grip.

'Where are your muscles?' Anahera asks them all. 'I want to see them.' Cynthia feels like a child but also sexy, like always at this part, and she tenses obediently. This is the sixth lesson of Anahera's limited participant class, and Cynthia's attended all of them, although she's known Anahera for longer.

Whenever they do weights the same 50 Cent song plays, and the same lady, Evelyn, puts out a small snooty puff of air about it. This time she exhales only three seconds in, long before the lyrics have even started. She's wearing a blue tracksuit, and Cynthia puts a glare on her. She's got a kid doing puzzles inside, but that's no reason to be superior.

The singing starts. 'Damn, baby – '

'Oh my gosh! I am so embarrassed. I really will sort this out,' Anahera says – like always, in a rush – picking up her bar and not moving at all to change it. Cynthia nearly laughs. 'Lower,' Anahera says, calm again. 'Yes, and lower. Hold.'

After twenty-five minutes with the weights they all lie down in the grass, even Anahera, who shows them how to kick their feet in a very specific way to work their abs. Cynthia closes her eyes and tries to keep moving in the same pattern. It feels right, it feels good. But, 'No,' Anahera's head says, appearing above her. She takes a firm grip of Cynthia's right foot, and moves it so it's no longer comfortable. 'Alright,' Cynthia says, because her whole body's been repositioned. Anahera gives her ankle a little rub before moving on, and when Cynthia closes her eyes again there's sun caught and sparkling inside them.

A car parks at the roadside, Cynthia hears it and looks up. It's a red Toyota, not so flash, but obviously regularly washed. That sort of guy then, and he is: a puffy, pinkish man with floppy hair and a fake pocket sewn at the left nipple of his shirt. He gets out and leans over Anahera's fence, sighing and impatient, waiting for her to notice him and stand up. 'Kick, kick, kick,' she finishes saying to the assembled exercisers, then looks up at him.

He sighs again, seeing that she's not going to stand. 'Ana, where's my laptop? I'm supposed to be at work.'

'Kick, kick,' Anahera says, nodding at Cynthia. 'Then go to work?'

'But I need my laptop. I'm just asking if you've seen it around.' His hair's a dull, light brown, the same colour as his chinos. His mouth hangs limp at the end of his question.

'I don't know, Simon, I'm instructing a class.'

'You haven't seen it then?'

'I don't know, Simon.'

'Bloody alright then.' He marches past them all, up the garden path and into the house. Anahera says, 'Kick, kick,' again, but stands to watch him go in, scratching her eyebrow. Cynthia tries to kick, but she's lost it now, completely.

Minutes later he comes out with nothing under his arm, looks at them all, and drives off.

What a bland man! Just another part of the world which simply isn't adequate, not for Anahera, and not for Cynthia either; not with all its roads leading to more roads, its lines and lines of houses, its dogs on leashes, and all these ladies in Anahera's class, on her lawn, so heaving and entitled. The feeling is boredom and disappointment to the point of excruciation, and Cynthia understands it absolutely.

She first attended Anahera's muscle class at the gym nearly a year ago, and she went to those classes for months. One day, and it was a bad day – the third in a row of non-stop rain – she heard

Anahera speaking sternly to the gym manager in the hallway. 'I don't care,' Anahera said, then, 'No, I'm not going to.'

He spoke sternly back. 'If you care about your job, you might –'

'I don't care about my job,' Anahera said, Cynthia heard it clear as day. Then she was coming down the hallway, towards the corner, and Cynthia ducked into the bathrooms. A week after that, Anahera left his employ and offered Cynthia and six other select individuals places in her limited participant class.

Once they've stretched, Anahera comes over to see how Cynthia's feeling. She pats her own hot cheeks, and Cynthia does the same. They exhale together. The only male class member's petting his poodle at the gate, with one of the ladies. Cynthia can't think of much to say, but she smiles and shrugs. Anahera grins back, and everyone follows her inside.

Anahera's house is quite big, Cynthia supposes, and there are things around: half-read books and not-completely-drunk teas. A big dog roves in circles at the edges of rooms, pausing at the doors, shut inside because of the poodle. The snooty woman, Evelyn, gives her kid a mandarin from Anahera's table.

Cynthia's about to go after Anahera, to help make everyone's drinks, but Evelyn sits down at the table and says, '*Hmm*,' in a very pointed way.

'*Mmm*,' another lady says, her friend.

'It isn't just me then?' Evelyn says. 'The quality of these classes is definitely slipping.'

'Sorry, um – you just stole her mandarin?' Cynthia says. She looks around the table but there are no expressions of outrage on her classmates' faces. Several people are nodding, slowly.

Particularly a woman in a bright orange sweatband, Evelyn's main friend, her sidekick.

'Well,' the friend says, her eyes glimmering with excitement, 'at the facility her classes were incredible. I mean, really, she was the *best –* '

'Excuse me, just a second,' Cynthia starts up, surprised at the high noise of her own voice. 'Anahera's mum died, do you know?'

'That was well over a year ago,' Evelyn says quietly.

Cynthia's loud this time, 'So? Her mum fell off a horse, rolled down a cliff, banged her head on a rock, and *died.*'

Everyone is silent. The man coughs, and Evelyn puts on her cardigan. They've all noticed at once, a moment before Cynthia, Anahera standing in the doorway. They all look away, at the table or out the window, except Cynthia, who can't. Anahera blinks, with her hands on her hips, waiting for an explanation.

Cynthia starts choking, but Evelyn interrupts and says in an aggrieved, solemn voice, 'Some of us have been feeling less than satisfied with your class.'

'Who?' Anahera says. 'Who else?'

Evelyn's friend tilts her head sideways, as if shy, and puts her hand up. Anahera taps the carpet with her bare foot. 'Anyone else?'

Two more ladies raise their hands.

Anahera nods. 'Okay.'

'I'm so happy with the class,' Cynthia says, breathing now. 'I actually think it's improved since we started at your house. You have a lovely garden, that's how I feel.'

'I don't garden. Those are overgrown bushes.'

'Oh.'

'Don't wait around,' Anahera tells everyone at the table. 'The tea and biscuits aren't part of your fee, they were complimentary.'

Then she says, 'Anyway,' and walks off down the hall.

'Well,' Cynthia says, 'that serves everyone right, I'd say.'

The man gives her a nod, or at least she can see him thinking about it, then goes out to his poodle. They all sit and watch him untie it through the window.

'It's another structural issue with this style of class,' Evelyn says. 'There's no way to place feedback anonymously.'

Her friend nods, and yanks off her sweatband.

'Does that thing even catch sweat?' Cynthia asks her. 'How much sweat do you have.'

'It's a sweatband,' the friend says, and she and Evelyn get up and leave.

The three remaining ladies look sadly at Cynthia, then they tidy themselves and go too. Just because they can afford Anahera's $75 class fee, doesn't mean any of them deserve even to speak to her, let alone learn her fitness skills, obviously. Cynthia picks up a *National Geographic* and moves through it quickly, looking only at the pictures: a series of frogs of varying colours, one of a couple of elephants trying to communicate, and then two of sand. She goes right through, then back to the frogs, and she's looking at an orange one when Anahera sits down beside her, sipping coffee.

'I'm pleased it's just you here now,' she says.

Cynthia nods and waits.

'I've noticed a definite improvement in you, you know,' Anahera says. 'You really are getting stronger.'

'Gosh,' Cynthia says, and feels herself rocking back and forwards in her seat. Her face is hot. She cradles her cheeks and they're lifted into smiling, warm and soft. 'That's an achievement you can feel amazing about, too,' she tells Anahera. 'I could never have improved without you. As for some of those other ladies.

Well. They'll just be fat forever, it's in their nature.'

Anahera nods and asks, 'Tea?' Then she goes to make it.

Cynthia sits, thinking. When Anahera comes back she's prepared. 'Okay, so,' she says, 'imagine for a second that you start another, even more private class? A one-on-one sort of thing. I could pay. My dad –'

Anahera interrupts. 'It's not sustainable, Cynthia.'

'I don't care about sustainable,' Cynthia mutters, and she squeezes Anahera's arm. It's astonishing, the solidity of it. Anahera lifts a long finger to her mouth, and bites the knuckle before turning to Cynthia. She blinks, as if coming out of a daze, and with a new, peculiar concentration, puts her hand on Cynthia's arm. Cynthia's skinny-fat, and Anahera's grip pushes through her like custard, and holds her bone.

'I have $30,000,' Cynthia says, 'and I've been thinking about leaving this dump-hole city. What do you say?'

Anahera shakes her head, and stands up. 'Class is on next week, as usual.'

Cynthia nods and moves to sip her tea, but it's too hot.

Anahera's trying to get her to go, she wants to be alone – it's obvious. But Cynthia stays sitting. She drinks a bit of the tea and it's definitely far too hot. While Anahera stands, still waiting, she prints her phone number out clearly on a scrap of paper, then double-checks it.

Cynthia misses her bus, she doesn't see it till it's already driving away, but she doesn't mind. She misses one more and walks home. Cars pass her but she doesn't notice a single one of them. She passes houses but doesn't see them either. At the traffic lights someone swears at her, but she doesn't hear properly. She should've waited, they were probably saying, but it doesn't matter. There's afternoon light all over everything, hitting the leaves from the sides and making patterns of glow and shadow. She picks several leaves and crumbles them up in her fingers to smell them, then drops some on the footpath, and more in her pocket.

For months or even for her whole life, Cynthia's felt a furious desperation to go somewhere, to feel things, and be a real person. Well, Anahera is the over-heated centre of the world, the point of rupturing where it becomes too big and too strong to hold itself, and Cynthia feels close to her now. At last, she's content.

2

When Cynthia got home she did things on Facebook, got in bed, did more things on Facebook, slept, and now it's the next day, afternoon, and she's still in bed. Nothing has happened at all. Anahera didn't call. Cynthia's struggling for hope, and looking at a picture of her own pool on Instagram. The underwater lights are turned on, so the water glows blue and purple. A very attractive, very tedious boy called Randy took the photo just a few days ago. Then they had sex, and afterwards she made him watch a documentary which he found boring. Actually, it was lurid. It was about a young soldier who met a girl on the internet, but really he was lying – he was middle-aged and dull. He'd never even shot a man. Also, she wasn't the girl – she was the girl's mother. But he didn't know that, and he killed another man in jealous rage. What Randy failed to understand was the doom bespoke by the middle-aged guy's smugness. After killing the younger man the older one was trapped in his own naïve satisfaction, and he will be forever; to think again will destroy him. Randy will never see that, and that's just typical. Cynthia has a lot of options in regards to boys, but none of them are able to comprehend depth.

When it finished she told Randy she's not interested in men who don't like educational television, and he went home. Earlier this morning he sent her a picture of a Labrador, but that's just more of the problem – that's the only way boys of his sort ever like to have sex.

Cynthia flops on her face, bends her knees to lift her crotch up, and throws it hard back down onto the bed. Her dog, Snot-head, was sleeping between her knees, and now he's flung off. He moves quickly, panting, in a hurry to readjust and settle back into sleep. Cynthia can't breathe so much in this position, with her face shoved into the pillow, but it hardly matters. Anahera hasn't called. Cynthia should probably text some boy. Her dad's away on business, in Australia, and if all her dreams aren't going to come true today, she should at least make some use of the house tonight. Snot-head lets out a big wheeze, and she breathes heavily too, out her nose against the pillow.

Snot-head snores, and she dozes. The bell rings downstairs. It twangs and hurts. Cynthia hasn't bought anything online lately, it won't be for her. It'll be one of her dad's employees, or some other ridiculous person. Still, it keeps ringing. She moves carefully, turning onto her back, this time trying not to wake Snot-head. He wakes anyway. He's a French bulldog, fat and de-testicled. He snorts and she adores him, even though she's not in the mood to. He wriggles under one of her knees, between her legs and up, onto her belly, lifting the blanket in a hump, then settles down to sleep again. Whoever's downstairs is rude. They knock now. Loud and then louder.

Cynthia topples Snot-head off, and heads for the stairs. He trots after her, hoping to be fed. The knocking continues, louder again. 'Yup!' she yells. Down the stairs, through a big pointless area, to the door. Her dad got a peephole put in, and she leans forward to look through it. Snot-head's butting her ankle, hungry, but she forgets him.

Standing right there, at the door, with her hair wind-licked and curling loose, is Anahera. There's no pause, the door is open. Cynthia deep-breathes twice. Anahera's car door's swung wide and her lips separate. Her eyes are raw, red. She's about to ask a big question. But then she only says, 'Is this your flat?'

'My dad's house. I, um, live here.'

Anahera steps back, towards her car and her own open door. 'Oh, ah – shit.' Snot-head runs out and licks her toes. She's wearing jandals. Cynthia wouldn't have thought she'd own jandals, but there they are.

'He's away,' Cynthia says.

'I'm getting a divorce,' Anahera tells her, then notices her car door and jogs back to shut it. When she returns she says, 'I just decided.'

Cynthia didn't know Anahera had a husband. It doesn't matter, she decides immediately. She looks up at Anahera, and all she wants is to put her in bed, then make her tea and carry it carefully up the stairs. She imagines Anahera not waiting for it to cool, just talking about being alone and how it feels. Cynthia's ready to see it burn her lips, and to understand burning. 'What do you need?' she asks.

Anahera glances up at the house, right at Cynthia's window, although she can't know that. 'Money,' she says, 'to leave.'

'Okay, me too,' Cynthia says. It's warm in the hall where she's standing.

Anahera pauses, then nods. 'Don't ask about him,' she says.

'I never will.' But what Cynthia means is, not until she's earned the right to.

3

Cynthia grabs Anahera's arm, and Anahera comes through the door. It clangs and the cold's shut out behind them. They look at each other. Anahera's lashes are long, and her head seems to be at a more accessible height now they're standing so close. She relaxes, she's indoors, and she leans against the wall with a hand holding up her head. 'Did I wake you?'

'No,' Cynthia starts, 'I was just – '

Anahera laughs, so Cynthia sees her tongue. There are some stray hairs at her eyebrows, and some tiny, soft, nearly invisible ones above her lip. Her eyes are bold and black in a way that makes Cynthia peer down and feel serious. She adjusts her pyjama pants, and looks back up. There are lines under Anahera's eyes. She's exhausted.

'We'll get a boat,' Cynthia says.

Anahera pauses, then replies, 'I need to go somewhere,' and that's agreement.

Cynthia makes sure to under-react. She waits, then, 'Okay!'

The fingers of one of Anahera's hands pinch the leg of her pants, and those of the other pull at the collar of her shirt.

'Okay,' Cynthia says again. 'I'm not sure how much I have, but we should be good.'

Anahera lets some air out in a surprised way, but that's all.

'We'll take care of each other, for a while?' Cynthia asks.

Anahera nods, and Cynthia sees she's waiting to be invited in further. In the living room, Anahera looks around briefly, then curls up on the couch to sleep. Cynthia doesn't touch her at all; she sits down in a chair opposite to think.

Once, late at night when Cynthia was twelve, she looked out her bedroom window and saw a woman in a navy blue jumpsuit and bangles standing on the driveway, buttoning up her coat. Her dad wasn't visible, but she heard him say, 'Yeah, alright. Good. Suits me.' Then a taxi arrived, and the woman was gone.

Before school the next day she asked him if the woman had been a prostitute. He said, *Well, yeah, yeah she was, sorry.* She didn't mind, she wasn't surprised. Her dad had always stood for long moments in the hallway on Saturday mornings before entering his home office; he'd always been a lonely man. She was proud of him for taking ownership of his needs and feelings, and she's even prouder now, remembering. Now she knows for herself how hard it can be, and how necessary. He said she couldn't meet the lady, and she understood.

You have to ask for love, and do anything for it. When Anahera's eyes blink open Cynthia tells her, 'I'm ready to do my best, and earn some respect.' Anahera nods and sleeps more, and Cynthia watches her till she feels herself less frightened, and then completely brave. She goes to sit down at the computer in her dad's office.

He doesn't leave it locked, and he's got an auto-login on his computer and a password saved online for ASB. She winces. There's only $16,650 in his cheque account, and nothing in the others. She transfers herself $16,400, and wipes her eyes.

Anahera comes in then, and stands tilting her head side-to-side, as if to tip the sleep out of it.

'$16,400,' Cynthia tells her. 'It's less than I thought, but I think it's enough. I took a bit from my dad.' She's trying very hard not to cry. She never planned to leave him with nothing. He probably has another account, she thinks, with another bank. She doesn't know him very well in some respects, she has to remember. After she finished uni, when she was looking for a job, he said he didn't have any contacts in the media industry. She's at least forty per cent sure he was lying. He'll have more money somewhere else, of course he will.

Anahera's looking at the hedges and the lawn, and close behind them, Auckland city. She doesn't ask another question, she says instead, 'We'll get jobs. We can pay him back if you want.'

Cynthia's not really interested in jobs anymore, so she waits.

'My husband caught me fucking a guy I used to know,' Anahera says. 'Everything's ruined for me now.'

Cynthia fries bacon so the fat crackles and drips, loud. Anahera can probably hear it from where she's sitting in the lounge, thinking, most likely about her marriage. Cynthia's always been what you'd consider a lonely person, but also, she's someone with a limitless sense of meaning. It wells up hot in her, and ebbs away cold, and she often does have to be careful not to get sad, but mostly she's able to make sure she feels inspired instead. Now, with Anahera in the next room waiting for her, the feeling comes easy.

She's made pancakes too, beautifully puffed, and she's pleased to bring them through to the lounge, balanced on her wrist, to present them to Anahera. Anahera doesn't want bacon, but Cynthia doesn't mind, she just gets some maple syrup.

'We'll leave tonight,' Anahera says.

Cynthia nods.

'Or tomorrow?'

Cynthia thinks. 'Tomorrow.'

'Okay.'

There's a pleasing dab of syrup on Anahera's lips, and a smile there too, maybe. Cynthia's not so hungry, she's just looking, and waiting for some nice new thing to do for Anahera, who pauses, then licks the syrup and says, 'Good.'

Cooking is not one of Cynthia's things, so this is an incredibly good sign. She watches the food admiringly on Anahera's fork, then at the entry to her mouth. 'Oh!' She jumps up. 'You need clothes?'

Anahera starts to say no, but Cynthia jogs off and up the stairs, into her father's room. She takes some navy blue pyjamas, a pin-striped shirt, an All Blacks one, and a cowboy hat one of his business friends gave him in Australia.

She dumps it all in front of Anahera, looks up at her face, and straightens it into a neat pile, with the hat on the top.

'Won't he notice?'

'Nope.' But Cynthia hopes he does, and knows that she left with someone.

Anahera puts the last of her pancake in her mouth and grins, rubbing the silk of the pyjama pants with her thumb. 'He definitely won't notice?'

Cynthia shakes her head vigorously.

'I feel better now,' Anahera says. 'Thank you.' She puts the hat on, and Cynthia begins to nod again, encouragingly. *This is who I'll love,* she thinks, then knows. Anahera stands up and does two very good lunges, tips her hat, and grins.

'I got into the postgrad thing I applied for,' Cynthia says, lying and surprising herself. She didn't apply. 'But I'd much rather come with you.'

Anahera does one more lunge, which isn't perfect because she's confused. 'Okay, good,' she says. 'Will we take some food?' She gestures to the pantry, which Cynthia's left open.

'All of it.'

'Okay, most of the things.' Anahera gets up and does the dishes – all of them Cynthia's, from when her dad left two days ago.

'You don't have to do that, you just put them in the machine,' Cynthia says.

Anahera keeps washing them, then puts them in the machine. 'What do we need to pack?' she asks.

'I have a solar phone charger, unopened,' Cynthia answers proudly, 'from when my dad nearly went camping. And I've got data-unlimited on my phone.'

'Cool,' Anahera says.

'Other than that, we'll be wild! We'll abandon everything, and everyone!'

'Canned food,' Anahera says.

Anahera finds a gas thing in the garage, and wants to pack food, but after she's packed her clothes Cynthia says, 'Will you lie with me a while, I'm scared.'

Anahera looks almost relieved – she must be a little nervous too – and follows Cynthia up the stairs to her bed, even reaching up for her hand. Snot-head hears their feet and comes too.

They all get in Cynthia's big bed together, warm like a family. Cynthia and Anahera don't touch directly, but Snot-head wriggles against Cynthia's belly, and he must be touching some part of Anahera too. Just in their togetherness, and their shared heat, it seems to Cynthia that they become a new place. A small home they'll take with them wherever it is they go.

4

They move forward in tired but certain silence. Snot-head sleeps and they let him. Cynthia picks up her duvet and sheets in a muddle, and at the car, whispering, Anahera tells her to fold them. 'It's easier if everything's compact, so we know where things are.' Cynthia finds this silly, but insignificant, so she puts everything down and picks it all up again, piece by piece, packing it neatly into the boot. They take all the food in the house except a bottle of wine Anahera says looks *very decent*, some bread, butter and coffee. Anahera says they should leave some canned tomatoes, but Cynthia's father doesn't cook. 'Then why does he have canned tomatoes?' Anahera asks, but it doesn't matter, they take them.

'The shop's just down the road,' Cynthia tells her. 'He can get apples.' She packs dog food, Snot-head's little spiky collar, and his lead with the hearts. They're quickly in the car and Anahera hands Cynthia some camembert from the fridge. Cynthia's got some cranberry juice.

A bit of cheese doesn't stay in Anahera's mouth and Cynthia picks it delicately off her shirt, careful not to push it in, then tongues it from her finger. Anahera's got a beautiful chewing smile, although it doesn't make sense to chew that sort of cheese.

They drive north. Cynthia checks her phone and there are five texts from Randy, the last three extremely sulky. How exciting for him not to matter anymore! She smiles brightly and they go down an avenue, between a line of trees. 'Both of us will become entirely new to ourselves! Just you wait!' she tells Anahera. 'We'll save each other from this ugly place.' The leaves shine in the new morning light, hanging like gems alongside the road ahead of them. It's when they reach the end of them that Cynthia remembers: Snot-head!

'We've got to go back,' she says. 'My dog.'

They've not driven far, only a few minutes, but Anahera pulls over instead of turning around. 'What?'

'My dog.' Cynthia enunciates very clearly.

'Your dog?'

'Yes.'

Anahera sits, licking her gums.

'There's no way I can go without him,' Cynthia explains. 'There've been times in my life with him as my only friend. He's always stood by me. I can't leave him there.'

'Cynthia, I thought we were getting a boat?' Anahera's using a patient, adult voice, tilting her head. 'That might not actually be so good for him.'

'All he does is sleep!' Cynthia holds her voice down, carefully. 'Sleep and love me, and he can do those things anywhere!'

Anahera sighs.

'I can't leave without him, simply.' Cynthia won't say more.

Anahera sighs again and gets back on the motorway, in the direction of Cynthia's house.

'Thank you.' Cynthia squeezes Anahera's fingers on the wheel. 'I can't say how much I appreciate this. Really, I can't.'

Anahera watches the road. But they're going back down the avenue, and when they're on a quiet street near Cynthia's house she turns and smiles.

'He's a great dog,' Cynthia says.

—

At Cynthia's, Anahera doesn't get out of the car. Cynthia feeds Snot-head, and waits impatiently for him to eat. He does so dutifully, staring forward for long moments after each swallow.

The car honks.

'Yup!' Cynthia yells back, pushing Snot-head's bum gently with her foot. He turns and looks at her solemnly, then continues eating at the same pace. When Cynthia loses patience and picks him up, jellymeat falls from his surprised mouth onto her white pants.

They're all together in the car, and Cynthia expects Anahera to say something. She doesn't, she looks at the dog and turns the key. Snot-head licks at the meat stuck to Cynthia's pants, and it falls onto the seat between her legs. He shuffles on the bone of her thigh and leans down to lick it from where it's fallen on the upholstery. Anahera pretends not to notice, which is good.

They drive for a while. Anahera's phone rings and she answers it. For a while she just makes annoyed noises, then she says, 'Paihia.' A sigh. 'Yes, with someone. Someone I know.' She turns and grimaces at Cynthia. 'Do whatever you like,' she says, and hangs up.

It must be her husband, Cynthia thinks. 'Paihia,' she repeats, and likes the sound of it. She's heard of Paihia. Part of *The Bachelor NZ* was filmed there. Beautiful scenery, and quite a historical focal point, actually.

They drive longer. Cynthia touches Anahera's arm, then thinks she's been touching it too long and stops. 'I've had this boy since I was fourteen,' she says proudly of her dog. Anahera doesn't seem that interested, but Cynthia continues anyway. 'I definitely noticed a big change in his personality when they lobbed off his testes. *Definitely.*' Anahera doesn't ask about the change, but that's fine. They're together, and what that means is potential.

They pass three KFCs and Cynthia points each of them out, but Anahera says things about saving money. They'll stop at twelve and eat stuff from their cans, she says, but then she looks at Cynthia and Snot-head, and pulls over so Cynthia can get two bananas from the boot. They eat them leaning on the car, and Snot-head trots around it three times, then pees on a wheel.

'Watch this,' Cynthia says, but then Anahera is watching and she's nervous. She hasn't done this in a long time. The ground's gravel, but she gets on her hands and knees facing away from Anahera. 'Ride,' she says to Snot-head. It seems he hasn't heard, or he's forgotten. She hears a rock shift under Anahera's shoes, and she says it again. Then, suddenly, she feels his weight land with his four paws on her back. Anahera laughs, and she keeps laughing. She gets on her knees beside them and Cynthia can feel his paws pressing down while Anahera pats him. 'Excellent,' she says, 'that's just excellent.'

Encouraged, Cynthia crawls in a small circle around Anahera, careful to make slow, even movements so Snot-head doesn't fall. Then she stops, and explains, 'It's really hard for him, with his weight and all, he doesn't always make it.' Anahera laughs again and there's a sound of her kissing Snot-head between the eyes. The gravel hurts her knees, but Cynthia stays there till Anahera's done patting him.

5

Cynthia suggests mini-golf, and Anahera reminds her of the money issue. 'But haven't we gone insane?' Cynthia asks. 'I mean, aren't we just doing whatever we like?'

It doesn't matter. Cynthia's never had a sister, and she thinks – Anahera will be her sister, a whole new half of her. She's letting her money go, letting it run to Anahera like blood to a cut-off limb. She's venturing into a new wilderness with a friend at her side, and she won't turn back. All she wants is to be physical and real, beside Anahera's body and entirely in her own.

On a corner there's a big, sudden thudding noise. 'My weights,' Anahera says. Cynthia soothes Snot-head. They pass two more KFCs, but she doesn't mention them. She pats her dog. They're going away, to where no one will look at them and they'll look only at each other. It's such joy to see Anahera's eyes narrowed on the road, and her hand hard on the gearstick.

'Let me know when you want to drive,' Anahera says.

'Oh, I don't – drive,' Cynthia replies.

'That's fine,' Anahera says.

There's a word in Cynthia's mind, an enormous one: divorce. They stop at a bathroom, and while she pees she says it to herself. She says it quietly, but it's loud. The walls are unpainted wood, and she rubs them with her hands till the fat of her fingers catches a splinter, then she bites it out.

When she comes back out she's still walking through the awe of it, and she's awed even more to see Snot-head sitting cosy on Anahera's knee. Perfectly, Anahera looks a bit embarrassed, coughs and shoves him off.

Three more hours of driving, and Cynthia says, 'I think with the way my dad is – I think we'd better get cash.' They'll stop in Whangarei, Anahera says.

In Whangarei they wait in a queue at ASB. Cynthia keeps thinking Anahera's leaning down to whisper something, or about to, but she never quite does. They shuffle forward, like everyone else.

The lady says hello.

'Cynthia would like to withdraw everything from her account, in cash,' Anahera says.

'Would you?' the lady asks. She's got blond hair, but it's cheap, supermarket.

'I've decided to purchase a boat,' Cynthia says, and hands over her card. She's shorter than both the bank lady and Anahera.

'She and her father have been discussing it for a while now,' Anahera tells the woman, and pats Cynthia's shoulder.

She nods. 'Well, good on you!' she says. She puts a phone to her ear and dials. 'Pete, yes, Pete – I've got a youth here – '

Cynthia interrupts her: 'I'm twenty-one.'

Anahera's pat becomes a squeeze. A man walks through a door, past the tellers. He's blond too, and very combed. The blond woman shifts off her seat so he can stand in front of her. 'She'd like to empty it,' she tells him from behind.

Pete looks at the screen and he laughs. '16,800, eh?'

'For a boat,' Cynthia says.

'Hi, I'm Anahera.' Anahera puts her hand through the gap in the glass. Cynthia introduces herself too, and when Pete's laughed some more he says, 'Look, ladies, it's a bit humdrum, but I'm going to need you to sit down and sign some papers.'

They stand where they are and wait for him to walk along, back behind the tellers and through the door he came from. The blond woman smiles at them, then at the man behind them in the queue. Anahera pulls Cynthia aside to let him past, and Pete appears from a different door. 'Follow me,' he says, and gestures towards a third door. It's windowed, and opens to a little room where they both sit in cushioned chairs and wait while he prints forms. The printer makes a rasping noise, but he speaks louder, saying, 'Now, I'm going to need some proof of identification.' He laughs. 'If that's not too rude a demand.'

Cynthia hasn't got it on her. Anahera hands her the keys.

When she comes back Anahera's touching her face, laughing, and he's laughing too, with his crotch forward, his shoulders back, and his two hands gently caressing his belly.

'She's just finished uni,' Anahera says, nodding at Cynthia.

'Yeah,' Cynthia says, handing over her 18+ card. 'I have a degree.'

Pete nods, and Cynthia signs the papers he slides her. He checks them, turning each one over although some aren't double-sided. 'Righto,' he says, 'and next time – you can trust us – but next time, remember to read the small print on any documents you sign.'

Anahera nods and pats Cynthia's hands, which are held together in her lap.

'Righto,' he says again, and goes off to put their forms somewhere, and presumably get their cash.

He comes back with a surprisingly large padded envelope. Cynthia squeezes it. There are five wads in there, rubber-banded. 'Why not just a cheque?' he says. 'What sort of boat is this?'

The envelope's clutched tight in her fist, and Cynthia wants it back in her account, or her father's; intangible again, put back into nothing. She wants to eat it. There's no wind on the street, and people are looking at her. Should she dig a hole and bury it, like a dog? Put it down on the street and piss on it? Anahera is waiting quietly. Should she run?

'I'm sorry about in there,' Anahera says.

'What for?'

'I don't know.'

Cynthia sees her properly then, and understands her own terror as a ripping, a new place being made in herself for love. Anahera must be feeling the same way. A car goes past them quickly, loudly, but Anahera doesn't seem to notice it, or the people all around them pausing to gawk. She's not looking down at the envelope either, but at Cynthia's face. Anahera's eyes are brown in this light, on the street. She's doing nothing but waiting, with the sun on her face, for Cynthia. Neither of them can run, or will.

'It doesn't matter,' Cynthia says.

'Do you still want KFC?'

'Nah.'

They get back in the car. The passenger window is fogged with dog breath, and imprinted by his nose. Cynthia hands over the envelope, and Anahera puts it in the compartment between them.

'What kind of boat do you want?' Cynthia asks.

'Probably the cheapest one.'

'Yeah.' Cynthia nods. 'A little one then. Good.'

Anahera laughs. The dog's quite heavy after all the sitting he's already done on Cynthia, but he's warm.

6

Cynthia's been trying to explain for a while precisely what it is that's so tragic about *Talhotblond*, the documentary Randy so pathetically failed to understand. Snot-head's wheezing gently, and Anahera's been mostly listening for twenty minutes now. Cynthia jolts Snot-head awake, remembering something that could be crucial. 'The spelling of *tall* in the title is actually incorrect, they miss one of the "l"s, because the lady herself misspelled it in her username! And then – in real life she was actually quite short, so.'

'Okay,' Anahera says.

Knowing Anahera gets it makes Cynthia get it even more. 'But they're in an impossible love!' she says. 'They can never actually meet each other, because she's too old and he's a loser! It had to end in death.'

'Don't you think people just need to make things work?' Anahera asks.

'What I know,' Cynthia says, 'is that there was no possible ending without Brian's death, and everyone else's heartbreak.' She looks at Anahera and sees she disagrees. She disagrees, but she understands. She's a force to be reckoned with.

'You know,' Cynthia says, 'I think we three are going to save each other.'

'From what?'

Cynthia doesn't answer, they won't know exactly till they're saved.

—

Cynthia gets out first at the boatyard, then Snot-head, then Anahera, then Cynthia catches Snot-head and puts him back in the car. She's got to hold his small body back after she's put him down, inch her hands out the door and slam the last gap quickly. Anahera puts the envelope in her hands. They walk together up to a brown box-shaped office.

A guy sticks his head out the door. 'Hi!' he says.

'Where's your cheapest?' Anahera asks him, coolly.

'Oh yeah, I got a little pretty one for $18,000? Come in and I'll show you a picture.' He shifts aside and lets them in first.

It's tight and tiny in his wooden office. He sits behind a desk and Anahera takes a plastic chair, gesturing for Cynthia to sit on a padded one. He pulls out a worn photo album with yellow and blue flowers on the cover, opens it and shows them a photo at the very back. 'Comes with plates, anchors, some buckets, bedding, spoons,' he says, and he keeps listing other things, but Cynthia is in love.

It's got *Baby* written in wispy orange lettering on the side. It's bluish-white, with dirty bits at the water line, and the sea clinging at its little hips like low-waisted pants. There are bigger boats around it, but *Baby* catches the sun better.

'That looks alright,' Anahera says.

'Belonged to an old couple,' he says.

'You'll have to reduce your price,' Anahera tells him.

'How much have you got?' He nods at the envelope in Cynthia's hands.

Cynthia's about to answer, but Anahera says, 'Doesn't matter how much we've got.'

He pauses, thinking.

'Cash,' Anahera says, and Cynthia's thrilled and proud to be with her, to be her girl. She shuffles in her seat and covers her mouth with a finger.

'$18,000,' he says.

Anahera shakes her head.

'We could sell your car?' Cynthia asks her, chuffed to have an idea and be involved.

The guy looks at Anahera.

'Do you have a wife?' Cynthia asks him, then. 'Kids?'

He laughs. 'My wife drives a better car than that.'

Anahera laughs too, but only for a moment.

'We won't do more than $15,500.' Anahera straightens her face. 'Looking at that picture.'

He stops laughing, and Cynthia can tell this is going to take a while. She goes out to find water for Snot-head. They sit and wait. 'Bureaucracy,' she tells him. 'It does go on and on.'

Eventually, the door opens and the guy emerges with Anahera. 'Ron!' he yells. 'Ron!' Then he looks down at Cynthia and grins. 'Not his real name, but you'll see why I call him that.'

A red-haired boy arrives from a back corner of the yard, he's excessively freckled, and eating Twisties.

'See?' the guy says, taking the packet.

'Yeah,' Anahera tells him. 'That's good, alright.'

'Look, Ron, buddy, you take these ladies in that car' – he points at Anahera's car – 'and show them where' – he's leafing through his notebook – 'thirty-three is. You know the one? *Baby.*'

Ron's watching his Twisties swing in the guy's hand. He looks up, squinting – he doesn't know *Baby.*

The guy says, 'Anyway, thirty-three,' and eats a Twistie.

'Can I keep the picture?' Cynthia asks the guy, nodding at the album hanging in a hand at his side.

'Yeah, that's ten extra. Nah, just kidding.' He slips the photo out, clumsily, then nods at her envelope. '16,000,' he says. 'Plus the car.'

That sounds good, so Cynthia opens the envelope and lays the notes out on the step, counting them. There's no wind, and Ron steps forward to shift Snot-head out of the way. Cynthia can feel Anahera standing above her, but she tries not to rush. It does take a while. She turns back, and hands the money to Anahera, who passes it on to the guy. 'Good,' he says, without seeming to look at the notes or the numbers on them. Then he yells, 'Ron,' again, jokingly, because Ron's already there.

Just before they get in the car to go, he trots back up to them. 'You people want a dinghy?' he asks, blowing air out his nose.

Cynthia shrugs and Anahera says yes.

'Yeah,' he says. 'You'll need one. I forgot. Nothing extra. You want a motor in it?'

Cynthia's about to say yes, but Anahera speaks first. 'A paddle is good.'

Ron puts an old dinghy on the roof of the car, and Cynthia stands holding Anahera's arm and looking down at Snot-head. When Anahera's moved stuff around in the back seat to make room for him, Ron says, 'Or should I drive?'

'Nah,' Anahera says, waves at the guy, and they go.

Snot-head snorts, snuffles, sniffles and finally settles on Ron's knee. He's quiet in the back. Cynthia turns and asks him, 'How old are you?'

'Sixteen and a half,' he says.

'You look nineteen,' she tells him suggestively, and turns back around to flash a smile at Anahera. Anahera looks very ambiguous, and flicks the indicator.

Ron and Anahera carry the dinghy down a metal causeway, to the jetty. It's narrow, so Cynthia walks behind them. They tie it up in the water, and when they turn around she's embarrassed to be standing there with nothing, so she marches back to the car. She opens a door, and as soon as she does Snot-head runs out and begins pooping. Anahera and Ron both nod to show they understand, he's got to do it. He starts and stops, first under the tree, then a rubbish bin, then back under the tree again. Anahera and Ron take a second load, then a third. Before he takes the rest of the stuff, Cynthia stops Ron. 'Give me your number,' she says. 'We're probably gonna throw some parties on there.' He does. Anahera pauses and goes off again.

'That's the thirties,' he says, gesturing off at some boats anchored a little way from the wharf.

'Right.' Cynthia points at exactly where she thinks he means.

Anahera comes back, and stands beside Cynthia. 'Maybe you'll show us how it works?'

'Um,' Ron says. 'I'm not too good with those older ones.'

7

Baby appears gradually from behind all the bigger, more robust boats, dancing like something imaginary. The water lifts her sometimes, then drops back under, exhibiting her dirty underneath.

Snot-head runs around fast, sniffing everything, and Cynthia watches on. Big houses with a lot of glass windows look down on them from the hills. That must be where the boat salesman lives, she decides.

Anahera goes back in the dinghy for the rest of their stuff. There are windows, curtains and lots of little cupboards for Cynthia to open. There's a trap-door in the ceiling, so they can keep things up there. A little cabin, with a short, narrow bunk bed. It's all wooden, which Cynthia likes. She finds that the tops come off the built-in seats on either side of the table, and that inside them are long panels of cushioning, presumably to make up another, third bed. Opposite the table is a kitchen sink, a small counter and some cupboards they'll keep food in. She opens a little door and finds a toilet, and a sink. The boat has everything a house would – a toilet, beds, sinks, only smaller and more fragile, like a tiny set of organs. It's all perfect for Snot-head; he's little too. At the back of the boat there's a steering wheel, and an unsteady seat that flips out under it. There's a ladder which can be pulled up or dropped into the water. Along the boat are bars to hold while you walk its perimeter, and a thin panel for your feet, one after the other. At the front there's a washing-line, and a flattish area underneath where they can lie down, although of course it won't be safe there for the dog.

This is what Cynthia has now: her boat, Anahera and Snot-head. Her money was like water, in its big nothingness and the way it slipped away before she really had it. She doesn't mind. Money runs downwards, and people are always trying to position themselves under it like drains, but she'll never involve herself in any of that ever again.

When Snot-head's sniffed everything twice, he goes to sleep in the cabin. Cynthia crawls in after him, to touch the lift and fall of his little ribs. He's a very soft dog, with a nose he only occasionally lets her touch and ears he can stick up but never does. He's golden, and wrinkly, with a diva walk; he's got a big little swingingly seductive bottom. Sometimes he likes to stretch his legs apart and press his crotch into the ground, that's one of his cutest things. She lifts his ears and looks in them. They need to be cleaned, she'll remember that. She shuts the cabin door quietly, and sits at the table to wait for Anahera.

They're together, newly, looking at each other newly. Cynthia doesn't know how to work the gas, so Anahera puts the kettle on, then she says, 'We might not have any parties.'

Cynthia shrugs, that doesn't matter. It was only something she said, not her dream. Anahera pours boiling water carefully over her coffee, and Cynthia's herbal bag. The boat shifts gently right and left, and Anahera doesn't adjust her body in any perceptible way.

'Do you know my dog?' Cynthia asks.

'Yup,' Anahera says. She's lying down on the wooden bench,

half obscured by the table.

'Well,' Cynthia says, and begins: 'When I was fourteen I cried every single day. Sometimes three times. I wasn't my best self then, and I was bad-looking. I had no friends. I looked at myself in the mirror every day, crying. Sometimes I'd watch myself cry for whole half hours, in my pocket mirror, in my bed. I caught my tears in a jar, but they always dried up.' She peers over the edge of the table to check Anahera's listening, and Anahera sees her and nods.

Cynthia's pleased. She continues: 'And one day, my dad asked me what I wanted, you know. It was our best moment of love together. He didn't hug me, but if he'd been that sort of guy I know he would have. He told me he'd heard my crying all that time. I felt better then, when I knew he'd been listening. He said, "What do you want? I'll give it to you."'

'And?' Anahera asks, although she must already know.

'So I got Snot-head.' He's on her knee, looking up at her and listening. He looks like he's been hit in the face with a plate, a bit. But that's how he always looked. He's just got a head that's squarer than other dogs, with their pointy noses.

Anahera sits up, and nods again.

'Yeah, and I still cried. But it was better. I always had Snot-head in bed with me, and he knew.'

'That's actually really nice,' Anahera says.

'Yeah. He's my true love.'

'Okay,' Anahera says. 'We'll keep him.'

Cynthia hadn't considered it up for question, but she nods.

'Where will he shit then?' Anahera asks, looking around their new boat.

Cynthia hadn't thought of this.

'In kitty litter,' Anahera suggests.

'We can get it tomorrow, he only needs to once a day.'

'Okay,' Anahera says.

The sea is gentle with their boat, and very blue. They find romantic novels in a little cupboard above the door, and read them together sunbathing on the deck, under the washing-line. The sun's going down – so Cynthia goes around the side of the boat for blankets. There's a loud thud, which Anahera says is just her weights. When it's too dark to see they go back inside and Anahera makes some miso soup with broccoli and other stuff in it. The thudding happens again while they eat, but Cynthia isn't frightened, she's expecting it.

While Anahera's cooking, Cynthia finds a small fresh circle of spew on one of the cushions in the cabin. Snot-head looks up at her, and she pats him three times slowly on his head. His eyes close and he nuzzles into her hand. Tomorrow she'll sneak the whole cushion into the water. He only needs to adjust.

She kisses him and leaves to ask if Anahera needs help with anything. She says no, but Cynthia sits and watches her cook. She cuts the broccoli quickly, then slides it into the pot. Everything's simple, when she moves.

They sit and eat. Anahera says not to worry about the dishes, and Cynthia stands back to watch her puzzle the table into a bed. There's a steel pipe holding it up, and Anahera loosens a screw so it can contract. Then, it's level with the seats. They lay the cushioning from inside the seats over it, and it's a bed. Cynthia gets their sheets and pillows, and Anahera sets it all up. It isn't till they're settled in and warm that Cynthia remembers Snot-head. He hates sleeping without her, but she's caught in Anahera's warm and quiet, and she says nothing. At ten, when Anahera's asleep and she almost is, she hears him under them, scratching. He whines. Cynthia's on the wall-side, so she's got to clamber over Anahera to reach him. Anahera shifts her legs, but stays mostly sleeping.

Snot-head twitches and settles into Cynthia's spooning, and Anahera lies close and breathes gently.

In the morning Cynthia wakes early, excited, and it's like she's slipped into reality, but not out of her dream. She moves quietly, and dumps the spewed-on cushion into the water outside. Under the sunrise, she eats a packet of biscuits and watches the cushion float, sink a little, and float away.

Anahera comes out, yawns in the sun, and gives Cynthia a good-morning smile. Her shoulders are postured soft, and her hair's a sweet mess on her head. She ties shampoo and conditioner to the corner of the boat – they'll be washing their hair in the sea. While she's back inside putting her togs on, Snot-head retches twice more on Cynthia's knee. Nothing comes out either time, which is great.

Anahera's togs are an old-fashioned black one-piece, which exposes the solid bones of her hips and the smooth of her back. She stretches her arms and legs, and her smile while she does so is peaceful and controlled, almost religious. Then she dives into the sea, cutting a smooth, perfect hole, precisely the size and shape of her body. She emerges metres away, and Cynthia and Snot-head watch the sun wrench the last of itself from the horizon while she swims towards it. When she's vanished, Cynthia takes her dog in to feed him. He doesn't chew, he just takes hunks of jellymeat between his teeth, lifts his head backwards so his neck squashes into rolls at the back, and lets them fall down his throat.

There are ten texts on Cynthia's phone, all from her father. They're all one long continuous message, split by his cellphone into parts. They say, 'Hello, Cynthia. Now, I see that you have stolen $16,400 from me, and some of my clothes. Without even mentioning the intensely hurtful nature of your behaviour, I must emphasise that I consider this a serious issue. I expect to receive contact from you in the near future, wherein you will apologise, and describe a detailed series of steps through which you plan to make this up to me. Sincerely, your loving father, Thomas.'

She reads it twice, and composes two draft replies but doesn't send either of them.

8

Anahera's back and she's saying all at once, 'Are you ready? Put a lead on your dog. We're going to town. Pants, Cynthia!'

Cynthia is wearing shorts, they're just tight and small. She puts on a sweater. Snot-head sees his lead and gets so excited it takes seven minutes to catch him. Anahera changes, then stands waiting. She's in the dinghy first, and when Cynthia passes the dog over there's a moment before she takes him. He trembles, and his legs wriggle in the air. 'We should definitely bring him along,' Cynthia says. Anahera takes him then, and he shakes in her hands. When Cynthia leans forward and pats his head his eyes stay wide open. Anahera paddles, and Cynthia holds him tight, tight enough to still him. 'I know how we'll make money,' she says. A gull swoops near their heads, the wharf's getting closer.

Anahera looks up abruptly from Snot-head. 'Oh, how?'

'Well,' Cynthia leans forward, over her dog. 'We'll sell undies online.' She pauses. 'Used ones.'

Anahera stops paddling.

'Horny men,' Cynthia says knowingly. 'We just have to photograph each other's bums in them.'

Anahera's paddles thoughtfully, slower. 'You've done this before?'

'Course I have,' Cynthia lies. Snot-head's a bit calmer. 'Our bums are quite different, but I've looked at yours and I think we'd do well.'

Anahera looks at Snot-head, but it's okay, he's not trembling so visibly now.

There are so many children, too many children. The footpaths are laden, and not a single person is walking down them with the same verve or purpose with which Cynthia follows Anahera, pulling Snot-head behind her. They all get out of the way. First thing, Cynthia shouts ahead to Anahera, they should stop at a café.

Some backpackers are at the table behind them. One says, 'You've just gotta breathe, man. That's all I do, breathe. And think, when has the universe not provided?'

Anahera lifts her eyebrows, and Cynthia suppresses a giggle.

'I was down to my last pair of shoes,' he says, 'you know, I was gonna have to cough up and buy some. But then – my buddy was like, he goes, "Hey, I found some shoes? I think you were saying you needed some shoes?" And, like, I'm not saying they fit me perfectly, but –'

Anahera's eyebrows are still up.

'Yeah, I can see,' the other guy pipes up. 'They've got Velcro *and* laces.'

'Mmm.'

A lady comes with Cynthia's coffee – Anahera isn't having one – and a bowl of water for the dog. 'So,' Cynthia says. 'We get G-strings, and cotton ones. Cotton ones are less sexy, but more absorbent. We make a $200 investment, and we start photographing tomorrow.'

A man comes out of a pub across the street while Cynthia's talking, and nods at Anahera, but together they ignore him.

'$200?' Anahera says.

The backpacker's pulling off the Velcro on his shoes, and putting it back down again.

'Yup,' Cynthia says. 'Gotta do it properly. Spend to make.'

'$200?'

'Alright,' Cynthia sighs. '$80.'

Anahera looks uncomfortable even with that.

It's a very small town, Paihia. Everything's either on one street, or in the little mall tucked in behind it. There's a shop with jeans, togs and two bras in the window. Cynthia walks straight in, with Anahera following. Then she has to go back out to tie Snot-head to a rubbish bin. '*Retirement knickers*,' she says under her breath to Anahera when they meet again in the lingerie section. The bras are mostly huge, and the undies too. A lady comes up to them so quickly Cynthia worries maybe she heard her joke.

'Can I help you?'

'G-strings,' Cynthia says, but she can't see any.

'Hmm,' the lady replies. She gestures to the rack they're standing beside, then wanders off a bit. They're all enormous. Cynthia wants to say *big old curtains*, but the lady doesn't quite leave. She nods at them, and adjusts some shapewear on the hangers. Because Cynthia's concentrating hard on not glaring at the woman, she's surprised when Anahera says, 'You'll look good in this,' and holds up a little red lace thing. Cynthia's head gets suddenly hot, and her shorts feel too tight. Still, she moves closer to Anahera, being careful not to look sideways at the woman who must still be there. 'So would you,' she says. Anahera holds up some blue cotton ones, jiggles them, and puts them back.

'Should we try them on?' Cynthia asks, but panics at the rasp in her voice.

'Go,' Anahera says, and hands her the red ones. Then, after thinking, the blue ones too. 'I'll find more.'

A sign says you're supposed to leave on your undies while you try on the shop's, but that's ridiculous if you're buying a G-string. Those rules are for people who aren't serious about making a purchase, not for Cynthia. They look good, both of them. Cynthia turns to see the red one from the back, and catches her own eyes in the mirror. The blue of them looks dark, she blinks. Should she call Anahera to come see? She's probably been in there a while.

There's a knock at the door. 'Are they good?' Anahera.

'Yup.' A pause. 'Do you want to –'

'Yeah, there's only one changing room.'

'So I'll get out?'

'Okay. Yeah, cool.'

Cynthia rushes with the undies, and they make a stretching noise like ripping. 'I've got the same ones,' Anahera's saying from outside. 'Just bigger and different colours.'

'Alright,' Cynthia says, sorting out her little shorts. They make brief eye contact on her exit, and she passes the undies under the door, then goes out to see Snot-head sleeping happily by the bin he's tied to outside. She's pleased to see where he's peed on it. He looks like he's melted into the concrete, he's so soft and wrinkly. His ribs are warm and she gets on her knees to pat him, and nudge his stomach with her head. Anahera laughs from above her, and touches Cynthia's bum with her shoe.

They cross the street, and Cynthia and Snot-head wait at a

picnic table while Anahera's in the supermarket. She puts him on the table so she can look at him. He's shy of the height and lowers himself to a grovel against the wood. As a youth he was very energetic, then he started humping Cynthia's legs while she slept and, although she told him a thousand times not to worry, her dad got the dog's testicles removed. Now he's very submissive and lethargic. His eyes are brown, and choc-chip flecked. She puts his head through the leg hole of the pink knickers, then the big one for hips, then the other leg hole. Anahera's taking a while.

The guy from before, who passed them while they had coffee, comes out from Countdown. Cynthia can't properly see his face, but from the way he holds his limbs he looks like all he does is walk around hoping someone will try and thump him; he's a smug, huge body with a big head settled on top. Snot-head feels the lack of her attention and panics at the tightness of the underwear. The man's pretending to watch a tree behind their table, but he's looking at Cynthia.

Anahera helps pull the last of the dog hair from the lace, then they have a biscuit each, with Snot-head looking from one mouth chewing to the other.

Either Snot-head trembles less on the way back or Cynthia's got used to it. Anahera watches, frowning and thoughtful. When they're back on the boat he won't sit down. He runs from one end to the other, snuffling and sometimes making little barks. Anahera leans back, closes her eyes, and scratches her neck. Then she opens them back up, black and bright, smiles at Cynthia, frowns, and shuts them again. 'Want to play cards?' she asks a little later.

Sure Cynthia does. 'Snap?'

'Nah,' Anahera says. 'It's always the same.'

'Aw, then nah.' Cynthia goes to the toilet, and when she comes out Snot-head's sitting on Anahera's knee, retching.

Anahera looks up. 'This doesn't seem normal.'

'Oh, it is,' Cynthia says. 'It's absolutely normal for a French bulldog to do that. They started with a very small gene pool you know, so there are those things.'

He quiets, and Anahera holds his head in the soft of her hands. 'I'm not entirely sure,' she starts saying.

'Well I am, and he's my dog,' Cynthia tells her. Anahera keeps patting him like he's nearly died, and Cynthia looks out the window, at its small cut of sky.

9

Cynthia thought they'd get right into the underwear and photographing, but they don't. Anahera joins her outside and says, 'You can have that boy Ron over, if you want?'

'Why would I?'

'I'll sleep in there,' Anahera gestures through the window, to the cabin. 'I don't mind.'

'But why would I?'

Anahera shrugs. Cynthia thinks she looks guilty, almost, but whatever she's feeling she doesn't hold it like guilt. Anahera has excellent posture, and a chin almost like a man's.

They read their books for a while under the washing-line, but Cynthia feels bad about leaving Snot-head alone and goes in to see him. She tells him to sit and he doesn't, so she squashes his bum down while telling him again. Dogs are like children's toys were in the nineties. They can only do about five things, but they still make you immensely happy. When he's stayed this way for one hundred seconds she kisses and lifts him above her head. He's got a pasty, pink bald belly and quite short legs. She loves him, and she says so a lot of times. His head crooks down and thrusts towards her face, trying to lick. He's heavy, and eventually she lowers him. He lands with his uncut nails digging into her chest, and tongues her face fast and wetly. Cynthia tries not to shut her eyes – this is intimacy – and to look steadily back at him. When he's done she wipes his spit off on her shirt.

She goes out to rejoin Anahera, but Anahera's coming back in.

—

'Business,' Cynthia says, sitting down at the table.

Anahera nods with a flirty smirk, and moves to sit, but Cynthia asks if she'd like coffee. So Anahera stays up and turns the kettle on, and Cynthia says she'll make them drinks when it boils. The slice of Anahera's mouth deepens, but her eyes don't lose their kindness.

'Alright,' Cynthia says. 'How many pairs of undies do you have, and do any of them look a bit new?'

'Five.'

'New-looking ones?'

'All together.'

That doesn't sound plausible, but Cynthia stays neutral. 'You should keep those for your own domestic use,' she says. 'I brought about, twenty?'

'Cynthia, if you brought twenty pairs, why did we spend $87 today?'

The jug boils. 'Okay. Okay, listen.' She'd thought it would be cool if they had matching ones.

Anahera does a listening face.

'Oh my god, I don't even know if I want tea now.'

Anahera switches the lean of her head from one shoulder to the other, and says, 'No, I'm sure you know what you're doing. You've done this before.'

'Well, yeah, I have,' Cynthia says, forgetting that she hasn't. She gets up to make the tea.

They sit, and Cynthia talks, making big gestures. 'Just think about it, I mean. It's money – what I'm seeing. Wads. I'm seeing our bums pressed together, you know, in one photograph. Two-packs could be a big seller. I don't think anyone's doing that. My undies and your undies. Two scents in one envelope. You know men. They're just' – Cynthia laughs – 'men are just, really.'

'How many of your own do you think we could sell?' Anahera asks.

Cynthia counts on her hands. 'Nine pairs, that's my surplus.'

Anahera spends minutes texting someone on her phone, then swims, and Cynthia sits down at the table with Snot-head to write ideas and do research. She looks at pictures on different sites: Perfect Panty Premium, Panty Deal and Stumptown Sniffs. She notes the names down to consult Anahera on later. In an article she reads, 'The inclination to smell is as natural as the urge to urinate. When you take raw meat from the refrigerator, you may smell it to determine if it's still fresh. Men approach woman in much the same way, and it's natural for them to find the scent of a woman arousing.' Snot-head's retching in the cabin, so she doesn't bother with the rest, which is about how to post things and use PayPal.

He spews only a little bit, and it's on an old blanket they got with the boat. She uses a jagged knife from the kitchen to cut the section off, and throws it into the sea.

He trembles and licks her hand while she holds him. 'Thank you' – she leans down – 'for everything you're sacrificing.'

When Anahera comes back she sits immediately, muttering, and writes down some numbers. 'Do you understand, Cynthia, that we're totally broke?' Two of her fingers rub into the fat of her cheek, but otherwise she holds her face still. She slides the paper over so Cynthia can see the figures, but Cynthia won't look away from her face. Her eyes are pierced, like a rabbit's. She's waiting for an answer.

Cynthia sighs gently and leans in. 'Don't worry, we can just float away. We'll end up somewhere.' They're not *totally* broke, she knows.

Anahera shakes her head, wriggling her hands inside each other.

'No. Hey,' Cynthia says, seriously. She needs to remember that Anahera was an adult, with a job and a husband, so she says the next part gently. 'I've been researching. We can make it extra big in the panty trade if we pee in them a bit.'

'A bit.'

'Yeah, you know, just a bit.'

'We own our own home,' Cynthia whispers to herself, twice, while Anahera sleeps. Soon, she knows, they'll talk about her father and about Anahera's divorce. She'll know who Anahera's been texting, and she'll know Anahera knows her. She's waiting patiently. Snot-head snuffles against her belly, and Cynthia's sure he's learning to hold his guts still.

There are little hills and islands all around them, and the water underneath lolls and loves them. In the bed, under all the blankets, in the warm with Anahera and Snot-head, it's like being in a tummy, under soft, mute fat and skin. During the day the sun comes through the windows and the way it yellows the old paint seems hygienic and purifying; simply healthy. Their togetherness is love or indistinguishable from love, and it's getting warmer, expanding like porridge and filling their little home.

10

Anahera goes swimming every morning and night, but that's fine. The waiting is exquisite. Cynthia's still not quite sure how to work the gas, but Anahera boils the kettle each time before she goes, and Cynthia drinks tea and watches *The Bachelor* on her phone. Snot-head spews daily, but Anahera stays out of the cabin, so it's easily handled. Her absences are also good times for Cynthia to use her face washes and pluck her eyebrows. Anahera's never gone longer than an hour, and they smell of the same soap and shampoo, so for a whiff of Anahera Cynthia only needs to sniff herself. Twice daily Anahera washes their dishes in sea water, so they dry salty, and while she's gone Cynthia licks the sides of cups like Snot-head, who, after she bathes, likes to drag his tongue down her now-spiky legs.

Each time Anahera comes back from swimming she's wet and shiny with new thinkings: 'We have to ration our food, Cynthia,' and, 'Do you want me to call your father? No, you're right, that would be inappropriate.' Mostly Cynthia isn't worried.

'You still look real good,' Anahera says one night while Cynthia's in bed watching her cook. 'Like when we left.' She flexes a leg, in Cynthia's dad's navy blue pyjamas.

'You too,' Cynthia says, and it's true. Anahera gets in with her, and hands her a bowl of something orange. 'You're good with cans.' Cynthia gestures with her spoon. Anahera's weights shift in the ceiling, gently but with noise. They must be dangerous, Cynthia thinks. This is how it must have felt for Anahera's husband, being married to her; risky and exhilarating. Cynthia doesn't mention it, instead she asks, 'How do you think a shark's stomach must feel, on the inside?' She imagines her own legs contained with Anahera's in the pyjama pants, and their breasts and arms buttoned in together under the shirt.

'I think they must stretch,' Anahera says, which is certainly right.

11

Cynthia leans in, with her mouth slightly open and her eyes a little popped, as if the tail of a fish were poking through her lips, and the fish itself were behind them pummelling her cheeks. She pushes forward, in need, with her face passive and open, held in quiet. She touches her own face, blinking for clear eyes. Her lips feel like they're plumpening, warm and tingling against the air.

It must make her even prettier, this leaning, this swaying in her body and blood. Pride swells her further. She thinks, *Here, I feel myself*, holds herself, and wishes to hold herself out for someone else. *I'm so warm*, she thinks, *who could not want this warmth of me; to take me home, and make a home for me, a home of me.* They're already there, in their new shared home, so it must have started – the looking, and leaning – the growing towards each other's light.

She touches her own warmth and softness, and doesn't see a need for it to be a secret. Still, she waits till Anahera's asleep.

Cynthia loves herself – it might be that. It's not so easy to tell the difference between self-love and a firm expectation of love from someone else.

12

It's the middle of the night. 'Cynthia,' Anahera says. 'Your dog spewed on me.'

'What? Sorry!' Cynthia says. She wriggles her hands around, trying to find her phone for light, but keeps hitting parts of Anahera's body.

'Cynthia,' Anahera says.

'Yes, Anahera, I know.'

'Yes, well, I have your dog's spew all over my stomach.'

Cynthia scrambles her hands faster, and scratches the back of Anahera's arm. She starts to apologise, but stops. 'Poor Snot-head, Anahera, I have to think of him too.' She wriggles her feet, trying to touch him, and kicks his skull. 'He spewed,' she says.

'Yeah, he spewed on me.' Anahera gets up.

'I know! That's how I know he spewed!' Cynthia moves down the bed to find him, and feels suddenly like he's running away. Anahera doesn't say anything, but goes outside. Cynthia hears the splash and slap of her wetting her shirt and leaving it on the side of the boat. She lies completely still, and after a while Snot-head snores lightly. Anahera comes back in to stand above the bed, in a different shirt, looking down. Cynthia can't see her eyes, but she sees her teeth, wet and white, in flashes as she speaks.

'This is probably not ideal for your dog.'

'No.'

Anahera waits, and so does Cynthia.

'So, just let him go, then?' Cynthia asks.

Anahera says nothing, and Cynthia's heart wrenches. She pulls at the skin of her neck and looks up. New, dim light falls through the window, on Anahera. She looks back. 'You don't like him,' Cynthia says, pulling in breath. 'You never did, and now he's puked on you.'

Anahera looks at the duvet, and the sheet, and pulls them back one at a time. Cynthia presses hard against the wall to give her space.

13

She wakes in light, to Anahera's humming. Right as she moves, Snot-head's on her face. His eyes come very close, and when she blinks he does too. She pushes him off, and sits up. Anahera turns with a warm bowl of porridge.

'I'm sorry,' Cynthia says.

'Me too.' Anahera puts some food in Snot-head's bowl and gets back in bed. 'Has he done that before, since we came?'

Cynthia shrugs, but Anahera's waiting. 'One other time, I guess.'

'Okay,' Anahera says, and her fingers are in Cynthia's hair.

Cynthia hasn't washed it, she pulls away. 'Dogs are really tough animals, and they love their owners.'

'He's real cute,' Anahera says. 'Nearly as cute as you.'

Cynthia puts some porridge in her mouth and quietly swallows it. Then she says, 'Are you even committed to this relationship?'

'What?' Anahera pauses with her spoon mid-air.

'With me and Snot-head. You haven't once suggested we photograph each other in the undies. You never pat him. Then he spews on you a little bit one time and –'

Anahera makes an interrupting noise, but then doesn't say anything. A moment, and she starts speaking but stops again. Then, 'Keep him,' she says. Immediately her mouth puckers in, surprised and regretful at what it's said. But she doesn't take it back, she adds, 'I thought we were waiting for you to join a site on your phone.'

'Well, I can't keep him if you're going to blame me and think I'm inhumane every time he spews for any reason at all.' Cynthia presses her head back against the wall, and spills a little of her porridge. Snot-head snuffles at her hip.

'We'll do it today, this morning. The photos,' Anahera says. She touches Cynthia's leg and her hand's warm.

'Only if you feel like it.' Anahera's overfed Snot-head, so Cynthia gets up and scoops meat back into the can.

Anahera goes off swimming, and Cynthia looks dumbly down at her dog. Would he prefer to die than spend another night with them, ill, on *Baby*? She's got no idea at all. They touch noses. Anahera's right; he wouldn't be alone, or even unloved for long. He'd only need to trot up to the right person. It'd take half a day. His eyes and nose are dewy, and he's excruciatingly soft. He's not obese, but certainly luxurious in figure.

Cynthia checks the cabin for more spew, and there's none. When Anahera comes back Cynthia holds her face blank, and says nothing about the dog. Anahera changes clothes and changes the table, then says, 'Right,' and smiles. 'Where do you want me to strip?'

Cynthia shrugs. 'Over there?' There's not much space, but she gestures towards the area in front of the toilet door, adjacent to the kitchen sink. It's near a window, so there's good natural light.

Anahera sticks her head in the cabin, looking for the underwear.

'I don't know if I'm in the right mood, sorry,' Cynthia says.

Anahera shakes her bum. 'Nonsense.'

Cynthia pulls Snot-head closer, and looks out the window. Anahera changes in the bathroom, and emerges in a T-shirt and the lace thong – sickly pink. She's embarrassed. 'Um,' she says, 'do I just turn around?'

It'll be fun after all. 'Yup,' Cynthia says, suddenly moving and disturbing Snot-head. He trots to the cabin. Anahera turns and takes awkward hold of the bathroom doorknob. Cynthia's not sure what the right, encouraging thing to say is, but it looks real good. She takes a picture. Anahera takes her shirt off then, so she's in just a bra, and shifts onto the toes of one of her feet so one butt cheek's higher than the other. 'Oh, yup!' Cynthia says, and takes another shot, then wishes she'd stayed quiet. But it feels weird to be quiet. Anahera turns and Cynthia says, 'Gosh!' then feels worse. She shades her eyes like the sun's in them, and squints.

'Alright?' Anahera asks.

'Oh, oh yeah!' Cynthia says. 'We'll roll in it. Money!' She takes one last photo, from the front, clipping out Anahera's face. Anahera laughs, relieved, and goes for her shorts and shirt. Photos in just one pair aren't enough, but Cynthia says nothing. They're only starting.

'Sorry if I made you uncomfortable.'

Anahera snorts gently, dressed now, and sits down to ruffle Cynthia's hair. 'You're doing it too.'

'I'll get rid of him,' Cynthia says.

Anahera's quiet, but they're sitting side by side, and Cynthia can feel through her arm that she's pleased. Neither of them looks to the cabin, where he's asleep. Cynthia shifts her eyes from her knees, suddenly, and stands up. 'Right then!' She gets the red underwear from the cabin, and changes in the bathroom. She adjusts the lace so there's no hair poking through, and pushes the tap-pump three times to wash her face in salty water. Then, she strides out.

Anahera's sitting on the bed in the still of the boat, waiting. She looks away from the window, at Cynthia, and Cynthia bursts into tears.

'Come here,' Anahera says, patting the seat beside her.

'It doesn't matter,' Cynthia says. 'My face won't be in the shots anyway.'

Anahera's face scrunches deeper with concern, but Cynthia ignores her and gets her phone. She explains how to work the camera. Anahera must already know, but she says nothing, nods, and takes a test shot of the kettle.

Cynthia makes a big smile, and gives two thumbs up. Then she stands and turns around, sticking her bum out. She waits, and Anahera doesn't take the photo. Snot-head's in the cabin with his ears flicked up; he's heard her sobbing. His eyes are wet and his wrinkles look particularly saggy. Cynthia only glances at him, then faces the wall again.

'Look, we can do this another time,' Anahera says.

'But we haven't done it another time ever!' Cynthia splutters. She doesn't move, gets herself quiet, and at last hears the camera go. That done, she turns and looks dully through the window behind Anahera's head, while she gets a photo from the front.

'There are other ways for us to make money,' Anahera says.

'What's wrong with this way?' Cynthia asks, holding her body still and barely moving even her mouth.

'Keep your dog,' Anahera says.

'Take the photo, Anahera.'

The clicking noise.

'Take another one.'

Anahera does.

'I'm not going to wear any other pairs today,' Cynthia says. 'I actually can't be bothered.' Anahera says nothing, which enrages Cynthia, but she holds in her rage, saying nothing either. Snot-head makes a little dry-heave in the cabin.

They both agree the milk smells fine and Anahera makes Cynthia a hot chocolate with it. She doesn't say anything more about the photos, the dog or money, she just watches Cynthia slurp up the drink. Snot-head watches too, from the floor.

'We'll do it tomorrow,' Cynthia says toughly, through her milky mouth, and nudges his ribs with her foot so Anahera can see what she means. 'And we'll get more groceries.'

Anahera nods, and rubs her back. The photos are good, but Cynthia doesn't get around to uploading them.

In bed that afternoon Cynthia runs her fingers through the crevices between Snot-head's wrinkles, and pauses every now and again to feel Anahera's own fingers wriggling through her hair. They are three spoons, but Anahera coughs and walks outside. Still, when she lies down again Snot-head makes a short lovely snuffle and she and Cynthia laugh against each other, his body a warm perfect nugget at their centre.

For dinner Cynthia asks if she can give him corned beef, even though there's jellymeat left, and Anahera says yes. After eating it, he walks in three little circles, slowly, then waits under the bed to be lifted up into it.

Anahera doesn't swim that night, and makes Cynthia a really nice soup. They wrap Snot-head in a blanket and eat it with him outside, under the stars, then a whole packet of Tim Tams.

14

The next morning Snot-head hasn't spewed anywhere at all. When Cynthia goes to the toilet, she lets him in after her and Anahera pretends not to notice. She sits with him on her knee after peeing, in privacy. After she's not sure how long, she stops patting him and forgets where she is.

When she comes back out, the bed's the table and they sit at it, side by side on the seat. Anahera stays out of the way. Cynthia writes a letter saying all the predictable things: How loved he is, and how lovely. That his name is Snot-head, and can it please not be changed? Also, you've always got to feed him less food than he wants.

The water under them is slow but rolling, so the note's a bit woozy. When she's done, she puts the paper aside and copies it carefully, pressing the pen down hard with each letter. It still doesn't look good, but you can see how hard she's tried by the pen's indent in the paper.

'He's very handsome.' Anahera puts her face close to his.

Cynthia shrugs.

'You have me,' Anahera says.

Cynthia pats him and doesn't look at her. Anahera always knows how to speak without promising.

Anahera waits a very long moment, then asks, 'Should we go soon?'

Cynthia says nothing, just affixes her note to his collar with some lace cut from her blouse.

'I just think, the sooner we drop him off, the more of today he has left to find somebody.'

They feed him and eat as quickly as he does. In her best clothes, Cynthia uses spit and her finger to clean gunk from the corners of his eyes, then her own, and they go.

In the dinghy she holds him tight – he's breathing deeply too. The water's slow, but the waves are big and moving up and down as well as towards the wharf. They keep coming up in leaps, and splashing Snot-head's tender face, so Cynthia takes her sweater off to wrap him up. Anahera pretends not to watch them, and makes a wince-smile when Cynthia catches her.

'Is it a weekday?' Cynthia asks.

'Thursday.'

'Then we'll leave him at the school. He likes kids.'

'That's a really, really good idea.'

Cynthia squeezes him, and smiles. 'I'll show him around a bit, so he knows where he is.'

They go to the supermarket and Cynthia picks Snot-head up and carries him inside. Anahera says nothing, and when Cynthia talks to her dog aloud to see if he wants the most expensive salmon, she stays quiet. 'Yes, of course you do!' Cynthia says, and she licks him between his two big eyes. On the checkout guy's request, she and the dog wait outside while Anahera pays.

She comes back out, hands over the can, and stands waiting. 'The school's just over there,' she gestures across the street, and moves her body in that direction too, suggesting they head off.

'We'd prefer to do this without you,' Cynthia says.

Anahera furrows her brow.

Cynthia doesn't watch her face for long, and busily fondles her dog.

'I'll get more groceries then,' Anahera says, and pats the pocket with her phone and card.

'Great.' Cynthia walks off.

'See you back here at twelve,' Anahera yells after them. She doesn't yell a second time, although Cynthia makes sure not to acknowledge hearing. After she's clipped the lead to his collar and put him down she notices a car's waiting for them to move; they're standing in the middle of the road. She's got no money for a snack.

They walk together past some quite nice houses, and Cynthia points each out to Snot-head. 'You see, that one's got a big deck, but the grey is no good. It'll depress you. Yes, it will. Yes.' Sometimes he looks where she points, or up at her when she speaks, but mostly he just sniffs the ground. 'That one's wood. Bricks, that one. Bricks are warmer. Three cars at that one. Yup, yup. *Three* cars.' When they've walked around two and half sides of the school they reach a carpark, which they hurry through. Cynthia doesn't want him hanging around that part of town.

Soon they're back at the dairy. It must be mid-morning. Over the road there's a bank at the bottom of which is the back end of the school sports field. She'll climb down it, wait for the bell to ring, eat a bit of salmon, and leave him on the field with the rest. The children will emerge yelling, and he'll trot to them. She'll be gone up the bank before he turns back to her.

She picks him up and clambers down, much quicker than she'd like to. He quivers in her arms. When she sets him on the ground he's very pleased, and she sees how small he is. She opens the salmon, and hits it hard against the ground so half falls out. There's less than she thought, and he eats quicker than she imagined. His share is gone, and he waits. She gets on her knees to kiss him goodbye and tell him not to worry, she loves him, but he won't look at her face. He gets up on his back legs and rests his front paws on her arm. 'No,' she says, careful not to be harsh because she thinks the bell will go soon. 'In a moment,' she tells him, and pushes his front legs gently from her arm. She holds him down while she kisses him, and cries a little.

When he hears her, Snot-head pauses and – this is his love – stops trying to reach the salmon. He looks up at her, confused. She pats his head twice more, and murmurs her love again. Silence, and he doesn't know why they're still there, or why he remains unfed. He uses his best manners and waits. Finally, Cynthia pats the rest of the salmon from the can onto the ground. He sniffs it, but decides he's had enough fish anyway. 'Yes, I love you. I love you more than her,' she tells him, but she can't make it make sense. He sniffs a second time, half-heartedly, and Cynthia remembers she was about to leave. The bell hasn't rung, he doesn't want the salmon. She touches her forehead, and scrambles up the bank. It's steeper than it looked. He's not eating, but standing with his head up, watching her, still waiting. She turns away, and struggles up the last bit in a big movement. At the top, she turns again, and he's left the fish to stand with his two front paws up against the bank. He sees her looking and struggles to follow her. Not hard, he's fat and lazy, and he doesn't know what her going means, but he tries. The bell rings then, but he doesn't look away. He's shuffling all his feet, the two on the ground and the two on the bank, and not moving at all.

Cynthia walks away, to wait for Anahera.

She sticks her head through the door of a bakery and sees she's half an hour early. She could go back now, to watch him meet the kids, but she doesn't. He'd see her looking, and she'd distract the children from petting him. He might run in the wrong direction, and what could she do to help, call him? No, she waits. She walks up and down the street and looks through the windows of a series of ridiculous shops. There are so many scarves for sale these days. Anahera arrives three minutes late. Cynthia knows, because when she sees Anahera coming she ducks her head through the door of a tourist shop and checks the time on a big paua-encrusted clock. Counting the time it takes them both to get back to the designated spot, Anahera might even be late by seven minutes. When they do meet, she knows better than to ask how it went. She's carrying seven huge bags of groceries, but she doesn't gesture for Cynthia to take any of them. 'I'm sorry,' she says, seeing Cynthia's face. 'You can go back and get him?'

They walk in silence back to the dinghy, and on the way Cynthia takes two of the bags.

That afternoon there's another text from Cynthia's father, split into five parts. It's the same one he sent before ('Hello, Cynthia. Now, I see that you have stolen $16,400 from me, and some of my clothes . . .') but he's added the words *very,* and *humiliating* so that the message now says, 'Without even mentioning the very intensely hurtful and humiliating nature of your behaviour, I must empha- sise that I consider this a serious issue,' before continuing on to inform her that he expects to receive contact in the near future. He's also included a postscript stating that he's 'sorry if she ever felt he didn't support her in whatever career ambitions she had'.

This time, he's sent the message as an email as well as a text. She's got to have courage, so reads it in each format only once and deletes his number. She doesn't say a thing for the rest of the day, and Anahera watches her cautiously, touches her gently, and doesn't ask any questions.

15

The next day, before Anahera goes for her swim, she says, 'I thought because I liked sunbathing with you so much, and reading those books' – and she hands Cynthia a stack of pink-edged paperbacks. Four of them. 'This guy's on a horse' – she shows the cover of one – 'and this one's a Wall-Street wolf.' She makes a little growling noise at Cynthia, leans down, and bites her gently on the ear. Cynthia shivers from the bite, and jumps a little in excitement. After a moment lifting up and down on the balls of her feet, she growls back. Being in the sun with Anahera, and under the sunsets, knowing they're both reading books the other has read, or will read – what could be more beautiful? The men on the covers are all shirtless.

'Thank you,' she says. 'Thank you so much.'

Anahera beams back, and retrieves a packet of Tim Tams. 'I don't need to swim this morning,' she says. 'I just want to be with you.'

They take blankets around the edge of the boat and lie on them. They have cups of cold tea and of rum, and even though it's a bit warm it's cooler than the air around them, and sweet. Anahera reads from the blurb of her book, 'His face is that of a millionaire magnate, yes – but heavy and low in his Armani trousers lurks the cock of a lumberjack.' Her voice is sharp and cool, like a knife in water, and she laughs. Cynthia's probably in love. She laughs too, and unsticks her sweaty legs. Anahera pats them and says they'll read a bit, then go in for lunch.

Cynthia gets stuck on one page for an hour, and what she's imagining is Anahera saving her from drowning.

Anahera's stirring whatever lunch is on the stove. Cynthia's lying on the bed, and she sticks her foot up in the air. 'What do you think of this?'

'What?'

'My foot.'

Anahera turns. 'It's alright.'

Cynthia raises her eyebrows and waggles it. She worms her body on the warm, sun-heated bed, into the blankets. With her eyebrows raised, she waggles it faster and faster till Anahera says, 'It's good.'

Cynthia stops then. 'Thanks. It is, yeah.'

Anahera turns the heat down on the stove and stands looking at Cynthia, at her body. 'I had bunions,' Cynthia tells her, provokingly. 'You wouldn't think it, but I did.'

Anahera leans back on the bench. 'Bunions,' she repeats.

'And I've got a sensitive tummy,' Cynthia adds quickly. 'Weird ankles, too. Sometimes I just fall right over.' She rests her foot down on the bed and pulls her shirt up to reveal her tummy. 'I can drink those big bottles of apple juice, but I'll tell you what – I shouldn't. If I drink a small bottle of apple juice I can't jog anywhere, or even walk quickly, or have sex with anyone for four hours afterwards, minimum.'

Anahera looks down tenderly, as if Cynthia's belly were a kitten, and nods.

'You can touch it,' Cynthia tells her. Anahera squats down, beside the bed, and puts her fingers lightly on Cynthia's stomach.

'My body's a real disaster, in some ways,' Cynthia tells her, not showing off, just stating a fact. Anahera nods, and shifts her fingers like a whirlpool around Cynthia's tummy button. 'Anyway,' Cynthia says, 'you can touch my armpits, through my shirt.'

Anahera looks at her and her fingers pause.

Cynthia feels her lips pull in, but she's making sure not to be embarrassed. 'I like it sometimes,' she says. 'I touch my own armpits sometimes.' It's hot, the blankets are so hot under her, and her face must be like a capsicum. She lifts her arm up above her head and smiles playfully. 'Come on, love,' she says in a fake man's voice. 'Get to it.'

Anahera pauses a moment, but doesn't laugh. She leans over Cynthia, and with the long fingers of both her hands touches Cynthia's armpit. It tickles splendidly, like Cynthia's a pet rabbit, but she makes sure not even to smile. She can feel her eyes and lips opening, and she touches the inside of her bottom lip with her tongue. Anahera pauses her fingers, and Cynthia nods for her to keep moving them. 'It's sexual,' she whispers bravely.

Anahera nods, puzzled and hopefully pleased.

'Okay,' Cynthia says. 'That's enough, they lose sensitivity after a while.'

They gaze at each other. Cynthia notices again four or five stray hairs at Anahera's eyebrows, and her long blinking eyelashes, and realises: she's in love, definitely. Anahera stays close for a moment longer, then goes to circle the spoon around in the pot. She shifts from foot to foot, like dancing.

16

They're having a fabulous conversation, where words mean more than they do, and everything is true. 'We don't always understand each other,' Anahera has said, very frankly, and Cynthia has nodded.

Now Cynthia adds, 'We don't, no, no, we don't,' and she laughs. 'We're very different, but I try, and you try, and that's what counts.'

Anahera sips her rum, and nods. They look at each other, and this is what Cynthia has always wanted to feel – that by making eye contact with a dear, special person, she might become eternal. She feels herself expanding, and the enormous water laps at their boat from below.

The sun returns to them stronger with each day, and Cynthia stops counting them. Quickly, they finish the first bottle of rum, and Anahera produces a second. They lie close, nearly on top of each other, and at every full stop, between the sentences in Cynthia's romance novels, she imagines rolling over against Anahera, and telling her the dirty, truthful facts of her desire. Sometimes, Anahera herself rolls over and she says nothing, but Cynthia thinks her eyes press forward, like fingers. She's sure they both know, and are both waiting.

Cynthia could list her needs, and all of them are love. She could list what she's paid, given and sacrificed to Anahera, and it's so much more than money now. It's everything.

Anahera's swims are longer, twice as long. But Cynthia's happy for her – she must be even fitter! – and the time between them seems to have expanded. When Anahera's gone, Cynthia remembers Snot-head and wonders where he might be. She plucks herself, looks in the mirror and feels sad, but each time Anahera returns she's always pleased, and beautiful again.

17

They're re-reading their books now, which is a bit boring, but in a lovely, predictable way. Anahera gets up, slowly and hardly using her arms to lift her weight, and goes around the side of the boat and into the toilet. Cynthia sits still and watches the door once she's shut it. It takes Anahera less than three minutes to re-emerge. When she does, instead of returning to the sun and to Cynthia, she sits down at the table and looks into her phone, then types something. A message, she's sent it. Then she looks up and sees Cynthia watching through the window. She looks back, and sets her shoulders.

This is the third time this has happened, but Cynthia knows that, if asked, Anahera will assert her right to text whoever she likes. So, Cynthia rearranges her book in her lap, and peers down into it.

When Anahera's settled back onto her belly and elbows to read, Cynthia gazes down into the parting of her hair, and sees it as a crevasse. She asks, 'Where do you swim to?'

'Oh,' Anahera shuffles up, and points in the direction of an island. 'There.'

'To that beach?' Cynthia asks.

'Sometimes just towards it.'

Cynthia settles down to read then. She will not be unreasonable, she takes a glug of rum. Anahera has every right to send text messages, and visit a beach. 'Do you want to watch *The Newlywed Game* with me tonight?' she asks.

'Yup, what's that?'

The Newlywed Game is Cynthia's current favourite. Some couples even got divorced because of it. They answer questions about each other, and have to predict each other's answers to win. It's good to watch on a phone, because the definition's bad.

For lunch, Anahera boils two-minute noodles and canned tomatoes together in a pot, and the result is good. While eating they drink more rum. Afterwards Cynthia does some dancing. 'Wiggle it!' Anahera shouts at her. Cynthia bends and shakes her bum harder. Laughing, nearly wheezing, Anahera takes her head, holds it still, and puts some raisins in her mouth.

Cynthia dances her plastic cup up to Anahera and it's filled right up. She drinks half, and she drinks more while undressing for her midday wash-swim. 'I'm too drunk,' she tells Anahera, laughing. 'Too drunk for swimming.'

'I'll watch you,' Anahera says, and Anahera is watching her.

Cynthia strips down to her underwear, like usual, to wash. But she can feel Anahera's eyes pulling her body, sucking at her, and she can feel her own desire prickling, trying to escape her skin. It's hot. She swallows more and watches Anahera gulp back twice as much, and even flinch a little after doing so. Then, she puts her glass aside and leans forward with her elbows on her knees. Cynthia turns around, in a circle, unthinking, looking for nothing. Then she stops. She's facing a little to the side of Anahera, looking at the island. 'What do you do there?' she asks.

Anahera shrugs. 'Sit, mostly.'

'And, are you watching me still?' Cynthia asks, but she can't turn the rest of the circle, she can't look at Anahera while she speaks. Instead she leans over the edge, to feel the water. Its coolness reminds her of her body, and how smooth it is. She wants to shift her hand and touch herself, her hip, her waist, her ass, but she can't, Anahera's looking. She touches her wet hand to her throat, waiting for an answer.

'Yes,' Anahera says, 'I'm still watching you.'

Cynthia will slip in, underneath the water. She's about to. She can see the ladder, and the shampoo tied to it where the water foams against the side of the boat. She will, but she can feel Anahera's eyes holding her, and all of her body tingles, ready to be filled up and loved.

'I'm still watching you,' Anahera says.

Cynthia puts two of her fingers under the elastic of her underwear and wriggles them, wriggles them down, then kicks her two feet out of the holes. Trembling, she unclasps her bra. She can't hear it, not quite, but Anahera is breathing behind her, sitting with her eyes open. It's good, standing there in the cool light wind, under the sun. That's all you have to do to find yourself; tear everything else away. The air shifts against her new wilderness hair and her hardening nipples. She won't be ashamed. She turns to look back at Anahera.

Anahera's eyes shift away first, and she says, 'You know,' then gestures to the other boats around them.

'So?' Cynthia stands for one moment. Then, in her usual slow way, she gets in the water, wetting herself in very small portions at a time. Anahera's still watching her, she must be, but when Cynthia turns back to see her she's drinking more, and staring down at her hands.

Cynthia's careful not to do anything faster than she normally would, to get the roots of her hair washed properly, and not to miss any sections in conditioning the tips. When she's clean and a little cold, she shifts to the ladder and hovers on it, halfway up.

Anahera's untangling her hair. 'I don't know,' she says. It's very tangled today, a huge poof on her head, and she pulls a strand through the larger mass thoughtfully.

'About what?' Cynthia says, touching her nipple and trying to adopt a similar, contemplative expression.

'I don't know if sex would really be good for us.' Anahera drops her hair and watches Cynthia's finger, moving in circles now. The sun caught in her hair is godly. She raises her eyebrows.

'But why are you thinking about it?' Cynthia asks. She shakes some water from her hair and climbs up into the cold, fresh air. 'I play fast and loose,' she says, 'and I have since forever.'

Anahera's laugh is like biting, but she says seriously, 'So you want – what?'

Cynthia feels like a dashboard dog, nodding. Then she hears the question. 'You,' she says.

'I'm not looking for anything.'

'Doesn't matter, I'm something anyway.'

Anahera touches her own neck, and Cynthia begins nodding again. When it doesn't seem right to nod anymore she goes to sit on the bed, hoping Anahera will follow her. Anahera stands in the doorway, looking all over Cynthia's body. She's wearing Cynthia's father's pin-striped shirt and her workout shorts. Her feet are bare, and the muscles of her legs look almost tensed. The shirt's not buttoned all the way to the bottom, and she's holding one side from underneath, scrunched up in a fist. Cynthia can see her tummy button, a rude-looking slight outie. She shifts one of her feet, but doesn't come forward or stop looking. Cynthia lies back and twists sideways.

'What do you like, Cynthia?' Anahera asks, with her voice quiet like she's trying to be careful.

Cynthia thought she knew this. They both wait for her to stop thinking, and say, 'Come touch me.' Just then something clangs outside, and Anahera looks up, but Cynthia says it again, and Anahera does. Cynthia fingers the collar of her father's shirt, and then the buttons. Her fingers slip between them, and she's touching Anahera's breasts. Anahera laughs, but doesn't move to remove the shirt. Blood rushes through Cynthia, and lands hard and thumping between her legs. She squirms against the pressure, then she's squirming against Anahera's hand, and her fingers. With her second hand, Anahera presses down on Cynthia's chest, pushing her into the bed. Cynthia pushes back, and then she doesn't.

Anahera leans down and kisses her mouth, then, smooth and sudden, her fingers are in Cynthia. Cynthia moans and thrusts up, but Anahera's hand is pressure on her chest, holding her down. Her eyes shut, and the feeling becomes bigger, and becomes everything she's ever felt, or could feel. There's nothing in her mind but Anahera's eyes, looking down, with her pupils big and seeming to grow, then more, more, and Cynthia's feels she's lost her whole body inside them.

She blinks, and feels she's falling upwards.

'You're cute,' Anahera says, and Cynthia wants to touch her nose. The air between them sparkles, or Cynthia has fallen into Anahera's eyes.

'Are you alright?' Anahera asks, which is peculiar.

'I am, I don't want to move,' Cynthia says. There's no blood in her head, only an enormous, expanding sense of meaning. She says, 'I keep dreaming of Snot-head.' She hasn't been, really. She didn't think of him at all yesterday, but now she hears his name the soft, wet memory of his face comes right back to her. His tongue licking her cheeks. She touches them, and they're wet with tears. 'I knew we were magic,' she tells Anahera, 'I knew everything would be worth it.' She dabs some wetness from below her eye, and puts it to Anahera's lips, hitting teeth. Anahera had looked fierce only a moment ago, while her hands worked on Cynthia and pushed her down, but now through Cynthia's tears her face looks pliant and dewy. Confused, even. She shakes her head a little, so Cynthia's finger is flung from between her lips, and she goes outside.

Cynthia lies a moment, still deep in feeling, then follows her. The weather's changed, the sun's behind a cloud and there's wind. The water's a voluptuous mess. 'You're like my hero,' she tells Anahera. She wipes her eyes with her wrists and looks up, but Anahera isn't looking down at her. 'I think it's around the time of Snot-head's birthday,' she says. 'Today might be his birthday.'

Water is flung against them, and Cynthia remembers she's naked. 'It's his birthday,' she says, insistent that Anahera understand. But he wasn't Anahera's dog. 'Let me do you,' Cynthia says, but the wind takes her words before Anahera's had a chance to hear them, and she can't seem to repeat herself. They stand together.

Anahera waits for two more waves to disappear before wiping her eyes and looking down as if puzzled. 'Another time. Let's watch your show.'

'You're cute,' Anahera had said, and it made Cynthia happy, but now she can't find her show because it keeps distracting her, playing back in her mind in a dull voice. The air's gone cold, but Cynthia feels if she gets up to dress something will be over, so she snuggles in towards Anahera's warmth, and eventually finds the link.

She points out the couples who've matched their clothes; they're the ones you have to watch. Another thing: 'They call sex "making whoopee"!' Cynthia repeats it a second time. 'Making whoopee!'

Anahera laughs then says, 'Okay.'

Cynthia's hungover, so maybe she's not thinking properly, but it feels like their bed's gone saggy. She waits for the feeling to pass, but it doesn't. She presses play.

Bob, the host, asks the husbands, 'What percentage of your wife's body is jawbreaker, and what percentage is jello?'

Anahera gets squinty at the little screen, at Bob. The men all answer, laughing, but Anahera doesn't seem to get the fun of it, so Cynthia turns it off.

'Aw,' says Anahera. 'Why?' But Cynthia feels the space in the bed between them, and Anahera's body already readying itself to stand up.

'Never mind,' Cynthia says, and goes for her clothes.

That night Cynthia sits out late, with more rum, under the washing-line and the stars, putting Burger Rings on her fingers and eating them off. She's thinking, if you stop waiting for something to happen it won't, and if you start wondering if it will happen, you'll stop waiting.

She goes back inside, and Anahera's lying with her eyes open. 'Excuse me?' Cynthia says.

'Yeah?' Anahera barely moves.

'I saw your husband in town, and I know you've been texting him.' Cynthia shifts her feet, but keeps her head up.

A noise comes from Anahera's mouth, but it's a time before she speaks. 'My husband will never talk to me again, because I took his car and sold it to buy this boat. And because – *Cynthia, as you know* – he caught me having sexual intercourse with another man. Now, I can tell you very definitively that I have not been texting my husband, and that you did not see him in Paihia.'

'Oh, sorry,' Cynthia says, shrinking.

But Anahera leans over and tugs Cynthia by her arm into bed. They don't touch, not properly, but Cynthia thinks of how their bodies are lying in parallel lines, and feels tremendous relief at knowing there's no one else, anywhere, equivalent to either of them.

18

The following day Anahera's swim takes longer than any other. The waiting drags. Even when she's back the hours feel limp. They lie on the deck, reading in the sun, but spend more time not reading, and not doing anything else. Cynthia joins Panty Utopia, uploads pictures and writes the listing. She can't tell Anahera, because Anahera thinks she's already done it. 'You think we need jobs,' she says instead.

Anahera's hands stay far away from Cynthia, and her body far away from Cynthia's hands. They go inside, then Anahera goes back out. Cynthia turns the table into the bed and gets in. It's shaky and wrong, she's never done it before, but she won't get out and fix it. She watches a *Catfish* episode about a guy who thinks he's dating Katy Perry. Anahera comes back through, looks at her, and goes to pee. Cynthia turns off her show – she doesn't need to see him click any more faulty links to know his Katy's false – and turns to face the wall.

Anahera opens the door. 'What do you want?'

Cynthia wets her lips then blows air through them. Anahera always acts as if things are simple.

'I'll watch the rest of your show with you? I thought it looked really interesting.'

Cynthia makes another noise with even more moisture, and her spit lands on the wall in front of her face.

'I'll make biscuits,' Anahera says.

Cynthia rolls over to look at her.

'Okay,' Anahera says, then disappears back into the bathroom, and releases the water from the sink. 'Alright.' She re-emerges and sets about the biscuits. Cynthia sits up on her elbows to watch.

'There's nothing wrong with you,' Anahera turns and says, 'at all.'

'I don't need you to say that,' Cynthia grumbles. But the biscuits already smell good. It doesn't take long, and they're in the oven. Anahera gets on her knees on the bed above Cynthia, and touches her forehead with a thumb.

'Sorry about yesterday,' she says.

'What part?'

'They shouldn't take long,' Anahera says, of the biscuits. 'I made little ones.' She moves back on her heels to watch Cynthia.

'You're right, I'm totally fine,' Cynthia mumbles. Anahera seems to be waiting for more, so she adds, 'I only know how to be myself.'

Anahera gets up then, to peer through the foggy window of their little oven. 'First time we've used this thing,' she says. While they wait she goes outside, and Cynthia watches her feet through the windows, walking around the edge of the boat in loops. On the fourth loop, Cynthia joins her, then they come back in together to check the biscuits. They're nearly done. They walk three more loops together, and the biscuits are cooked.

In bed beside Anahera, Cynthia pulls one apart in her two hands. It doesn't crumble, it divides. The chocolate's in big parts, and the biscuit's fudgy. Anahera puts her arm up, near Cynthia's head, so it's touching the fluff of her hair. Cynthia can feel her in the static. She shoves both parts of the biscuit in her mouth and holds them there.

'We do need to make a plan,' Anahera says. 'About what to do with ourselves.' She kicks the blankets to the ground, away from their feet. It's hot. The biscuit dissolves in Cynthia's mouth, moving towards her throat and between her teeth. 'I don't know what,' Anahera says, 'but something.'

Cynthia just feels tired. She runs her tongue between her top lip and gums, and she doesn't mention her father, or her dog.

Anahera can't lift her legs straight up, because the ceiling's low over the bed, but she stretches them with her knees bent.

Cynthia reaches for another biscuit.

'What do you think?' Anahera asks.

'I'll get mussels with you,' Cynthia says. This is something Anahera's talked about more than once, but it seems brutal and scratchy; unfun. Still, Cynthia will do it.

'Okay,' Anahera says, but Cynthia can feel her still waiting.

19

That night in bed, Anahera cries.

'What is it?' Cynthia asks, but Anahera pretends to sleep. 'Please,' Cynthia says, stroking her fingers down Anahera's back, but the muscles stiffen. She waits, maybe for an hour, and then Anahera really is sleeping.

She takes $20 from Anahera's wallet in the drawer under the cutlery. She's going to buy nice food things. Sweet buns, possibly. They'll eat happily in the morning.

With the money tucked in her bra, she gets in the dinghy and the darkness, then unties herself, holding tightly to the paddle. The moon is magical light on the water, every part of it glimmers and beckons. She's not far from the wharf, and it's lit. Still, it stays the same size for minutes and minutes despite her paddling. Sometimes the work is easier, and she forgets this means she's holding the paddle wrong. Suddenly, the prickle of the money's gone from her breast and she looks around – as if it will be the sole bright thing fluttering in the night, but it's nowhere. Also: she didn't pay any attention when she walked with Anahera, she doesn't know where the shops are. They won't even be open. She turns, thinking she'll go back, and finds she's moved farther from the boat than she thought.

She struggles forward, and arrives. When she's tied the dinghy up and retied it a second time, there's the sound of people talking. Comforted, she squeezes her bra and finds the money there, as crunchy as when she first shoved it in. She wipes her sweat proudly, and gets out. The wharf's still under her feet, a peculiar feeling, and the surety of it strengthens her.

At the top of the steel bridge she's right by the tree Snot-head pooped under when they first arrived. It was the last one she ever watched him do on land, so she stands a while. There's just enough wind to shift the leaves, silhouetted by the moon, and to touch Cynthia through her shirt, where she's wet with sweat at her armpits. It's cold, she's wearing only her pyjamas, and she must move on.

She thought she was leaving to buy nice food for Anahera, but then she's in a pub. There are two men at the bar. She sees them, and sees them shift towards each other and see her. They're not attractive, but Cynthia leans on something out of habit – a high table. One looks Samoan, about twenty-five, and his hat's on backwards. He's the better one. The other's thirty, white, and he's walking towards her.

She remembers the sweet buns. His eyes are brown and his cheeks pouchy. He's looking at her hard, through an odd soft face. There's stubble on his cheeks, which should be good but somehow isn't. Suddenly his hand's out between them, and he's still walking. She doesn't move towards it. He hurries the last step and finally arrives too close.

'Where have you run away from?' he asks her.

'I'm just looking for the supermarket.'

'What?' he says.

'They're probably all shut,' she tells him.

He nods, and moves to go back to his friend.

'I'm having trouble with my girlfriend,' she says.

He looks right back at her. 'What?'

'I gave up everything to be with her.'

He nods for her to follow him, and they go back to his friend. 'Having trouble with her missus,' he explains, and his friend adjusts his hat and nods. They wait for more information.

'I had to let my dog go.' She nods as she says it.

'Ah,' they say, as if they've lost pets to women too. It's a poorly lit establishment. They sit there together, leaning on the bar and thinking. Cynthia orders a beer and drinks it. She goes to the toilet, pees, and comes back to sit with them and think some more.

'Him and his girlfriend never have sex,' the white guy tells her of the Samoan one. He doesn't deny it, just looks glumly into his glass. Cynthia doesn't say anything, but she does feel better, and warm in a way she misses. 'He's single,' the Samoan guy tells her, gesturing at the white one. Then he says, 'Love is difficult.'

Cynthia nods. Eventually she says, 'Okay,' and leaves. On the way back she stops at a liquor store and buys two packets of biscuits.

In the dinghy the tide pulls her in the right direction, and she doesn't worry about finding the boat. That's a whole town Snot-head can poo on she thinks, forgetting the regulations. Anahera was right, he'll be happier on land. She paddles slowly and wriggles, mixing up the beer in her belly to keep warm. Then she sees it, in its splendid curling script. *Baby.*

20

Anahera's gone when Cynthia wakes. It's still dark, and she stares hard at the ceiling, thinking. Her feet have always fit perfectly in her shoes, and her socks were always white, all of them, perfectly. Her handwriting's as neat as her toes, and till less than two months ago her eyebrows were as elegantly articulated as the dots on her 'i's. Now everything's slackening, she can feel it. She's shed her father, her dog, and now she's shedding herself.

Things have been happening since before she was born, she understands, in places she's never been, and Anahera seems to know everything. Cynthia must step forward or lose her.

She's reached a time and a place; Anahera will be back soon, and Cynthia wants only to be obedient.

'I'm going to town today, to ask about jobs. You can come if you want.'

'I'll come,' Cynthia says. Anahera's breasts are visible through Cynthia's father's damp All Blacks shirt, and Cynthia wishes they were touching each other, and that she didn't have to speak. 'I know you want stuff,' she says.

Anahera nods, and says, 'Okay, that's great Cynthia!' but then she doesn't say anything else. She makes jam sandwiches, and Cynthia sits thinking of Snot-head. Her dog, walking up to door after door, sniffing and begging. You can't think about it sensibly.

You can't think of anything important that way. Someone will have taken him in, surely, and he'll be in a room sleeping with them now, while they knit or talk on the phone. You can't think about need.

Anahera hands her a sandwich, and then two more wrapped in a plastic bag. 'Lunch.' The bread's stale, but they'll get more today. While chewing, Anahera says, 'I think sometimes – why can't I belong only to myself?' She looks to Cynthia for confirmation, and Cynthia eats her sandwich. 'My husband looked so *aggrieved* when he caught me, and I just think, he didn't have the *right*.'

Cynthia would like to argue, actually, but she chews.

21

Cynthia watches Anahera paddle, trying to understand how she was getting it wrong the night before. How do you know where you're going without turning to check? Anahera looks at Cynthia, who has dressed up very tidily. 'Do you know how to ask for a job?'

Cynthia adjusts her blouse where it's tucked into her pants. 'Can I have a job?'

'No,' Anahera says. 'That's wrong.'

Cynthia stares up at the sun.

'You say, "Hi, my name's Cynthia."' Anahera puts out her hand and beams when Cynthia shakes it. 'Then you say, "I was wondering if you happen to have any jobs going?"'

Cynthia makes a joke. 'This isn't the kind of role-play I want to do with you.'

Anahera pauses, pursing her lips as if she doesn't get it, then says, 'Say it back to me.'

'Hi, my name's Cynthia. I was wondering if you happen to have any jobs going?'

'Sure,' Anahera says.

Cynthia squeezes her sandwiches in their plastic bag.

Cynthia crossed this very same bridge only last night. Now, she trudges over it mutely, bringing up the rear. They go right past Snot-head's tree, and she can't remember how she hoped things would go today. She looks down the street before they cross it, and remembers the glow of the streetlights and how they led her to the bar like they were taking her home. They're so high and dull now she'd miss them if she didn't look up.

They arrive in town, outside the tourist shops. 'Back at the wharf in an hour and a half,' Anahera says, 'and focus on restaurants and cafés, I think.' Then she goes off in a direction.

Cynthia stands outside a café, and looks in the window. There's a boy in there, grimacing and vigorously wiping a table. He looks up and smiles. She walks into a gift store next door and inspects a watch. A kindly grey-haired woman approaches, smiling.

'Can I help you?'

'Yeah, um.'

The lady waits.

'No.'

The lady smiles and tells her to have a good day.

Cynthia decides to go back to the school and have a lie down where she left Snot-head. Then she'll come back, and go into more places. It's a small town, and she doesn't want to ruin all her chances in a rush.

She settles on her back and eats her sandwich slowly. There's a boy squatting low under the slide at the playground. He's wearing very, very tight denim shorts, and a loose long shirt. She looks closely, and he's holding a spray can. He turns and pulls the fingers at her, then waits, struggling to maintain his balance, to see what she'll do. She pulls the fingers back. He's a cute kid. He nearly topples, but rights himself and keeps spraying.

This is where she let Snot-head go, and she wonders, where

might he be? What might he have eaten this morning? She makes sure not to think of the shops, the people in them, or of Anahera. She closes her eyes and breathes in, then out.

A breathing noise that isn't hers. She looks up and it's the boy, puffed from jogging over. She shuts her eyes into slits, and watches him.

'Don't call the police,' he says.

She opens her eyes completely. She'd never have thought to call anyone.

He's a bit tubby, and red from the short run. 'I'm quick, I'd just sprint off. It'd be embarrassing for you,' he says. His face is concerned, squinting.

'You're not quick.'

His mouth falls open. She half expects a glob of spit to land on her.

'What were you drawing?'

'Aw.' He's ashamed. 'Just a dick.'

'I'll come look at it,' she says, and gets up. He's much taller than her, but not yet properly formed. He doesn't know how to hold his elbows, and they jut out like they might injure somebody. His face looks like putty.

'Dicks are classic,' she says, to reassure him.

He covers his mouth with his hand, but smiles and lollops after her to the slide.

'Now listen,' she says while they walk, 'have you seen my dog? He's a French bulldog. Quite ugly, but you know – a sweetheart.'

He listens closely. 'Nah.'

The dick's black, and he's barely started filling it in. 'What does it mean?' she jokes, pointing at it.

He scrunches up his face, puzzled, and answers, 'It's a dick.'

She laughs to let him know she was kidding, and he smiles. Cynthia doesn't want to go and lie alone, guilty in the grass, and she certainly doesn't want to go into more shops asking for jobs. 'What hobbies do you have?' she asks him.

He starts spraying again. He's at a difficult age, and she can see him deciding whether to trust her. He finishes the left ball, and says, 'Creative destruction.' The huge shirt he's wearing has a picture of a dead duck on it. He taps the dick with his spray can to indicate it as an example of his activity. Then looks around, for witnesses.

'Seems good,' Cynthia says. 'I don't know too many people who're into that.'

He takes a big, proud breath and begins the second ball. 'Yeah, well, me and my friend were supposed to pee over the wharf onto the tourist boats last night, but he didn't show.'

'Aw.'

'It's okay,' he tells her. 'He's only thirteen, prob'ly wouldn't be able to reach anyway.'

'Did you go without him?'

He sprays a little over the line. 'Nah.' Then smudges it with his finger, making it worse, and pats the problem spot with the pad of his thumb. 'Keep an eye out for teachers.'

She nods and sits down in the bark, then asks him, 'Are you bored?'

He shrugs, but looks down at her, differently now. 'I'll give you forty bucks for a twelve-pack of Cody's.'

'Nah,' she says.

She hears him spray a little more, then stop. He coughs, and says, 'You want something, or . . . ?'

'No,' Cynthia tells him, adjusting herself in the bark. Anahera's probably found herself four jobs by now. He doesn't start spraying again, and she looks up at him for a moment. His hair's orange, a very bad attempt at blond. He almost definitely thinks it looks good. 'You don't have a job, do you?' she asks him.

His eyebrows scrunch down, and his mouth puckers for a moment, then he says, 'I wash the windows and sweep the floor at my house. And I go to school.'

'Okay.'

'Well,' he says, 'what do you even do?'

She should tell him off. Instead she says, 'I have a boat.'

'Whoa!' He lifts up and down at his knees. 'With Wi-Fi on it?'

Cynthia remembers she's wearing her best blouse, her best pants, and that her shoes are black leather with sensible but serious heels. 'Of course,' she says.

'Fuck!' He switches his can from one hand to the other, then back again.

'Yup!' Cynthia nods. 'It's quite big, I guess, too.'

'I'll bet,' he says, solemnly. He touches a finger to his mouth for a moment. Then asks her, 'Do you drive through the rock hole?'

Cynthia doesn't know what he means. 'I have a girlfriend,' she says. 'We live on it together.'

He nods, bored. 'Do you have a drinks cabinet?'

'Yes,' Cynthia tells him.

'Oh my fucking god!' he says. 'I'll give you my forty bucks if you take me through the rock hole.'

Something about the way his nose twitches reminds her of Snot-head. 'I'm not sure about the rock hole,' she says.

'Ah!' he laughs. 'Can't fit, eh?'

Cynthia scratches behind her ear, thinking. 'There's an island,' she says.

'Is it deserted?' he asks, and she nods.

'Alright,' he says, and takes two twenties from his pocket. 'I will give you my forty bucks if you let me come drink four beers on your boat, and take me to the deserted island.'

She looks up at him and his money. She doesn't want to be alone with Anahera. 'Two beers,' she says. It's probably time to get back to the bridge, so she gets up and walks that way. He follows, gesturing back at his dick. 'Can finish that another day.' He gives her the money, and she pockets it.

'You'll have to let me stay the night,' he says, trotting ahead, then pausing to wait for her. 'Can't go home to my mum *drunk*. I'll text and tell her I'm staying with my boy Roger.'

They're early, and wait at the metal bridge together, under Snot-head's tree. The boy lies down and sends his mum what must be a very carefully worded text message – it takes a while – then clicks a finger above his head. 'Done.'

Cynthia nods. He shifts his legs around, trying to get comfort-able, but he never will – not in those tight shorts. Snot-head's tree droops down and shades one of his legs. She points at its trunk. 'My dog pooed there.'

'Aw,' he says, and that's all. He coughs then, and she thinks he's faking. 'Is she coming?' he asks, of Anahera.

'Yes, I said she was.'

'Yeah,' he says.

'Um,' she asks him, 'what's your favourite subject in school?'

He grunts, and as he does so, Anahera appears around the corner with bags of groceries.

'Look!' Cynthia says, pointing at the boy. 'Isn't he good?'

Anahera peers at him for only a moment. 'Sure.' She looks bored, so Cynthia doesn't say more. 'There's nothing going,' Anahera says, about jobs. 'Nothing I want.' She waggles the bags. 'We're broke, pretty much.'

The boy's watching a seagull balance on one foot, pretending not to listen to them.

Cynthia presents the forty bucks, proudly now. 'I told him we'd show him our boat and some stuff.'

Anahera looks down at Cynthia for a long time. The seagull flies away.

'We're *broke*,' Cynthia mouths up at her.

'What?' But she got it. She walks off down the bridge to the dinghy.

'Don't worry about her,' Cynthia tells the boy, 'she's often quite obscure.'

He looks back at her, away from where the gull was. 'It's alright,' he says, 'my sister's a complicated person too, she says so herself.'

Cynthia can't help smiling. She tugs his shirt, and he follows her down the bridge.

In the dinghy he says, 'I can't see your boat.' He's big and he leans to the right, so the dinghy leans that way too. Anahera laughs and paddles.

Cynthia tells her, 'I thought we could go to your island, today or tomorrow.'

'Tomorrow,' the boy says. 'That's what I texted my mum.'

'He already texted his mum,' Cynthia explains.

Anahera nods. 'My island?' she asks.

'The one you swim to.'

The water's gentle around them, and the air's a little heavy and wet on Cynthia's shoulders; it'll rain soon. Anahera keeps paddling, and sucks her top lip. The boy looks at each boat they pass, craning his neck for the big ones, then back at Cynthia. She smiles.

'What sort of beer will it be?' he asks, and it starts raining.

Anahera swings her head around at Cynthia, glaring. Then back to the boy. She says, nicely, 'You won't be drinking any beer on our boat, sweetie.'

'That's fine, I guess,' he says. He frowns, and settles his elbows against his thighs.

'Do you want us to take you back?' she asks him. 'We'll give you your money.'

He looks at the water, and the rain falling into it in plonks, then lifts his shoulders and holds his hands together in front of him. 'No thanks,' he says. 'I want to go to the deserted island.'

Cynthia smiles at him, thankfully, and he grins back. Under his breath he's muttering the chorus from that one Kendrick song, 'Sit down, and drank. Stand up, and drank. Pour up, and drank.'

He's got the lyrics a bit wrong. Cynthia interrupts him. 'With most things, I'm allowed some part in the decision-making pro-cess.' The wind changes, and a lot of rain hits her face in a slap.

He waits till she's wiped her eyes and reassembled her face before nodding. Then he skips forward in his muttering to a later part of the song, 'I wave my bottles, and watch girls all flock. They all wanna – ' Mid-sentence, he looks up and sees her still looking at him. She smiles reassuringly, and he settles, quiet.

'Cynthia,' Anahera says, now he's stopped.

Cynthia waits.

Anahera turns to the boy. 'How old are you?'

'Sixteen.'

She keeps looking at him.

'Fifteen, and uh' – he calculates with his fingers – 'four months.'
Anahera looks back at Cynthia.

Cynthia shrugs. He leans forward and takes an apple from their
bags. His knees are high up, lifted at least level with his tummy
button. She notices his yellow hair again, and touches her nose.
It's got a spot. The water's a little rough, and the dinghy rocks now
they're out in it. He stretches his legs out, and they're scabby. Rain
runs down them in drops. He's got broad shoulders, strong thighs,
and a wider than average mouth. He shrugs for no reason.

Baby's much smaller with him on board. They sit around the table,
and he kicks the steel pipe holding it up. Anahera and Cynthia
watch him quietly while he crunches through a second apple.
When he's done Anahera asks him, 'What things do you like?'

'Uh,' he says, 'sports.'

'Oh!' Anahera jumps up a little in her seat. 'I'm a gym instruc-
tor, and I'm always saying to Cynthia, there's so much exercise
to be had here.' She gestures to the little window above the sink,
which is now being pummelled with rain. Cynthia nods, pleased
to see her all perked up.

He breathes in and touches his ugly hair. She gets up to show
him his bunk, in the cabin. 'It's a lot more comfortable than it
looks,' she smiles and tells him, although she's never slept in it.
As they're standing there, looking through the little door at the
bed, the boat shifts suddenly sideways. She slips onto him, and
he holds her up. His mouth smells thickly of lollies and Coke.
Anahera's weights are heavy and moving above them, and Cynthia
puts herself firmly on her feet.

'Cool,' he says, and laughs, then stands up on the table and knocks the panel in the ceiling. 'What's this?' Neither Anahera nor Cynthia answers, but he jumps up onto his seat, slides the panel back, and sticks his head through. 'You should renovate,' he tells them, echoing. 'Make up here a second floor for lying down in. Hot-box it. Shit-tons of cushions, I reckon. Psyche-fucking-delic.'

'No,' Anahera says, 'get down.'

'*Psychedelic*,' he repeats, as if he's not heard her. He thrusts himself up onto his elbows, so his feet dangle at Cynthia's eye level.

'That's dangerous,' Anahera says sternly. 'Get down.' Cynthia remembers her weights up there. He sighs, and his feet thump back onto the table.

Once he's sat laboriously back down beside Cynthia and taken a full minute to look around at everything in their one room, he asks, 'Where do you shit?' He's not looking at them, but up at the ceiling. Cynthia notices paint flaking there where she didn't before, at the edges.

Anahera gets up to show him the toilet and the bucket you dip into the sea for water to flush it with. 'It's on a string, so you don't lose it.'

Cynthia can't see his face, but almost hears his mouth pucker. Why did she invite him into their home? They come back and he sits again, beside her. She inhales and says, 'We're out of money,' dramatically, still trying to show him a good time.

'I know,' he says, 'I heard before.'

She forces a smile. 'Yes, well. We're unemployed.'

22

His name's Toby. There's a near continuous patter, louder than the rain, of gulls shitting on the roof. Periodically he gets up and swings around the side of the boat, trying to swat them with a rolled-up newspaper. The way Anahera looks at him when he returns from these expeditions is either indulging, or exasperated, Cynthia can't say for sure.

The weather gets nastier. Anahera bakes more biscuits, and he eats most of them. Cynthia eats most of the rest. They're delicious but he says so first. He goes to the toilet and doesn't flush properly. Anahera says nothing, and lugs in a bucket of water to do it for him. He doesn't seem guilty, or even to particularly notice.

They play cards. Toby only likes Go Fish, which Anahera seems to find endearing. Cynthia says, 'Maybe something a bit more grown-up?'

'You kept asking to play Snap before Toby arrived?' Anahera says.

'Snap is more grown-up.'

They play Go Fish. Anahera keeps smiling at Toby, then Cynthia. She seems to think Cynthia likes him, and that she's doing her a huge favour just by having him there. Cynthia goes for a lie-down in the cabin, in Toby's bed, thinking about her dog and almost pretending to be him. After a while she trudges past them, out to look at the water. It's filled with shit from the estuary.

At dinner, Toby's busy glancing around again, rudely, at the wood their home is made of – chipped in places, and blistering in others. Cynthia makes sure not to look at anything while he is. His eyes could pull her dream to pieces. She peers down, under the table, at his very clean high-top shoes. 'Are they leather?' she asks.

'What? Aw, yeah.' He rubs them against the steel pipe that supports their table.

'You definitely, actually want to come to the island?' Anahera asks him.

'Yeah, well . . .' He looks around some more. Cynthia actually wants to slam his head against the wall, a bit. 'I'm already here, and I already gave you my money, so yeah, I do.' Cynthia gives Anahera a look. He's not getting his money back.

'When I'm older I'll own an island,' he says.

After dinner they play more cards. Cynthia doesn't even nearly win, not a single round. She watches the rain fall against the window and the light fading behind the wet glass. Anahera shifts some hair from her eyes, and Cynthia waits for it to fall back. When it does she shifts it again. The boy tires quickly, and Anahera pays less attention to the game, watching him slump. The light falls lower, and soon they're not playing anymore, just all sitting there.

He sleeps in the cabin, and Cynthia and Anahera sit facing each other at the table.

'I went to places,' Cynthia tells her, 'but there were no jobs.'

'Yeah, well, we'll have to go back with lower standards,' Anahera says, not seeming to care if Cynthia's lying or what.

'You miss your husband,' Cynthia says.

'No.' Anahera doesn't ask about Cynthia's dog, or her father.

The next day Anahera wakes Cynthia, gently, with a hand on her arm. 'Let him sleep,' she says. Then, 'Why do you want to go to the island? Why does he?'

'Because we want to do something!'

Anahera looks for a moment like she's going to ask again, but Cynthia says, 'Please?'

'Okay, okay, sure.' Anahera shrug-wriggles, and gets quickly out of bed. 'We'll leave soonish, when he gets up. Make eight jam sandwiches, and cut one in half. You and I get two and a half, and he gets three.'

Cynthia lifts up on her elbows to see Anahera. She's being told off, almost. 'Please,' she says again. 'I really want to see your island. I wanted to anyway, before I met him.'

'Yeah,' Anahera says, 'well I said we would, so.'

Cynthia dozes for fifteen minutes, and while dozing she tells Anahera, 'I think about you a lot, and your needs.'

'Thanks,' Anahera says. 'We need jobs.'

They fix the table. There's noise from the cabin, Toby shifting into wakefulness. Cynthia makes the sandwiches, and Anahera sits out on the deck. While she's buttering, he walks in and opens a can of spaghetti, quickly, before she can comment. 'I'll only want one of those, thanks,' he says, nodding at the sandwiches. Cynthia shrugs and continues making as many as Anahera told her to.

When they're done she sits opposite him at the table. He's eating from the can with a spoon, and long strands dangle over the side. He tilts it so she can see how much he has left; roughly a third. 'They're so saucy,' he says disparagingly. It's on his face. He puts two more spoonfuls in his mouth, then tilts it again, grimacing; there's still roughly a third left. 'Can I have some bread?' he asks.

Cynthia hears herself breathe in. 'No, because you won't be hungry at lunch time, for the sandwiches.'

'I hate spag.' He stirs the spaghetti around, glaring at it.

'You have to finish it,' she says. 'We can't afford to waste food.'

He takes another spoonful, and fake gags. He's got spots on his forehead, and some on his chin. He gets up and walks outside, past Anahera, and throws the can into the sea. He comes back in and says, 'Now can we go? I want to see this island, but I've got shit to do today.'

'Actually,' Cynthia says. 'Do you know what? You told me you were into creative destruction, blah blah blah. I thought you were adventurous. Really, you're a little runt.'

He looks down at her quizzically.

'Psychologically – not in terms of size – you are a runt.'

He preserves the same expression. Anahera's looking in at them now.

'Okay,' Cynthia says, 'sure, we'll go. Whatever, but first you need to understand about our toilet, because it's very simple.' She makes him follow her to the deck, where Anahera's still watching them. She gives him the bucket and fixes the end of the string in his hand, then watches him drop it into the water. For a second she thinks he'll drop the string too, and she'll really have to ruin the whole day by making him swim for it, but he doesn't. The string's tied at three places, at opposing sides of the bucket, so he should be able to pull it up against the edge of the boat without losing too much water. However, as she knows he will, Toby yanks and three quarters of the liquid slops out. She looks him in the face, and holds the bucket between them. 'Now, is this enough to flush the toilet?'

'Should be,' he says. 'Or you'd have a bigger bucket.'

He's a typical teenager, a real little fuckhead. 'No,' she tells him firmly, and explains the string while he looks off into the distance, at the island.

'Cynthia,' Anahera says, 'what exactly is your problem?'

'Well,' Cynthia starts, 'I just don't like the way he's looking around our boat. He thinks it's crappy.'

'How am I supposed to look at it?' he says, far too loud. He's wriggling his arms, with his weird sticky-out elbows.

Cynthia doesn't want to answer. She loves *Baby*, it shouldn't be a problem if a teenager notices where the paint flakes, or complains that the toilet's laborious. But the ceiling seems lower with him under it, and the floor makes a noise beneath his heavy-stomping feet that she hasn't heard before.

'Okay,' Anahera says. 'Look, Cynthia – you can see he's sorry. He's embarrassed.'

His face is as red as blood, but that doesn't mean he's embarrassed or sorry for the right reason. Why doesn't Anahera understand how this matters? But Cynthia looks at her – standing there in her dad's Australian hat with the water moving behind her – and feels that if Anahera's not worried about it, she won't worry either.

'It's hot,' Cynthia says. 'It's so hot.'

Toby nods, relieved, and Cynthia sees Anahera watching her. She smiles back, and climbs up onto the edge of the boat, then jumps into the water. It's cool and fresh, and Cynthia doesn't generally jump off things. Toby jumps in after her. Then, after thinking about it, Anahera does too.

23

Even though he's in a man's body, Toby stands and watches Cynthia and Anahera drag the dinghy up the beach, twitching his foot, with the dark mass of trees waiting behind him. They put it down, and while Cynthia's puffing, he shoots Anahera a thumbs up and runs at a jog-trot into the trees. 'Go that way,' she yells at him, and he swerves to enter the bush where she's indicated.

Cynthia lets them go ahead together. Her feet are bare in the warming sand, and she hasn't been alone for so long. The water flickers. She'll have a new, fresh opportunity to understand Anahera soon, and she knows she can do better. Waves touch the beach and leave it wet, like licks over skin. She and Anahera will come back later, just the two of them, and the ocean won't have paused. She lies back to watch the clouds, just for a while.

Rested and warm, she follows their footprints along the beach, into the trees. In the clinging, striving mess of bush there's Anahera's bright orange workout singlet to follow, and then it disappears. When Cynthia sees it again it's stopped still. She can't see Toby. She concentrates on moving carefully, watching her toes and where she puts her feet, and holding the thicker trunks for support at the rocky parts. When she's closer she sees Anahera looking up, and she looks up too.

First she sees nothing but green, then – Toby's high in a tree. Anahera looks at her briefly when their shoulders touch, but turns quickly back to see him. This is the only way to admire people in his age group, Cynthia thinks: from a distance. He moves quickly and doesn't pause. He's done this before.

'Adults have forgotten the purpose of sports,' Anahera says. Cynthia looks at the side of her face and wishes she could be up there too; that she were a sportsperson. She can feel Anahera's arm against hers and, she thinks, a heightened pulse in it. The tree's high and tilting leftwards. He's near the top, at the surface of the canopy.

Down low, where Anahera and Cynthia are, there's no space for the air to move and they don't either. Anahera's breathing is steady. Cynthia knows what she wants, and she shouts up at him, 'Higher!' Her voice is a sudden break in the quiet, and she wishes she could suck it back in. It doesn't matter, he's too far to hear her, anyway.

He stops and waves, then looks down. He's ready to turn back, Cynthia can see it in his smallness, in how vague and unreal he looks. He lowers his left leg, and feels with that foot for a branch to stand on. 'To the right!' Anahera shouts, but Cynthia doesn't feel so patient. He's done now, he should just come down. He puts that foot back where he had it, and pauses, then lowers the other foot, and feels right. Anahera blows out air, and runs a hand through her hair. His hand slips as his weight shifts to the right, and she inhales again. He grasps again for the branch, but his left leg's shaking at the knee. He moves to pull his right foot back up, and the left slips. He's hanging from two branches, and one of them snaps. He falls, plonks.

The thud echoes, and the ground feels too solid under Cynthia's feet. Where is he? His tree, despite its height, has disappeared into all the others. There's no wind, and she forgets Anahera. For a moment nothing's alive, and all the trees might be made of plastic.

They're so still, and such pure green. Cynthia touches her eyes and they're dry. They blink. Her hands hang slack at her sides, like two wet towels. She sees his body then, a lump in the distance.

One of his elbows points skywards, she sees now, and his legs are tensed. A leaf shifts – and like that, there's wind again. The forest is alive once more with bugs, but when Cynthia touches her eyes a second time, they're still dry. Anahera's walking towards him. Cynthia follows, and when they arrive they see his eyelids. The right's shut, and the left's mostly open. Behind them, both his eyeballs stare up, and Cynthia and Anahera stand looking back down at him for a long time. His mouth is wide open and empty. Anahera squats for a moment, obscuring him with her back, then stands again.

Cynthia would like to know what to do. She moves away, and sits on a log to wait. She'd like to have a good thought, but she thinks only of how it wasn't her fault, or Anahera's. The sandwiches were squashed to mush in her fist while she stood looking at him, and she takes a bite of one now, chews, and spits it out. It sits in the dirt, as pink as guts. She pushes it aside with her shoe, and some gets caught on the toe. She won't feel guilty, she decides, and when Anahera sits down beside her, she pulls her sandwich apart and peers into it, to see the fleshiness, then takes a bite and swallows.

She can feel without looking how Anahera's lips are pulled in, and trembling like they'll be sucked down her throat. She tries to speak three times before she says, 'What can we do?' The edges of her eyes look sore, and her nose has swelled up red.

Only what they're doing, but Cynthia doesn't say it. She stands up and takes off her sweater, then walks to him. His mouth is slack at the corners, like it'll fall off his face. In his eyes, behind the wonky lids, there's a look she recognises from when he first arrived on their boat and looked about him. A slumped look, disappointed and aggrieved. She lowers herself to her knees on the rough, rock-studded earth. Her sweater is pink merino, thin and soft, and she puts it over his face. But his neck looks too exposed, pale, and his Adam's apple seems painfully sharp, like a stone pressed up through his body from the rough ground below. She piles leaves over him, so his thick limbs and neck are buried like roots. One of his hands sticks out, uncovered and limp, turned palm up, and she can see the veins running to it through his wrist. She's covering the hand when wind blows in a gust and exposes his knees and chest in patches. She piles the leaves back on, grazing his chest with her wrist. It's still warm.

She's finished, he's completely covered, and she sees the pink of her sweater and how wrong it is. It looks like the jam from her sandwich; it looks spat out. She can feel his face under it, can see the outline of his nose pushed through. There's still heat in him. In the dark under her sweater, behind his half-shut lids, he'll still have heat in his head. His brain, as pink as her sweater, is probably still twitching in the dark.

She takes it back. She doesn't want to look down but she does, and his face is exactly the same as before, except his mouth might have gone a little slacker. She goes back to sit with Anahera, and Anahera says, 'He's just lying there.'

Cynthia squeezes her sweater in her fists, it's still soft, and puts it back on. They sit for hours. She eats the rest of the sandwich she bit twice earlier, and it's too sweet. She used too much jam. She holds it between her teeth like a kitten in a cat's mouth, and leans backwards. She lands heavily with her head on the ground, and grabs Anahera's still, steady arm to pull herself back up. It doesn't work, she needs to be helped. Anahera doesn't move.

'Okay,' Cynthia says. The blood's all run to her head, and the jam's sickening in her stomach. She flops right down, and gets back up. Standing, she shakes her legs and stomps them into the ground to get the leaves off. She plucks every leaf from her sweater, and when she's done she drops it back onto the ground, back into the leaves. Anahera's sitting with her eyes closed, and her head lifted. Her mouth moves in little tremors. She's praying.

24

Cynthia pretends not to have noticed, and waits while Anahera mouths thousands of little words that can't mean anything. After hours, Anahera's eyes open slowly, but she looks down at her own hands, not at Cynthia.

Cynthia's lonely, so she gets up and walks. It's not a big island. She'll come back soon and they'll paddle home. She walks over lumps of roots and rocks, and through twiggy, sticky branches, falling and picking herself up twice without understanding that she's tripped.

He fell, and Cynthia thinks about the silent stillness of his body caught in the leaves. Now everything is moving again, there are sounds again, but that only means his quiet has turned into something else. She can't remember where he was. She looks up and feels she's being watched. She'd like to go back to Anahera now, but she turns and turns and every direction she picks feels the same as the one she came in. Then she sees something in the distance, blue, behind the vine-tangled trunks.

She walks closer. It's a tent. Beside it there's a dead campfire, dug into the ground, and a pile of wood. She approaches with her hands behind her back, and keeps them there, but bends to look closely. There's a pot, dirty with tomato sauce and dropped on its side. A stack of canned spaghetti and beans. Sloppy food, she thinks, and remembers Toby's fake gagging. The trees are loud around her.

She walks around the tent twice, then stops to touch its door flap with her fingers. It's unzipped and hanging open. She wants to hide, wrap up, and suck both her thumbs. Inside it's empty except for some blankets, a pillow and an exposed mattress. It would relieve her to crawl in, she thinks – maybe in there she'd cry.

But, Anahera. Cynthia didn't see her face when he fell, and not even for a time afterwards, but she saw the way it had swelled from crying when she left her alone on the stump.

Anahera doesn't look up, she hasn't moved.

'I found a tent, with a fire and a bed,' Cynthia says.

Anahera's twirling a leaf on a stalk, between her fingers. 'Did you.' She lets it go, and they sit longer.

Cynthia says, 'Do you think we should go back to the boat?'

She waits, but Anahera doesn't answer. It's getting dark, and quickly. Each tree has a shadow, long and distorted, mingling with the others, growing. She lifts Anahera by the arm, and leads her back through the dark mess of bush to the tent. They don't trip, fall or get lost, they simply trudge and arrive there, like they've been led. There's a can opener she didn't notice before, balanced perfectly on top of the spaghetti and beans stack. She opens some beans and they share them. Anahera weeps, and some fall from her mouth into the dirt. Cynthia wipes the sauce from her chin and asks, 'Do you want to sleep?'

The trees have disappeared into their own shadows. It's night. Cynthia leans closer, and asks again, quieter, 'Do you want to sleep?' but Anahera doesn't look at her, and shakes her head.

Cynthia crawls into the tent alone, and tidies the blankets as best she can in the dark. She'll give the pillow to Anahera.

'Anahera,' she says, and she says it again and again till she's not sure Anahera's still there anymore. She can't settle, and the blankets get messed up. She tidies them a second time, and leans out under the sag of the door flap. There's Anahera's hair, a dark mass looking so soft Cynthia thinks everything would feel okay if she could just touch it. She pulls at Anahera's shoulders, but they don't move.

When Anahera comes to bed she faces away from Cynthia, and Cynthia gives her as much privacy as possible, pushing herself against the side of the tent, so tight it makes a damp mask over her face.

Later she wakes and Anahera's holding her so close it hurts.

25

The next day Cynthia stirs slowly, and late, into the musk of the tent and her own sweaty heat. Anahera's gone. The nylon above her is illuminated in sections where light's struck through the trees. It's blue, and very bright in places. Lower down, it's mildewed, in some parts pure green. Her legs and arms are moist in the blankets, and she sniffs. The air's potent with the smell of mould, beans and something else. Anahera's left the door flap open, and through it Cynthia can see the pile of used cans. They're stacked, but most have fallen and rolled. A bird lands on top of them, and shoves its head inside so deep and quickly Cynthia worries it won't be able to retrieve it. A can shifts. The bird yanks its head out fast, and flies off. Everything is still again, but Cynthia thinks she can feel bugs on her. So many of them that they're like a new, thin layer of her skin. She looks at a plant so spindly it shouldn't be able to stand and remembers the boy, that he's dead. There are no insects to brush away, there's only Cynthia alone in the forest, and the time to wait before Anahera comes back, if she does.

The cans are still, and the trees shift only slightly behind them. Cynthia looks at the tent roof, then back at the thin tree. Anahera walks briskly into view then, and says, 'We're going. Get up.'

Cynthia does. There's nothing to bring with them. She follows as quickly as she can, not saying anything, but trying after each big tree they weave around to clutch Anahera's hand. Anahera's legs are her usual legs again, solid and abrupt, and when her hands swing back behind her they're fists. She doesn't look around, only straight ahead. They walk and walk, and the green brightens as they approach the edge of the bush, the beginning of the beach, and the sun. Cynthia thinks of asking about Anahera's feelings, but it doesn't seem appropriate. Anahera looks about suddenly, twice and twice again as if she's seen something. A pest, or a predatory animal. Cynthia looks too, at least three times in every direction, but only sees birds. The previous day she didn't notice them, but they're everywhere now. Some stop and peer at her, tilting their heads one way and the other. There are so many of them waiting along the path, and each flies off in its own direction. Then they all pause, even their necks with their shifting heads don't move, not at all. The leaves are bright, they're near the beach and it must be around midday. Cynthia's back is hot, and there's sweat on her top lip. She stops to suck it, and Anahera takes another step forward, and screams. There's a moment of her standing still, then she contorts and crumples.

The trees are huge above them. All of them loom. There's a steel trap clamped at Anahera's ankle. It's not bleeding, but the trap's made a horrifying dent in the muscle, and Cynthia's worried about the bone. Anahera moans, crying, and Cynthia squats down. She touches the metal and the skin, then sits back to look. Finally, with all her courage, she leans forward and pulls hard on the bars connected to the clamps. The trap comes out of her left hand, and her effort to open it slams it into the ground. Anahera screams again, for seconds and seconds, but there's nothing to help them. The trees grow more alive, closer. 'Shh,' Cynthia says. 'Hush, I'll take care of you.' Anahera looks at her, wild. The birds are moving again now, they're everywhere with their dark, darting eyes, watching. Anahera stares hard at Cynthia, and shakes her leg and the trap till she cries out again, and her elbows slip, so her head hits the ground with a thump.

Cynthia touches Anahera's hair, it's still soft, and she can still at least touch it softly, and says, 'I want to be good, I want to help.' But Anahera's moaning sharpens. Her whole body shakes, the foot most of all. The trap drags along the ground, lifting and thumping back down, and each time the sound Anahera makes is louder, and hurts worse.

'Please let me help you,' Cynthia says. Anahera's foot stops moving at a last thump after hearing this, but her screaming continues at the same aching volume. Her eyes dart everywhere around them. The birds are at a distance now, still looking and tilting their heads, but from behind leaves and branches. The noise is so much inside Cynthia's head. It goes on despite her.

Anahera stops suddenly and asks, 'How? How can you help me?'

Cynthia can't think. A hard, big reality has fallen on her. Might they die there? If they do they'll be alone, separated eternally by Anahera's noise. She moves forward gently, towards Anahera. It has to come off, so there must be a way to get it off.

'Don't,' Anahera says quietly.

Cynthia begins saying something about love, her love, and the anything and everything she's willing to do, but Anahera screams again, and her eyes bulge. She's looking behind Cynthia.

A person steps out of the trees. 'I am a German man,' he says, and comes forward. His moving is confident, his feet are big and in big floppy sandals but they fit perfectly between the rocks each time he puts them down. He touches the trees, but not for support; he touches them like loved and known furniture, like all of this place is his own bedroom. He's carrying a huge backpack with two pairs of shoes tied to it and holding a fishing line. He nods. 'A big one!' he says, gesturing to the trap. 'There.'

He's arrived and he's an answer, Cynthia understands. Anahera looks like she's about to pass out.

'Not legal,' he tells her sternly.

Anahera groans, glaring hard, but Cynthia sees she's looking at the man now. He's moving slowly. He gets on his knees beside Anahera's foot, without looking at her face. 'It's not serrated, you are alright,' he says. She yells and spits up at him, but it lands on her chest. He shifts back and waits for her to finish. 'Don't fight me.' He moves over her again, and Cynthia can't see the trap anymore. Anahera doesn't move, but she's breathing deeply, like something about to attack. His biceps flex, and Cynthia hears the metal pop open. 'This bad boy is not from this century,' he tells them, and he opens his pack and puts the trap inside.

'Have you already eaten?' he asks.

They don't answer.

'I have not,' he says, and takes a Tupperware container from his bag. It's white rice, drizzled with soy sauce. He brandishes a spoon from his pocket. 'I am a German man. Hello, I am Gordon. I'm only friendly. Don't fight me,' he says, then starts eating, ignoring Anahera as if she were an unnecessary table between himself and Cynthia.

Cynthia flicks her gaze from his spoon to Anahera's bulged eyes.

'Just sit quietly, you will be fine.' He nudges Anahera, and she moans again. Cynthia's very thankful he's arrived. He can carry Anahera back to the dinghy and paddle them home to their boat. She'll take it from there.

He talks through his food. 'I am on a nice-nice holiday with my girlfriend. But she left me on this island! For another girl! But I have all the money! You see, it is a twist. I am on a nice-nice holiday with myself!' He swallows and laughs, 'Ha ha ha. Ha. What am I to do with all this money which I have?'

Cynthia watches Anahera's face. She's not thinking, it's all scrunched up. Neither of them says anything.

'I am not even mad, you see? I am a friendly German man. But only a little stuck here, on this island.' He shrugs, and shoves another big spoonful in his mouth.

Cynthia laughs now, a hideous gulping noise she's been holding in since the boy fell. She laughs and she can't stop. Gordon watches her patiently. When she's done laughing she touches Anahera's arm, to show she's thinking of her. Then, 'You seem friendly,' she tells him. 'How much money do you have?' Anahera wrenches her body away from her hand.

'What are you girls?' he laughs, and looks down at Anahera, who's making a deep, hateful noise through her nose.

When he's finished his lunch and licked the edges, the corners and the lid of his Tupperware container, he moves towards Anahera, bashfully, with his hands.

'Under her knees, maybe? And her back?' Cynthia suggests.

But he picks her up instead so they're facing each other, and her legs are twisted around his stomach. 'Suck onto me like a mollusc,' he says, laughing. Cynthia can't see Anahera's face because it's pressed against his chest, but her nails are digging hard into his sides, and there's a rough, muffled noise coming from his torso, where her head is. 'You take my bag,' he tells Cynthia, and she does. It's big and heavy. She waits for him to start and walks behind.

They arrive on the beach directly in line with the dinghy, and stop next to it. He puts Anahera down on the ground, and she half falls, half sits in the sand. He turns to her kindly and asks, 'This is yours, yes?' pointing at the dinghy. She glares up at him, and Cynthia stands quietly alongside, out of sight.

'I am an abandoned man,' he says. 'I only want to help.'

Anahera spits again, in the sand, and tilts her head to one side. She makes a gurgling sound, and struggles to turn it into speech. In a dull voice she says, 'You only want to help.' Cynthia squats down next to Anahera and holds her face in her hands. Anahera looks right back at her, and says, 'I know this man. He only wants to help.'

Gordon laughs over them, good-naturedly. 'It's true!' he says.

Cynthia looks up at him, and sees he's begging like a dog. She's nearly waiting for him to get on his knees. He's lonely and lost, just like them. His face looks solid, as if beneath his skin are foundations of concrete, or carved wood. The skin under his eyes is baggy, but lifted by the hard muscle of his cheeks. There's a tough small line above his nose, and his forehead's another slab on top of it. His chin's divided into two parts. Above it his lips are fat, completely unlike the rest of his face, jutting out as if the wind would shake them; they protrude sweetly. His body's muscled, full, and strong. Cynthia estimates him to be about thirty-five. She stands up, and prods him in the sternum. 'What will you do for us?'

Anahera laughs cruelly, and bursts into tears on the ground beside her, but Cynthia thinks, *I am doing what's best*, and keeps looking at him.

He doesn't step back from her finger. 'Ah,' he says, 'I am a good company, yes, or you can tuck me away in a small place. I will give you a thousand dollars if you show me about to this beautiful environment.'

One thousand dollars! The man in sandals enjoys a moment of beauty in the sunlight, with the sea lavish and tumbling behind him. Then it's too long since Cynthia's spoken. 'Alright,' she says. Anahera will thank her later. She nods at him and says, 'Paddle us back. Our boat's over there.' She waves at it, pats him on the arm, and smiles comfortingly down at Anahera. He smiles too, then strides off and drags the dinghy down the beach.

Cynthia squats down to rub Anahera's back and listen while she says, 'He's a fuckhead.' The rubbing is light and smooth, but Anahera shrugs her hand off and says, 'Look at him.'

She looks, and he's just the back of a man, heaving their dinghy down the beach and to the sea. 'Try and be nice,' she says, and lays her hand back down, still, on Anahera's back. He's near the water now, and he turns and flashes a thumbs up. Anahera stands, and Cynthia holds her. It's a slow hobble, the leg is heavy and weak, and balance is difficult in the sand.

He jogs back to them, laughing. Cynthia steps aside so he can pick Anahera up. She doesn't fight, but he seems to anticipate it in the loose way he moves at her with his arms, then the tight way he holds her.

'Be gentle,' Cynthia tells him sternly, and he laughs and adjusts his hands. Anahera snorts. Cynthia wonders if she should carry her, or make Gordon put her down. But she doesn't, she runs ahead and pulls the dinghy into the water, then holds it still while he puts Anahera in.

26

Anahera shuts herself in the cabin, and Cynthia speaks with Gordon in hushed tones in the larger room. 'We're going through a difficult time,' she says. He nods sympathetically, and his kindness ruptures her. She's acting normal, she must be – he thinks she's normal, and that her problems are to the scale of a normal person's.

She pushes forward further, in relief. 'I was going to be on TV, announcing the news, probably. That was my dream, but I don't know if it will come true now,' she says. She's not as embarrassed saying this as another girl might be, she knows she's got a mostly stunning face and body, and that her elocution's good. The boy fell and hit the ground, but it makes her so happy to think of something else.

He nods. 'A worthy ambition.'

'I left everything for Anahera, we're in a real relationship. My father and I no longer speak,' she tells him, then realises Anahera can probably hear her through the cabin door, and rushes to change the subject. 'We could use some groceries.'

'Alright!' he says. 'That will be the first thing you show me of your beautiful land: the supermarket!' That isn't so funny, but they both laugh and laugh till there's no air left in either of them, and still laughter falls out of her. This is what she was waiting for in the forest, when she couldn't cry. She doubles over and bangs her head on her knees. He stops laughing first, and waits patiently while she continues to splutter.

She pats the cabin door, and whispers through to Anahera that they're off to the supermarket, and won't be long. There's no reply.

Gordon paddles Cynthia across the sea, grinning. His lips keep moving, as if he's silently practising to say something. She wonders if he's going to ask what they were doing on the island, but he doesn't. Instead he looks across at her suddenly, with his eyes clear, and asks, 'This water, do you look at it?'

The ocean is glimmering all around them, and how odd that Cynthia forgot all about it. She shuffles and peers over the edge of the dinghy, into the shifting murk. It must be in so many layers, like a pile of shadows, each with their own push. He nods when she looks back at him. He understands the water; he's an attentive sort of man, and his presence is comforting.

The beach is ugly, a lethargic expanse of grit speckled with bodies. Cynthia doesn't love everybody in the world, and certainly not in the way people at beaches expect to be loved. One of them gets up and strolls, then sits back down in a different place. She and Gordon share a look.

They arrive and the closest bodies are facing away from them: a middle-aged woman in a bikini with a bob haircut and man of the same age sagged onto his towel, asleep beside her. Gordon walks around so he's standing over her, but not too close. 'Hello,' he says.

She squeaks a little with fright – she was reading – but laughs.

'Will you be here for another hour? It is just, will you watch our dinghy?' He nods at it.

The woman looks at him oddly, and Cynthia almost explains:

He's German. But she smiles. 'Sure.'

Gordon shakes her hand and they move along, up the beach.

'I know this one, my girlfriend showed me the way.' His walk is big and confident. Cynthia hasn't been here before. She walks sometimes behind him and sometimes alongside, depending on his speed and the size of the footpath. 'You can take *anything* you like,' he tells her. 'Budget unlimited!' He's loud, but his snortle is cute. Before crossing the road they have to wait for a pair of police cars. 'Oh!' Gordon says. 'The justice system!' She makes sure not to turn to look at his face.

He takes a big family trolley, and Cynthia fills it right up. He drives it fast and zany, darting between people and around corners, and she jogs behind him, biffing things in. It makes her thankful to see his huge body jogging along in front of her, pushing the trolley and grinning, it makes her feel like she'll be alright. She punches him in the arm and he doesn't notice, he just keeps jogging. 'You have to try this! It's New Zealand's best stuff!' she tells him, dropping in a tub of hokey pokey ice cream, then two more.

'But,' he says, 'it will melt.'

'I don't care,' she tells him. 'We'll drink it.'

'You are a fun, adventurous girl!' he says. 'You are just getting *everything*!'

At the checkouts, they see four kids Toby's age smacking each other with Zombie Chews. One's been hit particularly hard, and he tries to make the others stop and look at the red on his leg. 'It's a welt,' he says, while the other three keep hitting each other. He's pulled his pant leg up around his hip, and he keeps saying, 'It's a welt. It's a welt, see,' but from where she's standing Cynthia can't see any discolouration in the private white of his thigh, and the other boys won't stop to look.

Their queue moves, and Gordon's hand grazes her shoulder. Remembering him, and herself, she looks away, and back at the old man grimly swiping groceries.

Gordon wheels the trolley right out of the parking lot, and down the footpath to the beach where he spoke to the woman. They take their bags in trips to the dinghy, and Cynthia walks behind, wondering if she's being too quiet; if she seems guilty. Before they leave he thanks the lady, and gives her a packet of Afghans. Cynthia waits with a foot in the dinghy, and thinks he might be flirting. The lady's beach partner is still asleep.

Anahera's on the big bed, with her foot raised high and a damp cloth over it. She doesn't watch the groceries as they unload them, or listen while they tell her what they bought. Instead she looks at Cynthia's hands, and at Gordon's big feet. Her eyes make it impossible for either of them to move properly in the small space between the bed and kitchen cupboards. Cynthia holds up the ice cream to tell Anahera how Gordon hasn't tried it, and Anahera says, 'Put some new water on this,' shaking her foot with the cloth on it. The foot, when it's revealed, is a blue-black mess with a mound at the front of her ankle, valleyed where the metal clamped down.

Cynthia comes back with the cloth, and Anahera's looking at the ice cream. 'Put it in the low cupboard,' she says. 'It'll be cooler there.'

Cynthia does so quietly, and Gordon moves apologetically to the cabin. He has to pull his shoulders forward and duck his head down to get through the door. Cynthia and Anahera sleep very early, at seven thirty. There's nothing left for either of them to say.

—

Cynthia wakes in the night, into musky hot air and Anahera's breathing. The blankets feel heavy, so she gets out and lies back down on top of them. Gordon shifts against the wooden walls in the cabin, and she's thinking about the boy. The weights move in the roof, and the water shifts below them. She never noticed Toby's eyes, but she remembers them now, blue, and in her memory peculiarly serious. She wishes, just for tonight, that she could lie alone, somewhere other than their boat.

27

It's afternoon, and Cynthia's talked to Gordon. They're taking him on an island boat tour. They're going to show him a lot of good things. First he gives her a lot of money, happily. He takes it in wads from different pockets on his pants and sections of his bag. It might be two, or eight hundred dollars. Certainly there are a lot of fives and tens. Cynthia takes it inside to Anahera, who makes a near-smile, and props herself up on her elbows to count it.

'The rest is, ah – digital,' he says, and having shed his cash, he gets down to just his underwear and into the sea to wash.

Cynthia sits on the edge of the boat, and looks down at him. 'You must have seen her before then?' she asks, gesturing back towards the bed, with Anahera on it.

'Nope.' He blows a lot of salt water out his mouth, then looks at her properly. 'Oh, who? No, nope – I was only on there for three days! How long do you think a man can survive!' His chest lifts and falls in the water, and she can see his legs green-tinted and kicking like he's running on the spot. They're like a frog's, thrusting out and bent. He's got long hairs on his chest, but not many of them. Cynthia makes sure not to stare. He's looking up, blinking from the sun behind her head. He chuckles at her imagining he'd been on the island for weeks; lived there. 'Also,' he says, still with laughter in his face, 'I would be so frightened at being alone with such a woman – I would shift my tent backwards, in terror, to the island's other side.'

He paddles with his hands and feet, and watches her face. After taking a big breath he says, 'I wandered in the forest all night, with my broken heart for my girlfriend. Then in the morning the light resumed with you two in it. I must now admit, I saw something beautiful, but oh, she was crying.' He shakes the water from his hair, and looks up at Cynthia shyly.

The tour's scheduled to begin tomorrow, when Anahera's better. They all sit at the table and pass around the last of the ice cream, which is a nice sugary slop. The gulls continue shitting and squawking, and Anahera's weights are gentle noise above them. 'These are things I will fix,' Gordon says quietly. He gets up and pours a little pile of peanuts in front of Cynthia, then Anahera, steps back with a flourish, and sits back down with the bag. 'Okay,' Anahera says. Then she turns to him. 'What do you know?'

He's caught, with a peanut only halfway between his lips, still supported by the finger he was using to put it in. It falls. 'Hey?' he says. 'Nothing.'

They're all of them reduced to their spit then; the almost-sound of it held in their mouths. Anahera and Cynthia share a secret look. Gordon's stomach makes a noise. He's clean after washing, and he's joined their pool of scent – he smells like peaches. Anahera separates her lips.

That night he goes to his little bunk again, and Cynthia sees briefly as he leaves the room that he's sad. He hasn't asked where he should sleep, just understood that the cabin's the only place available to him. Anahera's in bed, in the blue satin pyjamas, and Cynthia joins her.

'We can deal with him,' Anahera says. They're in sleepiness together. She touches Cynthia's hair, and throws an arm over her waist.

28

In the morning Gordon makes them porridge at the stove and they stay in bed. 'This boat is love music at night,' he says, sombrely. 'I couldn't sleep, I feel it all night.'

'No,' Anahera says.

'You do not think we are all in a big love?' He looks hurt.

Cynthia shuffles forward and touches his upper arm. 'It's just water, just lapping.'

'It's noise,' he insists. He's standing with a glass of milk and trying not to spill it. He puts it down and stirs the porridge. Cynthia's a bit miffed with Anahera. This is deep; this is a man sharing his feelings about the wide open sea and the silent noise of it. There is his heart and soul, displayed right there in front of them. That idea of music must have meant a lot to him; he must have been planning all night precisely how to phrase it, and Anahera's being very uninspired. Gordon inserts his thumb into his mouth and puckers his lips around it.

'What did it sound like – the music?' Cynthia asks.

He's confused by her English. 'Noise, I said.'

While they eat Gordon stands on their romance novels, and lifts the trap door in the ceiling up and aside. 'I will still those,' he says, gesturing up to where the weights are. Then, on his toes, he puts his head through the gap. Cynthia passes him her cellphone and he twists it back and forwards, trying to see them.

'It's probably very dangerous,' Cynthia murmurs to Anahera.

'One could just roll and knock him out.'

'Well, he doesn't *need* to be up there. I don't know what he thinks he's doing.'

'Ah, yes,' he says, muffled above them. 'I see, they have all rolled against that side, because of the tilt, and they are making the tilt.'

Cynthia looks at Anahera and shrugs, *What tilt?* Anahera grimaces back. It's like they're being accused of something. 'How's he going to get hold of them?' Cynthia asks, quietly.

Anahera answers loudly. 'He's going to catch them with his head, when they roll and hit his skull.'

Cynthia looks at her and she's unwavering. Has the boy's falling changed her? But it doesn't matter, if anything Cynthia loves her more. Gordon lowers himself back onto his heels. 'Pardon? What? Never mind,' he says. He steps carefully from the books to the floor, although they are only four and not high, and leans back against the kitchen cupboards, holding two by their small knobs.

'Cynthia! I know what you will do! You stand here, under the hole and wait for the weights to roll through it, then you catch them!'

Cynthia laughs, she won't do that.

He chuckles too. 'No, no, no. I am just funny. But you are very light, I will hold you up into the roof and you retrieve them.'

Cynthia's still laughing, she won't do that either, when Anahera interrupts. 'Gordon, how much money do you have?'

He shrugs, and laughs now at his own joke even though he didn't before. Anahera rolls her eyes and says she'll go swimming. She asks them to do the dishes. If they do remove the weights from the ceiling, she requests that Gordon put them back exactly as they were before she returns. They both nod, Gordon with his head right down, *Yes, of course they will.* She thanks them and sends them both outside so she can change into her togs. When she's done that she says it's cold, so could Cynthia find her wetsuit? It doesn't seem so cold to Cynthia, but she finds the wetsuit in a cupboard above the kitchen sink.

The foot is enormous, dark purple and blue, edged with green now. Anahera makes Cynthia hold the suit still, with the leg open, while she hoists the foot up and positions it in front of the hole. Gordon turns away to face the window, as he should. Cynthia stands with her legs wide apart for balance, and steadies herself, then nods for Anahera to shove it in. It doesn't go in, it might not have been lined up quite right, and Anahera howls and falls back against the table. 'I do not say it,' Gordon says, still facing away, 'but you should not be swimming.'

'Pah!' Anahera growls, and pulls herself up using the table. Cynthia's ready to get the hole positioned perfectly this time, but Anahera wrenches it from her hands. She shudders and breathes, and the suit stretches in stages as her foot moves through it, like a snake that's swallowed a rat. It's on, and she stands up suddenly, leaning hard on Cynthia's shoulder, then sits again to put her other foot through. Cynthia supports Anahera's balance while she gets it over her bum, then Anahera leans over with both hands on the kitchen bench so Cynthia can do the zip up at the back.

She doesn't say thank you. When it's on she limps to the deck and slips into the water with her bad foot first. Cynthia stands with Gordon to watch her go. She doesn't kick, so she's slow, and her damaged foot seems to drag her left side back, so she's crooked, but she's still got her powerful arms, and her determination. She absolutely remains an inspiration to Cynthia.

'I have been hit by a sudden love for that woman,' Gordon says. They watch several more waves fall in heaps over her body, and then she's out of sight.

29

It's quiet with just Cynthia and Gordon, even though Anahera wasn't talking very much. The weights have stilled, and Gordon's replaced the slat in the ceiling. Behind the window, in the distance, a flock of birds dive-bomb for little fish. They're the ones usually pattering about and shitting on their roof. Cynthia feels a new allegiance with Gordon; they both love a difficult woman. They wash the dishes together, as they were told to, and she asks him, 'What do you have in your bag?'

'Maybe a lot of shoes. I am a lot of men, sorry – man.' He laughs.

Cynthia's all hollowed out with her new knowledge of his love. She can see it's true. But he'll have to leave, he's too large – he's going to be hurt. She only wishes she could talk to him first, *really* talk, about everything.

Anahera returns, changes clothes, tells them she needs more time alone, and leaves again in the dinghy. The Island Boat Tour is postponed till the afternoon. 'Think up an itinerary,' she tells Cynthia before paddling off.

So, Cynthia watches a bit of *Bachelor Pad*. On season three there are three women whose heads and hearts boil with special love for Michael, a lovable goof from previous seasons. It's only a matter of time, and Cynthia observes carefully, looking for early signs of the downfall to come. Gordon boils the kettle so she can drink tea while watching. She sips, thinking – reality TV *is* society; it's about limited resources.

He grins charmingly and interrupts her programme, saying, 'You and I both know a thing in common?'

'What?' She pauses it. His arms are golden and she can tell from his face he's got no idea how bad his English is.

'Do you think it's about Anahera?' he asks her. It's the first time he's said her name. He pronounces it correctly.

'Well I do now!' Cynthia bursts out laughing. He looks at her, and she forces herself to be quiet.

'Oh,' he says, 'I can't say it, I'm very sorry.' He peers down at his knees.

Cynthia's giggling escapes her.

He laughs too. 'I am just funny,' he says. 'How would you know? You wouldn't want to know.'

Cynthia knows exactly. She laughs a bit more, and drinks her tea.

He retrieves some string from his bag and starts piercing holes in their used cans with a knife. Cynthia watches this during the boring bits of her show. Anahera will be annoyed about the knife. On *Bachelor Pad*, Erica's trying to convince Blake that they should spend the night together in the fantasy suite.

Gordon cuts his string into sections, and ties them to the cans. Then takes them around the side of the boat, clanging. Cynthia pauses her show and cranes her neck to see what he's doing. He sits them all upright, carefully, against the window at the front of the boat, then ties each to the washing-line. Two tip and roll away, and she's not sure if he notices. She could go and help him, but relaxes her neck and watches his feet.

When he returns, Cynthia's not sure why but she says, 'She and I made love, once.'

'Gosh,' Gordon says. One of his cans falls down from the line and clanks off the edge of the boat. 'For scaring birds, see. Yeah,' he says.

Cynthia changes the subject, to make it easier for him. 'I've thought of nothing for the itinerary,' she says, then waits for his reply. One of her friends got pregnant, and Cynthia went along to see it upside down in her belly, curled like a little moon. She touched her friend's stomach, and felt it hot with unfurling. Now, her boat's warm with Gordon. She watches, still waiting.

'Ah. Mmm,' he says. It's the beginning of his hatching, his clambering out. He says, 'Hmm,' and another of his cans falls and rolls into the water. He goes to tighten them.

Anahera comes back and says the tour can start whenever, it doesn't matter that they've got no itinerary. They'll just drive around a bit. She and Gordon fiddle with the motor out the back while Cynthia finishes her episode.

They have no petrol.

'That's okay,' Gordon says. 'I am very, very tired. Instead of having a good time today, could some of that money I paid be to sleep in the proper bed?' He gestures at the table, where Cynthia's sitting. Anahera's looking at him carefully.

'How long have you been up north?' she says.

'Less than a week in this area,' he tells her.

She says nothing, then shrugs – he's paid. When he's made the bed and settled in it they make tea and politely leave to drink it on the deck. They sit, and Cynthia waits for Anahera to say something about the boy, but his snoring starts, sudden and loud.

'Can I trust you, with the – ' Anahera finally says.

'Yes.' Cynthia interrupts her.

'But later, when we're separate?'

'What do you mean?'

Anahera looks away, off to sea. Her hair's pulled back, tight and smooth, and she touches her lips. Cynthia pulls her own ponytail, and waits for her to turn back. She doesn't, she pulls her good leg up to hug it near her waist, and sips the last of her tea. Cynthia finishes hers, and runs a finger around and around the rim of her cup. Eventually Anahera gets up, and goes inside. Cynthia follows her.

They look down at Gordon's body, splayed out with his mouth open. Cynthia's about to ask what Anahera meant before, when she snickers and says quietly, 'Would you eat him with me?'

'Yeah!' Cynthia giggles. She might, but Anahera's only joking.

'I know how to tie them up – pigs,' Anahera says. 'I used to hunt with my dad.'

'He'd have to taste better than he looks,' Cynthia says, although from some angles she's thought him quite handsome. The cans on the washing-line tinkle. Cynthia listens attentively, and believes she can hear his naïvety in their strange, sad music. Anahera nudges him with her foot. He doesn't wake. Cynthia can see it in the rise and fall of his chest – loneliness. She's seen it in continuous flashes since he arrived; in the way he rubs his own hair and head with his hand, and cradles his hands held together between his legs. He wants to be touched.

30

The sea is a continual yes. They flush their shit into it and it closes its arms around them perfectly. It's like the boy's falling, their disaster, was a question it didn't hear. Cynthia marvels at the ease of the water. Their mess disappears into its holding, and maintains its same motions. A fly lands on Gordon's body, his arm. His sleeping mouth opens. He's been touched like a button.

31

They tire, and wake him. He goes to the cabin so they can sleep, and Cynthia pats his head before he ducks through the door. In bed they hold each other, and Cynthia knows the answer to Anahera's question, from before, about if they're apart – they won't be, can't be, not after what's happened. 'I know what you believe,' she tells Anahera. 'You believe in independence and strength. Well, I believe in those things too, and I believe in them through love.'

Anahera says, 'Is that contradictory?'

'Might be,' Cynthia says. 'That doesn't worry me.' In a few days, Cynthia thinks, when they're lying like this she'll touch Anahera's thigh, and that will be the beginning. Not even a question; an announcement. But it has to wait till Anahera's completely herself again.

The next day nothing seems to happen. Anahera swims twice and Cynthia watches some things online that she's already seen. There's a good bit on *Bachelor Pad*, where they have a pie-eating contest and Tamley spews pie back into her pie and keeps eating it. Gordon borrows Cynthia's nail-clippers and uses them sitting under the washing-line.

Sometime after lunch she's on the toilet, just relaxing. It's the boat's most private area. The water's shifting, and the seat's unsteady under her bum. She touches the doorknob, it's really cute – less than half the size of a normal doorknob. She doesn't have to flush, she's only peed and not much came out. She adjusts and imagines Gordon where she's sitting, with his knees to the side so he can fit in the bathroom with the door shut, and a huge dick hanging down, nearly into the water. She wonders if he has to hold it out, or rest it on top of his legs so it doesn't get wet.

32

Anahera sleeps and Cynthia closes her eyes and doesn't move them. She only listens. It must be eleven o'clock. Gordon moves loudly from his bed in the cabin and the little door squeaks as he opens it. Cynthia thinks again about her boat, warm and soft like a belly, or yes – a womb. She can be kind to him. She doesn't need to worry; those warm organs are engines of expulsion; he won't be with them for long, and so there's no need to be cruel.

When she wakes again, Anahera's gone and he's fishing. She asks if he wants porridge, and he says he's had some, there are leftovers on the stove if she wants them. The pot's still warm. Cynthia eats outside, and stands beside him. Together they watch the water ripple where his line slits into the sea. He's earnest, looking down quietly. It's sad, but he won't catch anything. One thing she remembers her father saying is that no fisherman catches anything in New Zealand anymore. He owned a boat for a while. Gordon mustn't know what's happened.

The weights are silent, but the cans tinkle. Anahera comes out in her swimwear and Cynthia wonders passively if she's annoyed by the noise. 'You and Cynthia get petrol today,' she tells him. 'While I'm on my swim, and we'll take you on your tour this afternoon.'

'Ah,' Gordon says. 'About that – but I would like more sleeping. In the proper bed.'

Cynthia waits.

'Well,' Anahera tells him, 'then that's $500, on top of what you've paid for the tour.'

He shifts on his feet, looking at them like a sulky boy. 'Well. I would perhaps not want to go on the tour.' Then he turns and looks at Anahera, suddenly glaring.

'Our contract is that you would like to go on the tour,' Anahera says.

'There's a hefty fee to change the contract,' Cynthia pipes up. Neither of them looks away from the other, or moves to acknowledge her speaking.

Anahera's mouth sets and her eyes harden. 'Tell us about your girlfriend, then?'

He hardly opens his mouth for the word, but it's loud. 'Blond.'

'Tell us more,' Anahera says.

'Blonder than her.' He gestures at Cynthia's head.

Anahera doesn't look away from him. Cynthia touches her roots.

Then, he changes. 'Oh. I am so sorry. I have been grumpy. I am hurt, hurtful. I am so sorry, tired.'

Anahera's tone doesn't change, but she says, 'We're not trying to pick on you. But we made an agreement, and Cynthia's been very excited – making plans. We'd love to show you our country.'

'You are such a good woman,' Gordon says. 'Your forgiveness is an unctuous balm.'

Anahera pats Cynthia's shoulder. 'What do you say we let him sleep, eh? And we'll get the petrol. I can skip my swim.'

Cynthia nods, and Anahera gets the fuel can.

'There's no way his girlfriend was blonder than you,' Anahera tells Cynthia in the dinghy, then laughs. It isn't funny. It's exhausting for Cynthia, sleeping in the bed when she knows he wants it. Anahera keeps paddling, and says, 'He'll be gone soon. I think.'

Cynthia moves her hand forward, to touch some part of Anahera's body, but Anahera doesn't pause paddling, so she retracts it. Are they both thinking about the boy? Is Cynthia only thinking about him herself to wonder if Anahera's thinking about him?

'I'll just get all his money first,' Anahera says.

Cynthia desperately wants to tell her of his announced love. It's unfair that Anahera never has to acknowledge these things. Instead she asks, 'How much do you think he has?'

Anahera doesn't pause. 'Twelve thousand, or something.'

The rest of their little trip is quiet with Anahera's seriousness and Cynthia's excitement. Twelve thousand dollars! At the fuel dock Cynthia spills a bit of petrol, but none gets on her, and Anahera doesn't see from the dinghy.

When they return Gordon's dressed very formally, in black long trousers and a collared shirt. 'I am very excited to view the beauty in person,' he says, as if he's been waiting since they left, and planning this sentence, rather than sleeping as he was supposed to.

Anahera chuckles from her throat. 'Where should we start, Cynthia?'

'Yeah,' Cynthia says. Then, 'Oh, at the rock? That seems like a natural place.'

'Great.' Anahera unscrews a little cap on the motor and pours in some petrol. Gordon leans back, watching, with the legs of his nice pants well away. He says, 'Okay, ladies! Alright, ladies!' and salutes. It's cute. He wriggles his knees in his trousers, which look freshly ironed. When Anahera's set the motor up she climbs around the side of the boat for the anchor.

'Sorry about this morning,' he says to Cynthia. 'My girlfriend wasn't blonder. I was only lying.'

She pats his knee. 'It's alright. We'll do this trip and set you on your way.' But she remembers: that isn't what they'll do. They want all his money; they'll have to keep him longer. He nods, sadly – so unaware. Anahera returns and smiles benevolently at both of them, then she moves back, past Gordon, and holds a button down on the motor. It makes a sudden, big noise, and Anahera jumps away and bangs her bruised foot on the side of the boat. Cynthia jolts a little.

'Oh,' Gordon says. 'Do you not know how to operate?'

'Do you?' Anahera asks him, kindly.

'Oh no,' he says.

'Maybe pull the string?' Cynthia asks.

Anahera breathes in three times, says, 'I know that,' and pulls the string once, twice more, and they're moving.

'Wholly!' Gordon says.

'But I don't know how to stop,' Anahera tells them. Cynthia shrugs, there's no need to worry yet. It's all exciting, like a party. Anahera stumbles in a forward rush to grab the steering wheel, and Gordon and Cynthia make sparkling eye contact.

He's like a boy, she thinks – adorable. 'To the rocks!' she shouts.

'I thought it was only one?' he asks her.

'We just start with one,' she says, 'and then there are more.'

Gordon nods. His cans clang and fall as they drive, and Cynthia watches Anahera for a reaction but she doesn't even seem to notice. The direction she's picked should be good, they're going away from town, and also from the island.

'Already,' Gordon says, looking at Anahera, 'I see that the view is very much something, and extraordinary.' Cynthia nods. It really is. Anahera's hair is in a plait, and at the end under the ponytail it fluffs out in a tuft. The water's a foamy mess where the motor spits it out behind them and they're going fast towards a mass of huge, jutting rocks. It's rapturous to be finally moving away from those other, bigger boats, and where they go will be entirely theirs. Anahera's hands are confident at the wheel, and she and Cynthia stand together, blinking in the mist of the mussed-up water. 'Inside we go to make sandwiches. Nutella.' Gordon nudges her. It's a good idea. Cynthia touches Anahera's arm and follows him in to do that.

When they're halfway through sandwiching, and Gordon's cheekily eaten one, Anahera calls them out, and she's pointing to some rocks. 'There? You see? We can't get much closer, but we're going to drive alongside them.'

'All of my dreams!' Gordon nods excitedly. They're wet and shining, sharp like jewels. 'It is a beautiful country,' he says, and they both agree. Cynthia's really proud. When the excitement of the rocks subsides, and Anahera turns them off in another direction, Cynthia and Gordon head back in to finish spreading. 'Do you think we'll see a dolphin?' he asks. 'They are one of my great loves.'

After she's spread Nutella on each slice, and Gordon's slapped them all joyously together, they take them out to Anahera. She pulls the string on the motor again, and nothing happens. Gordon and Cynthia watch in silence. She looks the motor over on the side, then the top, then on the other side she finds a red button and pushes it.

It stops. Then, 'No offence to your good time,' Gordon says, 'but I am very sleepy. I might give you $200 to sleep in the bed?'

'Sure, $250,' Anahera says. It seems neither of them feels the need to check with Cynthia that everyone's had sufficient fun for the day. So Anahera goes to the front of the boat, under the washing-line, to read a book, and Cynthia sits down to watch a bit of *The Real Housewives of Auckland* on her phone, at the back, by the motor and the steering wheel. Nothing much is happening on *Real Housewives*, but most weeks nothing happens, and Cynthia enjoys watching it out of patriotic love.

After twenty boring minutes, she pauses on a shot of Angela smiling. Angela's smile always looks the same, all she does is turn her face at different angles. Cynthia peers deep in. It's not plastic surgery, she doesn't think, it's a more profound sort of tautness. The way Angela's features are set makes her think hard. There's something not quite right, some emptiness in everything. She puts her phone down, and gets up to walk around the side of the boat, to where Anahera's reading.

Anahera's lying on her front, with one hand supporting her chin and the other holding her book. She shuffles over to make room for Cynthia, but doesn't look up. Cynthia stands, looking down at the neck of her shirt and some escaped hair touching it.

'You could have told me,' she says. 'I would have understood.'

'What?'

'He's your husband.'

Anahera's mouth drops and her eyes widen, so Cynthia regrets saying anything. 'Cynthia, you saw my husband. At my house.'

Cynthia stands dumb, and shakes her head. 'Oh,' she says.

Anahera winces and pats her shoulder, firmly at first, then more gently. This Gordon character has thrown their relationship back at least a month.

No one remembers or bothers to put the anchor down, and they drift. When Anahera and Cynthia decide to sleep they do so separately, and not till late. Gordon moves peaceably from the bed.

33

There's a jolt in the night. Cynthia wakes and hears Anahera awake beside her. 'I'm sorry,' she says. She feels wonky. 'Sorry,' she says again. Another jolt, so she knows Anahera's awake. 'I shouldn't have asked,' she says.

'Don't worry about it,' Anahera tells her.

'Sorry,' Cynthia says again. She doesn't sleep again till much later, and then she wakes twice more, feeling crooked and squashed, but each time she hardly slips out of sleep before she's back in it. Then, later, in the almost-morning, Anahera's rolled against her. Her face is low, breathing warm wet air on Cynthia's chest, and one of her knees is bent up, pressing Cynthia's thighs.

Cynthia's pushed hard against the wall, and she doesn't move. She tries to release air slowly through her nose, and to keep her ribs still under Anahera's head. Anahera is warm, and very lax now. The silk leg of her pyjamas is scrunched up over her bent knee, so it rests bare against Cynthia's thighs. She's heavy. Cynthia squeezes her hands in fists and keeps them to herself. She's not quite breathing properly, and her bones feel compressed. Still, this weight and warmth is beautiful. Anahera breathes gently, and her feet move.

The air lightens around them, and Cynthia can see the side of one of Anahera's closed eyelids. Her lashes look like they've been drawn by a child, they're so thick and curling. So black. Cynthia looks around, the feeling's odd. Things are not at the angle they were when they went to bed. Everything is above them.

Gordon appears, and clears his throat. He says, 'Yes, we are run aground.' Then he pauses, and peers curiously down at her, lying as she is nearly underneath Anahera's sleeping body. 'Gosh,' he says. 'Are you happy?'

Cynthia doesn't answer, but notices one of her hands has moved, and is moving up and down along Anahera's neck. She stops. 'What?' she says, quietly.

'Yes, we are run aground,' he says again, louder. Anahera shifts and makes a gentle waking noise, rubbing her ear against Cynthia's chest.

He says it again. Cynthia glares at him.

'Well?' He looks back at her, astonished.

'What?' Anahera says, awake now.

'We are run aground,' he says.

Anahera gets up quickly, and stands beside Gordon, looking around. She shifts her feet. She's standing beside a plastic cup, in a small pool of bubbled Sprite. Cynthia sits up too. The boat shifts, and there's a crunching noise from beneath them. It's tilted. It's leaning sideways, so everything's up higher than her and the bed. Anahera's already moving for a sweater.

'We just get out, and we push it back in,' she says.

'Are you sure?' Cynthia asks. But Anahera and Gordon are already moving outside to look around. Through the window above the kitchen she can't see anything, just half-dark sky. A few stars. Their voices are outside, moving around the edge of the boat, behind her head. The window frame shifts a little, and Cynthia thinks their moving is pushing them deeper into the sand. Then, their voices are further away. They must have jumped off, onto the beach. Gordon says, 'Okay.'

She recognises the odd, weird feeling then. Static. The boat is so still. But why don't they sleep, and then shift it? Clearly they're not listening to her. She stands and wipes her eyes, then walks around the edge of the boat to sit and look down at them. They're just standing there for now, gawking this way and that. It's lighter. Cynthia looks up at the vanishing stars and understands – Anahera's afraid that they'll meet people, and have to speak to them. She's frightened of the police, and of their own foreignness to this place. It's a small town, and they'll immediately be registered as strangers, and so suspect. They're caught at the beach where Gordon parked the dinghy before they went to the supermarket. She can see some public bathrooms and a road with no cars on it. 'So you'll just push it, then?' she asks, sitting on the deck.

Anahera's standing with her hands on her hips, and she doesn't answer. Cynthia wants to tell her not to worry. There's no one around, they have hours. What they should do is think.

'Okay,' Anahera says, and she and Gordon both push.

'Alright,' Cynthia tells them, although it still seems like a nonsense idea. They should be calling in a person, a professional.

'Push harder,' Anahera tells Gordon.

He stops, shrugs, and pushes again, but his face doesn't change.

Cynthia pulls her knees up, near her chin, and holds her ankles. She notices her guts, caught inside her arms and between her legs like a huge fruit, whole, in a small jar. It makes her feel sick, all of that new fat. Sick, and hungry.

She bites her knee. If Gordon wasn't there she could tell Anahera how she feels and how sorry she is and Anahera would make her feel better. But no, there he is.

'Push,' he says to Anahera. She doesn't. She's stopped, and she's looking past Cynthia, squinting at the sea. She waves. Cynthia turns, and there's a yellow boat anchored near them, with a guy standing on the deck. He waves back, then disappears around the side of his boat.

'Well,' Gordon says to Cynthia. 'Do you know what this is? It is reality! We are out of your little-cellphone-little-TV, we are really stuck!'

'Excuse me?' Cynthia says. He very clearly knows exactly nothing.

'Well, that stuff's all, what is it? Devised.'

She stares at him, and he shrugs as if he hasn't said a thing at all.

'So?' Cynthia says, and feels her lips puckering.

Anahera's not paying attention, she's still looking at the other boat. Cynthia turns and the guy's paddling over in an inflatable dinghy. Gordon just stands there, looking up at her. She wants to put her fingers in his mouth and wrench the skin off his face. 'Do you think people aren't told what to do in real life?' she asks him.

He shrugs again, and looks behind her. She can hear the guy's paddling. Cynthia officially doesn't like Gordon now; he's not a person she can speak to. She gets up and goes inside for some breakfast. When she's got Nutella on her bread she realises she can't go out and eat it in front of them, not politely without offering them some. So she eats fast, wipes her mouth, and re-emerges to see what's going on.

He's so stupid and dumb. When she arrives back on the deck, under the washing-line, it feels like they're deeper in the sand. 'What did you do?' Gordon asks her. She ignores him. The guy's parked his dinghy, and he's standing with his hands on his hips beside Anahera, who maintains the same position. He's got on an orange singlet, and some little black elasticated shorts. Gordon's leaning on the boat, stretching one of his arms out after all the pushing.

'Gordon, I know you plan everything you say,' Cynthia tells him.

'I mean,' Gordon says, scratching his nose, 'we could just do more pushing.'

'Cynthia, why don't you come down and help?' Anahera asks her.

Cynthia starts. 'I hardly think – '

'I'll tow you.' The guy interrupts her, then touches Anahera's shoulder.

'Well, thank you,' Anahera says, and turns to him.

Cynthia goes inside again, to pull up her shirt and look at her stomach. She grabs what of it fits in her two hands and squeezes tight. It hurts, insisting on being part of her, and she squeezes harder, more hatefully. Her legs are bent up and she shakes them, they wobble under her knees. She pokes her stomach hard, trying to make a specific organ feel it, but it's all of her that's the problem. All of her is flab now. Suddenly, it's like she doesn't have organs at all, she's nothing but this new hurting excess. Only her breasts have stayed the same size. She tries to comfort herself with them but can only think of udders and cows. They used to feel better in her hands, warmer, maybe, and now they're just two flesh-sacs. The boat moves, Anahera and Gordon are clambering back on it. She tucks herself away, and it stills again.

They talk outside, on the deck, then they're talking to the guy again. He's handed them a rope. He must be in a dinghy. He says alright then, and they say alright then back.

A long moment while he paddles, then Cynthia hears his boat, and Gordon shouting something at him. He shouts back, and the boat moves in a shudder. There's a horrible scraping noise, and Cynthia worries about the bottom of her boat. Then, a gentle feeling. The back of the boat is on the water, floating, and the dragging feels softer. Through the window, Cynthia sees that a lady's stopped on the footpath to look at them. She glares back and hunches down. The tide must go out then, because it feels like they're flat again, and even sinking into the wet sand. She goes to stand on the back deck, by the steering wheel. Gordon and Anahera are there, staring forward, along a long, thick blue rope, attaching them to the guy's yellow boat.

The tide's left them. It's on its way back in, but they need to be out and away, in reliable water as quickly as possible. 'Pull,' she shouts at the guy. Anahera looks at her briefly, and Cynthia wonders what face she turns back to him with.

He makes a gesture to say he's waiting for the tide.

'Pull!' she yells again.

He shakes his head, they're waiting. The water's around them again, but not under them, as it was. They've sunk in.

'Pull!' she yells a last time. He does. The rope makes a strained, gratified noise, and she nods. Again, the boat lifts. It's floating. 'Faster!' she yells, she doesn't want another tide to get them. He maintains the same speed, and gives her a nice, placating wave. Cynthia grimaces back, it's important to get along with at least some people. Gordon's got his hands on the steering wheel.

It's okay, they're in the water and they move smoothly.

'Come for a coffee!' Cynthia yells at the guy, and he makes a smile so big she can see it through the distance. With a nice, jolly look about him, he gets in his dinghy and paddles over. Cynthia stands in front of Anahera and Gordon, smiling and encouraging him. He arrives and he's sweet, looking up at her. He's got a round nose.

'Do you want coffee?' she asks him, and he nods.

He ties his dinghy up to the ladder, next to theirs, and she waits while he struggles onto the deck. She can feel Gordon waiting beside her, before he interrupts the quiet and says, 'Thank you for helping us.'

Cynthia was going to say that when she'd sat him down inside. Anyway, it turns out he's boring, so it hardly matters. Still, Anahera gets perky talking to him, and Cynthia nestles in beside her, with a head on her shoulder. Their hair mixes together, into a shared soft mess.

'Sorry,' she whispers.

'It's okay,' Anahera whispers back, then shrugs her off.

'Not for not helping with the boat,' Cynthia murmurs, 'for –'

Anahera interrupts her. 'I know.'

'Northland College boy, me,' the guy's saying.

Anahera laughs. 'I went to Okaihau,' she says. 'We were afraid of you.'

They both chuckle away together, and Gordon looks back and forwards between them, smiling. Cynthia sits and waits for something she can laugh at too.

34

The guy goes, and Anahera goes for a swim. Cynthia gets back in bed but can't sleep. She gets up again and Gordon's fishing. His arms are huge and veiny. He's using ham, which is excessive, considering it's his hobby and an unattractive, unproductive one at that. There's porridge on the stove, but he doesn't mention it. She eats it straight from the pot, cold, and sits watching him. He lumbers, he's ugly and German. Anahera's a woman of dignity – Cynthia can't think how she imagined him to be the husband.

'Holy fucking shit,' he yells. She looks over, and his line's bent. He grunts and bends down, letting it run, then he grunts again and pulls it back. He doesn't seem to think she's watching him. This is his natural state, she thinks, swallowing a spoonful. How revolting. He's leaning back and pressing his crotch forward, against the edge of the boat. He groans now, like he's gargling a throat full of liquid. All his muscles are tensed, right down to his calves, and his bare toes press so hard into the floor the blood runs out and they look yellow. She shifts her porridge around and looks at it. His groan becomes a moan of release, and the fish slaps wet against the side of the boat. It's not humane, she thinks. He holds the line in his hands and pulls it up; the fish, in a twirling panic, gasps and wets everything.

'That is so not okay,' Cynthia says loudly.

'They don't have minds!' he shouts, excited. The fish swings and hits him in the leg. 'Get a towel and wrap it up!'

'We are not using one of my towels for that,' Cynthia informs him.

'Ah,' he says, with the fish still swinging. 'Hold this,' and he tries to give it to her. 'I will use my shirt.'

Cynthia won't take it. The fishing line looks sharp, the way it's digging into his hand. 'I'd prefer not to be involved,' she says.

'Well how can I take off my shirt?' he asks.

'Why would you want to?'

The fish is hanging from its lip, with two more hooks banging against its face. Blood drips from its puncture onto the floor of the boat.

'I will wrap it in my shirt,' he says.

'I'm not helping,' Cynthia tells him. 'I think you should put it back. That is my political opinion.'

He blinks, as if that doesn't make sense. The fish hits his leg again, leaving a red, watery mark on the side of his knee. Its lip breaks, finally, and it lands with a splat on his foot. He kicks it aside, laughing, and removes his shirt. Cynthia gasps, sickened. His chest is fatty and muscular at once, nearly bald, but with a few long hairs. She should leave, her presence is encouraging him in this behaviour, but she can't. The fish's eyes bulge.

'It is only like a plant,' he tells her, bending down to pick it up with his shirt. 'Read the science.' It writhes in his hands, but Gordon holds the fish tight, stands, and pulls it to his chest.

'You can't gut that on here,' she tells him.

'Anahera will gut it,' he says, with his simple confidence. He hugs the fish, and reddish water shows through the shirt.

Cynthia goes to sit in the cabin.

After a while she comes back out. She doesn't say anything to him, just sits watching the nearly dead fish make its last, sudden flaps on the floor. They're all three of them waiting for Anahera.

Gordon sees her first, and he stands and holds the fish for her to see. It's only now that Cynthia notes the size. It's at least forty centimetres. Its eyes still bulge, and its stomach's palpitating. Gordon shifts it up, down and sideways, as if it's tugged by waves. Anahera giggles and swims faster.

Cynthia takes her phone to sit at the front of the boat; she won't be there while they gut it. The washing-line's hard and thin to sit against, and the window's at a weird angle – she can't get comfortable leaning on either of them. She wants to go home.

The smell's as repulsive as she knew it would be. She imagines bones, and more and more of its blood. All their knives are blunt, Anahera's always saying so. How thick is a fish's skin? Or, maybe it doesn't have skin, maybe beneath its scales there's only a thin, papery film, like under the shell of an egg. She remembers Anahera's calm hands, and her long fingers. Where will she put the blade first? It might still be moving now, and it might still be moving when she kills it. She might have already killed it, and still it might be moving. Maybe Cynthia will become a vegetarian. She thinks about Anahera's nails and the webs between her fingers, sticky and wet with blood. If Anahera were to hold Gordon – if she put her fingers at the nape of his neck, or the top of his pants – there's a sheen all over him, and if Anahera were to touch it? Cynthia mustn't think of it.

She peers down through the window. Gordon's on the bed, under the covers, laughing and making jokes. Cynthia can't hear them, but there's a hum of Anahera's laughter under his. Her face isn't visible, but she's cut down the belly-middle of the fish, and

Cynthia can see her fingers inside it. It's pink. Neither of them looks back at her. He's oiled with something, false somehow; evil, even. For a horrible moment Cynthia thinks: Gordon is what they deserve, after the boy. But they weren't anywhere near him, he was too high to hear anything Cynthia yelled.

She stays there all day, even though her phone goes flat at two and she never finds a comfortable way to sit. She doesn't want to lie down. Anahera doesn't join her till four, and when she does she says, 'He's sleeping,' as if Gordon were a baby.

'I hope you charged him,' Cynthia says. 'Two hundred dollars, that's the price.'

'We have to think in larger terms,' Anahera says. Cynthia's ready to march around the side of the boat and tell him what he has coming. But Anahera puts a hand on her leg and says, 'To fund the sort of life you and I want long-term, we need money. Now, I can tell you for a fact that he's got $12,000, minus what he's already paid us.'

'How do you know?' Cynthia asks. The boat rolls over a wave.

'What do you think I've been doing in there?' Anahera gestures through the window. 'I'm doing everything I can to get us what we need.'

'I'll help you seduce him, if that's what's necessary,' Cynthia says sportively.

'I should be able to do it,' Anahera tells her.

That night they eat the fish. It's crumbed and crumbling, buttered, and so, so very good. Cynthia makes sure not to look at Gordon while she chews.

35

She's in a dream of custard, and the bed's empty. She rolls sleepily through the sheets and blankets, then gets caught in one and stops, waking. She remembers lapping the custard up in the dream, and loving it like a dog, but now the thought of lactose has sickened in her. Her feet are too hot. Her stomach's uncomfortable to lie on. Her face is against the pillow, and she's breathing back in the same air she breathed out.

Gordon's saying, 'Wonky, yes. That is it. Certainly it is on a lean, so I am telling you. But don't worry. It is taking on water.'

Then, Anahera's voice. 'What do we do?'

A masculine sigh from Gordon. 'I will tell you. I will lift the floor.'

Cynthia listens to Anahera snort, but then it's a giggle. 'She's awake, I think. We can do it now.'

Cynthia can't remember when they anchored, but the liquid feeling of her dream is underneath them, and the caughtness of waking in her tight sheets too; they're moving, but not really.

'Let her lie in her bed, and I will massage your poor foot,' Gordon says.

Cynthia waits for Anahera to say no, or that she has to go for her swim. But she says, 'Mmm,' and her voice is only slightly doubtful.

'Just give me a try,' he says, 'and we'll see how it goes.'

Anahera doesn't refuse, and there's shuffling, then quiet.

Cynthia thinks about waking up now, but it's too late, they must have started. What could she say?

'You see?' Gordon says. 'It is not so much a big deal, this foot. It is like I said.'

Anahera harrumphs, but almost happily, as if there's been a joke and she's taken a while to get it. Cynthia considers his repeated allegation of tilting. Does he think he's something special, or deserves something special for noticing it? No boat's going to sit perfectly straight. The real loss of balance is his weight, and their retention of him. Why do they need money at all? Cynthia refuses to think for an answer. She glares at the wall and thinks, *Whore*.

Anahera comes in to take a shit, and Gordon follows her. Cynthia lies silently, watching his back hunch to turn the stove on. He's lumpish, and his head looks small, bent down under the mass of him.

She leans over, slowly, and grabs his leg. He jumps.

'I love her, you know,' she tells him. 'But she's disappointing me. Breaking my heart.'

He regains himself and his hunched posture quickly, and shrugs so his shoulders obscure his head completely. 'She is a beautiful, cruel woman. What are we to do?' He chuckles. Then he's got the pot, and he's putting oats in it. He doesn't understand that Cynthia's love for Anahera is serious and adult. She desperately wants to tell him they don't want him, neither of them does, they only want his money. Instead she says, 'Your muscles aren't the hot kind, you know?'

He turns and smiles. When Anahera comes out of the toilet, Cynthia pretends she still has her dark black Gucci glasses, and that she's wearing them. She looks from one wall to the other.

'Tea?' Gordon asks her. 'You seem very stressed?'

'I am, yes,' Cynthia says solemnly, cryptically. He's standing up straighter now, and he's turned to face her.

'It's because the boat's on a lean,' Anahera says. 'I know it's been affecting me subconsciously.' She speaks like she's in a hurry to go somewhere.

'No,' Cynthia says. 'I've just been learning a lot about human nature recently.'

Anahera chews her lip.

Gordon says, 'It's okay, you are only young.'

He gives her some porridge and she eats it slowly. They don't have milk, they're out of maple syrup, and it's dry.

'Can you feel it?' Anahera asks her. 'The lean?'

Cynthia shrugs, and puts another glum spoonful in her mouth. It's hard to swallow, nearly impossible.

He turns and tells her, 'I'm going to take up the floor!' He's finished his porridge. It's easy for him, Cynthia thinks, because his mouth's so huge and spitty. Anahera's scraping the last of hers now too. Neither of them have noticed how much Cynthia hates her breakfast.

Anahera takes Gordon's bowl and washes it, then her own. Cynthia puts hers between her legs on the bed and looks at them.

'Are you alright, Cynthia-girl?' he asks.

'Yes, of course I am,' she says. 'I'm just sad at what I've learned lately, about people.'

Anahera doesn't turn, or even shift her head. When she finishes washing the pot, she says, 'Should we get started with the floor?'

Cynthia stands off to the side so they can switch the bed over. Anahera's quick at it now. Then, she and Gordon get on their knees together, with Cynthia watching, and begin on the floor. There's a layer of water-resistant carpet first, and under that panels of wood. One's painted blue, and they shift it aside to reveal a pool of thick, murky oil-water. Immediately the air is overwhelmed with oil and rot.

'You see, it is gunk!' he shouts, as if he's found something good. Anahera goes to get the flush-bucket from the toilet.

Cynthia makes a long, low, disgusted noise, and Gordon looks at her like he understands. They didn't have to smell it before, and they do now. Why should they not have left it? Anahera fills her bucket up and takes it outside. While she's gone, Cynthia notices again the silence of the weights in the ceiling above them. Gordon gets up and digs through the recycling. She asks him, 'Did you shift her weights, after she told you not to?'

'Oh,' he says. 'Oh yeah, I did.' He finds an old milk bottle and saws the top off with a butter knife, retaining the handle. When Anahera comes back with the bucket he uses the bottle as a scoop to fill it with muck. Cynthia sits down at the table and re-examines her porridge. She's hungry, so hungry now that she'd eat it without noticing the dryness. Now though, there's the air. She'd vomit if she tried to swallow anything.

She stares at Anahera's mouth and she doesn't like it. It keeps almost twitching. Anahera stands slowly, and goes to dump the slosh in the sea. Cynthia considers it: the dark, potent murk running into the water. She wishes she'd planned more to say to Gordon about the weights, but she didn't. Instead she goes and stands outside, watching the colours run and merge. Anahera comes out to rinse off the bucket, and Cynthia leans on the steering wheel. 'He moved your weights.'

'Oh,' Anahera says, unbothered.

'You know,' Cynthia tries again, 'I feel very ill. This is the second day in a row that he's really stuffed up the air quality on our boat.'

Anahera looks confused, so Cynthia says, 'The fish? The fish guts? I literally want to spew right now.'

Anahera shrugs. 'The boat was on a lean. Do you know what that means?'

It doesn't seem to mean much. 'Quite polluting,' Cynthia says, and nods at the water. There are flecks of rainbow on the surface, still being pulled away. Anahera puts an arm around Cynthia's waist, and says, 'What do you want to do today? Gordon's paying us $800 for the next part of the Island Boat Tour.'

'Why don't you go without me, in the dinghy? He'll pay more,' Cynthia says, watching Anahera's face. 'Actually, I need some time alone.'

Anahera purses her lips, concerned, but shrugs. They go, like Cynthia said. Anahera winks as they leave – she was right then; they did get a bit extra.

She spends the rest of the day in bed, lulled by nausea. The air is tight against her and terrible with oil. Her whole body feels invaded by the slick black of it, but her suffering is too deep, and she's too caught in it to move. She rolls onto her face. Then her side, her back, her other side, and onto her face again. She's watched the whole of *Bachelor Pad* twice now, and *Bachelor in Paradise* doesn't look as good. There's no prize money on the sequel show. She's tempted by an article on stuff.co.nz about a new Australian programme, *The Briefcase* (a take-off of an American one with the same name). Poor, suffering people are given money, but – *twist!* – they're then shown footage of other poor suffering people, and asked if they'll share some. Cynthia watches a trailer on YouTube. One family lost everything in a bushfire, and another woman had all her limbs amputated after a serious illness.

It's been hours since they left and Cynthia feels dizzy.

Now, this isn't why she's upset, but why would Gordon choose Anahera? She can't need or shiver like a girl, like Cynthia could, surely? Both he and Anahera are tan and muscular. What could be the purpose of a partnership between two people who both know how to lift things?

She gets up to pee, and checks her face in the mirror. It's been a while since she has. She's spotty and burnt now, with a dull, wild look in her eyes. Her hair's scraggly from being washed in salt, and she's got regrowth nearly two inches long. There's new fat all over her, expanding under her skin.

She thinks about going to sit under the washing-line, but she's worried that if they come back and she's out there they'll think she had a nice day in the sun. They don't return till night. Cynthia can't operate the gas oven, so she eats three packets of chips.

When they do come back Anahera brushes her teeth, then Gordon does his, although he doesn't have a toothbrush. 'So then, what did that guy Jason say?' Anahera asks him, continuing some conversation from earlier.

'Don't know.' Gordon pauses brushing to answer her. 'I stopped listening a bit before then.'

Cynthia hoicks up some plegm. She hoicks and spits five times over the side of the boat, and she hopes they hear it. Then she stands outside the toilet, waiting for him to finish.

36

Fear is only the healthy shock of remembering what's important. Cynthia's going to stage an intervention and sort out Anahera's priorities. She doesn't want porridge, so she asks Gordon to turn on the stove. He beams and does so. Anahera must be swimming. She makes omelettes. They look good, considering what she's got to work with, and she's proud. 'Has Anahera eaten?' She checks with Gordon.

He smiles again. 'No.'

'Have you?' she asks nicely.

'No.' He smiles bigger.

She puts a tea towel over them to save warmth, and gets back in bed to spend a little time on Facebook. She's turned chat off since they left, but she sometimes likes to scroll through the messages people sent her immediately after she did. They all say typical, lovely things: *Where are you? Are you alright? Wherever you are we miss you so much? Why don't you reply. Please, just let me know you're alright*, et cetera. Reading them is dreamy. She's already deleted the one obnoxious one from an auntie, which mentioned her father.

When Anahera comes back Cynthia is in the perfect mood. They set up the table together, and sit down to the omelettes. 'Delicious!' Anahera says, and Cynthia knows she means it because they really are good, and they're running out of food. Gordon nods and sits.

'Anahera,' Cynthia says. 'It would be really nice if you and I could spend some time alone together today.'

'Aha! Girl time!' Gordon taps the table with his fork.

They both nod and laugh at him. 'That's exactly what I've been thinking,' Anahera says.

He yawns, and no one mentions making him pay for the bed.

So they paddle together into the glistening water, and Cynthia's tempted to say nothing at all. When they're away from the boat, and nowhere in particular, she puts a hand gently on Anahera's arm, signalling for her to pause. She does. Anahera is beautiful and kind. It's hard to remember what she ever did that wasn't reasonable.

But she's looking at Cynthia questioningly.

'How's it going with him?' Cynthia asks.

'Good, I think. Just give me a bit and I'll have it.' Anahera rubs her thumb over the handle of her paddle and smiles.

'Excellent, because the police are after us, and he's a liability.'

Anahera shuffles back in her seat. 'Really?'

'Yep. Ron's been texting me. I mean, we'll be alright. But the last thing we need is Gordon coming along if we're questioned.'

Anahera shuffles forward again. 'What's he been saying? Ron.'

'His dad knows the family. They're making investigations.' As she's speaking Cynthia realises that they are, of course they are – a boy's dead.

'What do they know?' Anahera asks.

'Nothing. He was last seen at the dairy, by the school. There's a half coloured-in dick on the bottom of the slide at the playground, which they suspect is his. And an abandoned, nearly empty spray can there.'

Anahera nods, relieved, but Cynthia's tummy wrenches. What if they were seen with Toby? What if the police talked to the boat salesman? They'd know the mooring number then, and the name and colour of *Baby*. She's glad she took the photo from his office. Her face is hot, and suddenly she's crying. Anahera moves forward to hold her.

'It's okay, we'll send Gordon to get the groceries. We'll make him get a dinghy-full. We'll be fine. When we get enough money, and he's gone, we'll leave this place.' But she adds, 'Stop texting Ron.'

Cynthia nods. Maybe she should text him, just to check. 'Okay,' she says. 'And you finish up with Gordon. I don't care if we only get half the money, or three-quarters. This is important.'

Anahera nods seriously. They stay there for a long time. Cynthia puts her head in Anahera's lap, and Anahera runs her fingers through her hair and says, 'I'm sorry we didn't get to talk like this earlier.' Cynthia doesn't mention the weights, or the toothbrush. Anahera's saying the right things, and very kindly, but in a halting way. She keeps looking from Cynthia to the town, and back to the boat.

They paddle back slowly, with Anahera pausing intermittently to touch Cynthia's face and say, 'It's okay. Don't worry at all about it. We can go anywhere in our boat. Anywhere at all.' Cynthia wants to grab her head and hold it still so they look straight at each other up close. She wants Anahera to confirm it wasn't her fault, what happened with the boy. But she can't ask, she's too afraid. Something very good has happened between them, there on the dinghy, and she can't afford to tip it even slightly.

When they get back they leave Gordon sleeping and watch an Adam Sandler movie on Cynthia's phone. During a funny part, when they're both laughing, she puts a hand on Anahera's thigh. Later, when they're laughing again she shifts it up and in, so it's clasped between her legs. Anahera is beautiful muscle and clench, and she continues her laughing a moment after Sandler is off-screen.

37

The next day she scrolls through her contacts several times, and can't trust herself to trust Ron. Anahera's not making visible progress with Gordon, but that doesn't mean it's not happening. She watches him a lot, and feels the need to interrogate him. Where did he come from? What does he know? She understands; with every question asked she tells him something. He sees her looking, but stays friendly. That afternoon he catches another fish and Anahera guts it.

At night in bed Cynthia burns to speak, but she can feel Gordon alive in the cabin.

38

It's morning and he's brushing his teeth again, loudly. Cynthia gets a glass of water, and through the crack of the bathroom door sees his mouth in the mirror. His teeth are clamped hard together, and he's emitting foam through the gaps between them. She can't see his eyes through the gap, just his jaw in the mirror and his big arm moving.

Anahera's swimming. When Cynthia's swallowed her water she opens a jar of olives. 'I see you watching me,' Gordon says, coming back out. 'I see you watching me a lot.'

Cynthia shrugs, he's on her boat.

'It doesn't matter if you like me,' he says. 'I am a social scientist.'

Whatever, Cynthia thinks, and goes to eat her olives under the washing-line. When she's had enough and goes back in for something else, he says, 'She left again, in the dinghy.' Cynthia ignores him. He's deconstructed the bed and made the table.

'Look at this,' he says, waving the boy's cellphone.

'What?' She's horrified. Didn't he take it with him?

'Asses,' Gordon says, '*and,* tits.'

'Why are you going through our things,' Cynthia asks as calmly as possible. 'In what world would that be appropriate?'

Gordon's grinning and flicking through them. 'An amateur, someone is,' he says. 'All on the desktop, I found them. In a folder titled "Homework".' He laughs, hard.

'Anahera will be back soon,' Cynthia says, 'and I know she won't consider it acceptable that you've been snooping through our stuff.'

'Snooping!' Gordon whoops. 'I didn't know it was *your* item. I thought it was a thing of the boat, you know – came with the boat.' He gives her a sly look, and swipes right. 'Oh,' he says. 'Oh gosh, yeah, there is one.' He doesn't show Cynthia what he's looking at. 'Right under my sleeping bed, it was, in the cabin. Only my second night, I found it. It is the same charge-hole as my own phone.'

'You've got to buy us groceries,' Cynthia says. 'Anahera and I have discussed it. You'll fill up the dinghy. So you nearly sink.'

Gordon laughs. 'You're pretty interesting,' he says. 'There are some hugely interesting things here, to be found.'

She shuts herself in the cabin and weeps a bit. She'd like to have her crying done by the time Anahera returns, and to be engaged in an activity. But Anahera comes back sooner than expected, and immediately Gordon starts asking her things, and Cynthia knows he'll be touching things and touching her, so she stays where she is. He's unashamed, like a huge infant. When Cynthia does come back out, they're playing cards. Anahera asks if she wants to join in, but it looks hard, boring and stupid, so she says no. After dinner they play some more. In the cabin, waiting for them to finish, Cynthia looks at Ron's number again. When she's done more than enough waiting, she sticks her head through the door. 'Are you nearly done? It's a shit-hole in here. It stinks.'

Gordon laughs knowingly. It does.

Anahera scrunches up her face, as if confused. It doesn't matter, Cynthia doesn't move. Anahera says, 'If you want we'll pack up after this round, in say, ten minutes?'

'No,' Cynthia says, 'that's too long.'

She sleeps in the cabin.

Later, she wakes and hears them. There's talking she can't make out, then a sound of Gordon flopping over. They're in bed.

'Well, no. But – ' from Anahera.

'They all do the Tinder thing. It's their *normal.*'

There's a noise of shifting bedding, like Anahera's grabbed his head and moved on top of him. He groans, and she says, 'Gordon, you don't know a thing about women.'

He laughs in deep splutters, and Cynthia thinks there are thuds of Anahera pummelling his chest. Then she must stop, because he says in a deep, smooth voice, 'We all need someone, that's all I'm saying.'

Quiet, then, 'Hey,' he says. 'Hey,' and there's shuffling again. They've settled against each other. 'Hey,' he says.

'Yeah,' she tells him.

39

Breakfast is couscous with canned tomatoes. It must be an apology, and it's delicious. They eat together. 'Gordon, you're going to get groceries today, as many as you can. On your own card,' Anahera tells him. He salutes, and keeps eating. He's wearing Cynthia's father's pyjamas. Anahera washes the dishes, and he changes on the deck. When he's ready to leave he folds them and puts them in Anahera hands.

After he goes she tells Cynthia, 'If they haven't come for us, I don't think they will. We just need to get his money and we'll go.'

Cynthia shrugs, happily, but there's a change in Anahera's eyes. 'You must be tired?' she asks. 'He's big, I imagine, to be in bed with. You must be exhausted.'

Anahera sighs, like a mother or a cleaning woman, and gets up to dry the dishes.

'Don't you see? You don't have to dry them at all!' Cynthia says. 'There's a rack, you can just leave them on the rack! They dry themselves, effectively.' But she stops. Discussions on this subject only ever become sad and philosophical.

'This isn't a big boat, Cynthia,' Anahera says.

Cynthia doesn't mention that as the extra person, Gordon should be doing them. She says instead, 'We used to be such dirty girls, Anahera! Before he arrived.' She's embarrassed at the way Anahera's name seems to glug in her mouth, like it did before they knew each other. There's a hard clunk of her tongue over the 'r', and a quick 'a' at the beginning, like in the small, dismal word 'ant'. She knows, Anahera always cleaned. It just didn't seem like much till Gordon arrived. Still, as she must, she continues audaciously, 'We were kidnappers, and we suntanned, and we had better biscuits. He's going to come back with shortbreads, and they're so dry.'

Anahera flinches at *kidnappers*, but only says, 'I don't like Tim Tams, Cynthia, you like Tim Tams.' Then she sighs again, deeper and drier this time, and re-wipes a plate.

'I don't even know what biscuits you like!' Cynthia says, but it comes out more like wailing.

Anahera turns and shrugs in a cooperative way, as if it's not important.

'Tell me something,' Cynthia says quickly. 'While he's gone – who would you rather kiss: Katy Perry or Beyoncé?'

'Beyoncé.' Anahera puts the plate away, finally.

'Me too!' Cynthia's toes are wriggling. 'Do you miss our old days sometimes?'

Anahera pauses. 'Yeah.'

Cynthia beams. 'He's just so boring, and he's got a honky nose.'

Anahera looks at her, as if the word might still be hanging there in the air, in front of her face. She laughs. Cynthia blinks. Anahera likes her and that's the truth. They only need to get back to the island where everything went so wrong, and let destiny set it right. There, Gordon was nothing and they were in each other's orbit.

'We need to go back,' Cynthia says. 'To our island. To stretch our legs, because we can't go into town, and we can't be like this a moment longer.'

Anahera waves at the window, and the distance behind it. 'It's a crime scene. It's disappeared.'

This isn't true. 'Pussy,' Cynthia says quietly.

'What?'

She didn't mean it seriously, but the way Anahera's looking at her makes Cynthia feel like a rude, breast-sucking little boy. She's ashamed. 'Pussy,' she whispers, glaring at Anahera's face.

'We'll never find it again,' Anahera says definitively.

'He used your toothbrush,' Cynthia tells her.

Gordon returns in the dinghy, moving very slowly but paddling hard. He's red-faced, and Anahera gets him a cup of water. The dinghy's absolutely full, with food piled high around his sitting hips. Anahera ties it up, and it floats oddly, dangerously, as if it's on the brink of sinking. She unloads it, bending down towards him while he sits there.

Cynthia stands back and watches Anahera's hands move things from around Gordon's hips, then his waist, and finally his feet. There are ten big water bottles, the same number of instant pasta sachets, a bottle of dishwashing liquid, one of vodka, and a bag of apples. There's a way Anahera grabs the food products that Cynthia doesn't like, and she stops noticing what they are. When Anahera leans down, over the edge of the boat and towards Gordon in the dinghy, her breasts are at his face level. Her hands and arms graze him, and he sits there as solid and dumb as a post, still puffing a little.

Cynthia waits for some instruction, but it doesn't come. Not until Anahera's shifted every last thing onto the boat does Gordon, still with blood in his face, get out to help put it away. Cynthia swivels to watch them, now they're in the kitchen. Gordon's shoulders touch Anahera's, and a couple of times they each reach for the same item and Gordon beams so big that even though Cynthia can only see Anahera's back, she knows he's being smiled at.

Anahera pours three cups of Fanta, and drinks hers while making some mac and cheese with fresh broccoli on the stove. She uses three packets, which seems excessive. Gordon probably got too many. He swallows his Fanta in a glug, and pours himself some milk. 'Smells good,' he tells Anahera. Then to Cynthia, 'I am thinking,' he says, 'during my long paddle. You are a young woman, Cynthia, and I find your ambitions inspiring. Very.' He nods at her. 'To become a news presenter, you said to me. It was your dream.'

She ignores him. Anahera doesn't turn from her pot.

'I am thinking, we should act out our fantasises. Self-love is so nice here!'

There was another thing she told him: that she and Anahera were in a real relationship. It makes her want to drown herself, to slam her head down into the table like it's water. She bites forwards, but it's like apple bobbing, words are too big for her and slip away from her mouth. She can't breathe. She'd like to throw herself away, into the water, and to die. Still, she lies more. 'Yeah, my father thought I should do it. He knew the people. But then I got into a specific postgrad thing, and I felt that was more important.'

Neither Gordon nor Anahera asks a single question. Anahera slops mac and cheese into three plastic bowls and they eat it.

Cynthia's in the bathroom, examining her regrowth in the mirror. Gordon leans on the doorway and says, 'I invented a philosophy, it is: if you are not making your own dream, you are making someone else's. I ask you now, do you believe in your own self-love?'

She lets her hair go and looks instead at his eyes.

'Don't worry,' he says. 'I know your island. You will go back to it.'

She turns on him suddenly. 'How do we know we can trust you?'

'Oh!' Gordon shifts quickly backwards. 'Oh, for what?'

Cynthia pushes past him, to get out.

'I will think about it for you,' he tells her. 'I will think of a reason.'

They have tomato soup for dinner that night, with more broccoli, carrots and leek. Then sausages. After dinner, Anahera and Gordon play cards again. At ten, Cynthia tells them it's time to switch the table for the bed, she wants to sleep. They do, but Anahera doesn't lie down with Cynthia, she goes out to sit under the washing-line with Gordon, talking.

Cynthia creeps out into the deep night. The air and water are one big nothing, and her hands disappear in front of her, into the black. It's very difficult, but she plants her feet firmly onto the narrow walking platform along the side of the boat, one after the other, and holds tight to the support bar like it's a hand reached out to save her. The screws are loose, they must be, because the bar shifts when she does, but Cynthia doesn't worry or even think about drowning. She moves closer, slowly, silently, and hears Anahera say, 'All my problems, he solved them all. But he'd get this look on his face, you know, this smug-generous look. And it would just stay there for hours and hours, after I'd thanked him, thanked him twice and made his dinner, and I'd know he was waiting for me to thank him again.'

Cynthia clings tight. Her hair itches at the edge of her forehead, but she doesn't move her hands.

'Mmm,' Gordon says. 'I know what you mean.'

It's the boat that shifts. Cynthia's feet slip and she squeals. Neither of them says anything, and both stay silent while she makes her way back around the side of the boat, then to bed.

He's a mindless speaking thing; a tongue, and he's crawled out of the cabin and smeared his spit and noise all over Cynthia's boat, her home and Anahera. A tongue: a big flaccid muscle, out and wriggling too far from its mouth. He's not where he belongs, and because of him there's no place for Cynthia either.

40

The next morning Cynthia's desperate in a sexy way. She licks Anahera's neck, unabashed like a dog, from her collarbone to the lobe of her ear. 'You're nice, really,' she whispers. Anahera grins, still mostly sleeping. 'Yeah, I am.'

Cynthia snuggles her till they're both hungry.

'I am too!' Gordon shouts from outside, where he's fishing, and Cynthia's not at all surprised by his listening. Anahera gets up and makes porridge, then tells them to save her some while she swims. Gordon takes more than he should, and Cynthia has to take less than she wants so there's some left over.

'I've made up my answer,' he says, 'to your important question of yesterday. You can trust me because you can trust Anahera. She is pressed down on me like a thumb. She kissed me so good, hard, last night.'

Cynthia doesn't go cold hearing this, she settles into the cold she already is. She's calm. She knows – and Gordon must have his own inklings – that they're bad women, and dangerous. Some kissing is nothing. Cynthia shrugs.

He sits, still waiting for a response, but she's given one. She finishes her porridge and throws the bowl in the sink. It clangs but it's plastic. Anahera's a whore, but Cynthia's not worried. What she understands is this: their shame, and their pride too, are engines, whirring now. The game's started, and Cynthia will play it.

Anahera clambers back onto the boat and stands dripping in the same place she did when she first confessed her island to Cynthia, announcing their destiny. She looks around, and notices the lack of porridge in the pot, then Gordon's fingers at the elasticated collar of his shirt. She notices Cynthia too – Cynthia can feel her guts and posture under Anahera's eyes. The hard coolness in Anahera's glance makes Cynthia think of the moment just before Toby fell from the tree. There's something she didn't notice then, but she remembers it now all the same; Anahera's face just before he fell, enraptured. He wanted to impress her, and he did.

Anahera's neck stretched right back, her face lifted to him, and a twitch in her lip as if a hook were through it, pulling. Light falling onto her cheeks through the trees, and into her eyes. Her hands held slack in the shadows, forgotten, beside Cynthia. But her heart, and her blood! Anahera's blood must have moved so fast as they stood there together, quickened by seeing him, and Cynthia's sure she has more of it than a usual person. Murderess, Cynthia thinks, and who knows? Anahera might have been thinking the same of her for weeks.

Her love for Anahera is laced with something better than love: destiny, fate. Clearly, Anahera is some things. No matter. All Cynthia wants is to stand beside her again, amid the trees. Cynthia's regrowth is black, and long now. Her hair at the ends is dry from salt. Even her new fat is something; she only needs Anahera to bite it off. They're of the same wilderness; the same badness. She's proud, she won't be hurt. Gordon simply can't be with them.

She won't use her new knowing immediately. She's daring now, but also in new self-control. She smiles sweetly at Anahera, her partner and lover, and ignores Gordon, then holes herself up in the cabin under the light of her phone, with their three squeezy last apples. In that dark little space, with her phone's brightness right down to save power, her mind opens wider. Cynthia's at war – with a man – for a woman. She watches *The Bachelor* for three hours. It's all about how to fight your enemies by lying, kissing, fucking and dressing really well. All she needs to do is remember everything she knew in her old life.

Either Cynthia or Gordon will be humiliated. The water and sky don't care which, and Anahera doesn't necessarily either. It doesn't matter about the truth of anyone's love. You either have the gumption and talent to win a place for what you'll call your love, or you don't and it means nothing – if you can't swim, the water won't hold you.

The *Bachelor* girls fight and cry hard. Vienna wins even though she's got a bad face, particularly when she cries, but Cynthia knows she's tougher. She's a killer, with new tan lines and an oiliness that won't leave the nape of her neck. At midday, Anahera passes some canned soup through the gap in the door. Cynthia takes it, then takes Anahera's fingers and sucks two of them. She pulls them hard with her whole mouth, right into the back of her throat. When they sit down to dinner, she's going to tell Gordon, 'You're an ugly piece of shit and we all know it. Your ex-girlfriend knew it. Your time here is finite.' He'll act hurt and wipe his eyes, but she'll tell him not to bother.

She'll ruin him at dinner, and seduce Anahera at night. How it works is, you tell a person what they are, then you tell other people what they are, and if they become that thing by your telling, you win.

41

It's baked beans, dinner. Gordon comes in and wipes his brow as if fishing was a hard day, and sits opposite them both. He combs his fingers through his hair, then pats where he's growing a beard. 'So, ladies,' he says, leaning forward towards them, onto his elbows, 'I hear the police here are silly and willy-nilly. Arresting everybody all over the place.'

'Oh?' Anahera asks. 'Who've you been talking to?'

'Just at the supermarket, my friends there.'

Anahera laughs, so Cynthia does too.

He waits for them to stop. 'I am thinking now, we should make a practice. For if there is an emergency questioning!' He grins, ear to ear, like an infant who's just been changed and spitefully peed himself.

They say nothing. Anahera leans over and touches his elbow. He leans in and holds her shoulder, then pulls her forward. They kiss, gracelessly, over the table. Anahera shifts her bowl of beans aside so she can rest on her arm. Cynthia takes a bite of her bread, then puts in a spoonful of beans. She won't listen to their spitty tongues, instead she chews, loudly, so they can hear. Sadly, she knows, this will be her chief act of aggression this evening. She adds more bread, swallows half of what's in her mouth, and recommences chewing.

Gordon unlocks his lips from Anahera's. In a new, unaccented voice he says, 'Do you have any awareness of the incident?'

'No,' Anahera says, but there's a flinch in her neck, and Gordon's seen it.

'Where were you at the time of the incident?'

Cynthia begins swallowing to answer, but Anahera interrupts her. 'What incident?'

'Ah,' Gordon says. His accent and smile return. 'Good.' He looks at Cynthia. 'Will it be fine if I steal her away tonight, for a little ride in the dinghy?'

Cynthia looks at Anahera, and there's a slight nod. 'Whatever,' she tells him.

'Thank you,' he says. He stands up and makes a little bow. 'You are generous and mature.' Then he turns to do the dishes.

The paddle moves gently at the ends of Gordon's huge arms. There are no waves, and the boat slips through the water like a tongue into a mouth, silently. They stop. It's dark, they've not gone far. The moon falls on them like a spotlight. He's murmuring to her, Cynthia can't make out what, and Anahera murmurs back. It's his moment, he's alone with her. For all Cynthia knows he could be reciting a poem. She can't see Anahera's face, but she's wearing a singlet, her arms are uncovered. The moonlight, or some reflection from the water, has glazed the skin of her shoulders just slightly blue. One arm is bent back, its elbow pointing, to hold the edge of the dinghy, and the other is lifted to touch the skin behind her ear, where Cynthia knows it's soft.

Cynthia goes inside, into the cabin. There, she unzips his bag. First there's a pile of clothes, she shoves those aside quickly. Underneath them is a copy of *A Good Keen Man* by Barry Crump. Three cans of beans, and two of spaghetti. The gin trap, some keys, and a cellphone (charged). There's a fluffy teddy bear, wrapped up in plastic similar to cellophane. It's peachy brown, with a shiny red heart sewn on its belly. There are words stitched in silver on the heart, *Forever and ever*. Lower, there's a GPS (also charged) and a handful of pens bound together by at least three rubber-bands. An A4 exercise book, with the first third of its pages torn out. Under that is a box of chocolates. They're heart-shaped, in a red, transparent-topped box. Cynthia looks at them closely; some are dark and some white, and they've all got little smiley faces drawn on their tops in chocolate of their opposite shade. Some of the faces wink. Under those are chargers for the phone and GPS. She checks the phone, but it's locked. She puts everything back in the right order. When they first met he told her his bag was full of shoes.

42

The next morning they're drinking beer outside. Anahera swallows the last of hers and stands up. They watch her. Gordon tips the rim of his bottle against his lips, slowly. Anahera's already wearing her swimming shorts, but she turns to face the wall and removes her shirt and bra. Her breasts swing out briefly, but she puts on her bra-integrated swimming singlet easily and turns back around. This is how she changed before he came, as if her body were nothing, no secret at all.

The air around her is plump with every feeling Cynthia has. But inside that air, Anahera's the same woman she's always been: fit and moving, unblemished. She doesn't look any different for the salt air, or their separation from the supermarket. There's nothing to take from her. She's her own system of temperature and weather; abandoning Cynthia all the time, without any change of movement or breathing.

Gordon doesn't look away. He sits, dumb as a dog, while she looks back down at them. But why should he? How can he feel so safe? His brain's as slack as his mouth. If Anahera bent down and touched his thigh, Cynthia knows, if she grabbed it, he'd maintain precisely the same expression. His brain is a drainage system, moving fluid continually through the same place. He doesn't know where he is. Cynthia watches him watch Anahera straighten the underwire of her singlet, which is still wet from her swim yesterday.

He'd want her if she were anything. But Anahera is something;

Cynthia can't sit there like he does. She looks at the kettle, then the ceiling, and down again at their little wobbly table. The whole room of their home is small. He sits in it with them as if everything is nothing and they're only animals.

Anahera sits back down. She isn't smiling, but Cynthia thinks she would if she let herself. She's holding it, like she holds her muscles while she exercises. She stands again and grins in a way that isn't a smile, acknowledging there was no reason to sit, then walks to the back of the boat and dives off.

Anahera swims powerfully away. Cynthia gets up from the table and stands in the kitchen area. She's thinking what she might eat. She can't think what to eat. She notices with horror the way Gordon's muscles pull his shirt taut around his shoulders. His jaw is hard. It's because of his body, and the way of his body. Anahera's body is perceiving the threat of his, and it's lubricating itself *down there*. She's mistaking that for real attraction. Even his nose has menace about it.

He sees her watching him. 'I am not what you think I am,' he says. 'I am not a tourist.' Cynthia says nothing and stands to look out the little window above the sink. His lips make a wet, vibrating, in-suck noise. 'I am everywhere I go on business,' he says. 'I am a sociologist.' Cynthia fills a glass of water, drinks some, and tips the rest down the drain. 'What does that mean?' he sighs, then answers, 'It means my job is to watch people. To find a place and sit down with my eyes – ' He thinks for the word. 'Skinned? No, peeled. With my eyes peeled and fresh like a potato. Just my sitting here will change you. Is changing you. That is the power of me and how good I am with my eyes. I am like a potato, peeled by you. Bits of me are removed by your moving, as I come to new understandings. But you, too, you will lose your skins just as I look at you. Do not appear alarmed! This is not flirtatious. But sociology will leak in here, through me, through my eyes opened into an opening. We will all be washed clean, understand? And see the water in our filth. Won't that be healthy, Cynthia? When we, all three, are bare to each other.'

Cynthia hardly waits for him to finish. She says, 'You're not what you think you are. You're a moron, actually.' Then, without changing, or even letting him see her remove her socks, she goes outside to wash in the sea.

When she clambers back up the ladder, he's standing above her. 'I will give you the forecast,' he says. 'I am going to ask her the right question soon. It is not much I wait for.'

Cynthia pushes past him for a towel. It's her responsibility now, she understands, to save Anahera from unimaginable shame. She goes on Facebook, and Gordon fiddles with his fishing equipment. Together, they're waiting for Anahera. 'She doesn't owe anyone a thing,' he whispers loudly, out of nowhere.

A gull shits on the window. Cynthia understands, as suddenly as a slap, that *waiting* isn't enough. She crawls into the cabin and dresses herself, starting with a push-up bra and an invigorating thong. Then she pinkens and wets her lips, and puts on a short, frilly dress. Her dulled cellphone screen acts as a mirror, and she gets everything exactly right. After considering pigtails she settles on a high ponytail. Her eyes are lined.

Sexy isn't when you want sex, but when you offer it; sexy is what oozes from you when there's none of you left. She lies back in the dark, and she knows. She's going to stuff his rude, under-educated tongue back in his mouth and watch him choke on it. She'll seal the cranny in Anahera's mind before it cracks, before he can press anything through.

She looks at herself more – she knows what she can trust. Yes,

Cynthia has gained weight and got hairy, but she and Anahera are the same sort of woman, and those aren't the things they care about. By her own standards, and certainly by Anahera's, Cynthia's still a definite nine. When she's lounged and loved herself adequately, she emerges, tripping a bit on the second anchor, but righting herself.

She's surprised – she was paying deep attention in there – to find Gordon at the table, eating a four-layer club sandwich, oozing jam. 'Ah!' he says, with his mouth very full. 'You have made, what is it? An effort?'

She ignores him and sits down. 'Knowing what I do, I advise you to leave.'

Gordon laughs. 'What do you know.'

She says nothing, only stares back.

'Oh, never mind!' he says. 'Wow, you are so little. How could you become bigger? Make a huge deep breath of your lungs, I tell you! Breathe in power! You must! Are you breathing at all?'

'Turn this on,' she tells him, standing and gesturing to the stove, which she still can't operate herself.

'Sorry, you are a weakling,' he says as he passes her, like he's hurt her feelings. Still, he lights the thing and turns the knob. Cynthia's not afraid, she looks right up at the back of his head.

Anahera's going to be hungry when she comes back, so Cynthia makes porridge and slops it into two bowls. He clearly wants some, but says nothing. She makes custard in another pot with milk powder from the cupboard. She also finds a can of lychees, and puts them aside with a can opener. She'll open them for Anahera later, if that's the way they feel. She slops the custard on the porridge, and goes to wait with it on the deck.

43

Anahera's minutes away, swimming slowly. Cynthia's been waiting a while, and her hip hurts from leaning over the edge. Anahera flicks her head to keep some loose hair from her eyes, and a moment later, flicks again. She flicks twice more before Cynthia decides she's close enough, and tells her, 'I need to be alone with you.'

Gordon's doing something inside. It doesn't matter what – he'll be listening. Anahera tilts her head to show she hasn't heard, and Cynthia leans over further to repeat it, not louder, but with more obvious movements of her mouth. After a moment, Anahera nods. It's perfect; it's all going perfectly.

When Anahera arrives, finally, she's flushed and panting. 'I didn't know how far I went,' she says.

Cynthia laughs knowingly. 'I made you breakfast, I thought we could eat alone together in the dinghy. I'll paddle.'

'Sure, sweetie.' She looks into the bowls and raises her eyebrows. 'Looks good.'

Transferring everything from the boat to the dinghy was difficult, but it's done now. Cynthia beams, sitting close. She hasn't bothered to paddle them anywhere. He can hear them; she doesn't care. 'I got these things too,' she says, nodding to the lychees and forgetting what they are.

'You sure did,' Anahera says.

It's hard, opening them in the dinghy – there's a balance problem for one thing – but Anahera doesn't watch and Cynthia gets it.

Then, she realises – she didn't think of spoons! She says nothing of it, and hands Anahera her bowl. Anahera has an odd, curious look on her face, but she holds it out, waiting. Delicately and stickily with her fingers, Cynthia slops some lychees into Anahera's bowl, then her own. She ends up with more than she wanted – she's not really sure what lychees are – but doesn't worry.

Anahera's waiting for a spoon.

'Um,' Cynthia says. 'Yeah.' She nods at Anahera's bowl, and her fingers holding it.

'We could ask Gordon. We're not far – ' Anahera starts. They haven't drifted much, they're only a few metres away. Cynthia shakes her head, No. Then she picks up a lychee with her fingers, squeezing it confidently. The bowl's resting between her legs, nearly at her crotch. Anahera laughs and shakes her head a little, flicking some water from her hair. She lifts a smear of custard to her mouth and says, 'Good, with only milk powder.'

Cynthia nods, relieved. She's got a whole lychee in her mouth, and it's a lot, but she's deciding she likes the taste. She bites and it's hollow in the middle. When she's swallowed she lifts the bowl to her mouth and slurps some custard-porridge. Anahera laughs so she does it again, louder and slurpier.

Anahera doesn't laugh the second time, but her smile stays. 'What is it you want to say then, Cynthia?'

Cynthia pauses a moment, then leans her head on Anahera's shoulder, not heavily, but enough to be felt. Anahera slurps some porridge herself, and it's a loud noise in her mouth, right near Cynthia's ears. 'I've been thinking about me and you. I mean: men, what did they ever do for us, huh?' Cynthia murmurs.

'Hey? I didn't get a word of that,' Anahera says.

'What did men ever do for us?' Cynthia says.

Anahera laughs, slurping again. 'Your dad's –'

'No,' Cynthia says. 'I mean really *do*. We find this whole place' – she gestures around them, not at the other boats, but at the sea, sky and hills – 'then he comes. They're just lumps, I think. Men.' Anahera's hand pats her head, so she says, 'That's just my opinion.'

'I'll speak to him,' Anahera says.

'It's important to me.' Cynthia puts her bowl aside and nestles in closer. 'All the male race ever does is walk into beautiful scenery and ruin it.'

'Did you have a boyfriend, when I took you?' Anahera asks.

'No, because I knew I was waiting for something.' Cynthia takes Anahera's hand, which is now resting on the seat beside her, and moves it to her waist. Something momentous.'

'Something momentous,' Anahera repeats. Her face is still, and her hand motionless above Cynthia's hip.

'It's just, I always felt I knew you. From the very beginning at the gym.'

'You're alright, Cynthia.'

'But you noticed me, you saw me in a special way.' Cynthia's voice breaks and she shifts. The hand at her waist feels dead like a fish.

'We had several extremely good moments, and you're definitely attractive, but Cynthia, that's not enough – not, you know, when there are all these other things.' Anahera's voice is steady, low, and she shifts her hand up and down along Cynthia's side in time with her speaking.

'What other things! What other things can matter?' Cynthia's sobbing now, in quick little heaves.

Anahera doesn't answer. Clearly, she thinks the things are too obvious: Gordon, Toby, the dishes, their respective levels of maturity, and money – of course, money. Instead she says, 'I'll never in my life forget the way you looked in my classes when you were proud. When you'd achieved something, even something small, and you beamed. You were an extremely satisfying student' – she pauses – 'I'd say my most satisfying, Cynthia, even though you never lost any weight, or gained even a bit of muscle.'

Cynthia giggles, looking up at her. Her cheeks are wet, but the sun's hot, warming them. Their faces are close, she only needs to move forward a little. They touch lips gently. Forget Gordon.

Anahera maintains her hold on Cynthia's head when they pull their faces apart. 'There are things,' she says. 'You know there are.'

'They're nothing,' Cynthia tells her.

'It's been something for a while,' Anahera says.

'He's nothing.' Cynthia leans in again, and puts her lips around Anahera's bottom one, holding it. She shifts Anahera's hand inside her shirt, and bites her tongue.

'Will you take care of me?' she asks.

'I am,' Anahera says, indignant. 'I'm trying to.'

Cynthia puts her hand at the nape of Anahera's neck, and pulls it forward. This may not be going so badly after all. This time she bites a little harder, still only inquisitively, and Anahera's hand tightens on her waist.

Now's the time – Cynthia grabs Anahera's hair and pulls it back, hard and suddenly. Anahera begins to say something, but Cynthia says, 'No.' Anahera starts again, but Cynthia tells her, 'Listen up. I know he's a fake – he's got no feelings.'

Wind comes past them in a rush, then they're sitting in simple, hot sun again. Anahera says, 'He knows.' The boy falling. The dinghy lifts and lowers on a wave. Anahera won't look at her eyes.

'I'm not saying you can't have your pet,' Cynthia says. 'I'm saying, train him.'

Anahera maintains the same face; Gordon knows.

'What do you think I'm afraid of?' Cynthia asks. 'Him? The police? I'd rather be arrested ten thousand times than let him own you.' Anahera starts to speak again, about what he knows, but Cynthia stops her. 'He's a dog, and I respect you.'

'Cynthia, you're not being reasonable.'

The boy falling, and all the trees. The wind's gone. The water holds still for a moment. 'He watched us, do you know that? He watched you grieving, and he watched us sleep together in that tent.' Cynthia understands now. 'He waited.'

Anahera holds her breath patiently.

'He set the trap.' For days Cynthia's been having visions of Gordon tied up like a dog, eating all different colours of boiled gruel. They make sense now.

Anahera doesn't look so astonished, she already knew.

Cynthia makes sure to proceed calmly. 'Okay,' she says. 'He needs to give us all his money. Then we give him an allowance for shopping and if we can't afford the good corned beef, he steals it.' He'll be their criminal slave, that's the only way they can survive him.

Anahera nods to show she's heard.

'He's an evil degenerate,' Cynthia says.

'I don't know abou –' Anahera starts to say, but Cynthia stares at her hard and won't stop.

'Okay,' Anahera says, looking down into the water. 'I'll talk to him.'

Cynthia nods. It's not enough, but it's a start. She wants to kiss again now. Anahera feels Cynthia leaning and turns back from the water to reciprocate. Her tongue is almost utterly still, but Cynthia bites and sucks. Then, she slides down in Anahera's arms, and lands softly in the cushion of her lap. There she watches the water move, and feels it under them. She looks up sometimes, at Anahera squinting, as if to interpret some code in the waves. 'I mean it, what I said about prison,' Cynthia says. 'I mean it even more now.'

Anahera doesn't reply directly, but she does say, 'Tell me about your dad.'

'Eh.' Cynthia makes a deliberate noise. 'He bought me a lot of Barbie things.'

'Mmm,' Anahera says. Right in front of Cynthia's eyes are two bare knees, brown, one with a freckle-thing. She feels just as she imagines Snot-head must have, and closes her eyes, rubbing her head gently against the bottom edge of Anahera's shorts. Neither of them say anything else, but it doesn't matter. It could be an hour, two, or only fifteen minutes before Anahera says, 'Well, we'd better get back, I suppose.'

44

Cynthia did gymnastics for a while as an adolescent and it's definitely her best sport. While Anahera makes lunch, she invents an entirely new series of positions using the washing-line for support. The gymnastic feeling comes right back to her, and a blue pair of Anahera's underpants brushes against her shoulder. She hopes Anahera's watching. After ten lunges and ten squats, she lies down. It's a hot day. She rests and watches the shifting patch of water where, less than an hour ago, everything changed.

Canned tuna and tomatoes on rice. Cynthia muses quietly while she eats, and Anahera doesn't say a thing to Gordon. When they're nearly finished, Cynthia asks them, 'How are we all?'

'Exhausted,' Anahera says.

Cynthia nods, and looks at Gordon.

'Whatever, white girl.'

After lunch the dishes sit by the sink. Eventually Anahera and Gordon go do stuff, and Cynthia makes the bed from the table and lies down on it. She relaxes her eyelids, and her eyes under them, then her toes. The two of them come back in, occasionally, and move around her. She twitches her knees, and her glutes too. Anahera's going to speak to Gordon; she's probably speaking to him right now, telling him what Cynthia says is what.

Anahera taps Cynthia's forehead with two slim fingers, and Cynthia opens her eyes happily.

'What is it you think you do, Cynthia?' Anahera asks, peering down.

She looks up, dazed.

'You can actually be a very difficult person to get along with.'

'What did I do?' she asks, astonished.

'Firstly, I've washed the dishes once today. Gordon's been fishing since this morning, and the least you could do –'

'Is wash the dishes?'

'And flush the toilet,' Anahera says.

'What? I always flush the toilet. When have I ever not flushed the toilet?'

'But properly, Cynthia. So the bowl's full of entirely new water. You have to fill the bucket up, then tip the whole lot down. I don't think you've ever done the pump more than twice.'

She hardly opens her mouth, and Anahera says, 'Don't try to blame Gordon.'

Cynthia's shocked. This has never been a problem before. She turns over and pushes her face into the pillow. The boat shakes gently as Anahera walks away.

What's wrong with this picture – the answer is oafish and obvious – Cynthia, Anahera and Gordon? The weight distribution is terrible. Someone sits alone and two people share a seat. It won't float.

Cynthia doesn't open her eyes for practically the whole afternoon. There's nothing she wants to see. You can't move the seats around, they're fixed on the boat.

She shifts onto her back and presses her palms against her eyeballs till the blackness hurts. After a while of this, Anahera's fingers tap her again, this time on the shoulder. Cynthia doesn't move. More tapping. 'What?' she groans.

'Look, I am sorry.'

'Doesn't matter, what's said is said.' But Cynthia removes one hand from over her eyes. Anahera laughs a bit, and Cynthia covers it again. She's ashamed of the voice she uses, it's moany, but still she speaks. 'You think I'm just silly and white and too much mess.' Anahera will say, *No, of course not*, but Cynthia's prepared to listen through to the truth.

'Well,' Anahera says, as if the whole thing is a joke.

'But – you know – you don't know anything about me.'

'What don't I know?' Anahera says, like she's being really patient. It's confirmed; the worst. Cynthia removes her hand, briefly, and sees Anahera's kind face looking down. She slaps her eye covered again. Anahera sees her only as what she is, as if that's all she is.

'I'm really complicated,' Cynthia mumbles, almost gurgling.

'What?'

'I said,' she says clearly, and louder, 'that I'm really complicated.'

'Yeah, well. Of course you are,' Anahera tells her.

Cynthia's not going to speak for the rest of the day. Enough's been said, more than. She clamps her lips together and closes her eyes. Anahera rubs her shoulders a bit, then goes away.

Gordon's captivated her. There must be something in the way his muscles tense when he hauls fish in from the sea; he must have a proud, boyish smile when he turns to her, with them still flapping on the end of his line. His lips peel back in Cynthia's mind now, and the teeth behind them are big and white.

—

That night she and Anahera share the bed, but it means nothing. Cynthia's body is weighty with new fat, and it pushes her down.

45

She wakes at her usual time; something like eight. She's in bed alone, which is typical, and the sun shines on the boat, coming strong through the windows like always. But, there's no noise at all. Gordon's gone too. She fills a cup with Coco Pops and eats them un-milked. They make a good noise between her teeth. She fills it twice more. When she's done she doesn't wash it, but bangs it on the floor twice so the leftovers fall out, and puts it back in the cupboard. She feels weird and jumpy, and gets up to pee. The boat doesn't move, even when she does.

She watches a video on her phone. It's of a woman in front of a blackboard in a pencil skirt. She writes 'Penny Lee, substitute teacher' on the board, and giggles. Beside the blackboard there's a poster with an apple on it. After Penny Lee flicks her hair – which is a very good part – Cynthia skips forward.

'It's your what?' Penny Lee's mouth drops. 'Your big cock?' She puts a lot of emphasis on some words and looks offended, but also aroused. In the moment before this, Cynthia remembers, Penny's just asked why all the girls want to sleep with the student, who's in detention for sleeping with all the girls.

Penny Lee touches her top, then flicks her hair again. There's no one else in detention. They're away. She's on the boat alone. She doesn't know where they are or what they're doing, but she knows exactly what Penny's about to say. She never leaves the guy time to reply, or even for Cynthia to think what he'd say if he did.

It's big, anyway.

Penny strips unhurriedly, while keeping Cynthia abreast with the situation. The guy's wanking his big cock, and Penny admits it's only fair that she should get completely naked. She's got a British accent, she says com*plete*ly naked. Then there's a good bit where she shows her bum, and Cynthia pauses it there.

She looks at it for a long time, and slowly it begins not to look like a bum at all. It becomes two lumps of flesh, and then a mass of beige like an old pudding. Cynthia looks out the window at the water – still barely moving – then back at Penny's bottom, and she cries a bit. She gets up for more Coco Pops, but sits again. She's crying a lot. Penny's bum's blurry through her tears, and liquidy. The water outside stays silent and static, ignoring the small heaves of Cynthia's body.

She gets the whole bag, even though they're stale and dry. Then, back in bed, she pours them in her hand carefully. It's full of them, but – they'll never fill her up; they're hollow, milkless. She shoves the fist of them against her mouth, but it can't open wide enough to receive them all. About a third are crushed against her face, and fall down her shirt, onto her legs and the bed. She fills another hand with them, then swallows what she's got in her mouth. After putting the second load against her face and in her mouth, she shakes her top out, so the crumbs fall onto her belly and stick there.

What are they doing? Talking about? Cynthia doesn't know anything at all. When Anahera goes to the toilet, or swimming, or even just looks at Cynthia, Cynthia forgets that their love isn't a mutual love. When Anahera does anything at all Cynthia forgets. It's only Gordon that reminds her, and with each remembering she finds herself newly abandoned, floating alone on the vast loneliness of the sea. It swells and settles, and once it's settled she forgets again that it's right there beneath her.

Cynthia hears the splashing and laughter of their return, brushes most of the Coco Pops from her face, and settles in sombrely to wait for them. Anahera takes a hand off his arm before coming through the door, but Cynthia saw it. They stand together above her, dewy, salty and fresh with the calm morning.

'Have you eaten?' Anahera asks.

'No.'

Anahera begins making porridge.

'Do you think you might get up? I will make this table,' Gordon says, scratching his head. He sits at the foot of the bed, and Cynthia pulls her legs quickly up and away from him. 'Okay,' he says, and shuffles away too.

'What does she see in you, do you think?' she asks him, quite loudly.

He recommences scratching, now at his ear, and looks at the wall. Anahera turns and says, 'I thought we might all have breakfast, Cynthia. At the table. Gordon has something he'd like to tell you.'

'Oh?' Cynthia says, wriggling her feet so they take up more space, and glaring at him. 'Yes?'

'Cynthia, get out of the bed. Gordon's going to make the table. We're having a meal,' Anahera says, scooping porridge into three bowls.

Cynthia giggles and says in a husky, kinky voice, 'Yes Ma'am,' but really she's annoyed. She stands back and watches Coco Pops fall everywhere while Gordon pulls the bedding off.

They all sit down, with a bowl of porridge each. Behind the

window the yellow boat that pulled them off the beach only three days ago sits gently on lilting water. Cynthia moves her finger towards the glass. Anahera and Gordon eat, and watch her. When she hits it, he says, 'Oh, sorry.'

'What?' she doesn't turn, but pushes harder. The finger bends at the first joint, and goes white at the tip. Further down it's red. *Interesting*, she thinks, but it isn't.

'Oh, nothing anyway,' he says.

She shrugs, removes her finger, and slams it forward again as suddenly and hard as she can.

'Yes,' Anahera says, putting her spoon down. 'Something.'

Cynthia's listening now, but she doesn't shift or lessen the pressure of her finger on the glass.

'Ah,' Gordon says. 'Yes, it is that. I am to tell you. My game I have been playing is irresponsible. Ah, cruel. I am to stop immediately.'

Cynthia sucks her finger, it hurts now. She doesn't look at him, but at Anahera, who looks back and fills her mouth with more porridge. Gordon makes a noise as if to say more, but Anahera turns – suddenly – and says, 'Nothing else. That's it.'

'Should he apologise?' Cynthia asks.

Anahera nods, and says, 'He will apologise.'

Gordon is red. Little veins are visible in his cheeks. 'I will apologise,' he says.

They both look at him, with eyebrows raised, waiting.

'I will say – ' he begins.

'No,' Cynthia says. 'Say it.'

'I am sorry.' He looks down into his porridge, and scrunches his face up as if very confused.

'Good,' Anahera tells them both, looking from one to the other.

46

Right after dinner, Gordon tugs Anahera outside by the arm, to watch the sunset. Cynthia makes the bed and gets in. She stretches her four limbs out tight so they hurt. There'll be no space for him. They stay out there for minutes, and Cynthia's thigh cramps. When Anahera does finally come back in she appears shocked at seeing Cynthia so aggressively star-fished.

'Oh!' Cynthia says. 'There's room for you.'

She shuffles over quickly, but Anahera says, 'It's only eight?'

'That's fine,' Cynthia says, shifting her arm and leg back, lest he attempt to slip in.

He strolls back in and stands beside Anahera, looking down and yawning, 'Gosh,' he says. 'Do you want to play cards?' he asks Anahera.

She looks again at the bed, there's no table.

'Oh,' he says. 'Want to go for a paddle about?'

Anahera nods, goes out, and he follows her. Cynthia lies, waiting. If she goes to pee, even with him in the dinghy, even as quickly as she can, he'll attempt to claim it. He knows how much it means now. She lies there for at least an hour, then sleeps.

Her hand touches a leg, rough and hairy: his. It moves.

'Gordon!' she hisses.

'Yes. Oh, yes – she said, she will take a turn in the cabin.'

'Excuse me?'

He repeats himself.

She logs in to Facebook. There's no chance of sleep now.

'Are you scrolling through a wall?' he asks, immediately.

She's turned away from him, blocking the screen with her body. He'll only see the light. She moves down the page silently, and thinks she can feel his eyes blinking behind her back in their slow, dumb way. 'You all just post pictures of things,' he says. His lips are as wet as a baby's, she can hear it in his voice when they separate. 'Things you think are pretty.' His mouth is a pond of spit.

Cynthia raises her eyebrows in the dark, and likes someone's link to an article about sugar taxes. If she leaned over with a knife right now, and stabbed his throat, would he gurgle? She scrolls. He would.

'Are you afraid of drowning?' he asks. 'Or have you already drowned in your social media device?' The blankets shift down low, near his muscled toes. He's wriggling them.

She could conk him on the head with something. 'How would I drown in my phone, Gordon?'

Anahera shouts at them from the cabin. 'Little bit quieter, guys.'

'Righto!' he yells back. Then he whispers to Cynthia, 'Ah, I mean, metaphorically. In the *feed*. Are you hungry, Cynthia, or are you *fed?*'

She hears his age. When they first met and he seemed wild, he seemed young too. As young as Anahera. That was a long time ago now. He's acquired a decade from nowhere, and he's weak.

He very diligently ignores her lack of response. 'You don't believe in reality,' he whispers. 'You believe in *reality TV*.'

He's naïve. Cynthia remembers when he dressed in a suit for

their Boat Island tour; he combed his hair. She likes a picture of a three-legged dog.

'If I threw you over' – his whisper is even quieter now – 'would you be afraid you might drown? No? Because you can swim?'

'I can swim,' Cynthia turns and hisses back at him. 'It's just fucking boring.' Her face is much too near to his. She can feel him breathing.

He clears his throat; a deep, reverberating noise, like a rock falling in a cave. 'Because you think Anahera, that nice strong girl, would save you? You think you know she'd save you?' She can feel him grinning now. His lips are stretched. 'Think of Anahera – she is a lion. She would murder a goat with her mouth and eat it. And she knows how to speak nicely to people.'

'Guys,' Anahera says from the cabin. 'Quit muttering.'

Cynthia closes her eyes. Not to sleep – she won't surrender – but to rest. He's probably a farmer in Germany, she thinks. He's got the waiting intelligence of a dog, and the muscled tongue of a bull. Here, he has found himself so at home in New Zealand, our dirty country of animals. Cynthia doesn't know any farmers, but you only have to watch the news to know what sort of place this country is.

47

In the morning she wakes in bed alone.

Gordon is clean – his clothing and his smell, his articulation and the way he moves through the boat. His body's sectioned into tidily cleared parts like those of a Ken doll.

He's clean, but Cynthia finds a bottle of piss in the cabin where he sleeps. It's tucked away, where the walls narrow and the ceiling meets the floor, behind some cushions they don't use. She opens it and peers in. It's a big old Fanta bottle, nearly full. At its neck the liquid's surfaced with five or so little bubbles. She takes a whiff – *putrid* – then screws the lid back on tight, and replaces it behind the cushions. What a revolting man he is, she thinks again and again, kneading the cushions with her feet.

For the rest of that blessed afternoon she ponders what to do about it. During dinner she decides that at their next meal time she'll pour it very gently under the table onto the crotch of his pants. She only needs something good to say afterwards. Something he can't reply to.

The piss bottle is from when he first arrived with them. When he stayed in the cabin at night, unsleeping. He behaved properly in their home then.

48

The next day Anahera's swimming and Gordon's having breakfast; it'll have to wait till lunch. When Anahera comes back Cynthia's having seconds.

'You look cute,' she says. 'Happy.'

Cynthia nods, it's true – she does and she is. 'What will you do today?' she asks.

Anahera shrugs and leans forward, towards her. 'You?'

'Just some stuff,' Cynthia says.

Gordon's standing at the back, shouting at the guy on the yellow boat. It's closer now, not twenty metres away. He's so noisy, Anahera rolls her eyes.

'Hey!' Cynthia giggles. 'Hey, hey – wait a sec.' She touches Anahera's nose, and clambers into the cabin. It's the perfect time for the chocolates. He's distracted, and she and Anahera are both beautiful today, and near love, or just near each other.

He's folded the clothes in his bag, and she doesn't want to mess them up and disturb him prematurely. The chocolates are right at the bottom. She's got the bag on the floor, and she's lying on a lower bunk with one of her legs sticking through the cabin door. Anahera taps her foot with something cold, like a spoon. Wet, maybe – with Anahera's spit, maybe. Cynthia stops worrying about the foldedness of the shirts. She pulls out the chocolates, then fists everything back in. The spoon taps her again, and she turns to see Anahera's face smiling through the gap in the door.

'Yeah?' Anahera says.

'Yeah!' Cynthia throws the box at her.

They sit opposite each other. Gordon's yelling at his buddy. 'Women!' He laughs uproariously. 'They're always screaming! Ha!'

Anahera hasn't opened the box. Cynthia wants to take them back and do it. She wants at least ten chocolates in Anahera before Gordon says they're his. But, Anahera's examining the little smiley faces. 'These look expensive,' she says, beaming.

'Yup,' Cynthia nods. She can feel herself squinting, and she's pulling at her thumb with her fist, so it aches at the socket.

'What?' Anahera asks. 'What is it?'

'I just want to see you eat five at once,' Cynthia says, still squeezing and pulling. She looks behind Anahera, through the door at the deck, but she can't see Gordon. He's quiet now, he must be listening, either to them or his friend.

Anahera's only silent for a moment. Then she laughs and rips the box open. 'Five?' she asks.

Cynthia nods, waiting.

'Do you want one?' Anahera pauses.

'I just want to see you,' Cynthia tells her.

Anahera laughs again, in a lovely flattered way, and puts one in her mouth. Then, counting them, four more. Her cheeks push out huge, and her eyes seem pressed from the insides into a new, splendid brightness. She laughs more, and chokes a bit. Cynthia's very satisfied. 'Are you going to swallow?' she asks, taking one herself and looking at it. They're quite big, the size of your average marshmallow. She looks down at the little iced wink on the one she's holding.

Anahera's trying to swallow, but laughs too hard. Her shoulders lift up and down, and the chocolate shows in flashes in her mouth.

Some falls on the table. She moves for it, but Cynthia gets there first. She wipes most of it up with her fingers, it's wet and spitty, and puts it in her mouth. Anahera smiles. She's stopped laughing now, but she's still breathing loudly through her nose.

They might be a bit off. There's a slightly metallic taste, but Cynthia thinks that's Anahera's spit. She doesn't swallow, she just sits there and meanders her tongue around, tasting. *I love you*, she tells Anahera with her eyes, and she sucks each syllable.

'Alright, friend!' Gordon shouts, and Cynthia remembers him. Anahera gives her a meaningful look back.

He re-enters, stomping loudly. Neither Anahera nor Cynthia turns to see him, but he arrives, standing right over the table. 'Oh,' he says. 'You have stolen my love gift.' He turns immediately to Cynthia, who looks back at him, empty-mouthed now, and defiant.

'This boat is private property,' she tells him, smartly. 'It got mixed up with our stuff.'

She hears Anahera's effortful swallowing of the chocolate, but doesn't look to her for support. She won't shift her eyes from Gordon.

'You bitch,' he says, laughing. But then he yells. 'You fucking little bitch!' His accent is gone.

'Gordon!' Anahera says, loudly. 'Stop that immediately!'

He says, calmly, accent returned, 'Hello there, Cynthia, you fucking little bitch. I am going fishing.' Then he walks back out to the deck, presumably to set his line.

Cynthia snorts, noisily, so he can hear. But she looks at Anahera, and says, 'Did you know his accent was fake?'

Anahera holds her face deliberately, and says, 'I had some idea.'

49

Cynthia finishes the chocolates and makes plans. At lunch she'll tip the piss on him. Then, when he jumps and shouts, she'll say in a calm, almost maternal tone, 'Are you okay, Gordon?' When he says no, he's covered in two litres of his own piss, she'll explain back to him concepts he's spoken of earlier, of self-love, and breathing deeply. Cynthia won't laugh at all when he jumps up screaming, but Anahera certainly will, because it'll be very funny.

He'll be driven wild and reveal his true nature. She imagines his big hands squeezing their frail table-bed so hard it crunches, then smacking her across the face. If he hits her she'll cry and Anahera will comfort her, ignoring him. He'll shout for hours without stopping, dripping piss, then eventually collapse on the floor in a drenched puddle. He'll cry louder and longer than Cynthia, because he's a man and when they get started that's how they are.

When her eyes are dry, and they've let him go on for a while, she and Anahera will share a look. A look communicating Cynthia's plan: Anahera forcibly ejects him. She biffs his wet, angry body into the bigger, wetter rage of the sea. He'll be weakened by his own stench and shame, and the sight of seeing Cynthia hit will propel Anahera, she'll be at her strongest. Cynthia will then zoom the boat off. That bit's a concern, actually – Cynthia's never operated the motor, she might have to step aside and let Anahera do it.

Gordon's shouting again, at his friend, but she doesn't pay attention. His whole life is meaningless.

———

She's just eaten the last chocolate when he comes in, with his buddy. 'Sit, please,' he says, ignoring the empty box. 'What can I get you?'

The guy's wearing the same little black shorts and orange singlet as he did when he pulled them off the beach. He sits at the table opposite Cynthia, and shrugs. 'Coffee?'

Gordon does the thing with the gas then the lighter, and the kettle hums.

'He doesn't own this boat,' Cynthia tells the guy, gesturing at Gordon's back. 'Or a single thing on it. He's a guest who will be uninvited soon, probably tomorrow.'

Gordon turns and says, 'You've already met Cynthia, and you know what? She's only fourteen.' His fake accent's vanished again.

The guy looks from Gordon to Cynthia, and back. If it were a room he'd leave. She gives him a smile, she understands. Then she gets up and stands behind Gordon. He's hunched down and bent over, into the small gap between the raised kitchen cupboards and the bench. She turns briefly back to the guy, and pulls her fist back, ready to punch, then gives him a nod. She makes sure he's watching properly, and with all the force she can muster she slugs Gordon in the back of the neck.

'Ow!' He stumbles, and bangs his head on the wall. The boat rocks at his movement, and Cynthia waits patiently for him to regain his balance. When he does, he doesn't turn back to look at her. She punches his lower back twice, but it does nothing, he's holding the bench to steady himself.

'I know you're not German,' she snarls.

Gordon turns to look at her then. 'I'm not German,' he repeats, as if mildly surprised. His eyes are white, and he looks dully down with them for a long moment, and blinks twice. Then, he looks over Cynthia, to the guy sitting at the table. 'Good day fishing?'

Cynthia returns to her seat, across from the guy. He's scratching his chin, and looking at the door.

'What are your interests?' she asks, to make him feel better.

'Aw, fishing, I guess.' He shifts his singlet, so the areas around each of his armpits are equally uncovered. They're very hairy, like he's hiding mice.

'Cool,' Cynthia says. 'Do you want coffee?'

She can see Anahera's ankles through the window behind Gordon's head, coming around the side of the boat.

'Yeah,' the guy tells her.

'Cool, Gordon's making you one. Do you want sugar in it?'

'Yeah,' he says. 'Or, either or.'

'Gordon, put sugar in it.' Anahera's off the edge, and must be on the deck.

He turns and stares at her, then spits in the sink.

Anahera sits down beside the guy. 'Hey there.' She gives him two friendly, hard pats on the shoulder.

Cynthia notices Gordon not adding sugar, but says nothing. His friend can suffer the wrong sort of drink, she doesn't care. 'This guy enjoys fishing,' she tells Anahera.

Anahera laughs. 'I know.'

He makes a crackly chuckle too, and finally settles into his seat a bit.

Gordon puts down three coffees: his own, one for Anahera and another for the guy. 'I didn't know if you'd want tea,' he tells Cynthia. Then, 'Caught much?' he asks the guy.

'Nah, but I took a nap.' He shrugs.

Cynthia looks straight forward at his pecs, still flabbily

exhibited at the big arm holes of his singlet. Is now the time for the pee? It doesn't feel right. She waits patiently. Anahera and orange-singlet both know a family in common: the Henares. How boring.

Orange-singlet asks Gordon, 'How long have you been around here?'

'Only months.' Gordon shrugs.

'He got dumped,' Cynthia says.

'Should I make lunch?' Anahera asks, smiling broadly.

'Aw, nah. Don't trouble yourself,' the guy says, but he's leaning forward a little. He likes her, he's been running a hand through his hair and smiling since Cynthia mentioned Gordon's having been dumped.

'Lunch'd be pretty good right now.' Gordon rubs his belly.

Anahera opens a can of corned beef, then their last loaf of bread. She boils the kettle again, and they have sandwiches and tea. 'Victoria Beckham kissed her daughter on the lips,' Cynthia tells them. 'Then posted it on Instagram.'

Anahera says, 'That's nice.'

Cynthia thinks it's gross, but she lets them do the talking, chews her sandwich, and checks Facebook instead. When he finally leaves, she looks up at the guy and says, 'Pleasure.' He nods and smiles, and Gordon shows him out.

'Interesting man, that,' he says when he comes back in.

Anahera agrees, and says she'd like to have him over again. That doesn't seem consistent with their plans of not getting arrested, but Cynthia doesn't worry. She only needs to wait a few hours till dinner.

50

Dinner is canned peas, canned corn and more corned beef. It looks nice and tidy, all scooped out in sections on their plates. Cynthia and Gordon are waiting for Anahera to finish washing her hands in the bathroom. The bottle's behind the cabin door. She knows she can reach it from where she's sitting, and doesn't think they'll see. She sections her foods off from one another with careful scraping movements of her knife. Gordon tells her to stop, and she finishes the corn, then she does. The peas roll a bit, but the water's okay tonight, so not too much. She puts one between her lips, a pea, and holds it there a moment. She sucks it back in and says, 'Will you wash your hands, Gordon?'

'No. Will you?'

'No, I never do. Before dinner.'

Anahera joins them, and Cynthia wonders how she's even going to manage this. The excitement and nerves are making her hungry. She eats a large mouthful of peas. They're actually not good, very watery. She's got the bottle behind the cabin door, and Gordon's beside her, between her and the wall. How to unscrew the lid without them seeing? She just has to do it, she decides. She won't put it off.

She puts some corn in her mouth and it's sweet. She smiles at Anahera, then turns the same face to Gordon.

'Definitely an interesting guy, your friend,' she says. 'What with how he liked fishing and all.'

'I wasn't so sure about his politics,' Anahera says.

Gordon laughs, as if he understands her or New Zealand politics at all. Anahera and Cynthia let him. He's eating quickly, he'll be done soon. She didn't account for his way of swallowing without chewing. She shuffles sideways and down, towards the cabin door and the bottle behind it. He's still laughing.

Anahera's looking at her corn. 'We won't get these peas again,' she says.

'Nope,' Cynthia agrees, and she's got the bottle by her fingers. She lifts it a bit so it's not dragging loudly along the floor, and gets it through the door. She can't go back now. She's not sure if it's visible from where Anahera's sitting or not. 'Not *these* peas,' she agrees a second time. It's under the table, touching her left foot. She shifts the foot, so the bottle's between her two feet. It's much bigger than her feet, and she's worried it could topple, but she uses her ankles and calves to hold and shift it. It makes a dragging noise, but she's watching their faces, and they don't hear it.

Gordon extends his plate towards Anahera, and she lifts her own and shoves the peas over. Cynthia rests her head on the table, so she can get her arms low to the bottle. 'I'm bored,' she says. 'I get bored with politics.'

Anahera nods at her oddly. That's not what they're talking about anymore.

'Also, these peas,' Cynthia says, smiling. 'Gordon, you can have my peas too, they're so tiring.' She slides the plate towards him, still concentrating on shifting the bottle.

'I don't want your peas,' he says.

She's got her fingers on the lid now, and she's turning it carefully, and holding the bottle still with her calves and feet. She shrugs her shoulders as if to say it's fine about the peas, and she's nearly got the lid off. Neither Anahera nor Gordon reacts to her shrugging, so she does it again. The lid's off. A bit of pee spills. Her fingers are wet. She thinks she can smell it, but she's careful not to sniff. The bottle cap falls to the carpet then, and makes a soft sound.

Anahera looks at her.

'*Peas*,' Cynthia says. '*Peas, peas, peas.*' She nearly sings it.

She's got to move quickly, they're watching her now. Or, Anahera is. She can't see Gordon's face, and she's worried if she turns she'll tip the bottle. Anahera puts a fork of corn in her mouth. Then, quickly, Cynthia lifts the bottle and it shakes in her hands. It's going to fall, so she half throws, half shoves it at his crotch.

'What the fuck?' He wrenches Cynthia around to face him. She pulls away. The smell is deep, musky and acidic. Anahera's head tilts and her eyes stare hard. Cynthia's legs are wet. She can't remember what to do now. 'Breathe deeply?' she says, and she's shocked by the height and panic in her voice. Her legs are warm and dripping.

'Pardon?' he asks her.

Cynthia looks at Anahera. Her eyes widen, and her eyebrows lift right up. It smells citric and rotten, like an off lemon.

'Cynthia,' Gordon says, in a measured voice. 'Did you just tip piss on me? Old piss?'

Anahera waits, with her eyebrows.

'Yep,' Cynthia says. 'I did.'

Silence.

'Why?' Anahera asks.

Cynthia says nothing.

'Cynthia, do you know how disgusting it is?' Gordon says. Cynthia doesn't turn to look at him, but he's swivelled right around to stare at the side of her face. All she can think is that he phrased the sentence wrong, he should have said 'this' and not 'it'. He leans forward, closer. 'I am dripping urine,' he says.

Anahera drops her head into her hands.

'It's your own piss,' Cynthia tells him. 'It's you.' She looks down at her corn, and wishes they were still eating.

'Cynthia,' Anahera asks through her fingers, 'have you done this to make a point?' Cynthia can't look at her either. She stretches her neck right back, so quickly it hurts, and stares at the ceiling. The piss is sinking in, she can feel it tingling around the hairs on her legs. 'You already know what my point is,' she mumbles.

'Excuse me,' Gordon says, standing up. He shifts past her. 'I am going to wash.'

Cynthia puts some corn in her mouth, but Anahera looks up, and looks like she's waiting for something, so Cynthia shrugs and gets up to wash too.

Gordon's already in the water. He says nothing, and turns away towards the sun. It's setting and the water's not warm. She gets in and out quickly, and goes back in to change. Anahera watches her dripping on the carpet, but says nothing. Cynthia finds a shirt and shorts, and changes in the bathroom, dripping more water by the toilet.

She doesn't say another thing to either of them, and goes to sleep alone in the cabin. If Anahera isn't prepared to stand up for her ever, why sleep together? She can get squashed to death under Gordon for all Cynthia cares.

Anahera knocks on the door three times, but none of them to apologise. Twice to ask if she's alright – Cynthia doesn't answer, and Anahera doesn't open the door – and once to leave water outside the cabin, which Cynthia ignores.

She lies like a corpse, caught in an understanding as simple and putrid as death: some truths are not to be accepted as facts. A fact brings with it a horde of contingent truths, more potential facts. If you don't stop accepting them, you might never. Then you're in an ocean. Anahera never loved Cynthia, and Cynthia stops thinking at that.

On silent, she watches a girl shove a huge dildo in her mouth, then her vagina, then her bum. She turns it off and they're talking about her. He says, 'Where did you find her?' His voice is muffled, like he's talking right into Anahera's chest.

There's shuffling, then, 'Gordon, probably just don't touch me. I can smell it on you.'

He mumbles, still against her, 'I can wash again. If you want me to, I'll go out into the cold water and wash?'

'I just want to sleep.'

Cynthia doesn't breathe or move in the husk of the cabin. She waits.

Gordon's voice is clearer, and sudden. 'What the fuck is your plan now, tell me?'

'Gordon,' Anahera says, 'no one invited you here. You got urine tipped on you, whatever. Don't think it's my problem.' The boat shakes, and Cynthia hears Anahera stomp out and around to sit on the deck. Then she stomps back and says, 'Gordon, you ruined everything for me, do you know that?'

51

Cynthia lies awake, thinking of Snot-head, and her father. Randy. Ron. All of them, boys; such innocence, so loving and lovely and Cynthia's thrown them all away, for what. She mustn't think of Toby, and his elbows. She remembers Snot-head's legs instead, and the bones in them. So short and knobbly; little grandad bones. His big tongue, big eyes, and the heat of his nose and panting mouth. The thought of him in someone else's bed is all she has left to make her happy, but she keeps crying and imagining him dead, then getting sadder when she realises he probably isn't; he most likely really did find somebody.

Gordon's mouth asks her through the door, 'What will you do with your life?'

'Fuck off.'

'I had a job when I was fourteen.'

Cynthia very deliberately says nothing. Anahera must be asleep.

When she left university, she applied for jobs at McDonald's, Burger King, Pizza Hut and Kmart. She didn't get work anywhere, but McDonald's had her fill out a questionnaire online that, in response to her answers, gave her advice on becoming her best self: she needed to develop a can-do attitude, and care more about other people.

'Let me guess? There was a boy and he didn't love you, so now you *mope* – so now you have taken it upon yourself to destroy my relationship.'

'Oh, with who?' She looks deep into the dark.

'There are a lot of boys who don't love you, Cynthia,' he tells her. 'And a lot of women who aren't your mother.'

The survey said to Cynthia, 'Consider how you would feel working in an environment where open and honest feedback is a regular part of your day.' They asked how she'd respond to someone stopping her on her way out for her lunchbreak with some constructive criticism. She answered honestly: she'd rather eat. They replied in kind: they found her unreceptive to love. Food is love, and they questioned her right to handle theirs.

Gordon says, 'You think because you have a little body, a child-ishly taut body, that people will continue everlastingly to spoon food into your mouth, and carry you about on their shoulders?'

'No,' Cynthia says, alone in the dark. She feels stupid, but continues, 'I expect to die.'

He goes on as if he hasn't heard her: 'She will not want you now, or even me, after what you've done. But after your murder of the teenager, you see – oh yes, I know you know that I know – we're all together now, probably forever. Breathe, Cynthia. It's important that you breathe.'

She clamps her lips shut, to spite him.

'I saw her face when she smelled it. Every love opportunity is over.'

The smell, the rank, deep, sharp smell, and Cynthia remembers how it felt lukewarm on her leg. She wasn't looking at Anahera, not when it first poured out. She can't remember where she was looking. At the wall, probably.

'You must be going limp,' he says.

But she's hard, strained; the air in her is stalled. She scrunches up tight against the cabin wall. His is the language of debtors and employers – love yourself, it says. Make yourself contented. She listens to him settle back into the bed. Anyway, Cynthia never got a job.

When he's silent she stands on the deck, watching the water. In the dark it's only more darkness, and that's all water is. Transparency and transparency on top of itself until you can see nothing through it. Her father was moustached and rich and distant. She never saw him in shorts, and she can't imagine him with tanned legs or pale ones. He hasn't texted her in over a month, no one has. She remembers her old bed, and how soft it was. The laxity of Snothead's sleeping limbs, and his gentle breathing.

There's sound from inside. Cynthia peers through the doorcrack and can see only the lines of someone's limbs moving through shadows, but they're Anahera's. Things are being picked up, and there are shuffling sounds. The noise of a zip, and the thump of a full bag being put down on the ground. Anahera's packing. Cynthia squeaks, her knees are weak. She holds the doorknob for support.

Anahera lifts her head up into the light from the window, big-eyed, and says, 'I thought we might have a day out tomorrow, hey?'

Cynthia bites her cheeks and stares back.

'I've just got some Weet-Bix, Nutella and a sweater,' Anahera says.

Cynthia says nothing, and continues to stare while Anahera puts the bag down, gives her a nod, and gets back under the blankets with Gordon.

She needs to regain the bed immediately, by force if necessary. She stands in the doorway to examine the situation. They're each lying at far edges of the mattress. All she needs to do is place herself between them, and sleep. She pees first, even though she doesn't need to, so that after claiming her position there'll be no need to relinquish it. Then she steps, carefully, over Anahera's body so she's standing on the bed. Gordon rolls and moans by her feet. Silently, she lowers herself down, onto her knees, then her elbows, and finally her stomach. There she is, then – that easily! – lying between them.

She doesn't really sleep, her tendons feel tight and weird. She just lies there, tensed and breathing. He smells salty. Then, when the morning light is still only arriving, Gordon rolls onto her, opens his eyes and yells. He doesn't make words, only a deep, long roar. When he's exhausted and regained himself, he looks at her and says, 'Creep.' He shoves her hard against Anahera, and Anahera pushes back silently. Cynthia struggles for breath between them.

'I'm sorry, excuse me,' he says. 'I do not feel comfortable with your body so close to me in bed.'

Cynthia pulls in as much air as she can – they're still both pushing – and says, 'Then you know what to do, Gordon.'

He stops pressing. 'Oh, I'm not sure?'

It's still dark, but Anahera fake yawns and gets up. 'Well,' she says. 'Today we're going for a trip. All of us together. Confined space clearly isn't aiding our psychological health.'

Gordon gives Cynthia a hard shove, and she falls onto the floor. Immediately, she clambers back up and over him onto the good side of the bed – the safe side, by the wall, where he was, and where she won't be expelled nearly so easily again. He doesn't fight her, and she doesn't know why till she sees Anahera's backpack, visible from where he is now, leaned against the kitchen cupboards.

'Is your plan – extensive?' he asks Anahera.

She nudges the bag with her foot and smiles, very nicely. 'I've packed some food and things. I couldn't sleep last night.'

She's lying. Cynthia moans and bangs her head against the wall.

'You see,' he says, speaking over her, at Anahera, 'you are giving us agony.'

Cynthia hears herself moaning and moans louder. He's turned to face Anahera, and his back obscures her from Cynthia's view. All she can see is wall and ceiling; all that flaking paint. There's more light now, it's nearly daytime.

'What do you mean?' Anahera says.

Cynthia watches his mountainous back shrug.

'Well,' Anahera says, 'I'm awake now. Thanks to both of you. So I'll go for a swim, then when I come back we'll go?'

The lump lifts and fall again, another shrug. His muscles ripple. Anahera goes, and Cynthia and Gordon lie still for twenty minutes. Then, she reaches up and digs her fingers into his back. His muscles are hard, her fingernails can't find purchase. Then, one of them catches on a mole. 'I'm not giving you my bed back, ever,' she says. 'You came here, and you ruined my life.'

He slumps onto his back, and covers his face with his hands. 'No,' he says. 'Nothing that happens to you means a thing, you are too young. Your life is not possibly ruined. Do you have a father? It is my life that is a great heap of ball-sack. It is you who have ruined my great dreams.'

He's pathetic. She looks at his body. His thighs are thick, and his chest's very solid. She leans over, and touches his stomach with a fist. She presses it down hard, but nothing happens. He doesn't have any squishy part at all. He opens his eyes, and tells her, 'You know she thinks she's going to run from us?' He laughs and laughs. 'She will not run from us,' he says, and he twists and resettles himself under her fist, still pressing. She lifts it up and punches him once in the stomach, so he makes an 'Urrgh' sound.

Satisfied, she lies back to watch the ceiling for twenty minutes more.

'A lot of boys would like you, Cynthia,' he says casually, 'but not me. There are specific qualities I look for in a woman.'

How annoying, and after that he pulls one of his knees up, and squeezes it against his chest. He releases it, blows out three short, sharp breaths, and looks at her sideways. 'Well,' he says. Cynthia wishes she knew a stretch she could do lying down. She can't copy his, but she feels very tense. He does his other knee, still looking at her.

'Anahera practically said I was allowed to make you my criminal slave,' she tells him.

He raises his eyebrows and releases the second knee.

'But you're just too shit. I was going to make you steal corned beef, and steal that guy's yellow boat, but you're just too shit.'

'Where would you contain me?' he asks.

She doesn't hesitate. 'I'd tie you to the table.'

'But then where would Anahera sleep?' He lies there, ogling her.

She's about to say that, actually, she'd lock him in the cabin, when he puts a finger to his lips and nods towards the door. Anahera's on the ladder. 'See how mature I am,' he says. 'I will give you the whole bed.'

He gets up and pours the last of the Coco Pops onto his face, and into his mouth.

Anahera arrives in the doorway and looks down at the carpet

where a good deal of them have fallen. He stamps them in with his bare feet, and says preemptively, 'There were a lot already spilled there.' The big toe on his right foot twitches, and he grabs it by the ankle to lift it and remove a half-crushed Coco Pop from the crevice between that toe and the ball of his foot. Having flicked it away, he tells Anahera quietly, 'You won't leave us.'

'What? Why?' she asks, panicked.

'What, or why?' There's a fleck of Coco Pop caught in the slight hair above his lip.

Anahera gives him a reducing look, then goes back onto the deck. 'Cynthia,' she says, loudly. Her voice is bright with deceit, but Cynthia comes, like a called animal. 'There's the busy town we've been going to,' she explains, pointing to Paihia. Cynthia nods, she knows. 'But then,' Anahera shifts her arm, so she's pointing in the opposite direction, 'on the other side of the estuary is a much quieter place, Russell, with secluded beaches. I thought we could all go there for the day.'

It doesn't make sense, what Gordon's been saying. Anahera could have left on her own in the night, in the dinghy. She could already be gone. She moves behind Cynthia now, and touches her hair. 'I'll plait it,' she says. There's no wind, it's quiet, and her voice sounds almost girlish, sweet in the cool, still air. 'Fish-tail or French, you pick?' Cynthia's thinking of Snot-head. He had very watery eyes, some days. The hair's pulled softly at her scalp. The tips of Anahera's fingers slide under Cynthia's ponytail and wriggle, loosening it. 'Fish, then,' Anahera says, and Cynthia can't help her posture rising up towards her touch.

52

They're silent and squashed in the dinghy like sardines. 'So,' Anahera says, and neither Cynthia nor Gordon says anything. 'Well,' she says. Then, finally, 'Alright then.' Gordon paddles. The sky's thick and weighted with waiting rain. Cynthia and Anahera sit side by side, and Anahera's arm twitches.

When they arrive, Anahera tugs Cynthia up, and they walk to sit on some grass at the edge of the sand. The only visible buildings are high above them, on the hills. Gordon joins them after shifting the dinghy from the sea, yawns loudly, and lies back. His shirt lifts right up and shows his hairy belly-button. Around them, the grass is rough, and in patches it's beige like skin. The water's grey, and tides heave up onto the beach, one after the other, near to where he's left the dinghy. He didn't drag it far.

Anahera's looking around, worried they'll be seen, but Cynthia doesn't bother. Let them take us, she thinks, and lies back as peaceful and loose as Gordon, to imagine herself being caught, photographed, shamed and locked away forever.

Rain falls on them in plops. 'The town's over there,' Gordon says, shuffling up on an elbow to point where the beach curves around, away from them. Then he lies down again, and brings his lips to Cynthia's ear. 'This place connects to the mainland, you know,' he whispers.

Anahera's sitting up, and she turns back to them with a lazy, forced smile, then unpacks the picnic. They're nearly out of food.

There's a Weet-Bix for each of them, and Nutella to spread on top. 'We can put it on thick,' Anahera says hopefully. 'And to wash those down . . .' She presents a huge bottle of water, one of their last ones, almost grimacing. Gordon takes a Weet-Bix gingerly in his big fingers, and slathers it like he's been told to.

'I always loved these,' he says.

Cynthia ignores him. No one loves Weet-Bix.

He laughs hysterically. 'Just kidding, I am German.'

'Fuck off already, Gordon,' Anahera says. She's been sitting, looking dumbly at her own wheat biscuit, and now she throws it into the sand and stands up. She walks to the water.

'Boof!' Gordon puffs out after her, but quickly all his attention is on the Weet-Bix, and he's brushing the sand off with the careful soft of his fingers. He places it down at his side, away from Cynthia, on his cardigan. Only then does he screech after Anahera, 'What do you know about the incident, woman?'

She doesn't turn.

He yells again, 'Suspect!'

Cynthia couldn't care less about any of that nonsense; the boy, the police or anything. He makes a little wheezing laugh under his breath, and together they watch Anahera ignore him.

Water laps at her feet.

'Killer,' he says.

'You're a child if you think we'll be hurt that way,' Cynthia tells him, and begins to crunch through her Weet-Bix, dry.

He laughs, and nods at Anahera. 'She will be hurt, she is that way.'

Cynthia wants to tell him what sort of person he really is, but there's not enough saliva in her mouth to swallow what she's chewed. Anahera's kicking the water, and she stops to squat down and look at it. Cynthia takes glugs from the water bottle, and swallows her mouthful in three portions. When she's done the moment's passed, and she and Gordon watch Anahera together. The air between them feels peaceful to Cynthia, as if there's no truth left to be spoken or changed.

'We were going to take all your money,' she tells him. 'Before we knew you knew about the kid.'

He shrugs. 'You thought that.'

She narrows her eyes so Anahera becomes a dark blotch before the reflected light of the sea. But, what else would she expect him to say? She closes her eyes and lies back. 'You see?' he says. 'She is a sweet woman. She could have paddled off, but then you and I would have no dinghy. So she took us here, so she could run, and we could use it to get back to the boat. A real darling, she is.' He yells at her, 'You're a real fucking sweetheart, are you not?'

When Anahera does come back to them, she says, 'I thought I might just go for a little walk.'

'Where?' Gordon asks.

Anahera waves her hand off to where the land curves away, behind a corner.

Cynthia wriggles her feet, thinking to get up and go with her, but Gordon speaks. 'You can go,' he says, coldly. 'You can go wherever you like. I will not follow. I will not tell the police any bad thing of a good woman like you. You can trust me.'

Anahera squats down, grasping her thighs and looking hard at him. Cynthia sits quietly alongside.

'It is Cynthia,' he says, 'that you cannot be sure about.'

Anahera swivels, and she's looking at Cynthia. Her lip twitches. Cynthia tries to look up sweetly, to push all her generosity and love into her face, but it doesn't seem to be working. Anahera blinks, and wipes some hair from her eyes, then continues her deep looking. A laugh-choke comes out of Cynthia.

Gordon adjusts himself in the grass. 'Cynthia,' he says, 'I put it in her bum, in my tent.'

There's not a thought, just dull, vicious noise. Anahera's eyes, nose and mouth are all Cynthia sees. They turn away from her, all at once, to face Gordon.

'Fuck off,' Anahera says.

She turns back to Cynthia, but Cynthia's eyes have opened so wide they hurt. Her guts are rising in her throat, and all she can think of is vomiting on Anahera's so-close face. 'What?' she asks Anahera. What he said is true.

'Please, ignore him,' Anahera whispers.

Cynthia shouts back, spitting, 'What?!'

Anahera says nothing.

'What? So you can run off and leave me with him? So when you leave me I won't call the police on you?' Cynthia spits more.

Anahera doesn't move or wipe her face till Cynthia's done. She waits, and says, 'Right, I think we should all head back to the boat.'

Cynthia's fingers are in her mouth, and she's pushing them back. For a moment she finds them there, pauses, then continues pushing deliberately. Anahera grabs one of her elbows, trying to pull them out, but Cynthia slams her head against them, harder. She doesn't think why; doesn't think. Bile comes up and touches her fingers. Her fingertips are wet and her throat burns. Anahera pulls Cynthia's arms harder, so the joints hurt, and their faces are near each other again. 'I'm sorry,' Anahera says. 'I'm sorry, I'm sorry.' She's crying. She's going to say more, so Cynthia throws herself up, out of Anahera's arms, and runs.

Gordon's ahead of her, putting the dinghy back in the water.

She runs past him, screaming, into the sea. She trips and falls when it's at her knees, cries out, stands, and continues running, but falls again.

Anahera's yelling, 'Don't, don't,' then she *catches up and grabs* Cynthia. 'Don't,' she keeps saying.

'Don't tell me don't!' Cynthia kicks at her legs, but Anahera's holding her by the stomach, and her grip tightens. Cynthia swings her arms, still kicking, not touching the ground anymore, and screams louder.

Gordon looks over, from where he's waiting now at the dinghy. 'Just let her go,' he says. 'She'll come back.'

Cynthia bites, but she's only biting salty air. Anahera lets her go, and she runs, struggling against the tides, till she's in water too deep to stand in. She can't see a thing through her tears, the water and her hair which has slapped wet in one mess over her face. There's water in her throat, her mouth and her eyes. She's heavy, but she tries to swim back to the boat. She remembers waiting for Anahera outside Countdown with Snot-head, and a man coming out and looking at her, and she thinks, Of course, of course, over and over again.

Anahera's voice isn't far away, calling her name. She looks sideways and the dinghy's right there, floating gently in the water beside her. Anahera's hand's out, waiting. Cynthia doesn't want to touch it. She swims over, and struggles to pull herself up, out of the water, but slips four times. Before the fifth, Gordon offers his hand, and she takes it.

He paddles. The water all around them is unbearable green. He's sitting opposite them, and his whole body rolls forward and back with each stroke. Anahera's hands are on her thighs, and her knees press tightly together. Cynthia looks at her, then at the water again, and her throat burns with salt. She swallows to soothe it, but it won't feel better. Anahera leans forward, with her hands and her fingers spread, murmuring to comfort her.

'Anahera,' Cynthia says, 'who did your husband catch you having sex with?'

Gordon coughs and stops paddling. Anahera's hands are up, suddenly at her hair, pulling it back so violently her eyebrows wrench up. One side of the paddle catches in the water, and they move in a slow, wonky circle.

53

In the cabin, Cynthia just sits. She's got the last of their food: one more Weet-Bix, and a can of peas. What she feels is almost boredom. She knows everything now; it can only go on as it is forever. The bedding's still moist from the night before, and she can feel it getting wetter. She's sinking in.

She coughs like a dog coughing up a dog. He's listening – she listens back. They don't knock and ask for food, but still. She knows him, the way he lounges all over things and people with his big, ugly body, and she knows Anahera now too. They fucked. He slid his cock into her, and now Cynthia can't let them live unwatched.

She opens the door and finds Anahera at the table with her head in her hands. 'Cynthia,' she says in a pinched voice, 'will you please join us for dinner tonight?' Cynthia thinks they just want her peas, and she's about to say Anahera can get stuffed, she already ate them, but Anahera says, 'Gordon found some beans.'

'Oh, Gordon found some beans. Wow.'

Anahera nods dumbly, she's got nothing else to say.

A dead bird floats up against them. 'A bird corpse,' Gordon says. 'Come look!' Cynthia and Anahera stand at his sides while he pokes it with a broom handle. 'What do you think?' He turns between them. 'Dead?'

54

Rain falls in a continuous thud on the roof. They're inside, at the table. Gordon's philosophising and Anahera's acting interested because, as Cynthia now knows, that's what she does. He says, 'I'm not the police, as you know. But I could have been.' Anahera turns to Cynthia, probably expecting solidarity. Gordon registers the loss of her attention, and changes tack. 'Alright,' he says, 'I have a scary story. It starts with a boy – '

'You're being lame,' Cynthia interrupts him. 'Honestly, neither of us feels bad about that anymore.'

Anahera gives her a look.

'What?' Cynthia asks. 'It wasn't even our fault.'

Anahera wipes her face, and when she removes her hand her expression is neutral again.

'No,' Cynthia says. 'What?'

'Well, it was a bad idea,' Anahera says. 'To take him.'

Gordon's head swivels, from Anahera to Cynthia and back again. Cynthia feels herself make a noise, and goes to stand outside on the deck. The sky and water are separate blues, then a ways away you can't see the line between them. She cleans her ears with a pinky and wipes it off on her pants.

She's going to do it soon, and she won't feel guilty. The sky's heavy, deep and dark above her. She's going to wipe her boat clean of fluff and spillage, and see clearly what she and Anahera are; really are to each other. She doesn't need to talk to them anymore.

She reads one *of her* romance books on the deck.

55

Anahera calls the two of them to dinner. Cynthia sits, looks at it and says, 'Gee, thanks a lot. This looks like shit.' Anahera smiles anyway, and shrugs. Gordon says nothing. They're the beans from his bag.

'Cynthia,' Anahera says. 'We're both really, really sorry.'

'Oh, for what?' Cynthia looks up, and pauses briefly from spooning them around. 'I'm not into beans,' she says.

'It isn't that I didn't want to tell you. I wanted him gone, you remember, but then' – she looks at Gordon, and he nods – 'he knew about the boy, and my feelings changed independent of my control.'

'Independent of your control?' Cynthia slaps her spoon against her beans. A nice splat comes up, and some lands on her collar-bone. Anahera's mouth is open, she's about to explain herself more, so Cynthia asks, 'Have you been fucking often then, since he, uh, joined us?'

'No,' Anahera says. 'No, only once.'

Gordon shuffles quietly in his seat. Cynthia looks, and his face is a deep mauve.

'Hmm,' she says, turning to face him. 'Not much luck then?'

He looks down at his beans. His eyes are scrunched up, and his bottom lip's pushed over the top one, like he's sad and only ten years old. Cynthia chuckles at that, and leans over to slap-pat the side of his face. Her hand makes a good, sharp noise against his cheekbone. He looks up at her then, and says, 'It's your fault.'

Cynthia laughs, harder, spitting some beans on her shirt. 'Where are you from?' she asks him.

'Palmerston North.'

They sit, waiting, as if sense is going to arrive to them on their boat in the post.

Cynthia sleeps in the cabin that night, because it doesn't matter. She's ready to destroy herself to sink him. She only needs to wait for the decision to move from her mind to her body.

56

She lies all day in the cabin listening to splat after splat of bird shit fall on the roof. At five o'clock he shoves his monstrous head through the door. 'Peas and corn,' he says. 'I found some cans.'

They all sit at the table in front of their portions. 'We'll be hungry after this,' Cynthia says, although they all know. Tonight the water's rough, an aggressive mass moving beneath them, so they eat their peas first. There's rain on the roof. One pea rolls from Gordon's plate and off the table, and he doesn't move to pick it up. He finishes first, then Cynthia. 'Well,' she says. 'Do you have more up there?' He looks right back at her, with his mouth closed. His eyelids blink, slowly, three times.

Cynthia checks in the cabin, and her peas were the ones they just ate – he must have taken them last night, while she used the toilet. She has a look through the cupboards. There's nothing, and they swing closed loudly.

'Cynthia, go easy on those,' Anahera says.

'Why?' Cynthia asks, not turning. 'They're my cupboards.'

'We all have to live here.'

'Oh? Do we?'

Anahera and Gordon get up and look too. Cynthia sits back down to watch them. The answer is simple: his death. He squats to look in the lower cupboards, and she notices him being as rough with the hinges as she was. He finds a chip packet she missed, pinches some crumbs in his fingers, and lifts them to Anahera's mouth. Anahera ducks her head away and steps back, then puts out a hand for him to place them on.

'You need to shop, Gordon,' she tells him, after swallowing.

'Yeah,' he says, not looking away from the empty hole of the cupboard. 'We have porridge.'

Cynthia was thinking that.

'That's morning food,' Anahera says. 'We need it in the morning.'

He looks at her hands, near the handle of the cupboard with the porridge. Cynthia knows what he sees. Anahera's fingers are purposeful and quick. Coloured like copper, strong and elegant. 'Tomorrow,' Anahera says. 'Tomorrow, before you get groceries.'

Gordon nods without looking up at her face.

'This is shit planning,' Cynthia tells them.

'What should I get?' he asks Anahera in a dreamy voice, ignoring her.

Anahera turns suddenly, and smiles. 'Get whatever Cynthia wants.' Cynthia stares at the wall and nods, pleased.

She goes to bed early with a dry, hungry mouth. There she waits, for an hour, or hours, holding her hands up in the dark above her face and letting them touch each other. Anahera never snores, so there's no way to tell if she's sleeping. Cynthia's hands tire, and she lowers them to her face. She'd like to know what expression she's making. She touches her lips, but they only feel mouthy.

Anahera stays silent, but Gordon wheezes. The door opens gently. Their cabin's lighter than hers. The curtains are thin, and shifting gently. She waits in the doorway for the right feeling. She should know what to do before she moves, she thinks. But then she doesn't know, and she moves anyway.

Anahera's beautiful with her body so still; the blankets rise at her breasts, and dip in at the gap between her legs. Her eyelashes fan out towards her cheeks, and her nose has a smoothness Cynthia never noticed before. Beside her, Gordon's face twitches in the forehead, but otherwise he's still too, like calm water. She wants to touch both of them.

All their knives are blunt, she's heard both Anahera and Gordon say it. She looks around, and considers the kettle. She can't see anything else. When she lifts it from the stove it makes a metal noise against the element. Anahera moves, but doesn't wake. Gordon's still. It's filled with water. If she tips it in the sink, they'll hear it, and if she tips it outside, they'll hear that too?

They will, she decides. It's heavy, but how much of that is liquid? Should she just whack him with it full? Would the extra weight help her? No, she bends down and pours the water into the carpet. She's careful with the angle, so it runs out slowly, and she doesn't hear a thing. When she stands back up there's a noise from one of her knees. They both shift in bed, just a little, and she stands back and waits for them to settle. The kettle's too light now, and she wonders briefly – should she go outside and fill it again with sea water?

The skin of his eyelids looks incredibly soft, and his eyes form perfect mounds beneath them. The edges of his nostrils, too, appear extremely delicate. Perhaps she could lift him, so quickly he'd not have time to wake, and slam his head against the wall? She'd have to knock him unconscious with the first hit, then slam him five or so times more to kill him. It seems improbable. The moon moves and the light in the cabin lessens. She's standing in the water from the kettle, and her toes are wet. She struggles to think harder. There's nothing of the necessary weight on their boat, she thinks, but – there must be?

The anchor. She opens the cabin door carefully. It's dark in there, completely. She knows the spare anchor's on the floor, tangled in a lot of rope. She's careful picking it up, but still, it scrapes a little on the wooden floor. She doesn't think it's loud enough to rouse him, but Anahera? She turns, slowly, with her feet gentle on the ground. There's rope coiled around the anchor, and it tangles with her hands and hangs on her feet. She moves back through the door so she's positioned above him, then looks down. His eyes are open, and they open wider.

She slams the metal down on his face. He moans, and pushes her back with a big, meaty hand. The anchor drops, and hits her hip as it falls. There's still rope caught around her arms, but she limps as quickly as she can to the back deck, dragging it. It scrapes along the ground, banging at the step before the doorway. He's in the cabin behind her, moaning and moving. Cynthia pauses, and thinks she hears Anahera cooing to comfort him. The dinghy's adrift, tied to the boat with a long, white rope. She pulls it as fast as she can, and gets in.

She's struggling with the knot in the dark, and in panic, when she hears him clear his throat. He's on the deck, smiling, just behind where she was a moment ago, with his hands on his hips. She can't see his face well, but she thinks his lips are hanging oddly, and that one of his eyes is shut. His nose looks weirdly flat. He'll raise a hand soon, she feels, to wave her off. *He knew all of this would happen.* But he doesn't, and something moves in the shadows beside him. Anahera's hand reaches up. Her face is there too, only slightly behind his, with its mouth hung open slack, and her hand continues to reach up, so slowly, to touch her cheek. Unable to settle, it drops back down, to swing limp and graze his hip.

The knot comes undone, no one says anything, and Cynthia uses the paddle to push herself away from the boat. The moon's strong, and the water pulls her out of *Baby*'s shadow. Water ripples between Cynthia and her home, and she feels herself leaving faster and faster.

57

Because of the rain, the dark and her own drifting, Cynthia can't see *Baby* anymore. She doesn't want to. She curls up, and hours pass. The rain stops and the sky lightens. She looks around and sees nothing but water. She's got dandruff. She scratches her head and watches pieces of scalp twirl in the new light before her eyes. It's because she hasn't been shampooing often. She digs her nails in hard, as if peeling an egg. He's better than her. He fucked Anahera, and she couldn't kill him. Now she's alone.

Anahera could never have loved Cynthia, or made any serious love to her at all. She'd never have seriously touched Cynthia's so, so white body, with its pale stomach and pink elbows and knees. Cynthia remembers her own smugness at first imagining herself small under the older woman, squashed. Now she's left only with her shame; her desire's run forward and away from her, as helpless and dumb as a bug.

There are hours and hours, marching past like ants. The sun arrives, and quickly there's too much of it. Cynthia leans, slowly at first, one way then the other. The dinghy shifts, gently then violently, and water slaps both its sides. The sun's up now, on her back, watching her curiously, and Cynthia feels she's watching herself as she tips the dinghy. It flips easily, it'd been waiting to all along.

She's only under it a moment. The water moves. All of it shifts aside in a tide past her, and she's in the sun again and breathing. She holds its side and it settles. The water sparkles, wet and blue like an eye, wanting her. If she softens, it says, it will be soft against her. She only needs to breathe in three times, relax, and accept that Anahera doesn't love her, and never did. It'll be kind. She sees every curve of Anahera at once, but not her eyes, not their colour or anything at all behind them.

Her tears disappear into the sea. It shifts at her hips, appreciative. She closes her eyes and tips her head back, giving the nape of her neck to the water. It licks, cooling her. Cynthia doesn't mind, she doesn't mind anything. She stops kicking and lets her arms go still. She holds her eyes open while she sinks, to see the blue and the blue getting darker. Her toes are cold, numb, then her knees, her hips, and her whole body.

The water doesn't end. She stays loose, with her fingers hanging from her hands, and her hands from her arms like string. There's no bottom, only quiet. She can't remember how long she's been sinking, or feel her toes. Water presses her ears and nostrils. Her lips will quiver open soon, she feels, suddenly, and it will all come in.

His laughing, a deep noise in the murk like he's about to choke, but he won't – she will. She's going to die – that's the cold certainty at her toes, what she's sinking to. She panics, her mouth opens. Water floods down her throat and she can't close her lips against it, her body's sucking the liquid down. He laughs on and on, all around her in the water, burning her inside. He's alive, still so alive. She coughs and she's sucking in more.

She kicks, but can't feel herself moving. There's too much weight above her. The water's still, down low. She slaps at it with a hand and fingers herself in the eye. Cynthia kicks, and kicks harder. Then her hands, she remembers them and cups them to pull water down beneath her.

The water thins, the blue becomes lighter. Her toes return to her feet, and her feet are attached to her legs. She struggles higher and higher, towards the sun. There's warmth at her head and she moves through it.

She arrives – slows her limbs and breathes. The water's shifting gently, and Cynthia can look around and see the surface of all of it. Light and warmth are incredible all over again, and she throws her hands up in the air so the water falls off them and rolls down her arms in droplets. She'll survive.

The dinghy hasn't floated far, and it's hardly rocking in the water. She swims slowly, and slowly her survival becomes humiliation. They fucked. She's only moving, like food in bowels. She gets near the dinghy and it's upside down and still nowhere. There's going to be a long time waiting, she knows, and after that she doesn't care what happens. She rests against the dinghy, then tackles it the right way up.

The paddle's floated a few metres away, and she settles in to watch it move further. It doesn't, hardly. She waits hours and it only moves three metres. After a while she's sunburnt. She's only got a shirt and a bra on, and there's no way to lie properly, so she's red all over.

Of course, Cynthia knows that elsewhere there are bellied and pimpled girls who love themselves and are right to; girls who are perfect and enough just as they are. She tries not to think of them. Her stomach's cooked, searing hot, and she squeezes it tight between her fingers.

They'd have eaten together. She imagines him with one of his cans in one hand, spooning spaghetti into her open mouth with the other. In Cynthia's mind Anahera lies supine and he puts more and more in her mouth so it spills all over her, and heaves up and down on her chest as she wriggles – loving it – with her breasts shifting, and her lips spreading wider as if her mouth could hold more.

Cynthia remembers a noise from when she used to have sex: the wet unsticking of two sweaty bodies coming apart, and the feeling to that sound; the disappointed satisfaction of it being done.

Anahera and Gordon would have overexerted themselves every time, both being so into sports, and what was Cynthia doing? She was in the boat, waiting, watching nonsense on her phone and dreaming of Snot-head, who was almost certainly dead, even by then.

After resting they'd have walked back to the beach together, and looked at *Baby* moving on the waves. He'd have touched Anahera's arm to send her home, and, sated, she'd have swum through the water Cynthia floats on so glumly now.

58

The yellow boat settles not far away, under the sun, and rocks patiently for several moments, thinking. Gordon's friend peers through his window at Cynthia in her dinghy, then vanishes and reappears on the deck. The guy shouts something, and waves his arms, then revs his motor and putts closer. 'What are you doing?' he yells again, a hand alongside his wide-open mouth.

Cynthia shrugs, what does it look like.

'Do you want some sunscreen?'

She doesn't answer, but he gets some, and throws it at her. It hits hard against her burnt thigh. He's waiting to see her squeeze and apply some, so she turns away, scraping her raw torso on the bottom of the dinghy.

'I'm going that way,' he yells, stupidly – she can't see where he's pointing. 'Towards your friends, I could give you a tow.' His nose balls at the end, she remembers. He yells again, 'I could give you a tow.' Tow; his nose is round at the end like a toe. It's hard to think. Does he want his sunscreen back?

'What happened?' he shouts.

Anahera fucked Gordon. The boy fell out of the tree. Cynthia waits minutes for him to leave, and he coughs. It's agony, the way her sunburn's lying against the wood, but she doesn't want him to see her move. 'Ah, alright then,' he yells. But still, she doesn't hear him go. Then, with rasping anger, 'What do you expect to happen to you, like that?'

His boat splutters off, finally. The sun loosens its grip, and tightens again. That's all, the time for one cloud to pass and there's more shouting – Anahera. 'Cynthia, are you alright?'

No sound of Gordon. Cynthia's eyes must have been shut, because they open. The boat's coming towards her. It stops and starts in gentle fits, till it's positioned alongside the dinghy. Anahera cuts the motor, and Gordon stays unmoving where he's stood against the door. 'Boil the jug,' she tells him, but she's looking at Cynthia.

Cynthia's curled on the dinghy's small floor, and Anahera doesn't look away from her as she moves around the edge of the boat, then lowers herself down. A silky leg arrives at each side of her shoulders, and Cynthia squirms up to see Anahera's face, hallowed by sun. 'It's very hot,' Anahera says, and squelches something. The sunscreen from the floor, and she rubs it on Cynthia's cheeks, chin and forehead. She's looking down intently, but not at Cynthia's eyes. Cynthia chokes a bit and swallows it.

Anahera stops rubbing. 'Are you hungry?'

Cynthia swallows again. Chocolate snaps between Anahera's fingers, and it's in Cynthia's mouth. Cynthia darts her tongue out of the way of it, and the fingers, and tries not to suck. Anahera makes a soft sound, and squirts more cream on her hands. 'Sorry I let you go,' she says. 'I was frightened. I didn't know what to do.'

His eyes are peeled. Cynthia looks up, and there he is, staring down through the window. Gordon doesn't blink.

'I really did like you,' Anahera continues, 'when you came to my classes. I always noticed you.' She rubs Cynthia's shoulders, smoothing the cream in and stopping just before it hurts. She does her arms and even her fingers, although they're not burnt at all.

'You know sunscreen's to prevent sunburn, not to – ' Cynthia starts, but Anahera shushes her, and rubs her tummy and waist. The sunscreen's sticky and warm, dried out a little. She can feel lumps of it, congealed and rolling, between Anahera's hands and the fat of her belly. 'Look,' she says, 'why don't you stop?' She's still wearing only a bra and shorts, Anahera didn't think to bring her clothes.

Anahera does, and wipes her hands off on her pants. 'Sorry, I really just don't know what to do anymore.'

'Yeah, well,' Cynthia says, and stands up. The dinghy rocks, and she grabs Anahera's head for balance. The side of the boat's too steep and smooth for her to climb, so she sits again.

After waiting for her to settle, Anahera dives off after the paddle. She doesn't come back to the dinghy; she goes to Gordon, on the boat. He looks sideways at Cynthia, only briefly, before asking Anahera, 'Well?'

Anahera touches his wrist and Cynthia hears her say, 'Listen, Gordon,' before following him through the door. Once they're inside, there's her voice making statements, and his moaning. Cynthia rubs a wet patch of sunscreen with her thumb, where it's caught between her clavicles. The boat rocks beside her, he's stood up from where he must have been sitting at the table, and he's looking down again through the window. He marks a point where they make eye contact with a finger, and slaps it covered with his palm. He holds it there for several minutes, shifts it briefly, and winces to see Cynthia still looking back.

When Anahera's told her to, and Cynthia's climbed up the ladder, she stands waiting, touching her own elbows. Anahera and Gordon are side by side with their hands hanging down, quiet and looking a bit confused.

'Hello,' Gordon says, after a moment. 'Anahera doesn't take a single concern of mine seriously, and so here you are!'

'Leave, if you'd like to,' Anahera says, and she hands Cynthia the hot chocolate he boiled the kettle for earlier.

'Oh boy, I would like to,' he says, shaking his head. His bottom lip wobbles at the right side, and his eye on that side is swollen shut. The hot chocolate is delicious. 'But,' he tells Anahera, 'I am worried for you.'

Cynthia shakes her head. 'That's not why,' she says.

'Gordon, I'm trying to do the right thing.' Anahera rubs her own wrist, nervously or impatiently, Cynthia can't tell.

He's standing with his elbows tight at his sides, staring at Cynthia's forehead. 'Anahera wore my backpack, swam and got us food,' he says.

'Cool.' Cynthia's not listening. She's proud to see his baggy lip shake as he speaks, and the swelled mound of his eye lift into a bulge when he pretends to smile.

'How's your brain?' she asks him, swallowing the last of her drink.

He laughs, sudden and loud. 'How would I know!'

She can't help it, she laughs too. He listens and watches her eagerly. Anahera goes in to sit at the table, and they follow her, him standing back to allow Cynthia through the door first.

He stands, and picks up a soggy box of Baked Oaty Slices from the table, but he's like an animal – too frightened to look down and eat. 'She's clever, you see,' he says, nodding at Anahera. 'The box is cardboard, but they're each inside plastic packets.'

Cynthia nods, waiting for him to open them.

He changes tack, trying to be funny again, and says, 'Hmm. How does it feel to have nearly killed a man?'

'I can't remember,' Cynthia says, and it's the truth.

'Hmm,' he says again. He's scratching the damp corner of the box, afraid to look down and tear it.

'Gordon,' Anahera says, 'give it to me.'

He doesn't look at her, throws it, and misses. Anahera gives one bar to Cynthia, and one to him. He struggles with the wrapper, and most of his crumbles to the floor, but he puts what's left in his mouth and chews, gaining confidence.

'Anahera thinks it would be good for us all to do an activity. Yoga, she thinks. Her friend who found you is coming back for yoga.'

'Probably not into it,' Cynthia says.

He shrugs, and then, while chewing, looks at Anahera. Cynthia turns too, and Anahera's looking back at him. His face is wiped blank – they've communicated something and she missed it. He steps back towards the cabin, where it's darker.

'Do you want to sleep?' Anahera asks her.

'No.'

Anahera's face is disappointed; wincing. Cynthia can feel his new, loose lip twitching behind her, where he's standing in shadow. Anahera summons a smile. 'I could make the bed up,' she says, even though Cynthia's already said she doesn't want to sleep.

A noise from his mouth. A cracking noise, maybe from his nose. Cynthia turns to look at him, and he pulls his face together again, waiting for her to speak. She takes another slice from the box.

'You got burnt,' he says. The lump of his eye pulsates.

She chews. Eventually he goes to sit on the deck. She chews that mouthful for a long time, and Anahera goes out to join him, and murmur things. Cynthia can't quite make out what she's saying, but he interrupts her quick and loud: 'You don't take what I'm telling you seriously.'

She keeps talking, at her same calm volume – Cynthia imagines her with a hand, placating and cool, on his thigh or shoulder – and he keeps interrupting, saying, 'She won't, you know that she won't.'

Cynthia eats two more slices.

59

'It really isn't difficult,' Anahera says, and Cynthia can hear the instructive smile in her voice. Yoga. She's watched their three sets of feet troop around the side of the boat, through the windows. Now she turns to see them through a different one, at the front, where they've all stopped to stand in a collection at the washing-line. There can't be much space. They remove their shoes and wiggle their toes. Cynthia watches Anahera's, then Gordon's, then the other guy's. The guy's are pasty, with dark hairs, and she'd know Gordon's anywhere; he's the first to stop wiggling.

She grabs an Oaty Slice and goes to sit on the top roof and look down at them, squashed on the deck. 'I could make space?' the guy asks her, gesturing beside him as if he could move further that way without being in the water. She shakes her head and settles in. Anahera says, 'Downward facing, we'll take turns.'

'Dog,' Cynthia murmurs. She knows this one. The men step back, against the bar edging the deck, while Anahera demonstrates. The downward dog is one of the most nauseating yoga positions. Cynthia eats her slice.

'Good circulation,' Anahera says, pausing before she begins. The deck is sloped, high in the middle and falling off at each side. She gets on her hands and knees with her fingers spread wide. Then, quickly – Cynthia's never sure how this bit works – she lifts her bum right up in the air. She looks up through her legs at the men, and they're both standing back, mindfully quiet.

Gordon scratches his nose, and Cynthia remembers why he should be killed. Anahera looks up, specifically at him, and says, 'If your hamstrings are tight, bend at your knees.'

He nods. Then she says, 'My hands are engaged,' and he nods again.

'Righto.'

She stands back up, and waves her hand for the guy to take her place. He does, and she sits down beside Cynthia. She touches Cynthia's ankle.

'Thank you,' Cynthia says. 'Just watching this is making me feel better.' It takes a while for the guy to get it right, and Cynthia can't think what time of day it is. Gordon's being patient, with his hands clasped behind his back. When he's finally in position, the guy deep-breathes, goes red, and stretches his neck. Anahera lets him finish after only twelve seconds.

'What?' Gordon says. It's his turn. He does it quickly, and wrong.

Anahera says, 'Your knees. I said that with hamstrings like yours, Gordon, you should bend your knees.'

He turns his head sideways, and makes a pouty face.

'What you're doing right now is actually bad for your back,' she tells him.

He makes a big exhale, and adjusts his feet.

'Don't bother,' she says.

He bends his knees, then. 'Feels weird.'

'Looks stupid,' Cynthia says, and gets up to go back inside. There, she takes two Oaty Slices and a packet of chips, wobble-squeezes her belly, and goes to eat in the cabin.

Usually at the doorway she bangs her feet on the spare anchor, but it's not there. They leave her alone, and she concentrates on chewing. The sunscreen's dried up and turned oily, and it's flaking off with bits of her skin into the bedding. She rolls a large conglomerate between her fingers, and it disappears. They're talking again, behind the door, but she doesn't bother listening.

She's got a notification on her phone from Panty Deal. Someone wants to buy the G-string Anahera wore. Cynthia's remembering how pink it was when the door opens. 'Dinner time,' Anahera says. 'We're having potatoes, gravy, sausages and cauliflower.'

'Cute,' Cynthia says, and rolls onto her guts.

Anahera doesn't quite shut the door before saying to Gordon, 'It doesn't matter if that's true, that's what I've said. That's what I'm saying.'

Cynthia gets up, bangs her head on the ceiling, opens the door, and there they are; both of them at the table, waiting, not even touching their cutlery. She sits by Gordon, and he grasps his fork. Anahera's watching, so they eat.

'Oh, Cynthia,' he says, pausing, 'don't worry about all the chocolate oat bars from the box.'

After dinner, Cynthia goes back to the cabin and sleeps. She doesn't know what time it is when she wakes, but they're quiet. She's pretty sure he won't attack physically, not in cold blood. Perhaps it'd be easier to think outside, under the stars, but she presses her feet against the wall and stays where she is.

There's some noise outside, in the bed. Moving. Then the cabin door creaks and opens. Cynthia's blood quickens. She watches the gap, waiting for a face, but sees the eyes first. Anahera's. For a moment this is more alarming than if they'd been Gordon's; what could Anahera want? Then the door opens wider, there's more light, and Cynthia sees her face. The eyes twitch, and Cynthia understands – Gordon's afraid, and Anahera's been sent to watch her and protect him. Anahera asks, 'Is there room?'

Cynthia squishes tight against the wall and there almost is. Anahera says nothing of how half her body must be hanging off the side of the bed. She wriggles, trying to find balance. Eventually Cynthia hears her put a foot down on the floor, and they can both relax.

Anahera's fingers aren't in Cynthia's mouth, or on her body; they're not in or on her at all, but somewhere in the little bunk Cynthia knows they're there, resting. Everything's waiting, Cynthia feels it all over again. Her mouth is full of teeth and she roves her tongue through it.

'He's going to apologise to you tomorrow,' Anahera says.

'Cool.'

When Cynthia first thought of killing him it was a dream of gushing blood and screaming. It was like a movie with her arm, and her whole body, going *stab-stab-stab* like a boy's hips fucking something. Now, she only feels quiet. He'll wheeze soon, sleeping, and when Anahera hears him she'll leave. They both wait. Then, there it is, guttural puffs of air blowing out his nose. Anahera says nothing, but Cynthia hears her foot adjust on the floor. 'Maybe go back to your own bed, Anahera, so we can both sleep,' she says, but Anahera lies silently for several minutes. It's too hot. 'I'll sleep, don't worry,' Cynthia says. She's tired.

Without saying a thing, Anahera goes.

Cynthia lies, waiting, then moves quietly outside to look at the sea. Anahera's silent, and the sun's just now beginning to press the horizon and the surface of the water. Cynthia's eyes are hard, she can feel them, boiled. Anything, that water would take anything.

She thinks she's dangerous now, standing where he did while she floated away a night ago, but is she? She steps back, through the door, towards him, and he doesn't wake. He stays with his blood soft and slow and his muscles relaxed in his fat. He's got a knife there, sticking out from under his pillow. She touches the blade and it's sharp. The blanket's pulled up around his neck and under it, unconscious and breathing, he looks like something natural. He must be warm, beside Anahera. His eyebrows are soft, and full, and his top lip waits for the bottom one to stop sagging, and join it in smiling. He looks young again, boyish.

She leaves him to wheeze and goes back to the cabin, but she can't sleep. She's thinking of Anahera's eyelids flickering, the lashes twitching – her sleep was fake.

60

She wakes late, with her leg bent weird against the wall. She opens the cabin door with her other foot, and he's sitting at the table eating Nutri-Grain. There's the knife again, black-handled by his plate. He nods down at it. 'I sharpened that.' Then he puts his spoon in his mouth and stares at her.

'Okay,' Cynthia says, and sits opposite him. 'That's the first helpful thing you've done since you arrived.'

'Who ever loved you?' he says, spooning up more.

'Excuse me?'

He refines his gaze and holds the spoon steady in front of his lips. It's piled high, and she thinks he must be concentrating on keeping it steady and watching her simultaneously. His mouth opens much wider than necessary, and he puts it in.

'I've been assured of an apology from you,' she says.

One of his bloated fingers lifts and taps the table gently beside the knife. After a long, slow swallow, he says, 'Look at Anahera,' and gestures at the empty seat beside him. He looks from Cynthia, sideways, at the empty space, but only for a moment. She looks too, at the seat. Anahera's face, her body, her hands. A light falls on her, a gorgeous beam of it; their attention. Gordon, seeing that Cynthia's looking where he's pointed, chances a second look that way too. He gestures with his hands, adoringly, at the air where he says Anahera is, indistinguishable from the space in which he plans to make his point. It's Cynthia's hate that she sits in. But she sits comfortably in all that empty air. It seems she's revealed now – that this is what she always wanted; to be wanted this way, so hotly. To have everything waiting for her, because of course, Anahera's gone swimming.

'You see, Cynthia? Her parents had to go to WINZ, you know.'

'Her dad was a logger,' Cynthia says.

'Doesn't matter. I gave her her first fitness job.'

Cynthia gasps, appalled.

'That's right,' Gordon says. 'I instruct too. Women have sex with me because they respect my skill set.'

She gapes at him.

He laughs. 'They're cutest when they beg. Anahera, in particular, is inclined to say a lot of special things.'

Cynthia begins taking twenty big breaths.

'Do you not eat, Cynthia?' He's excited. He's using his stupid fake accent again.

She stops at seven. 'Gordon, I know you're from fucking Palmerston North.'

He ignores her. 'It is because you were beautiful, now you don't have an idea. Where's Louise gone, Thelma?'

Cynthia walks past him to stand on the deck and consider the sea. She watches the water shift and remembers how the blue nylon of his tent caught light, and how fecund and green it was with moss lower down. There wasn't much space in there, but in all that dark moisture, under that blue, Anahera moved so Gordon could insert himself into her. He stands near Cynthia now with a hand at his chin, pretending to think. What he's said doesn't hurt her, not particularly. What hurts is the size of him, his slow-moving strength, and knowing that however strong she is Anahera let herself be less in comparison, under him, or maybe as a game on top.

He coughs, he thinks he's thought of something. 'You could never be on television,' he says, excited again and gesturing with his knife. 'You are not flirtatious.'

'You're right,' Cynthia says, 'and I lack practical skills.'

'It's more than that,' he says.

'Yeah, I lack other things as well.' Having observed the repetitive swell of the water, Cynthia turns back inside, to the table. 'I'm not always good at following through on stuff, and sometimes people think I'm boring.' She sits down again, where she was.

He follows her, and sits too. 'It's not boring, exactly,' he says. He looks at her thoroughly, trying to think of a word more precise. Then, thinking harder, his head shifts slightly so he's looking out the window behind her head. His fingers flex around the knife. 'Hmm,' he says, then he gets up, and takes it with him to the toilet.

She hears him in there, loud like a horse and humming. Then he stops. 'Cynthia?' he says.

'Yes?' she answers, sweetly. She gets up and moves the slat back in the ceiling. Standing on the table, she struggles to lift herself up, and inside. The first time she doesn't make it, and twists her ankle when she lands back down on the table.

'Oh, nothing,' he says. He recommences peeing, and after that, humming. He's lost the tune and he stops and starts. 'Cynthia,' he says again.

The second time she struggles harder with her fists and wrists, and gets herself rested midway through the hole on her elbows and belly. She wriggles her hips and struggles forward. 'Yes, Gordon,' she says when she can breathe again. Her voice is muffled and echoing. There's not much room in there, or light. She can only lie on her belly, and see nothing, but she throws her hands out and forwards.

He stops peeing.

'Yes?' she answers again, puffing, in case he didn't hear her.

He hums, deliberately ignoring her. She wriggles her hips forward, and throws her hands around, then hits them. The weights. She clutches them, but they're tied together and the rope is nailed down.

The toilet door opens. He says nothing, but she can hear him breathing, standing in the doorway. She pulls her feet up, out of reach.

'What are you doing, then, Cynthia?'

'Sorry,' she says.

'What?'

The nail won't budge. She can't see the knot to untie it.

'Cynthia, how safe do you think it is up there? That is frail wood.'

She doesn't answer. She's chewing on the string, but she can't get through it. She should have taken a knife from the drawer.

He knocks on the wood under her. 'Excuse me, what are you doing?'

She feels where the string's tied around the weights, it's tight. 'Gordon,' she says down at him. 'How do you feel?'

'Oh, good, for sure.'

Then his hands are pushed up, through the hole in the ceiling. One of his blind fingers hits her thigh. She's careful not to move it, as if she hasn't noticed. She grabs a weight and pulls as hard as she can. It feels like something's about to snap, but that might be her arm. She stops, and touches the nail and the string around it. It's hammered in at the centre of the knot, not all the way in – the nail doesn't hang through the bottom of the ceiling, but enough that she can't pull it out. She takes one of the weights and bangs it against the nail, from one side then from the other.

'Cynthia!' he yells, and whacks the ceiling under her so it shudders.

'Yes?' she says, still banging at the nail. It's loosening. She hits it from each side, trying to enlarge the hole. Soon, she can take it between her fingers and tilt it in different directions. The wood's old. She spins it in circles, each time pushing it further outwards so the circles grow. Then, she can squirm it up and down.

It comes out smooth. She lifts the weights up, the big tied-together mass of them, as carefully and quietly as she can, and shuffles to reorient herself, so her head's at the ceiling-hole.

'Gordon,' she says.

He looks up. His teeth are bared, and his good eye squints meanly. 'Oh,' he says, 'you are unhinged.'

She lifts them, and plonks them onto his face. He falls with a thud to the floor. He's won't be dead, not that easily. She half falls, half clambers onto the table, and lands on her knees and chest. On the floor, his neck's bent and his head's propped up against the table-pole. One side of his face has collapsed completely, and only his bulged eyeball looks as it did earlier in the morning. Cynthia doesn't waste any time, she gets on her feet, squatting above him. Then takes his knife and stabs him three times in the chest.

The blood doesn't gush, it seeps. Twice the knife doesn't seem to go in properly, it just hits bone, but the third time she feels it move past that, into something soft.

She drags him by the feet through the door and onto the deck. His head lifts and falls, banging against the floor the whole way. He's heavy, but she doesn't rest. Anahera will be back any moment. She pulls him up to the side of the boat, then lifts him over the edge so he's face-down and his head's hanging towards the water. His knees are crimped up, and his feet are set on the floor. She pulls his shoulders over, and from there the work is easy. She gets a knee between his legs, and hoists the rest of him off the edge and into the water. One of his bare feet kicks out when he falls, and he floats. His head, hands and legs sink lower than the rest of him, so his back seems to balloon up and curve down into the water. It settles around him, and gains colour. His centre discharges a hazy red cloud, brownish and disappearing.

She can't have Anahera swimming through his blood, so she gets in after him, and grabs him by the arm. It's twitching. He's half sunk and hard dragging, the water's against her, but after minutes and minutes she gets him around the side of the boat.

61

There's blood on her shirt, so she takes it off and uses a clean patch to smear around the red on her arm. She throws it out the window, and sits down for a breather in her bra. Anahera will be back soon, and Cynthia would like to be doing something relatable. Gordon's gone, so she skips putting on a new shirt and gets breakfast. Nutri-Grain. Before pouring it, she remembers the knife on the floor. She stops, and takes it outside to drop into the sea.

Anahera's only metres away, treading water and staring. All that's visible of her is her head, and where her hands push the water away in ripples. Cynthia shouts, 'Hello!' as brightly as she can, and bends casually to slip the knife into the water, where it can stay.

Anahera doesn't reply, or come closer, but Cynthia can feel her eyes. She wishes she still had the knife in her hands, so she could stay bent, and drop it again. 'Hello!' she yells a second time.

'Hi,' Anahera says back, and when Cynthia looks up she's swimming forwards, but slowly, not even kicking her feet.

Cynthia's plan was to be sitting down, with a spoon on its way to her mouth when Anahera arrived. Then she wanted to look up, as if surprised. Now that's all ruined – before even touching the boat, Anahera says, 'Where is he?

Cynthia stands, still waiting, with the tendons stretched in her legs, before realising that the question's already been asked. 'What?' she says.

'He said not to worry, he was going to make it okay with you.' Anahera grips the ladder, and begins climbing up.

'I think he ran away,' Cynthia says. 'Before I woke up.'

'He had a knife.' Anahera's standing beside Cynthia now, damp and smooth in her togs. 'I thought it would be alright.'

'Did he?' Cynthia remembers his blood, and the wet noise of his mouth when she dragged him and his head banged on the floor. 'Maybe he'll go back to his girlfriend in Germany.'

Anahera doesn't shift or blink. After a long moment she shoves Cynthia aside and dives back into the water. It's still brown with his blood, and the murk reforms quickly after her body's cut through it. Cynthia waits, but there's nothing. The air's windless and the water stills. There's no sound but her own breathing.

Then in the distance, screaming. Anahera's head's bobbing up and down twenty metres away. She stops and sobs, then she's silent. Cynthia can't make out her eyes or nose, just her hair hanging wet over her face like a curtain. Her head's small and isolated, lifting and falling like a toy in the water.

She shifts to face away from *Baby*, and after twenty minutes Cynthia goes into the cabin and finds the bear in his bag, to comfort herself. She tears the plastic away gently and touches her nose to its soft face. She'll give it to Anahera later, maybe tomorrow. The heart on its belly is made of silk, which Cynthia thinks is real. She reads the words sewn there, *Forever and ever*, trying to forget Anahera's head, silent and caught in the water's moving.

After a while she sits the bear down and goes back out to stand on the deck. Anahera's spreadeagled on her back now. Her arms lift while her legs fall, each wave moving under her body in parts. Cynthia stands there, looking sometimes at her, and sometimes at the ocean or sky. The blood vanishes, and the water's clean again.

Then, Anahera swims back.

After climbing the ladder, she wipes the hair off her face. Her eyes are red, and her teeth bared tight. She says, 'We got Nutri-Grain. He wanted Nutri-Grain.' Her hair drips.

'Cool,' Cynthia says.

'He was good to me when I was your age.' Anahera pushes past and lays out two bowls on the kitchen bench. She takes up the whole kitchen and doesn't even let Cynthia pour her own milk. Cynthia holds her bowl and looks into it. All the pieces are floating. Some aren't wet, because they're sitting on top of other floating pieces. She lays her spoon on them, and applies the tiniest amount of pressure so they absorb fluid. Then she spoons a single piece into her mouth. She sucks the sweetened milk out of it, and lets it soften into mush. 'I saw him looking at you a lot of times,' she tells Anahera, 'in a way I didn't think was appropriate. A sexist way, actually.'

Anahera hasn't touched her own breakfast. She says nothing.

'He always turned to face you. He's like a dick you only saw when it was hard. But I saw him all droopy and evil, from behind.'

Anahera swallows in a way similar to choking. Then, 'What do you want to do?' she says.

'Go back to the island.'

Anahera can't have any spit left to swallow, but her throat's still moving.

When Cynthia was younger, only months ago, she wanted to become an animal, eating, fucking and wild. Now, though, it seems she is one, and wild isn't it. Animals move as slowly as humans when they're comfortable. She stands and goes to find a sweater.

The pink one. She sits wearing it with the last few Nutri-Grains in her mouth, sucking milk. Her dream again – barer now

– Anahera licking her forever in a way that will give her something better than cumming, and Cynthia licking back, again and again till it isn't even tiring. On the island.

62

Cynthia watches the distance between them and the land. She feels Anahera propelling them, against the water and through it, and she says, 'You know he's just a silly old thing that escaped from the meat factory.' Anahera looks sideways, away from her, and keeps paddling. Cynthia looks that way too, but there's nothing there.

If Gordon climbed out of the water, and appeared again, she'd leap on him with her mouth wide open and chew right down his body, starting at his head. She touches Anahera's arm. 'Someone wants to buy your thong. The pink one.'

Anahera looks back at her, like she can't remember.

'The pink one.'

Anyway, might they not make love? Cynthia looks up and watches the clouds moving. It's not hard to see two merging into one. Anahera might lie down on the beach, and Cynthia will crawl along the sand to her. If the wind blows and she gets grit in her mouth, Cynthia will swallow it. She'll arrive to Anahera with a clean, smooth tongue. The clouds continue to merge. Cynthia looks away from them, to Anahera, and when she looks back they don't seem to have shifted.

Anahera's hair is mostly settled in the calm air, and her shoulders are soft like the hills behind them. Her eyes are dewy and glinting, deep. Water surrounds and lifts them, shifting through blues into greens, and now Cynthia knows how far down it goes. Anahera looks past her, over her shoulders, and paddles in regular, strong strokes. The bones and muscles in her face are unmoving, set.

There's only a short slice of sand at the edge of the island, and at either side of it are sharp rocks and trees balanced precariously on cliff edges. Closer, and the water lightens. The tide pulls them in.

63

Anahera forgets to shift the dinghy from the water, and Cynthia follows her into the bush. The air glows green with leaf-filtered light, and fades into moss and darkness lower down. Sun pierces through the canopy, falling on Anahera as if God's just opened his eyes and noticed her walking through Cynthia's love. She moves in deeper, quickly. Cynthia watches her step easily over roots and trees, away and into the centre of the island, to where Toby must still be.

How must it feel to be in her body? The trees are high and noisy with birds, but in her new way Cynthia doesn't feel below them. 'Forget him!' she shouts. 'We both know he's nothing.' Anahera doesn't hear, and walks faster.

There's a damp earthy smell, and Cynthia stops to breathe and touch the bark of a tree. Her throat had been feeling taut, but it's okay now. Soon she'll push forward. If the bush hurts her it doesn't matter, she only needs to reach Anahera's body with her own.

For now, she sits on a log to rest.

Encircled by gently leaning trees Cynthia is in her own small room of dappled light. The log is covered in dewy, airy mounds of moss. Cynthia thinks of Snot-head with his wet little nose. Wherever he is he'll be loved. Cynthia is giving Anahera space, which is what she needs, and while waiting she feels beautiful. Blond. She'll give Anahera time to tire herself out, then catch up with her. They'll go back to the dinghy together.

For now, she shifts her head from one side to the other, resting it. Time passes and the trees are silent. A small winged bug lands on her wrist then flies away. She doesn't notice.

ACKNOWLEDGEMENTS

Thank you Nick, for every draft you read and every tangent you waited to hear the end of. Thank you so excruciatingly much to my class (2016!), for talking about Cynthia as if she were a real person before she was even a proper character, and for being such a team. Thank you very much to my teachers: Emily, Pip, Anne, Robert and Ellie. Thank you very much also to my earlier teachers: Beth, Ms Evans and Jill. Thanks enormously to the people at VUP, Holly in particular. Thanks Fergus and Tracey. Thank you Verna and Denis Adam. Thanks James Daly! Thanks Jona and Danielle. Thank you Kirsti, for helping me grow up, and thank you everyone I studied with at MIT. Thanks Huntleigh. Thank you to my family. Thanks Mum, and thanks Dad.